LLOYDS BANK
IN THE HISTORY OF
ENGLISH BANKING

HOWARD LLOYD, 1837–1920
From the painting by Percy Bigland

LLOYDS BANK
IN THE HISTORY OF
ENGLISH BANKING

R. S. SAYERS

SIR ERNEST CASSEL PROFESSOR
OF ECONOMICS IN THE
UNIVERSITY OF LONDON

OXFORD
AT THE CLARENDON PRESS
1957

Oxford University Press, Amen House, London E.C.4

GLASGOW NEW YORK TORONTO MELBOURNE WELLINGTON
BOMBAY CALCUTTA MADRAS KARACHI KUALA LUMPUR
CAPE TOWN IBADAN NAIROBI ACCRA

PRINTED IN GREAT BRITAIN

PREFACE

LLOYDS BANK has its main root in a substantial private bank founded in Birmingham nearly two centuries ago; one hundred years ago this bank had still only the one office in Birmingham, with a related private banking house in Lombard Street. But by process of amalgamation it has absorbed scores of other eighteenth- and nineteenth-century banks, both private and joint-stock, and at least two of the former reach back into Restoration London, possibly Cromwellian London. It might be supposed that a bank with these many and deep roots would possess a wealth of archives from which its comprehensive history could have been written. This, unfortunately, is not the case. Whatever may have been the position fifty years ago, the salvage campaigns of two wars and the bombs of one have ensured that no systematic story should be written.

Nevertheless, rich material has turned up here and there, sometimes covering a considerable period, sometimes an important range of business. Recognizing that further lapse of time would mean further dwindling of these sources, the Bank a few years ago invited me to put their records to the service of English banking history. The present book is the outcome: it is essentially a picture of English banking development, mainly during the nineteenth century, as it appears in the records of Lloyds Bank and the host of other banks from which Lloyds Bank has grown. Within the limits set by these records, I have tried to make the picture a rounded one. It is a picture of the bankers and their employees, and of their relations with their customers, with other banks, and with the Bank of England. It portrays the bankers tackling the problems of organization as they enlarged their business in the nineteenth century, and how they joined up with each other to form the nation-wide Lloyds Bank of today. There are, alas, serious gaps: most of all, I regret the lack of material on the Lombard Street business before amalgamation swept it into the structure of branch banking.

Conceiving the book in this way, I have inevitably said much that will strike a familiar note to students already well versed in the history of

English banking. The more novel material for them will, I believe, be found in the Chapters dealing with the staff, relations with the Bank of England, organization, and the employment of funds, though I hope that some of the other chapters, particularly 5, 7, and 12, will fill out what has hitherto been somewhat sketchy. I hope that not only social historians but also those in the Bank of today will find interest in the chapters portraying the bankers, the staff, and the customers of earlier centuries; I am sure that in these and other chapters they will constantly feel that, however much its outward structure has changed, the spirit of English banking has hardly changed at all.

I have written it, and the printers have printed it, as a book to be read, but as it must serve also the reference purposes of historians and others both inside and outside the bank, the volume contains more than my twelve chapters of straightforward text. The information marshalled in the appendixes adds substantially to that appearing less systematically in my chapters. These appendixes have been prepared by Mrs. S. M. Johnson with the assistance of Miss J. Benge and many officers of the bank. The chapters have also been relieved of all the footnote references to evidence, except where the evidence is in published sources. All the other evidence is contained in the archives of Lloyds Bank, and the footnotes referring to this evidence are given in a booklet, copies of which are being deposited in the British Museum, the Library of the London School of Economics, the Marshall Library of Economics at Cambridge, the Bodleian Library at Oxford, the Library of the Institute of Bankers, London, and the City of Birmingham Public Library. For access to the books and papers referred to in these notes, research workers should apply to The Secretary, Lloyds Bank Limited, 71 Lombard Street, London, E.C.3 (where a copy of the reference notes is also available).

Information and suggestions have come from many quarters, and I have many debts to acknowledge. Mr. H. H. Lloyd has watched over the references to the Lloyd family with loving care. Mr. R. L. Lloyd provided invaluable papers from the bank's early days. Mrs. S. F. Lloyd lent her late husband's memoirs. Mr. Cyril Lloyd, Mr. S. L. Lloyd, and Mr. C. D. S. Lloyd all helped. On the other founder's family, Mr. Arthur Taylor gave information and advice, and has allowed reproduction of two portraits now in his possession. On the Hoare family, I have had help from Colonel R. R. Hoare, the Rt. Hon. Viscount Templewood, and Mr. Edward Press, M.C. Information on their families and family banks was freely given by Mr. Lloyd H. Fox, Sir Thomas Salt, Bart., Mr. Halsey Janson, and Captain H. M. K. Moilliet. Messrs. Wragge & Co., of Birmingham, provided information that opened important trails. Alderman T. Hannam-Clark of Cheltenham allowed me to draw on his store of local knowledge for my account of early bankers in Gloucestershire. Mr. C. Reginald Fox provided information on the foundation of the Plymouth and Devonport Banking Company, Mr. A. M. Stevens on South Wales banks, and Mr. A. G. E. Jones on banks in Suffolk. The Governor and Company of the Bank of England have allowed me to use (in Chapter 6) correspondence in the Bank of England's archives; I may perhaps be allowed to mention the courteous attention Mr. J. A. Giuseppi gave to my wants in this matter. Messrs. Glyn Mills & Co. helped similarly with their end of other correspondence, Mr. S. W. Shelton's kindly help being continually available. Many retired officers of Lloyds, the Capital and Counties and other banks had something to contribute, particularly Mr. S. P. Cherrington, Miss E. Edwards, and Mr. W. J. Braham. Mr. C. N. Ward-Perkins has an unrivalled knowledge of the personnel of the old private banks, and brought this to bear on some of my puzzles. Many libraries have been drawn upon, and I must acknowledge particularly Mr. F. J. Patrick, City Librarian of Birmingham and Miss I. Shrigley, Librarian of the Institute of Bankers. To all these, my very warm thanks for what they have contributed to the book; I remember also the hospitality I enjoyed.

Thanks are also due to Sir Thomas Salt, Bart., for allowing reproduction of the portrait of his grandfather, and to the Editor of *Punch* for permission to reproduce the cartoon opposite page 98.

Inside the bank, a large number of present officers of the bank, both at the branches and Head Office, have helped in one way or another; though unnamed, their co-operation is not forgotten. Mr. W. S. Hill-Reid was appointed at the very beginning to collect the material from the branches; through his efforts, what at first glance seemed a desert was soon a garden almost choked with fruit and flowers—and weeds. His practical experience in the bank helped in the rejection of the weeds and was at my disposal in discussion of innumerable problems. At the next stage, Mrs. S. M. Johnson (Miss Knight) sifted the material to illustrate the points that were emerging, and she did some preliminary drafting. Secretarial work (of an extraordinarily high standard) was undertaken in the early stages by Miss J. Upshon (Mrs. Gander) and later (including the preparation of the printer's copy) by Miss J. Benge. I deeply appreciate how much all these have done and how they have done it: although they shared in the delights of the chase, they did take huge burdens from me, and at the end they have allowed me, indeed enabled me, to write about what I liked and in the way I liked.

I have been fortunate in having the typescript read by Mr. L. S. Pressnell, so drawing anew upon his great knowledge of country banking. Mrs. Johnson has corrected the proofs and made the Index.

Finally, I must acknowledge my debt to Lord Balfour of Burleigh (at the time Chairman of the Bank) and Sir Jeremy Raisman (Deputy Chairman). They were the chief instigators of the work, and the generous interpretation they put upon my task alone made it possible for me to write this book. If the book proves of interest both to those inside the Bank and to those outside the Bank, their intentions will have been fulfilled.

R. S. S.

London School of Economics
April 1957

CONTENTS

LIST OF ILLUSTRATIONS

═══

PLATES

LIST OF ILLUSTRATIONS

Lloyds Bank. Constituent Banks founded before 1800

1

THE ROOTS OF LLOYDS BANK

LLOYDS BANK since 1919 has reached into every part of England and
Wales, though north of Mersey, Trent, and Humber Lloyds branches are
numerous only in the West Riding and in the Tyne–Tees area.[1] This
nation-wide structure has its historical nucleus in the Lloyds of Birmingham, a Birmingham private bank with a single office as lately as the early
sixties, but this gives a misleading idea of its roots. A fairer picture is
given by the map opposite, on which are marked all the towns that before
1800 had banks that sooner or later came into the Lloyds group. The
group around Birmingham—Coventry, Warwick, Rugby, Stafford,
Bridgnorth, Wellington—is prominent here, but other early banks are
well scattered about the Midlands and south. There are eight 'roots' in
London and quite a number in the southern counties, from Truro in the
west to Margate in the east. In Wales there are Cardiff, Swansea, and
Brecon in the south and Caernarvon in the north. Essex, Hertford, and
Cambridgeshire are blank, but the four chief towns of Norfolk and
Suffolk are included. In the north country there is only Newcastle; other-
wise Chester, Blackburn, Wirksworth, and Boston mark the northerly
limit of the roots of today's Lloyds Bank.

These early private banks generally originated as the ancillary business
of traders, manufacturers, and mining concerns. Sometimes the banking
business arose almost imperceptibly while the major business continued;
in other cases a definite date can be put on the opening of a new bank.
Lloyds themselves, as we shall see below, came from the Birmingham
metal trades and went deliberately and more or less independently into
banking in 1765. Stevenson Salt of Stafford developed banking business

---

[1] In 1954 there were only 213 branches to the north, but over 1,500 to the south, of
Mersey–Trent–Humber.

out of a successful mercer's business, its banking operations dating from about 1737 and being closely wrapped up, for nearly a century, with the profitable business of collecting 'Brief Money' for the Church of England.[2] Messrs. Garfit Claypons at Boston (1754) was started by a corn-merchant. I. and I. C. Wright at Nottingham traded in timber, iron, and hemp with the Baltic countries before opening their bank in 1760.[3] Haydon Smallpieces at Guildford (1765) was founded by a draper. Another of the earliest banks, Berwicks of Worcester (1772), was founded by Joseph Berwick, who as Receiver-General of Taxes was able to use as his capital sums awaiting dispatch to London; his family fortunes had been built in the drapery business and he took as a partner in the banking business a member of another firm of linen-drapers and haberdashers.

The last twenty years of the eighteenth century saw a huge crop of new private banks in almost every part of the country. Of these, forty-two, by one way or another, eventually came into the Lloyds group. Several of them had been grocers: Grant and Burbey at Portsmouth (1787), St. Barbe Daniel at Lymington (1788), Wyatt, Inge and Lant[4] at Coventry (1790), and Thomas Rickford at Aylesbury (1795). Walters Voss at Swansea was established some time before 1799 by a draper. Another draper became a partner in Micklem, Stephens, Simmonds and Harris of Reading (1790). This firm also included a 'mealman', but their most important connexions were with the local brewers. Another brewer-banker was in Toomer, Bunney, Slocock and King, bankers at Newbury from 1791. At Margate Cobbs were brewers from 1760 and regular bankers from 1785. Other banks were offshoots of manufacturing or mining concerns: Fox and Company (1787) grew out of—and remained closely connected with

---

[2] A 'Brief' was in form an instruction from the Crown to parishes to subscribe towards some good cause—church repair, extraordinary local distress through fire and flood, &c. The parson would read the brief from the pulpit and 'a retiring collection' would follow. After the Restoration the administration of briefs and the collection of the money raised were farmed out to professional undertakers. About 1754 the administration of briefs came largely under the control of Messrs. Byrd, Hall and Stevenson of Stafford. This firm and its successors remained the principal administrators until the virtual abolition of briefs by 9 Geo. IV, c. 42, 1828 (see W. E. Tate, *The Parish Chest* (Cambridge, 1951), pp. 119–24, on which this note is based).

[3] Some account of the early days of Wright's bank and particularly of Ichabod Charles Wright (1767–1862), written by Dr. J. D. Chambers, appeared in the *Nottingham Journal*, 29 June 1949.

[4] This is the firm which became Beck and Prime (see below, pp. 64 and 243).

—the wool-weaving business at Wellington; Cunliffe Brooks at Blackburn (1792) had been calico manufacturers; Gill and Morshead (1791) at Tavistock had woollen-mills and an iron-foundry; and Williams and Co. at Holywell and Caernarvon (1792) were connected with the copper-mine in Anglesey. Sometimes these men, going into the banking business, saw safety—doubtless also extension of business—in variety of partners' origins. The Lincolnshire bank of Peacock, Handley and Kirton was founded (1792) by a woollen-merchant in conjunction with a man described as 'attorney' or 'scrivener'. Lambtons of Newcastle was founded in 1788 as Davison-Bland and Company, of which one partner was a leather-merchant, another was in the hardware trade, the third a land-owner, and the fourth a barrister. At Farnham James Stevens was a hop-grower and wool-stapler, and after a narrow escape from highwaymen when returning from market, he employed an armed servant; his friends thereupon entrusted their money to him, and he thought it safer to turn banker.[5] In 1806, therefore, he opened for banking business in Castle Street, where the Farnham branch of Lloyds Bank now stands. Early in the nineteenth century the bank was taken over by the Knight family, wealthy local brewers.

The spate of new foundations in the last twenty years of the eighteenth century continued into the first decades of the nineteenth, and we find equally in these later years a wide variety of trades represented among the men who became bankers. Fosters at Cambridge (1804) originated in a millers' business; T. and R. Strange at Swindon became bankers in 1807, but remained coal-factors. Addison and Co., grocers of Wednesbury, were transformed in 1809 into bankers and in 1851 became P. and H. Williams. Nathaniel Hartland at Tewkesbury (1809) was a tanner; the Beechings at Tonbridge (1815) were drapers,[6] and Symons of Symons and

[5] This is the local story, but there may earlier have been a bank which James Stevens now joined. The story goes on that after carrying his friends' cash for a little while, he said 'Look here, this is all very well, but any highwayman will know that I am carrying considerable sums and if anybody is going to be held up by them it will be me, pistols or no pistols.' He determined, therefore, to open a bank so that these cash movements could be replaced by paper transactions.

[6] A print of their shop-front at Tonbridge shows the words 'Salesman. Linen Draper' over the shop, 'Hosier & Hatter' on the windows, and below the windows, 'Variety of Elegant Prints' and 'India Muslins & Shawls'. The business had been established in 1789 by Thomas Beeching, who from the outset cultivated relations with smaller drapers and

Soltau, Plymouth (1809) 'a merchant'. Paget at Leicester was a wealthy stockbreeder who had family connexions with an important firm of lace and hosiery manufacturers; in 1811 he went into partnership with a local banker, but in 1825 opened independently. The Hentys of Worthing (1808) were rich in land. Anthony Cox at Harwich (1807) was government agent for the packet-boats, an important business in those days. Cecil Parsons, a considerable character at Presteigne (1837), was a wealthy solicitor, in the habit of looking after monies and deeds for his friends. The only real oddity in the list was Fryers Bank at Wolverhampton. Richard Fryer, an innkeeper, in 1807 discovered that a large oak chest left at the inn for safekeeping and never reclaimed contained a fortune in French gold coins. The story goes that the chest had been left in 1745 when the Young Pretender was encamped near Derby, the money being allegedly on its way to France in the Pretender's interest. It is surprising that successive innkeepers remained incurious for over sixty years. However, Richard's curiosity was rewarded with such wealth that he was able to set up as the local banker, and the bank he founded was still in sound condition when absorbed by Lloyds sixty-five years later.

Changes of partners were inevitably frequent and, although the ravages of time could in this way be a source of weakness in the old private banks, the opportunity of bringing in new blood, new wealth, and new business connexions was in fact often taken. The link with the brewery, brought by the Knights to the Farnham Bank, was just such a case of strengthening from without. Another was in 'The Birmingham and Warwickshire', Birmingham's first recorded bank. Robert Coales, merchant and sword-cutler of Bartholomew Row, opened it in the 1770's;[7] in 1800, 1807, and 1812 new partners were brought in and of these nothing is known, but in 1815 an important new 'dynasty' joined the firm. This was by the introduction of John Lewis Moilliet, who had come from Geneva at the age of 16, was naturalized in 1801 when he

other shop-keepers in neighbouring villages. For these neighbours Beeching was soon doing some kind of banking business; the date 1815 refers simply to his first issue of notes.

[7] In 1770 the Directories listed Robert Coales as sword-cutler and merchant or factor; in 1789 he had become 'banker and sword-cutler', and in 1797 he was simply 'banker'. A newspaper obituary notice in 1804 said that he was 'highly respected for his liberality in a public capacity and his benevolence in a private one'.

4

married a Birmingham lady,[8] and was subsequently described as 'a Foreign Merchant in New Hall Street'. He and his descendants dominated the banking partnership until, as a business whose goodwill was valued at £25,000, it was merged into Lloyds when the latter became a joint-stock company in 1865.

In the variety of origins of the wealth and business connexions that men brought into the foundation of these country banks there is some slight justification for the picturesque phrases used by Lord Liverpool in 1826. But Liverpool was making a case, the case for joint-stock banking companies, and his words carried the clear implication that these founders of banks were little men of no substance. 'Any small tradesman,' he said, 'a cheesemonger, a butcher, or a shoemaker, may open a country bank, but a set of persons with a fortune sufficient to carry on the concern with security are not permitted to do so.'[9] Such details as have survived suggest that the private partnerships that went into banking were rather of substantial tradesmen who were not merely established business men but also men who brought considerable wealth into their new firms. Our sample is of course biased, in that these firms were those that survived long enough to enter, in one way or another, the Capital and Counties or Lloyds itself. But at least it can be said that England outside London had, by the time Lord Liverpool was speaking, a good number of banks which, though tiny by modern standards, were strongly founded on wealth and business experience.

The foundation of country banking upon a fusion of wealth and business experience and connexions is excellently illustrated in the Birmingham firm of Taylors and Lloyds, which is the real parent firm of the present Lloyds Bank. This private partnership entered the business of banking in Birmingham in 1765. The original partners were Sampson Lloyd (Sampson Lloyd II), John Taylor, Sampson Lloyd junior (III), and John Taylor junior, each of whom provided one-quarter of the £8,000 capital. Although he was the younger man, Taylor's name took precedence in the title of the firm, presumably because he was wealthier and

---

[8] She was Amelia Keir, daughter of James Keir, a chemist, friend of Joseph Priestley and an eminent member of the Birmingham Lunar Society.

[9] *Hansard Debates*, vol. xiv, col. 462. The passage has been frequently quoted in the literature of English banking history (e.g. Feavearyear, *The Pound Sterling* (1931), p. 224).

better known in Birmingham; but there is justice in posterity's alteration, for Sampson Lloyd II was the real inspirer of the foundation and he alone can be called the father of Lloyds Bank.

If a Lloyd was the founder and Birmingham the parental home, the iron trade was the business out of which the original money—and many business connexions—principally came. Sampson Lloyd and his elder brother, Charles, sons of the Charles Lloyd who was the first Quaker Lloyd, married two sisters, Mary and Sarah Crowley, sisters of Ambrose Crowley the famous iron-master; business ability as well as a valuable connexion probably came through these marriages. A sister of Charles and Sampson married John Pemberton, a wealthy iron-merchant from a Quaker family important in Birmingham life in the seventeenth and eighteenth centuries.[10] Perhaps it was this sister who impressed on Sampson Lloyd the tolerance Dissenters found in Birmingham, or perhaps his own acumen told him that Birmingham was a town of opportunity. Anyway, in 1698, at the age of 34, Sampson Lloyd moved to Birmingham, setting up as an iron-merchant in Edgbaston Street. He was soon described as an 'iron-founder', and added a water-powered slitting-mill in Bradford Street. When he died in 1724 he had become a man of very considerable property.[11]

The story of rising family fortunes continues with Sampson's third son, Sampson Lloyd II, the founder of the bank.[12] After apprenticeship to a Bristol merchant, Sampson II returned to the family business in Birmingham and through the next forty years he was well to the fore in the tremendous growth of the iron trade. Eventually three sons, Sampson III, Nehemiah, and Charles, were in the business with him.[13] The earliest record of the banking project is a letter dated 10 December 1764 from Samuel Garbett, an eminent Birmingham business man:[13a]

[10] John Pemberton's father and grandfather had been goldsmiths. John, the iron-merchant, lived at the top of Bennett's Hill, away from the industrial town in the valley below. He made his mark as a developer of this upper district and many of Birmingham's leading men in the next century came to live on property developed by Pemberton.

[11] A Birmingham historian in 1781 wrote: 'The proverbial expression, as rich as a Jew, is not altogether verified in Birmingham but perhaps time is transferring it to the Quakers' (W. Hutton, *History of Birmingham*).   [12] For Sampson Lloyd II see pp. 24–25 below.

[13] Just how rich Sampson Lloyd II was at this juncture is not known; he was certainly 'a man of substance' who had built an imposing mansion just outside Birmingham.

[13a] For Samuel Garbett, see T. S. Ashton, *Iron and Steel in the Industrial Revolution* (2nd edn., Manchester, 1951), p. 49.

6

JOHN TAYLOR, 1711–75
Founding partner of Taylors and Lloyds
From the miniature by W. Hedge, 1750

Some of the capital people in this town are establishing a Bank, viz.,
  Abel Smith, Esq., Banker of Nottingham
  John Taylor, Esq., our great Button maker
and
  Sampson Lloyd, an Ironmonger in this town. He is a man of unques-
  tionable substance, a most amiable character.

It is notable that the Birmingham writer of this letter put our Sampson Lloyd last, and thought it necessary to say a little more about him than about the well-known characters with whom he was joined. Abel Smith's presence in the trio is easy enough to explain. He was the most active member of the family that had established a bank in Nottingham a hundred years earlier;[14] he was a co-founder of Smith and Payne, bankers in London from about 1758, and founder of banks later at Hull and Lincoln. He was in fact an eighteenth-century forerunner of the 'bank promoters' prominent in the 1820's and 30's. John Taylor was a Unitarian who had started life in Birmingham as a cabinet-maker—'a mere artisan', according to a Birmingham historian[15]—but was soon in partnership with John Pemberton (brother-in-law of Sampson Lloyd I) as a maker of buttons and japanned goods.[16] At the age of 23 he was one of the 'valuable acquaintances' made by Dr. Johnson, though it must have been in the light of subsequent history that Boswell wrote that Taylor by 'his ingenuity in mechanical inventions, and his success in trade, acquired an immense fortune'.[17] Evidently he had a flair for picking the markets for typical new Birmingham products, for he became most widely known for his snuff-boxes, recognizable by their pattern and soon part of the essential equipment of the mid-century beau. He became a substantial owner of local property, including the manor of Yardley, and in 1756 he was

[14] Among those with a continuous history to the present day this was the first country bank in England. Like the London firm of Smith and Payne, it merged into what is now the National Provincial Bank. For Abel Smith as a founder of banks cf. H. T. Easton, *The History of a Banking House*, p. 14, and H. Withers, *National Provincial Bank 1833–1933*, p. 78.

[15] R. K. Dent, *The Making of Birmingham* (Birmingham, 1894), p. 94.

[16] John Pemberton's son, Thomas (brother-in-law of Sampson Lloyd II), succeeded John as Taylor's partner (Raistrick, *Quakers in Science and Industry*).

[17] Boswell's *Life of Johnson*, Oxford Standard Authors edition, p. 61. Many years later (1776) Johnson visited Sampson Lloyd III at his house in 'The Square', part of the district developed by John Pemberton (ibid., p. 6). On his death in 1775 John Taylor left about £200,000.

High Sheriff of Warwickshire. Taylor's business reputation, his great wealth, and perhaps his Unitarianism, were substantial assets for a new banking partnership, as was recognized when his name was placed first in the bank's title.[18]

Which of the three men took the initiative it is impossible to say with certainty, but there is some evidence supporting Lloyd's claim, and none supporting Taylor's—and whereas Taylor might not have hit on Lloyd as a partner, Taylor's wealth and reputation would have been an attraction to Lloyd, if he was the one casting round for a partner. The growth of trade in Birmingham generally would have attracted many towards, and may have caused Abel Smith's interest in—even origination of—the idea of a bank in Birmingham.[19]

Further light on the interest of Sampson Lloyd comes from a letter from his eldest son, Sampson Lloyd III, to one of his brothers. He (the son) was impressed by the difficulty of establishing the bank in Birmingham: '. . . the Success cannot be presently determinable but if found at all it must seemingly be the consequence of pretty great application everybody here being Strangers and the nature of it [the business of banking] different to what it is in London if not in most places'. Then he goes on to account for his father's willingness to enter such a difficult venture: 'My Father is actuated chiefly with a view to thinking out somewhat that might afford employment and advantage to his young family on which account I also confess my own diligence has of late been pretty much awakened especially as the Old Channel of our Trade has been considerably obstructed.' The iron trade was indeed going through a lean time, after the collapse of demand at the end of the Seven Years War.[20] And Sampson Lloyd did have a numerous family to put out in trade. Though the younger boys could be apprenticed in various places, father was no doubt keenly aware of the advantage of having some opening for them in Birmingham. In the event three came into the bank: Sampson III

[18] See pp. 27–30 below for the history of the Taylors in the bank.

[19] A Birmingham historian, W. Hutton, writing in 1781 of the foundation of Taylors and Lloyds, said that before 1765 the town was without 'a public bank'. 'To remedy this defect', he continued, 'about every tenth trader was a banker, or a retailer of cash. At the head of these were marshalled the whole train of drapers and grocers . . .' (*History of Birmingham*, p. 129).

[20] This depression in the iron trade and its effect in the Birmingham area are referred to by T. S. Ashton, *Iron and Steel in the Industrial Revolution*, pp. 132–3.

(writer of the letter just quoted), who became an original partner, Nehe-miah, who also remained active in the iron business, and Charles, who was only 17 at the founding of the bank.[21] These were the three who were then with their father in the iron business, and it is hardly surprising that Sampson Lloyd II was anxious to establish some alternative outlet for their energies when his original trade was shrinking.

As Birmingham was at this time virtually without banking facilities, there was everything to be gained by seeking the widest possible clientèle. Abel Smith from Nottingham, not himself a Quaker, no doubt urged upon Lloyd the necessity of allying himself with men of other religious views in order to attract customers from beyond the somewhat exclusive circle of Quakers in which the Lloyds moved. Thus Quaker energy, busi-ness experience, and the pressure of a growing family were eventually allied with the Unitarian wealth and local reputation of John Taylor.

Abel Smith, who did not eventually join the partnership, probably concentrated his energies on arranging London connexions for the new bank. Before the bank opened Taylor was busy in London and the Lloyds were considering the establishment of a partner in London. This step was not at once taken, but Taylors and Lloyds opened an account with Smith and Payne, the firm Abel Smith had founded in Coleman Street, Loth-bury. It was only five years later that the two junior partners in the Bir-mingham house (Sampson Lloyd III and John Taylor II) decided to set up their own house in London.

Messrs. Taylors and Lloyds, bankers at Dale End, Birmingham, opened their accounts in June 1765 and were paying interest (at 2 per cent.) on deposits from September 1765.[22] Ten years later they had 277 customers on their books. In the Lloyd family the tradition is that it was the Quaker connexion that really made the bank, and it is a little sur-prising to find that only about 40 of the 277 were Quakers. The 40 were, perhaps, particularly valuable to the bank both for their reliability and

---

[21] According to E. Allison, *Fruitful Heritage*, p. 64, Charles was sent to Freame, Barclay and Freame, in which his brother-in-law, David Barclay, was a partner, to learn banking.

[22] The local newspaper (Aris's *Birmingham Gazette*) published a bare announcement of the opening of the bank and made no comment either then or at any time in 1765. Bee-hives were a prominent subject of the *Gazette*'s front page on the day the bank opened, and it is tempting to suppose that the adoption of the beehive as the bank's emblem was not a coincidence. There is, however, no evidence of its use until 1822, when a highway robbery of notes led to a new and distinctive issue.

for the closeness of their connexions with Quaker business men else-where: certainly there are many indications that the Quaker connexions of the bank were both continuous and widespread.[23] Astonishingly enough, 72 of the 277 customers in 1775 were ladies—this not in a quiet residential town but in a jumped-up industrial city. The trades of the 205 men included a wide range of typical Birmingham trades.[24]

The methods of making up accounts in these early days do not allow summary in terms readily understood today, but it appears that in 1771 the balance-sheet total was £85,000 or perhaps rather more. Customers' credit balances totalled £43,000 and £33,000 of notes were out. There was also a candid item 'Error not found out, £33 7s. $8\frac{1}{4}d$.'[25] On the other side, £45,000 was due from customers, there was £13,000 of 'Bills, Notes and Cash in the House', and £27,000 with the London house—Hanbury, Taylor, Lloyd and Bowman. There had already been investments in India Bonds and in South Sea Annuities, to which Birmingham Canal Navigation Shares were soon added; not until the War of American Independence did British Government securities begin to predominate among the bank's investments. Among the advances to customers there was always, in the first decades, a large item due from the iron business 'S. N. and C. Lloyd'.[26] Nehemiah and Charles reduced this to £8,000 two years later by ploughing in the profits divided by the bank. The profits had in fact been substantial: after the first six years £10,500 was set aside as an addition to the original capital of £8,000. By the last decade of the century the annual profit was generally £6,000–£8,000.[27]

Meanwhile the London business also had been getting on its feet. In 1770 the two younger partners in the Birmingham house—Sampson Lloyd III and John Taylor II—joined Osgood Hanbury, husband of Mary, step-sister of the former. Hanbury had been in the family business, a tobacco

[23] Until 1845 the months of the year were never named in the bank's account books but were, according to the Quaker custom, referred to by number (I to XII) only.

[24] Among the descriptions were watch-chain-maker, hinge-maker, plater, thimble-maker, file-cutter, toy-maker, butcher, publican, victualler, whip-maker, factor and chapman, split-ring-maker.

[25] Another early balance-sheet entry is: 'By Sundries that should not have been entered on the other side, viz., etc., £1,025 12s. 6d.'

[26] i.e. Sampson III, Nehemiah, and Charles Lloyd, the three sons whom Sampson II had with himself in his iron business when he founded the bank at Birmingham.

[27] 1793 was an exception—£2,775 was allocated to bad debts and losses, and only £3,000 profit was declared.

empire, but this was not as prosperous as it had been and he was no doubt glad of another line of business.[28] For a fourth partner, William Bowman was brought in from Smith and Payne. There he had been cashier, and his experience of Lombard Street must have been invaluable.[29] Each partner provided £5,000 capital, and premises were taken at No. 14 Lombard Street. There the bank as Messrs. Hanbury, Taylor, Lloyd and Bowman opened in 1770, with William Bowman as manager living on the premises. In 1779 they moved to No. 60 Lombard Street, and there they stayed until their amalgamation, in 1864, with Barnetts Hoares. Throughout this period—and afterwards as Messrs. Barnetts, Hoares, Hanburys & Lloyd at 60–62 Lombard Street—'the London house' continued to act as London agent of 'the Birmingham house', but the family connexion between the two houses loosened. The Taylors combined partnerships in Birmingham and in London simultaneously, until the family left both, completely, in 1852.[30] Neither Hanburys (who remained in the London house throughout) nor Bowmans (who dropped out in 1814) were ever represented in the Birmingham partnership. The Lloyd family remained in both houses, but the last Lloyd to be a partner in both was Sampson III who died in 1807. Thereafter his descendants, Henry, Richard Harman, and Richard Borrodaile, were successively partners in London, as were John, a younger son of Sampson II, and his son Corbyn. The Birmingham partnerships continued to be held by the elder branches of Sampson III's family and by the descendants of the Charles who had been one of the founder's three sons in his iron business back in 1765.

The amalgamation of Lloyds Banking Company (as the Birmingham partnership became in 1865) and Messrs. Barnetts, Hoares, Hanbury and Lloyd of 60–62 Lombard Street, in 1884, brought all the bankers of the Lloyd family once more into a single concern. The connexion has con-

---

[28] Osgood's father, John Hanbury, 'had been well-known throughout Europe as the greatest tobacco merchant of his day'. His own fleet of ships included one named *Osgood*. The decline of the firm appears to have been connected with the war in North America which became part of the Seven Years War.

[29] There is an ambiguous reference to Bowman's value to Smith and Payne in H. T. Easton, *The History of a Banking House*, p. 73.

[30] The second John Taylor's two sons, James and William, were both in the Birmingham partnership; James alone in the London. William died in 1839; when James committed suicide in 1852 his widow persuaded their son, William Francis Taylor, to refuse partnerships both at Birmingham and at London (see p. 29 below).

tinued to this day, the partnerships of earlier times being followed by the directorships of nowadays. J. W. Beaumont Pease, Lord Wardington, Chairman of the bank from 1922 till 1945, was descended in the female line from Samuel (1768–1849) and so from the founder Sampson Lloyd II and the Bristol lady to whom he returned to press his suit. Mr. Cyril Lloyd, who retired from the Board in 1956, and Mr. F. N. Lloyd, now a Director of the bank, are both descended from Samuel Lloyd and so from the founder of the bank.

The 'London house' which the Taylors and Lloyds had established in Lombard Street in 1770 was by no means the only, or even the oldest, London root of the bank of today. Barnetts Hoares can be traced back, with some interruption, to Lombard Street in the early years of King Charles II. The firm of Bosanquet Salt and Co., absorbed by Lloyds simultaneously with Barnetts Hoares in 1884, derived from Bosanquets, a foundation of the 1770's (first in Exchange Alley and then in Lombard Street), and from Stevenson Salt and Co. established in London in 1787 and in Lombard Street from 1799.[31] Willis Percival and Co., of Lombard Street, absorbed in 1878 into what became the Capital and Counties, also goes back into the mists of Restoration London. Thus walking along Lombard Street in the early years of the nineteenth century, a man would pass five separate banks that were destined to come eventually into Lloyds Bank. A little later he would have seen another in the next street: in 1813 a group of Leeds men, then founding a bank in Leeds, opened at 75 Threadneedle Street the bank that was to become Brown Janson and Co. of Abchurch Lane. This, like the Taylors and Lloyds Birmingham and London connexion, was maintained as a Leeds–London connexion until both London and Leeds banks were absorbed in 1900 by Lloyds with whom the Jansons had become related by marriage. Another such London–provincial dual business was that of Cunliffe Brooks and Co. They were founded in Blackburn in 1792, and in the 1820's a London house was founded by a Cunliffe of the second generation. In 1864 this London house was merged in Alexanders, the discount house, but at the same time a new London house, Brooks and Co., was opened by the sole partner in the Blackburn bank.[32]

[31] Bosanquets amalgamated with Stevenson Salt & Co. in 1867.
[32] The first London foundation was at 29 Lombard Street and later at No. 24. It

Farther west other constituent banks had established themselves in the latter half of the eighteenth century and the first years of the nineteenth. In Fleet Street the Praeds from the Cornish Bank (which went back to 1771) established themselves in a building designed for them by Sir John Soane, the Bank of England's architect. Close to Temple Bar Twinings in 1824 separated their banking activities from their famous tea and coffee business, though direct access to the tea warehouse remained.[33] In the West End there were some rather different establishments, catering mainly for the aristocracy and landed gentry who kept 'the London Season'. Among these West End banks some had highly specialized origins. Cox and Co., opened in Albemarle Street in 1758, was at first simply an agent for the payment of Army officers; a character it retained throughout its independent existence. In 1772 Robert Herries opened at No. 16 St. James's Street, in order to introduce travellers' letters of credit which other banks could not then be persuaded to adopt; as Herries Farquhars the business became one of the leading 'West End bankers' until it was absorbed by Lloyds in 1893. Henry S. King from 1816 did some banking business; eventually the firm had banking offices in Pall Mall, in Cornhill, and in India, though the business was still quite small when it went, with Cox's, into Lloyds in 1923. In Bond Street from 1773 there had been the little bank of Call Marten;[34] this was absorbed by Herries Farquhars in 1865.[35]

A quite different type of London bank was that of Hill and Sons, up by Smithfield market. This had been founded in 1825 by the manager of an earlier bank in the same place, which had been among the victims of the 1825 bankers' tornado. Hill's customers were always predominantly from the meat trade, and branches were for this reason opened in Islington, Deptford, Romford, and Liverpool. They were very proud of their

was employed as London agent not only by the parent firm at Blackburn but also (1836–49) by the powerful Liverpool Union Bank. Its interests appear to have shifted, however, and the 1864 amalgamation was virtually that of one discount house with another.

[33] In the early days of Twinings Bank cashiers were often called upon to change cheques partly in coin or notes and the balance in tea or coffee.

[34] This firm had begun as Pybus, Hyde, Dorset and Cockell, in New Bond Street; by many changes of partnership and at least one change of premises it became by 1830 Call Marten and Co., in New Bond Street.

[35] On the West End bankers, see Chapter 9, below.

specialist service to the trade, and it was not until 1911 that they gave way to the amalgamation tide.

More will be said in later chapters about the business of these banks, of the men who ran them, and the customers who crossed their thresholds. For the moment their names have been brought together in order to show how many and varied have been the roots of Lloyds Bank, even within the Metropolis. Including Lloyds themselves there were fourteen 'roots' in London, two dating back to Charles II, six to the eighteenth century, and six to the nineteenth. Of the fourteen, four were provincial trader-bankers setting up London houses: Lloyds the iron-merchant bankers joining with a London tobacco merchant; Stevenson Salt, mercer-bankers from Stafford; Brown Janson from wool and Leeds; and Brooks from cotton and Lancashire. Another provincial-come-to-London was Praeds, but its parent Cornish Bank (a landed-gentry bank) had been an offshoot of a typical West End bank of the eighteenth century. Bosanquets was a typical foundation of the 1790's and Call Martens an equally typical little West End bank. Cox was primarily Army agent, Herries the circulator of travellers' cheques, and King a shipping and forwarding agent as well as banker. Hill was a professional banker serving a special trade and Twining a successful London merchant with banking as a sideline.

The remaining two of the fourteen were the seventeenth-century foundations Barnetts Hoares and Willis Percival. Which was the first cannot be stated with assurance; both existed in Restoration Lombard Street, and both had their origins in the shops of the goldsmiths. Willis Percival begins with Thomas Williams, noted as a goldsmith in the 'Little London Directory' of 1677. He was said to keep running-cashes (i.e. current accounts) at the sign of the Crown in Lombard Street. In 1701 the second Benjamin Tudman was carrying on the business now described as 'Goldsmith and Bancker in Linnen'. For a few years, about 1708–18, a Stephen Child, son of Sir Francis Child,[36] appears as a partner. Through the eighteenth century the name of the firm frequently changed as new partners came in; not until 1814 did it settle to being Willis Percival and

[36] F. G. Hilton Price, *A Handbook of London Bankers*. Stephen had been in Childs Bank prior to this and probably resigned from Tudman and Child after inheriting money under his father's will in 1713.

Co. Under this name the firm spread its interests widely in London's foreign trade; misadventures gave it a narrow squeeze in 1857 and in 1878 the collapse of some Greek importers caused Willis Percivals to suspend payment for the first time in 200 years. The Hampshire and North Wilts Banking Company, anxious to become the 'Capital and Counties' by getting into Lombard Street, took it over at once.

In the pedigree of Barnetts Hoares there is a break between 1698 and 1728, though there is reasonable probability that the descent was in fact continuous from Samuel Stoakes, goldsmith, living in the parish of All Hallows and buried in 1669. Humphrey Stokes or Stocks,[37] goldsmith and banker, whom Pepys knew in Paternoster Row in January 1665, removed in the first half of 1666 to the sign of the Black Horse in Lombard Street. It seems likely that this Humphrey was the son of Samuel and that he took over the business when his father was getting old; if so, the use of the Black Horse as a bankers' sign goes back to whatever date—under the Commonwealth or the very early years of Charles II—can be put to Samuel's entry upon banking transactions. But its first home was a victim of the Fire of London in September 1666: on 2 September Pepys saw 'my little goldsmith Stokes receiving some friends' goods whose house itself was burned the day after',[38] and a tax list of Lombard Street immediately afterwards included no Mr. Stokes. But apparently Humphrey carried on business elsewhere, for in November Pepys noted: 'This day I received 450 pieces of gold more of Mr. Stokes but cost me $22\frac{1}{2}d$. change.'[39] By 1673 he was back in Lombard Street and was still there in 1689, but in a tax roll of 1692 the occupants are 'Madam Stokes, goldsmith, her son and two children',[40] and a lodger, Mr. Dodson, with his servant. The son referred to was Robert Stokes, who became a liveryman of the Goldsmiths Company in 1698.

There is then a gap in the record until 1728 when John Bland, goldsmith, appears at the sign of the Black Horse in Lombard Street. In the meanwhile the name Stokes frequently appears in the All Hallows vestry

[37] Various spellings—Stoakes, Stoaks, Stokes, Stocks—appear in the early parish registers, in tax lists and in Heal's list of London goldsmiths; Pepys used 'Stokes'.
[38] George Allen & Co.'s edition of the Diary, published 1911, vol. ii, p. 387.
[39] Ibid., vol. ii, p. 441.
[40] According to the tax roll for 1690 Humphrey Stokes was there with 'his wife and 3 children'; 'her son and two children' in 1692 presumably means 'her son and her two other children'.

books, until in 1712 he fled from his debts and the hue and cry was ordered to be raised after him. This disgraceful Stokes must have been either our Robert or the Joseph Stokes recorded as a goldsmith in White Hart Court, Lombard Street, from 1704 till 1709. The only ground for presuming that Joseph was the black sheep is that nothing further is recorded either of him or of anyone else as a goldsmith at White Hart Court, whereas a goldsmith-banker, John Bland, appears at the sign of the Black Horse in Lombard Street in 1728. On balance we prefer to suppose that Robert Stokes continued his successful career long after 1698 and that at some date before 1728 John Bland took over from him.[41]

Thenceforward the succession is clear. John Bland, two of his sons, his widow,[42] and possibly another relation carried on the business under the Black Horse sign at No. 54 (now Barclays Bank) until 1749, when 'Bland and Son' removed, taking the Black Horse with them, to No. 62. In 1761 the name Barnett[43] was added, and when Samuel Hoare[44] joined in 1772 the firm became Bland, Barnett and Hoare. In 1788 John Bland, Quaker, spent an evening transacting parish business at the Jamaica Coffee House and then dropped down dead at his club; this terminated the Bland connexion.[45] The firm's title was not, however, changed until 1826, when it became Barnett Hoare and Co., a title that lasted until the amalgamation in 1864 with Hanbury Lloyds and Co. It was this amalgamation that brought the name of Lloyds and the sign of the Black Horse together, though at Nos. 60 and 62 Lombard Street and not at the present Head Office site. When Lloyds Banking Company of Birmingham took over both 'Barnetts, Hoares, Hanbury and Lloyds' of Nos. 60–62 and 'Bosanquet Salt and Co.' of No. 73 in 1884, No. 73 was pulled down and on an

[41] F. G. Hilton Price, in his *Handbook of London Bankers* (enlarged edition, London, 1890–1), has a list for 1725, 'Compiled from data at the disposal of the Author', in which he includes Robert Stokes, at the Black Horse, but this appears to be mere repetition from the preceding list, which repetition Hilton Price thought justified by the absence of evidence of any intervening change.

[42] For the second time in its history the firm was for a brief period controlled by a widow. Like the number of women among early customers of Messrs. Taylors and Lloyds (cf. p. 10 above) this suggests that women had an appreciable part in English business life before 1800.

[43] Both the father and the grandfather of Benjamin Barnett (b. 1735) were naval officers.

[44] On the Hoare family, see below, pp. 43–45.

[45] John Bland's only child, Priscilla (aged 16 at the time of John's death), later married Charles Hanbury, brother of Osgood Hanbury II, partner in Hanbury, Taylor and Lloyd at No. 60 Lombard Street.

extended site a new building was erected for the amalgamated London office.[46] This new building was the No. 71, with the Black Horse sign, which Howard Lloyd thought would last for fifty years. It did, and was replaced in the 1930's by the much larger building outside which the sign of the Black Horse hangs today.

All these older roots of the bank, both in the country and in London, were of necessity private partnerships, since the Bank of England retained until 1826 its monopoly of joint-stock banking. In that year Lord Liverpool, the Prime Minister, sponsored a new law permitting the establishment of joint-stock banking companies (with unlimited liability) except within a 65-miles' circle round London. In 1833 joint-stock banks were allowed inside the circle provided they did not issue notes; then in 1844 a stricter law almost stopped further foundations. During the intervening years some 120 'joint-stocks' were established in England and Wales; of these, twenty sooner or later came into the Lloyds group. All of them were outside the 65-miles' circle and were, in fact, well scattered to the north and west.

Among the first was the Halifax Joint Stock Banking Company—naturally enough, after the slaughter of the 1825 crisis among the Yorkshire private banks. In the boom of 1836 Halifax saw the establishment of a rival, the Halifax and Huddersfield Union Banking Company, and these two joint-stock banks stood independently, competing with each other, through the rest of the century. In 1910 they joined forces, becoming the West Yorkshire Bank, and for nine more years resisted the rising tide from London. Another early comer after the Act of 1826 was the Plymouth and Devonport Banking Company (1831) which changed its name to the Devon and Cornwall Banking Company when its vigorous policy of branch expansion made the old name inappropriate. This survived as one of the strongest 'country' branch systems; when it joined Lloyds in 1906 it brought fifty-five offices scattered over Dorset, Devon, and Cornwall, and was a major extension of the Lloyds network.

There were also, among these twenty, some important nuclei of the stronghold that Lloyds was to build up in 'the West Country'. Three of them centred on Gloucestershire—the Gloucestershire Banking

[46] Nos. 60–62 were used for a time by the bank but has since become the London office of the Commercial Bank of Scotland.

Company (1831), the Gloucester County and City Bank (1834), and the Cheltenham and Gloucester Banking Company (1836). The Gloucester County and City Bank two years later joined with a long-established private bank at Cirencester to form the County of Gloucester Banking Company and within a month absorbed a private bank at Dursley. Later it absorbed private banks at Stroud and Swindon, and in 1856 absorbed one of its most important competitors—the Cheltenham and Gloucester. Forty-one years later the County—now extending into Wiltshire, Berkshire, and Oxfordshire—in turn was absorbed by Lloyds. The Gloucestershire Banking Company—which had, besides absorbing five private banks, opened branches as far afield as Monmouth and Abergavenny—in the early eighties felt the need of outlets in Bristol and London, and in 1886 sold out to the Capital and Counties.

This—the Capital and Counties itself—had its main roots in this group of joint-stock banks founded in 1826–44. The Hampshire Banking Company was founded in 1834 at Southampton. Two years later a local rival appeared—the Southern District Banking Company, which proceeded to open branches in the Isle of Wight. In 1840 the Southern failed and most of its offices were taken over by the Hampshire Banking Company; then in 1873 the Hampshire rescued the English and Jersey Union Banking Company from the difficulties into which it had been plunged by its rivals in the Channel Islands, and so brought the first Channel Islands connexion into English banking. Meanwhile the North Wilts Banking Company, founded in 1835 on the basis of a Melksham private bank, had by absorption and by opening new offices built a county network of twelve offices. In 1877 these two compact networks, in contiguous counties, joined forces as the Hampshire and North Wilts Banking Company which quickly changed its name to the Capital and Counties Bank, and bought an old Lombard Street business, Willis Percival, in an unsuccessful attempt to gain admission to the London Bankers' Clearing House.

Other early joint-stock banks in the west were the West of England and South Wales District Banking Company (Bristol, 1834), the Shropshire Banking Company (1836), the Warwick and Leamington (1834), the Coventry and Warwickshire (1835), the Wilts and Dorset (Salisbury, 1835), the Glamorganshire (1836), and the Worcester City and County (1840). Of these the Wilts and Dorset had been an aggressive opener of

18

branches from its earliest days—the Select Committee of 1836 was told that it had already twenty-four branches—and by this means and the absorption of ten private banks it had by 1914 (when it joined Lloyds) a network of a hundred branches in Wiltshire, Dorset, Somerset, Hampshire, and Gloucestershire.

In Warwickshire the boom of the middle thirties produced two joint-stock banks that eventually came into Lloyds. In Warwick a private partnership, established in 1791 and known as The Warwick Old Bank, blossomed out in 1834 as The Warwick and Leamington Banking Company, with an office in each town and one at Stratford. Through thirty-two years it had its ups and downs without having much changed its character. At one time its shareholders had an unpleasant experience of the meaning of unlimited liability, and when taken over by Lloyds in 1866 there were some bad accounts in the building trade. The lending policy had probably been too venturesome because deposits came easily in the residential area of Leamington, and absorption in a larger bank which had plenty of outlets for the money undoubtedly made for sounder banking. The other Warwickshire foundation, the Coventry and Warwickshire Banking Company of 1835, was based on a private bank going back to 1790. It absorbed another private bank in 1839, but remained a purely Coventry bank, and in the seventies built for itself the office in High Street that remained the bank's principal office in the town until a move was made to the present building in the 1930's. Coventry was not in the nineteenth century the flourishing city it has since become, and Lloyds quite deliberately left it alone for some time. When the Birmingham Banking Company failed in 1866 and customers of its Coventry branch asked Lloyds to provide for them, the business was handled with extreme caution; both of Coventry's principal industries—silk and watches—were going downhill[47] and its destiny as a flourishing seat of the bicycle and motor industries was yet to appear. In 1874, however, Lloyds took courage and opened a branch; then in 1879 the Directors were surprised to receive an approach from the Coventry and Warwickshire Banking Company. The amalgamation that followed gave Lloyds

---

[47] The silk business had declined particularly since the Anglo-French commercial treaty of 1860; the watch industry was feeling Swiss and American competition (Howard Lloyd, *Notes and Reminiscences of Lloyds Bank*, p. 39).

a strong position in the city; in contrast to the 'Warwick and Leamington', the Coventry business brought borrowers more easily than depositors.[48]

To the west the Shropshire Banking Company had been founded in 1836 on the basis of four private banks, with extensive business—a switchback of profit and loss—in the iron and coal trades. It was gravely weakened by internal troubles as well as the vicissitudes of its major industrial connexions, but had its head above water when, as an organization of four Shropshire offices, it came into Lloyds in 1874. Of early joint-stock banks founded in Lancashire some retained their independence of the London giants until a late date—the District and Martins still stand aloof. But one did succumb to the blandishments of Lloyds in 1900. This was the Liverpool Union Bank, with which relations had always been close. An entirely new foundation in 1835, it had no branches at all until 1877. In the next few years it modified this policy, but only to the extent of bringing eleven branches—nearly all in Liverpool and Birkenhead—when it joined Lloyds in 1900.

In the south-west one of the most energetic young joint-stock banks was the West of England and South Wales District Bank. This was established in 1834 at Bristol by professional promoters of joint-stock banks (two from Manchester and one from Leeds), without any private banking basis. From the first it pushed out branches over a wide area—Exeter and Swansea were two of the earliest. By 1860 it had sixteen branches, including one at Plymouth, one at Gloucester, and a number in South Wales. It failed in 1878, but part of its business was reconstructed in 1879 as the Bristol and West of England Bank. When it joined Lloyds in 1892 it brought twenty-two offices, mostly in South Wales, Devon, and the Bristol area. The Glamorganshire Banking Company, founded in 1836, occupied a much more compact territory. Originally based on two private firms, one at Swansea and one at Neath, it absorbed another Swansea firm in 1841 but went practically no farther until after 1883. The branches established in the next few years brought the total number of offices up to eight when the bank was absorbed in the Capital and Counties in 1898.

In the Midlands there were foundations, all on the basis of private

---

[48] 'If a Coventry man can save a little money', noted Howard Lloyd, 'it is promptly required in his business, or for some other form of investment.'

banks, at Burton, at Daventry and Northampton, and at Nottingham. The Burton bank, based on two private firms, was at first called the Burton, Uttoxeter and Staffordshire Banking Company. In 1843 'Ashbourn' replaced 'Staffordshire' in the name, which in 1893 was shortened to the Burton Union Bank Limited. Eschewing branch expansion until comparatively late, it brought eight branches, a compact territory in Derbyshire and Staffordshire, into Lloyds in 1899. At Northampton and Daventry the private firm of Watkins and Co. had been in the banking business since 1783; in 1836 this became the Northamptonshire Banking Company, but it remained a purely local concern and brought only five branches into the Capital and Counties in 1890. Another converted private bank was Moore and Robinson's Nottinghamshire Banking Company with thirty-four years of history before it 'went joint-stock' in 1836. It continued to confine itself to Nottingham until 1875, when it absorbed an old private bank in Wirksworth: with these two offices it came into the Capital and Counties in 1901. None of these banks was much different in size or scope from contemporary private banks, nor indeed were they greatly different from the private firms they succeeded except in their broader ownership.

The Worcester City and County Bank was the last of this group to be founded. The craze for forming joint-stock banks was thoroughly exhausted long before 1840, and the fact that nevertheless this important local bank could then be founded gives a hint of the sound further development that might have proceeded in the absence of the restrictive legislation of 1844. This bank was opened, without any basis of private business, in a town with two old and respected private banks besides other banking offices. It provided for a predominantly agricultural clientèle, but the town had (and has) a variety of minor industries. The new establishment later absorbed one small joint-stock bank and one private bank, but for twenty years its growth was intensive rather than extensive. After 1860 it became more venturesome, and when it came into Lloyds in 1889 it brought twenty-four branches, scattered over and just beyond Worcestershire and into the home ground of the Lloyds in Birmingham itself. Howard Lloyd thought it 'a very important and promising territory' and its annexation a 'valuable addition to the strength and progress of the Bank'.

The twenty joint-stock banks noted above, all of them formed between the legislative changes of 1826 and 1844, had between them some 350 offices by the time they lost their separate identities. Their importance as roots of the present bank may be judged by comparing this number with the total of 888 Lloyds offices and 473 Capital and Counties offices which together became one of the 'Big Five' in 1918, and with the 1,700 Lloyds offices of 1956. They did not touch east or south-east England, and not one of them touched London until the Hampshire and North Wilts Banking Company went there just before it took its new name of Capital and Counties. But they covered nearly all of the west and south-west, most of the Midlands, and two islands of the north. Although the old private banks—at any rate those that survived to come into Lloyds Bank—deserved better than Lord Liverpool's innuendo in 1826,[49] it was inevitable that their joint-stock rivals should have been the more aggressive, the more minded to grow, and above all that they should have been stronger. The tendency has therefore been for the ways of the joint-stock banks to dominate the development of the bank. But the private banks, if less strong as business organizations, have produced some tough dynasties of bankers, and partly for this reason the Lloyds Bank of today has been able to retain much that was good in the old private banks, and to draw strength from the immense variety of the roots from which it has grown.

[49] Cf. p. 5 above.

2

THE BANKERS

In the banks whose origins have been traced in the first chapter, history has been made by the combined activities of three parties—the bankers, their staffs, and their customers. In Chapter 3 we shall be looking at the history of the clerks and others who worked in the banks, and in Chapter 4 we shall have something to say of the banks' customers and the business the banks did with those customers. In the present chapter our concern is with the bankers themselves—the men who built the business and remained responsible for the organization and conduct of the banks, and who for a long time were also financially responsible for all the liabilities of their banks. It is quite impossible to mention, much less to notice at any length every one of these men. Some of them have left little trace in the records, although they may actually have had great influence both upon the conduct and growth of the business in their lives and upon the traditions that extended into the generations after they themselves were dead. Others must go unchronicled because their careers fell so much into a common pattern that their stories would involve wearisome repetition: reading a succession of obituary notices of nineteenth-century bankers, the historian encounters over and over again all the virtues of Victorian England—the personal integrity, the singleness of purpose, the industry and thrift, the interest in charities, the tenacity of organized religion, the family solidarity—these virtues appear again and again, until the reader longs for a really black-hearted villain.

Our references to the bankers must therefore be selective: this chapter is confined to a few outstanding characters and a handful of others who were typical of the hundreds of men who have deserved the description 'banker' in the history of these banks, and whose lives left some clear trace in the records. In Appendix 3 the reader will find a directory of all the

23

bankers of whom there is appreciable trace in records surviving within Lloyds Bank.

Precedence must be allowed to the Lloyds from whom the bank takes its name and whose Birmingham connexion was in many ways the bank's strongest root. The true founder of Lloyds Bank was Sampson Lloyd II (1699–1779). The third son in a large family, Sampson was, like his brothers, apprenticed to Quaker business men before joining his father's firm. Sampson, at the age of 17, was to go to Bristol merchants, with whom the family iron business had regular dealings. John Andrews, who was to be his master, apparently asked a Quaker committee, presumably in Birmingham, to vouch for the boy. In October this preliminary was completed and the way was clear for Sampson to go to Bristol:

Sampson Lloyd   Bristoll X^{br} 20 1716

I have at last recd ye Committees answer in respect to thy son which is thus, they thinke as the fayer is soe near at hand & that being thy usual time of comeing mayst thou bring him with thee by which may have an opportunity of seeing him & settle ye subject matter with thee, I am with respects

Thy Lo: frd

Jo^n Andrews

Further correspondence reveals the satisfaction Sampson gave to his Bristol master. But the young man had more strength of character than of body: the following letter refers to a weakness that troubled Sampson for a long time:

Bristoll feb^r 26: 1718

Respected frd
S. Lloyd

Perceiving thy son Sampson to look ill I enquired respecting his wellfare but could not get from him any satisfaction, though I have been informed by another y^t he is much disordered of late he hath complayned of ye soreness in his back bone, and a pain in his stomach succeeding that, & then a sickness & loss of appetite this is what am told but thou knowest it must be got artfully from him & in his time & way, for he doth too much hide his indisposition, for w^n ye Doctor asked him lately how he did he would acknowledge nothing, this is what thought proper to advise thee, give my respects to thy family J P & his & J T & spouse accept ye same from

Thy frd

John Andrews

24

The obstinacy with which the boy concealed his troubles perhaps signalized the will-power that helped him through. At any rate, it was not long before the Bristol merchant was giving better reports to his 'Respected Friend' in Birmingham. Exactly when Sampson returned to Birmingham is not known, but it is clear that when he did he took with him valuable trade acquaintance and an astuteness in business that together gave a new impetus to the family's position in the iron trade.[1]

Sampson II was twice married, and both marriages contributed to the second generation of bankers. In 1727 Sampson and his cousin Thomas Pemberton married the sisters Sarah and Jane Parkes, quarter-heirs of the rich Quaker iron-master, Richard Parkes of Wednesbury. Mrs. Sampson Lloyd died in 1729 leaving a son, Sampson III, who became with his father an original partner in the bank of Taylors and Lloyds when they started business in 1765. In 1731 the young and now wealthy widower, Sampson II, returned to Bristol, whence he had perhaps brought romantic memories as well as business training. The lady whom he sought— Rachael Champion—at first rejected him, but as he rode back towards Birmingham he found fresh courage. Having ridden beyond Gloucester 'he could not divest himself of the persuasion that she was the proper person for his wife insomuch that notwithstanding his repulse he determined immediately to return and renew his solicitations'.[2] The resulting marriage proved happy—and fruitful in bankers: two sons became active partners in the Birmingham bank and one in London, while one daughter married a Hanbury, partner in the London bank, and another married David Barclay, partner in the Lombard Street bank of Freame, Barclay and Freame.

When the bank was founded Sampson II had become 'a man of unquestionable substance, a most amiable character'. The children of his

---

[1] The connexion with Quakers in the West Country (and elsewhere) remained of great importance to the development of the banking business. When Richard T. Cadbury came to Birmingham in 1794 he dined with members of the Lloyd family on each of his first two Sundays in the town; to this day the great chocolate firm's main account is kept in the Colmore Row office.

[2] Sampson Lloyd's conduct on this occasion may be contrasted with that of a later Lloyd, 'Charles the Poet', at the end of the eighteenth century. Finding it 'impossible to remain insensible to the charms of Sophia, daughter of Samuel Pemberton of Birmingham', Charles went so far as to make her an offer in a letter, but 'thinking it premature he hired a post-chaise, overtook the mail, and got it back again' (S. Lloyd, *The Lloyds of Birmingham* (1907), pp. 155–56).

second marriage were growing up and were, like the earlier generation, apprenticed to Quaker merchants in various places. Still following in father's footsteps, some of them returned from these apprenticeships to the family business in Birmingham—to which the banking partnership with the Taylor family had now been added. Nehemiah appears to have devoted himself mainly to the iron business; Charles (1748–1828) became with his half-brother Sampson III (twenty years his elder) a mainstay of the bank while John entered the London banking house. Sampson III held the family property at Farm,[3] while Charles became a man of property by a marriage to Mary Farmer, heiress of Bingley House. From these two—Sampson III and Charles—the two main streams of the banking family spring—the 'Farm' line and the 'Bingley' line.

Of Sampson III little is known, except that he was fortunate in his encounter with Dr. Johnson. Johnson and Boswell were entertained 'with great hospitality' by Sampson Lloyd in 1776.[4] There is a family tradition that Johnson, losing his temper in argument over a Quaker book, threw the volume on the floor and put his foot on it; afterwards, at dinner, he continued in such an angry manner that the frightened children wanted to escape. However, next morning Johnson called at the bank to make an apology: 'I say, Lloyd, I'm the best theologian, but you are the best Christian.' Lloyd was also the more successful as a family man: eventually he and Rachel (Barnes) had sixteen children.[5] One of the daughters made a Gretna Green marriage to her sister's widower; apart from this disturbance to his serenity, the third Sampson appears to have passed an uneventful life, leaving to his descendants the memory of a 'venerable and loving countenance' surmounting his uniformly grey clothes.[6]

His half-brother Charles ('Charles Lloyd of Bingley', or 'Charles the Banker') was evidently the more powerful personality; he was described to a later generation as 'far away the greatest man the Lloyd family had ever produced'.[7] His extraordinary memory allowed him to repeat

---

[3] 'Farm' resulted from Sampson II's purchase in 1742 of 'Owen's Farm', on the outskirts of Birmingham. It comprised 56 acres with a farm-house and other buildings. The residence generally mentioned in the family history was not built until 1758 (Rachel J. Lowe, *Farm and its Inhabitants* (1883), pp. 29–30).

[4] Boswell's *Life of Johnson*, Oxford Standard Authors edition, p. 702 (22 Mar. 1776).

[5] This is according to the list in *Farm and its Inhabitants*, pp. 46–48.

[6] He thought it right to wear wool undyed: 'dyes were vain things' (S. Lloyd, *The Lloyds of Birmingham*, p. 103).   [7] Ibid., p. 133.

'several entire Books of the Old Testament and the greatest part of the New'. He knew Virgil and Horace well and amused himself in his later years in translating Homer and Horace. He read several European languages and a wide range of subjects in his own. His interventions in public affairs included an effort to mediate between Franklin and Lord North in 1775, and later a prominent part in the anti-slave-trade movement. The General Hospital at Birmingham was yet another of his interests. In the last years of the eighteenth century and the first of the nineteenth Charles was the dominant figure in the Birmingham bank. In the London house he had no place; he shared the profits his half-brother Sampson drew from partnership in London, but this connexion ended with Sampson's death (1807), much to Charles's annoyance. Thereafter no Lloyd was partner both in London and in Birmingham; London became broadly the preserve of the younger branch of the Farm line, while Birmingham partners came from the Bingley line and the elder branches of the Farm line. His own successor in the bank at Birmingham was one of Charles's most difficult problems. His eldest son, also Charles, was put into the bank straight from school. But great efforts on the father's part made no banker of the boy—he had inherited his father's literary interests rather than his business capacity and soon dropped out of the bank to become known, in family circles, as 'Charles the Poet' who became a close friend of the Lake Poets.[8] The succession in the Birmingham bank went eventually to the second son, James,[9] who became a partner in 1802 and was followed in the middle decades of the nineteenth century by his own sons, James II, Thomas, and Francis. This second James lived just long enough to assist at the preliminaries to the conversion of the Birmingham house into a joint-stock bank in 1865.

For eighty-seven years in Birmingham and for eighty-two in London the Lloyds had as partners successive members of the Taylor family.

---

[8] There is frequent mention of this Charles Lloyd (1775–1839) in E. de Selincourt, *Dorothy Wordsworth* (Oxford, 1933), and in E. V. Lucas, *Charles Lamb and the Lloyds* (London, 1898).

[9] This first James Lloyd was at one time engaged to Elizabeth Gurney, subsequently Elizabeth Fry. There are many references to this engagement in Janet Whitney, *Elizabeth Fry* (London, 1937). The statement on p. 36 that James's father 'was the founder of Lloyds Bank' is inaccurate: James was grandson of Sampson Lloyd II, and James's father was only a junior partner in the early years of the bank.

John Taylor, 'our great button-maker',[10] who with Sampson Lloyd II and their two sons had been the original partners at Birmingham, was already 59 years old when the London partnership was established in 1770. He was, moreover, very wrapped up in his Birmingham business affairs and in local life and evidently felt it sufficient that his son, John Taylor junior, should join with the Lloyds and Osgood Hanbury in the London partnership. This second John Taylor, born in 1738 and therefore 27 when the Birmingham bank was founded, was a Justice of the Peace and inherited from his father Bordesley Hall and other very considerable property, to which he added by marrying (when he was 40) a rich heiress, Sarah Skeye. He is chiefly known as the central object of the mob's fury in the Birmingham riots of 1791. These riots were excited by a dinner to celebrate the second anniversary of the storming of the Bastille, and the mob attacked the property of prominent Birmingham citizens believed to be the enemies of 'Church and King'. Mosley Hall and other property known to belong to John Taylor was burnt down, and his net loss was substantial, even after compensation amounting to some £10,000 had been paid to him. Exactly why Taylor had this unenviable prominence is not known; it seems probable that it was as a Unitarian that he was distrusted, his extreme wealth and ownership of big local properties naturally focusing the attention of the mob.

The second John Taylor remained a partner in both the Birmingham and London banks from their inception until his death in 1814. His father had died in 1775, and from that time until 1804 John was the only Taylor in either bank. In 1804 he brought his second son, James Taylor, into both partnerships, and after John's death in 1814 the third son, William Taylor, then aged 25, was brought into the Birmingham bank but not into that in London. The eldest son, the third John Taylor, born in 1780, did not at any time join either partnership; shortly after his father's death he bought Strensham Court in Worcestershire, and there he remained, a bachelor landed gentleman. The two who came into banking, James and William, proved to be the last Taylors in this bank. Very little is known of them—nothing at all of their banking activities— and the only real interest in them revolves round the question why the Taylors dropped out of this flourishing business. The answer seems to lie

---

[10] See p. 7 above.

28

in a combination of circumstances: partly that the family tree was running thin, partly that those remaining were inclined to settle as landed gentry to the exclusion of any commercial activity, partly perhaps there was some discomfort remaining, through nobody's fault, from an unhappy episode in 1852.

Of the three sons born to John Taylor in the 1780's, only James had children. His younger brother William died in 1839, aged 50, leaving James as the only Taylor in the bank. The natural sequel would then have been for one of the next generation to be brought in—with a partnership either immediately or in early prospect, according to age. The next generation was limited to James Arthur Taylor, then aged 22, son of James by his first marriage, and William Francis Taylor, aged 9, son of James by his second marriage. Why did James Arthur not come into the bank? He was heir to his bachelor uncle's estate at Strensham in Worcestershire, and this alone may have settled the question; he is also known to have been, at some time, a gambler who left Strensham heavily mortgaged. Whether his habits of life already ruled him out of consideration is not known; what we do know is that neither at this nor at any other time does he appear to have been considered as a possible partner in either of the two banks. So James alone represented the Taylors, while his younger son William Francis was emerging from childhood and he himself left middle age behind. In the autumn of 1852 James's health broke down; in his last weeks he became quite irrationally worried about his business affairs and this worry hastened his end. It would have been timely for his younger son, William Francis, to be brought into the banks —he was now 22 and there is evidence that his father trusted him in business matters. But before James could take any such step or his partners discuss matters with him, he came to an unhappy end. William Francis was thereupon offered partnership, both at Birmingham and at London. He declined both—the latter only after hesitation. His decision is believed to have been due to his mother's aversion to any commercial attachment, an aversion that may have been heightened, if not originated, by the imaginary worries of her husband's last weeks. Possibly the son's inclination, nevertheless, to take up the London partnership was due to the slightly higher social standing of a London banker, but in the end mother's wishes prevailed. There was no mention of his half-brother,

James Arthur Taylor of Strensham Court, as an alternative successor in the banks; and so Taylors and Lloyds of Birmingham became Lloyds and Co., while the London firm became Hanburys and Lloyds. It is notable that in the private ledger of the London house James Taylor had some years previously[11] directed 'that in the case of his death, the old name should be continued for 6 months after his decease'. Evidently he had contemplated the probability that he would be the last of the banker Taylors, and perhaps it was his wish that this should be so. His sister had for many years been Lady Winnington, his elder son was a landed proprietor with tastes quite inconsistent with banking, the rise in Birmingham properties inherited from his father and his mother made commercial pursuits unnecessary, and the family had almost certainly by this time joined the Church of England.[12] It was a far cry from 1791, when a 'Church-and-King' mob had thought John Taylor the proper object of their wrath. It was time too, so the family seemed to think, for the Taylors to leave the banking business to other people.

The death of James Taylor in 1852 brought to an end the last common partnership of the banks at Birmingham and at London—the Lloyds in the two houses had for some decades belonged to different branches of that family. In 1865 the private firm of Lloyds and Co. at Birmingham consisted of three partners: Thomas of the Bingley line and Sampson Samuel and his brother George Braithwaite Lloyd, great-grandsons of Sampson III (the Farm line). The ages of the three Lloyds in 1865 were 51, 45, and 41 years respectively. Thomas's elder brother James (the Second) died during this year; his death was bound to leave a serious gap. Possibly the political differences between the three remaining Lloyds[13] helped to precipitate the change of status; but the really important influence was the general movement in English business life, and particularly in banking, towards the joint-stock form of organization. The collapse of a powerful private bank in Birmingham precipitated local developments. When the change came, it was made the occasion for the

[11] This would be while William Francis was still a child, though James Arthur had reached manhood before James Taylor became the only Taylor in the business.

[12] The next generation was definitely Church of England.

[13] Howard Lloyd, referring to the reasons for the reorganization, said that between these three Lloyds 'perfect uniformity of view was not always possible'.

infusion of fresh blood from powerful business circles in Birmingham. The initiative appears to have been taken by the Lloyds themselves, but some of the new men soon took the lead. They belonged to the great Unitarian connexion, unrepresented in the bank for many years: the three Lloyds represented Quakers and the Church. The new-comers evidently meant to take a serious part in the conduct of the bank, for although Sampson S. Lloyd became the first Managing Director, and Thomas became Deputy Chairman, the Chairmanship was voted to one of the new men. Joseph Chamberlain, one of the new directors, was rather too young—he was 29 and still making his fortune in Nettlefolds —but a man of the requisite standing was found in Timothy Kenrick.

This Timothy Kenrick, first Chairman of Lloyds Banking Company, was born in 1807, one of the two sons of Archibald Kenrick who had founded a successful iron-foundry and hardware manufacturing business at West Bromwich in 1791. Both sons entered and remained active in this business. A Unitarian by descent, Timothy was a prominent member of the New Meeting Congregation. He was an active and generous supporter of the local Education League and the General Hospital; the *Birmingham Post*[14] described him as practically the founder of the Nurse's Training Institution. In 1858 he became a Director of the Midland Railway Company, of which he later became Deputy Chairman. By 1865, when he was 58, his position as a business man in the Birmingham Unitarian circle was outstanding. He had no banking experience, though he had married into the family of a Leicester banker.[15] Living in Church Road, Edgbaston, he must have been known as a neighbour by G. B. Lloyd, the youngest of the surviving partners.

There is evidence that as Chairman Kenrick was no mere figurehead— in 1866 he engaged in negotiations with a correspondent bank about the discounting of bills—but just how he shared the real power with Sampson S. Lloyd, the Managing Director, is not known. In 1868, presiding at the sixth general meeting of the shareholders, Kenrick made an odd announcement: the *Birmingham Post*[16] report runs as follows:

---

[14] Obituary notice, 24 Feb. 1885.

[15] Paget and Co., the Leicester bank, was absorbed by Lloyds in 1895. Timothy Kenrick married a Paget and of their six children, two married Chamberlains (Joseph and Arthur).

[16] 7 Aug. 1868.

The Chairman announced that in consequence of public matters and circumstances to which he need not more particularly allude, Mr. Sampson S. Lloyd had sent in his resignation as managing director of the company. He had consented to continue in that office till the bank should make necessary arrangements, and he had also agreed to accept the chairmanship of the Board. He hoped that, whether Mr. Lloyd remained in Birmingham, or should be translated to a higher sphere, the directors would still have the assistance of his advice and ability.

Sampson S. Lloyd did in fact become Chairman in succession to Kenrick; his election at the age of 48 set a record for youthfulness unbroken even by the present Chairman[17] of the bank. Sampson Samuel Lloyd was born in November 1820, the eldest son of George Braithwaite Lloyd[18] who, like his forefathers continuously back to Sampson II in 1765, was a partner in the Birmingham bank. After education at Grove House, Tottenham (a Quaker school), Sampson Samuel Lloyd entered the bank at the age of 19. He became a partner in 1843 (aged 23) and, as we have seen, Managing Director when the bank became a joint-stock company; altogether he spent sixty years in the bank.

His resignation as Managing Director (to be quickly followed by election to the Chair) was evidently due to a determination to enter political life. A staunch Conservative at a time when in Birmingham 'to profess oneself a Tory was to almost court derision and abuse',[19] he unsuccessfully contested a local by-election in 1867. Then came the General Election of November 1868, the first after the Reform Act of 1867 whereby Birmingham became entitled to send three members to Westminster. As each voter was allowed to vote for only two candidates, there was room for entirely new organization of a party's supporters, and it was to exploit this situation that 'the Birmingham Caucus' was formed. Its success meant the return of all three Liberal candidates, to the exclusion of the two Conservatives, one of whom was our Sampson S. Lloyd. The election was long remembered as one of the stormiest Birmingham had known:

[17] Sir Oliver Franks.

[18] The name 'Braithwaite' came into the family through the marriage of Samuel Lloyd (1768–1849) to Rachel Braithwaite of Kendal in 1791. The younger brother of Sampson Samuel Lloyd was, like his father, named George Braithwaite Lloyd; he was the last survivor on the Board of the joint-stock company from the former partners of the private bank.

[19] *Birmingham Daily Gazette*, Obituary notice of S. S. Lloyd, 4 Mar. 1899.

SAMPSON SAMUEL LLOYD, 1820–99
Chairman, 1868–86
From the cartoon by 'Spy', Vanity Fair, 11 March 1882

it was the last occasion of nomination at the hustings, and Mr. Lloyd needed some courage to stand before the 'perfect storm of yells and groans' rising from a crowd of 30,000. Eventually he entered Parliament as member for Plymouth in 1874, and exerted himself in the House chiefly on commercial matters and on behalf of the Royal Marines. He sat through only the one Parliament, though he was an energetic candidate for a Warwickshire seat in the eighties, and became a great campaigner for 'Fair Trade' and for Imperial Preference.

Though his parliamentary career was not eminently successful, he remained for some time a prominent figure in public life. Particularly he was active in that middle ground between business and politics: he was a founding member of the Birmingham Chamber of Commerce (1856) and at a later stage became Chairman—for several successive years—of the Associated Chambers of Commerce, where his strong political views were often heard. In 1865 he travelled to Moscow to visit the Industrial Exhibition.[20]

As a banker he first made his name by his participation in a scheme for a country clearing system. With W. Gillett of Banbury, F. Bassett and Theodore Harris of Leighton Buzzard, O. Heywood of Manchester, and W. C. Tunstall of the Gloucestershire Banking Company, Lloyd planned to establish in London a separate Country Clearing House. It was, however, superseded by Sir John Lubbock's scheme when the Country Clearing was established in 1858 as part of the existing London Bankers' Clearing House. While Chairman of Lloyds Bank he became Deputy Chairman of the Alliance Bank Ltd., a small joint-stock bank with offices in the City and West End of London.[21] When Lloyds in effect came to London by the important amalgamations of 1884 (in the arrangements for which he had taken a leading part), Sampson Lloyd naturally had to give up his Deputy Chairmanship of another bank established in London. Two years later, when he handed on the Chairmanship of Lloyds Bank to Thomas Salt, Sampson Lloyd became a Director of the Ionian Bank. He remained a Director of Lloyds Bank until, a few days after attending

[20] Possibly his marriage (his second) in this year to the daughter of a Prussian Lieutenant-General had some connexion with his travels.

[21] The Alliance Bank was amalgamated with Parr's Bank in 1892 and so found its way eventually into the Westminster Bank of today. For its history see T. E. Gregory, *The Westminster Bank* (London, 1936), vol. ii, pp. 45–50.

the annual shareholders' meeting in February 1899 at Birmingham, he died at his home at Woking at the age of 79.

The third Chairman of the bank as a joint-stock company was Thomas Salt, who had been brought into the bank by the absorption in 1866 of the Stafford Old Bank in which he was a junior partner. In the range of his activities in public life Salt surpassed all his predecessors and most of his successors.

His family had been in banking for some generations before Thomas appeared on the scene. His great-grandfather (also Thomas Salt) had married into the Stevenson family which had founded a banking business in Stafford in 1737,[22] and the firm was known as Stevenson Salt and Co. through most of its independent existence; from 1787 there was a parallel London house, Stevenson Salt and Sons. The Thomas Salt who was to become Chairman of Lloyds was born in 1830, the son of another Thomas and Harriet Petit, descendant of a Huguenot family. From Rugby, where he won the English Essay Prize, Thomas Salt went to Balliol College, Oxford, where he gained a First in Law and History. On coming down from Oxford he entered the family business, then Stevenson Salt and Webb, and at the same time took a commission in the 2nd Staffordshire Militia.[23] Almost at once he became a figure in the county: going into politics as a moderate Conservative he entered Parliament as member for Stafford in 1859. But at this stage—perhaps because marriage claimed him in 1861 and a succession of children followed—he felt unable to cope with a variety of activities, and he took the opportunity of the 1865 dissolution of Parliament to withdraw in order to give closer attention to the banking house.

It was not long before extensive rearrangements of the banking business enabled Salt once more to spread his wings. In 1866, the elder Thomas Salt being an old man, the business at Stafford (with offices at Lichfield, Rugeley, and Eccleshall) was sold to Lloyds Banking Company, the younger Thomas Salt joining the Board of Directors. In the following year arrangements were made for the London house to amalgamate with Messrs. Bosanquet and Company, although these arrangements did not become effective until the elder Thomas Salt died in 1871.

[22] See p. 1 above.
[23] The regiment was embodied and called out for garrison services at home during the Crimean War.

As a Director in Lloyds Banking Company (Birmingham) and a partner in Bosanquet Salt and Co. (Lombard Street), Thomas Salt felt free to re-enter Parliament. In 1869 he again became member for Stafford and, apart from two brief interruptions, remained so until 1892. From 1875 until 1880 he held a junior office in Disraeli's Government, and was unpaid Church Estates Commissioner. He showed much interest in education and in church questions; one of his later parliamentary interventions was to move the rejection of the Deceased Wife's Sisters Bill in 1887. He became Chairman of the Lunacy Commission, and was an Ecclesiastical Commissioner and a Public Works Loan Commissioner. Just to fill up his time he was interested in railways: he became Chairman of the North Staffordshire Railway and of the New Zealand Railway Company. He was a County Alderman and in the Commission of the Peace for Staffordshire.

All this Salt made consistent with such attention to banking that he succeeded Sampson Lloyd as Chairman in 1886. In 1884 Lloyds Banking Company (of which Salt was a Director) had merged with the two London houses, Bosanquet Salt and Co. (in which Salt was a partner) and Barnett, Hoare, Hanbury and Lloyd. This combination took the title of Lloyds Barnetts and Bosanquets Bank Ltd., with Sampson S. Lloyd (from Lloyds Banking Company) as its Chairman. Although the Head Office remained in Birmingham the centre of gravity was shifting rapidly to London, and Sampson Lloyd soon gave up the Chairmanship in favour of Thomas Salt. Early in Salt's term of office the bank took its present title of Lloyds Bank Limited. It also began to assume something of its present character, for under Salt as Chairman with Howard Lloyd as General Manager the absorption of smaller banks became a common event. Both believed in extending the business of the bank by absorption, particularly of the old private banks. Not that the bank under Salt and Lloyd was aggressive in its amalgamation policy: rather it was a case of being receptive to the initiative of private firms who were feeling more and more that the future lay with the great joint-stock banks.

The progress of the bank in the twelve years of Salt's Chairmanship may be judged from a few figures. In 1886 the paid-up capital and reserves totalled £1,110,000, and the bank's assets £11,000,000; in 1898 capital and reserves stood at £2,400,000 and total assets at £40,000,000.

In 1886 the bank had 61 offices and 257 in 1898. Growth at this pace must have meant a busy time for Thomas Salt as Chairman of the bank, and he gave up parliamentary duties finally in 1892. When, getting towards the end of his sixties, something else had to go overboard, his railway interest finally claimed him. In 1898 his duties as Chairman of the New Zealand Railway Company necessitated a visit to that country, and he made this the occasion of his retirement from the Chairmanship of Lloyds Bank, although he retained a seat on the Board until his death in 1904.

By this time the amalgamation movement, prompted by Goschen's words after the Baring Crisis, had gathered speed. In Kenrick's Chairmanship Lloyds had absorbed four banks; in the eighteen years of Sampson S. Lloyd, seven (including the two very important mergers which brought the bank effectively to London). In Salt's twelve years there had been fifteen, by which the bank had both strengthened its hold in the Midlands and London and reached out into new areas in the south. Among the banks absorbed in Sampson Lloyd's time was the little 'Shrewsbury and Welshpool Old Bank', the family business of Messrs. Beck and Co.; it was by this amalgamation that Lloyds Bank secured John Spencer Phillips, who became in 1898 Thomas Salt's successor as Chairman of Lloyds Bank. Phillips was the son of a rector of Ludlow and was educated at Shrewsbury School and Trinity, Cambridge. After coming down from Cambridge he went into the Shrewsbury and Welshpool Old Bank and was taken into partnership by the two Becks. On the death of the senior partner in 1880 P. A. Beck and Spencer Phillips decided to sell out to Lloyds. P. A. Beck retired and Spencer Phillips was given a seat on the Board. Eight years later he succeeded Brodie Hoare as Deputy Chairman (under Salt as Chairman) and in 1898 followed Salt into the Chair.

While he was a Director during the eighties Spencer Phillips found a new neighbour in Shropshire in Joseph Beattie, the Managing Director of the Birmingham Joint Stock Bank and now in failing health. The two men were attracted to each other, and their friendship greatly facilitated, and perhaps was responsible for, the negotiations which ended in the acquisition by Lloyds in 1889 of the Birmingham bank, hitherto the 'powerful opponent and competitor' of Lloyds in that city. This was only one of many amalgamations in which Spencer Phillips took a leading part, and in 1903 the Board granted him a special allowance of £1,000 in recognition of his extraordinary exertions in this direction.

As Chairman of the bank—a bank now outstanding though not yet gigantic—Spencer Phillips was the first to use the annual meeting as an occasion for substantial commentary on the economic affairs of the nation. Salt, who had been something of a public figure, made only the brief references that any company chairman might make; Spencer Phillips, purely a banker, ventured into longer reviews, referring to the economic effects of the Boer War or the 'cyclical depressions of trade' until he approached the later style of bank chairmen deliberately reviewing the economic state of the nation. He also had much to say on broad matters of banking policy. He expressed in no uncertain terms the view that many of the smaller country banks were carrying on their business with too slender a basis of cash, and went so far as to advocate legislative interference in default of amendment from within. He constantly urged the desirability of some arrangement whereby all banks should publish frequent statements of accounts based on averages, and believed that this would of itself go far to settle the question of the alleged insufficiency of London's gold reserves.[24] Since Goschen's famous speeches of 1891 there had been no novelty about such views as these—even the confusion between internal bank reserves and London's international reserve came from Goschen—but it was something of a novelty for the Chairman of one of the biggest banks to preach with determination and vigour the gospel of banking reform.

As a young man Spencer Phillips had been a keen cricketer and a good oarsman. As a huntsman he was active in his native north Shropshire almost to the end of his life. For this and other reasons there was no realization, when he fell ill in the spring of 1909, that the bank was so soon to lose its Chairman and the Institute of Bankers its President. Indeed, he missed only two Board meetings through that last illness, and died on 31 May 1909 at the age of 61.

After twenty years under Birmingham Chairmen (Kenrick and Sampson S. Lloyd) Lloyds Bank had gone first to Stafford and then to Shrewsbury for their successors (Salt and Phillips). Still true to the Midlands-and-West-Country, in which most of the bank's roots lay, the bank found

[24] Obituary notice, *Journal of the Institute of Bankers*, 1909, p. 503.

its next Chairman in Vassar-Smith from Gloucester. But this time there was no family background of private banking. Richard Vassar-Smith, born in 1843 and educated at the King's School, Gloucester,[25] joined his father's business, in that city, of general carriers and agents for the Great Western Railway. By 1870, when he became head of the firm, he was prominent in the district and he eventually became Chairman of the Gloucester Railway Carriage and Wagon Co., the Port Talbot Steel Co., and the Gloucester Gas Light Company. In the Queen's Jubilee Year, 1886–7, he was Mayor of Gloucester, an office his father had twice filled. When Lloyds Bank absorbed the Worcester City and County Bank in 1889 Vassar-Smith had been for three years a Director of the Worcester bank, and was one of the two selected to join the Board of Lloyds Bank. In 1909 he succeeded Spencer Phillips as Chairman.[26] Lloyds was by this time one of the largest banks in the country, and Vassar-Smith was inevitably heavily engaged in discussions with the authorities regarding war-time arrangements. In recognition of these activities he was created a baronet in 1917.

Nevertheless, he retained some of his industrial activities, and in 1917–18 he was President of the Federation of British Industries. In earlier days he had, besides his local trade and banking activities, some interest in public affairs in Gloucestershire. He was on the Council of Cheltenham College and from 1897 he was a member, and later Chairman, of the Councils of Cheltenham Ladies College and of St. Hilda's College, Oxford.[27] For some time he was a member of the Gloucester County Council; he declined several invitations to stand as Conservative candidate for Parliament. He was a strong churchman and a freemason.

After he became Chairman of the bank he continued to own Charlton Park in Gloucestershire, but his activities in the county necessarily declined. His office did not, however, monopolize his attention, and he is particularly remembered for his great interest in the sports and other outside activities of the bank's staff. As a man he was noted for his calm, conciliatory manner: 'I never saw him ruffled', was a typical comment among those who had worked with him. When he died, still in office in

---

[25] In Vassar-Smith's time the school was generally known as 'the College School'.
[26] Unlike most Chairmen, Vassar-Smith did not have a period as Deputy Chairman.
[27] Cf. p. 47.

1922, his colleagues felt that they had lost a great Chairman. The staff of the bank subscribed over £10,000 for a memorial; this was devoted, as Vassar-Smith would have heartily approved, to a benevolent fund for the staff and their dependants.

Throughout Vassar-Smith's tenure of the Chairmanship he had been supported by J. Beaumont Pease as Deputy Chairman. With the succession of Beaumont Pease (he became Lord Wardington in 1936) to the Chair in 1922, the past knocks at the door of the present and must be left for a later generation to chronicle.

Leaving the line of Chairmen, we turn back to a few of the less central figures among the many who fostered the development of sound banking in particular localities. The seven bankers recalled in the following paragraphs are perhaps not all typical of the general run of nineteenth-century bankers: it is often because a man is something of a 'character' among his own kind that a story is told for later generations. But of the first of these men—Joseph Berwick of Worcester—there is no lively story to tell; we have simply the outline of a career showing how a young man could, in the hurly-burly of English business in the late eighteenth century, become the founder of a family banking business.[28] Joseph Berwick was born in 1751, son of John Berwick who was at once a draper and His Majesty's Receiver-General of the Land Tax for the City and County of Worcester. When Joseph attained his majority the local attorney was able[29] to secure the transfer from father to son of the appointment as Receiver-General. The Receiver was able to keep the taxes collected for at least six months before remitting them to London, and the use of this money for lending locally gave Berwick the basis of his banking business. There is no evidence that his father had made similar use of his opportunities; this may well be ascribed to his being a new-comer to the town, having arrived from Stroud only in 1766.[30] But Joseph, being known as the successful son of a successful father, could venture into the banking business, and it is believed that he did so simultaneously with his assuming

[28] The following sentences are based largely on A. W. Isaac, *The Worcester Old Bank*, printed for private circulation, 1908.

[29] For a commission which was to be £100 or less if the land tax collections should immoderately fall.

[30] The family had been cloth-makers in Gloucestershire over a long period.

the Receivership of Taxes in 1772. Certainly he was well established as a banker by 1778, for a notebook shows that 9,020 of his own notes were presented over his counter between 29 May 1778 and 7 October 1780. In 1781 he took as partners Samuel Wall and Elias Isaac. Wall, from an old Herefordshire family, was a local haberdasher who is believed also to have done some banking business as a sideline to his haberdashery. Isaac came from the Marshfield[31] banking firm of Isaac Baldwin and Shapland; his elder brother succeeded to the partnership in the Marshfield bank, while Elias Isaac, after marrying the daughter of his brother's partner, came to Worcester to join forces with Joseph Berwick.[32] After an experimental four years Berwick, Wall, and Isaac renewed their partnership in 1785. The capital was fixed at £20,000, of which half was subscribed by Berwick and a quarter each by Wall and Isaac. As salary Berwick (holding the Receivership) took £1,000 per annum, while Wall and Isaac took £150 each; profits thereafter were to be shared in proportion to capital holding.

As London agents the new partnership employed Messrs. Cocks, Biddulph and Co., who had acted both for Joseph Berwick and for Wall in the past. But in 1791 Berwick took a one-fifth share (in a total capital of £50,000) in the new partnership of Robarts and Company at 35 Cornhill, London.[33] The London account of Berwick and Company was thereupon transferred to Robarts and Company, and this connexion remained until the Worcester business was bought by the Capital and Counties in 1906. Joseph Berwick for a time held a third banking partnership, with Messrs. Wakeman, Farley and Turner in the Worcestershire Bank at Kidderminster. He parted company with them when they decided to open at Worcester a bank which could—and did—become a serious rival of Berwick and Company in that city.

Like many others of his kind Joseph Berwick held many local Treasurerships, especially for charities. In 1782 he was appointed High

---

[31] Marshfield is 12 miles from Bristol, on the road to London.

[32] Elias Isaac (c. 1775–1803) became Mayor of Worcester in 1799 after having filled every intermediate post in the Corporation.

[33] Robarts and Company about 1797 moved to Lombard Street where they remain to this day as part of Coutts and Co. As London bankers the name of Robarts goes back much before 1791; there appears to have been a Worcester connexion in the eighteenth century which may have led to the formation of the partnership mentioned above.

Sheriff: in the evening of Commission Day 'he gave an entertainment in the Town Hall, where elegance, plenty and harmony presided' over the gathering of judges, 'gentlemen, clergy, freeholders and capital citizens'. Presumably certain others also concerned in the Assizes enjoyed neither the elegance nor the plenty nor the harmony; but they were not always forgotten—a local press note in 1789 says 'Prisoners in the Castle return thanks to Mrs. Berwick for her humane gift of bread and beef'. The local *Journal* also reveals Berwick as Steward at Worcester Races in 1783 and a Director 'of our intended House of Industry' in 1792.[34]

Berwick was twice married. His first wife died in 1771, before he became a banker; then he married again in 1782. His only daughter, Mary, married Sir Anthony Lechmere, Bart., who succeeded his father-in-law both as banker and Receiver-General; the bank was known as Berwick Lechmere and Company for the remainder of its independent existence. The partnership in Robarts and Co. lapsed with Joseph Berwick's death, and the connexion thenceforward was purely that of country banker and London agent.

When Joseph Berwick and his partners were busy with taxes, haberdashery, and banking in Worcester, the partnership of Richard and John Twining was expanding its tea warehouse from Devereux Court into the Strand.[35] The Twinings had been in Devereux Court since the beginning of the eighteenth century: 'Tom's Coffee House', with the sign of the Golden Lion, attracted the custom of Queen Anne's aristocracy and made rapid progress. Its founder is believed to have been purveyor of tea to Queen Anne and, as tea became more popular, the Twining name became popularly associated with tea even more than with coffee. By the end of George III's reign the Twining family had established themselves in Twickenham, whence Richard Twining (1749–1824) in his last years would drive his pony carriage up to Temple Bar. The business then passed into the hands of his three sons, and it was they who added the business of banking in 1824. At first intended solely to provide facilities

[34] The 'House of Industry' would more commonly be called a 'workhouse'; its establishment at this time was presumably in accordance with the permissive powers under Gilbert's Act of 1782.

[35] The following sentences are based largely on Stephen H. Twining, *Two Hundred and Twenty-Five Years in the Strand*, published by R. Twining & Co. Ltd., 1931.

for the Twining family and their connexions, the bank consisted of a safe, a desk, and one clerk in a small room adjoining the tea warehouse in Devereux Court. Five years later the third Richard Twining, then aged 22, became a partner; he saw the business into Lloyds and into another century.

A few words on Richard's brother and two sisters will show the stuff of which this family was made. William lived to be only 35; after Rugby, Balliol, and Barts he took a leading part in bringing before the public the needs of idiots and the feeble-minded. Elizabeth (1805–89) organized 'Mothers' Meetings' in London; she was associated with the foundation of Bedford College for Women and with philanthropic works in Twicken-ham. Besides a number of books and pamphlets on religious subjects she wrote books on botany, of which the best known reached a second edi-tion in 1868. Louisa, the youngest, interested herself in Poor Law Reform and especially the provision of trained nurses in workhouses. She founded a House for Epileptics in Queen Square and, with Baroness Burdett-Coutts, an Art Students' Home. Like Elizabeth, Louisa was a prolific author; most of her pamphlets and books related to workhouses. Richard Twining, the elder brother, also had his philanthropic interests—among other activities he was President of King's College Hospital. He followed his father and grandfather as Director of an insurance company and was Chairman of the Equitable Life Assurance. But his main con-cern was the family business, of which he was senior partner for forty years.

Through the century the tea business grew enormously, especially after the Indian teas came in during the forties and the Ceylon teas in the last quarter of the century. The bank in the thirties was no longer con-fined to a small circle of family and business connexions, and larger pre-mises became necessary. A new building was erected in 1835–7 at 215 Strand: it had an inside door connecting the tea shop and the bank, and the association of the two businesses remained so close that cashiers con-tinued willing to change cheques partly in notes and coin with the balance in tea or coffee. In 1869 H. H. Twining, the eldest son of Richard Twining's cousin, came into the banking side, and a few years later his brother Samuel joined him. Thereafter, the banking business continued to be under the guidance of Richard and these two members of the younger generation[36] until the bank was amalgamated with Lloyds Bank in 1892. Richard Twining wrote to many of the customers a personal note warning them of the impending amalgamation; in their replies many emphasized their appreciation of the personal consultations they had always been able to have with Mr. Twining in the past. These personal contacts were maintained for a few years longer, for though 85 years old Richard Twining continued in charge, jointly with H. H. Twining, of what now became 'Lloyds Bank, Twinings Branch, 215 Strand'.[37] He also became a Director of the bank, and Howard Lloyd described him at this time as enjoying 'health, vigour and capacity in full equality with younger men. It was a pleasure to do business with him.' He retired in 1897, aged 90, and lived almost to complete his century.

Another notable family whose connexion with Lloyds Bank results from the amalgamation of Lloyds with a London bank is the Hoare family, belonging to Barnetts Hoares of Lombard Street. This Quaker family traces its origins back to Cork, prior to 1690, where the Hoares were merchants and bankers.[38] The modern English history of the family begins with Samuel Hoare I (1716–96), son of Joseph Hoare of Cork and Margaret Satterthwaite. Samuel I came to London and entered the Quaker firm of Gurnells, merchants who dealt in money as well as goods.[39] Towards the middle of the eighteenth century Samuel became a partner and cemented his partnership by marrying the daughter of the house; like her mother-in-law, this lady was one of the great wives-and-mothers who have distinguished well-known Quaker families. When he died at the age of 80 the *Gentleman's Magazine* described Samuel I as 'possessed of an ample fortune'. Twenty years earlier his son Samuel II (1751–1825) had married into another Quaker family of wealthy merchants, the Gurneys of Keswick and Norwich, just turning bankers.

[36] Richard Twining III had no sons, but sons of his three daughters became active in the tea and coffee side of the business.

[37] In 1895 the branch was moved to 222 Strand, and it is now merged in 'Lloyds Bank, Law Courts Branch'.

[38] These paragraphs are based entirely on Viscount Templewood's *The Unbroken Thread* (London, 1949), chaps. 1–3, and on information received from Colonel R. R. Hoare to whose courteous assistance the bank is greatly indebted.

[39] Whether Gurnells could ever be described as a bank is doubtful, though a wealthy Mr. Gurnell of Ealing described himself as a banker. The firm is said to have had important Russian connexions, and to have disappeared before 1850.

This marriage linked two families already close to each other as fellow Quakers; followed by another Hoare–Gurney marriage in the next generation and a later marriage between a Hoare and a Barclay, it brought the Hoares into relationship with the families that formed the core of Barclays Bank. But the banking careers of four generations of Hoares were determined neither by this connexion nor by the earlier connexion with Gurnells, but by a circumstance that must be told in the words of the family's historian:[40]

When the time came to decide upon his future, it was typical of the Quaker outlook that, as a life's work was too grave a matter to be imposed upon any-one from outside, the father solemnly consulted the son about his intentions. It was also significant of the precocious independence of character that was often produced in the hothouse of Quaker education, that the young man, after the most methodical deliberation, chose his own line of business rather than an almost automatic entry into the Gurnell or Gurney firms. While acci-dentally turning over a directory, he observed that there were only two part-ners in the house of Bland and Barnett, 62 Lombard Street, and told his father as the result of this remark, that he should like to be a banker.

The father at once agreed, and in view of his wide business connections had no difficulty in arranging for the young man to become a third partner with Messrs. Bland and Barnett. This was the beginning of a banking association that, under the name of Barnett and Hoare, continued until my own life-time.

And so, in 1772, the name of Hoare was added to the Lombard Street bank whose roots went back to Pepys's London.[41] After his marriage in 1776 to Sarah Gurney Samuel II lived for most of the year in Broad Street —and there the young couple found themselves in 1780 at the very centre of the burning, looting, and shooting known to history as the Gordon Riots. Sarah's letters to her mother, giving daily reports, survive to give an eye-witness's vivid story of those days: a phrase added at the end of a letter,

All well in Lombard Street

stands by itself to commemorate the relief when the troops at last had the situation in hand. Lombard Street survived to be the scene, for genera-tions to come, of the activities of Hoares, Gurneys, Lloyds, and the other great banking families—but ever since that night the Bank of England

[40] Viscount Templewood, op. cit., pp. 33–34.
[41] Cf. p. 15 above.

has been guarded by the little body of soldiers who march through the City as the offices are emptying.

Through the next forty years Samuel II built a great name for himself in the City. Through those troubled decades his serenity must have been a great asset. Even 'the astonishing tidings . . . that the Bank of England had stopped payment' in February 1797 left him relatively undisturbed.[42] It appears, however, to have stimulated his interest in the inner working of the system; he spoke occasionally in the General Court of Proprietors of the Bank of England and sometimes wrote in the newspapers. Outside the City Samuel threw himself heart and soul into philanthropic interests; 'The Heath' at Hampstead (now known as Heath House), home of his later years, became a meeting-place for abolitionists and penal reformers, the whole family being 'recruited into the movement'.

The tradition of humanitarian reform was carried on by Samuel Hoare III who married Louisa Gurney of Earlham, sister of the Elizabeth Fry who had nearly been Elizabeth Lloyd.[43] He followed his father as a senior partner in Barnett Hoare and Co. until his death in 1847. Samuel IV died young, after taking a brilliant degree at Cambridge, and the headship of the house passed to his brother, John Gurney Hoare (1810–76), and then to the latter's son, Samuel V, first baronet. J. G. Hoare (who married a Barclay) maintained the family eminence in the City of London and he read—and left his marginalia in—the pamphlets that in his day formed the main literature of monetary economics. But he was the last of the family with a real banking interest, and in his time the two neighbouring houses of Barnett Hoare and Co. and Hanbury and Lloyds, both becoming rather short of bankers in the families, joined forces to become Barnetts, Hoares, Hanburys and Lloyd. Of this firm Samuel V became a partner, but he was going into politics and no great turn of circumstances was necessary to persuade him to give up the family business. On its amalgamation with Lloyds Banking Company in 1884 both Samuel and his cousin Edward Brodie Hoare became Directors, and another Hoare remained as City Manager, but the main family interest had turned from banking to politics.

Among the personalities in the country joint-stock banks founded in

---

[42] This was the suspension of convertibility of the notes into gold, by Order in Council (see Sir John Clapham, *The Bank of England*, vol. i, pp. 271–2).   [43] Cf. p. 27 above.

the 1820's and 30's two of the liveliest were in one bank: Samuel Baker and Nathaniel Hartland of the Gloucestershire Banking Company. Born in 1791 and 1793 respectively from rather different stocks, they became in their quite different ways leading spirits in the development of this typical example of the sound institutions established under the legislation of 1826 and 1833.

Samuel Baker came of a Bristol family of shipowners and West India merchants and he himself followed these trades in London and Gloucester before joining the Gloucestershire Banking Company. He was not one of the original founders (in 1831), but as a very active local business man —with London experience—he was brought on to the Board in 1836. In 1837 he was appointed Managing Director, 'to devote his time and mind to the affairs of the Bank so as to gain a thorough knowledge of them in all their bearings and to superintend, regulate and direct in conjunction with the Manager all its transactions'. After about a year he found the bank too close a tie; the distribution of duties was reviewed and Baker was left in charge of the bank's interests 'out of doors', the arrangements made in London for the employment of surplus funds, negotiations with the Bank of England, inspection of collateral securities, and supervision of the branches at Stroud and Newnham.

When Baker came into the bank Nathaniel Hartland was already established as one of the most powerful directors. He had the advantage of a Quaker father who added banking to the successful tanning business at Tewkesbury.[44] Branches or agencies of the bank were later opened in Evesham, Cheltenham, and Upton-on-Severn. Nathaniel entered the business as a boy and was well acquainted with all its ways when it had to put up the shutters in the great crisis of 1825. The suspension lasted two months, but the firm paid 20s. in the pound and, as Hartland, Prior, Proctor and Easthope, got going again. From this date the bank confined itself to Evesham, Cheltenham, and Tewkesbury, Nathaniel Hartland living at and being specially concerned with the Evesham office. When the Gloucestershire Banking Company was founded in 1831, Hartland was in some difficulty through the death of his partners, and his bank was at once merged in the new company, though he apparently meant to keep

---

[44] Hartland senior had been a customer of Berwick Lechmere and Co. at Worcester (see p. 3 above); he removed his account when he set up as a banker himself.

the Evesham branch as his private empire within the wider organization.

The founding directors of the company to which Hartland had committed his fortunes were a mixed bag. Thomas Brown and James Daniell were simply described as 'Gentlemen'. William Gibbins was a 'Banker', brother of Joseph Gibbins well known as a promotor of joint-stock banks,[45] and a trustee of the new company. William Montague was a 'Merchant' and Samuel Bowly a 'Cheese-factor'. Most colourful of all was Maurice Shipton, who in the original deed of settlement was described as a 'Timber Merchant' but was also Lieutenant, R.N., retired. Still in his thirties, and not long retired from the Service, he was evidently brought in as an energetic local business man who wanted something more to do; certainly he took a very active part in the conduct of the bank's affairs and was taking the chair at Board meetings in 1837. In 1885, well past 90, he was still busy—taking part in the negotiations for the amalgamation of the Gloucestershire Banking Company with the Capital and Counties Bank. Two of these founding directors—Gibbins and Bowly—were Quakers; it was only their confidence in their friend Hartland—'a good banker and a very prudent man'—that overcame the Gloucester bank's reluctance to accept an office as far away as Evesham. Twenty-two miles was in those days a long distance between Head Office and branch— quite a hard day's ride out and home for an elderly banker.

Not that all these bankers, by any means, were elderly. Shipton, as we have just seen, was still a young man, but Samuel Baker was already 44 when appointed Managing Director. A year before this appointment Nathaniel Hartland had been called from Evesham to become General Superintendent of the affairs of the company. Having to move nearer the company's centre of gravity, he settled in Cheltenham. Here he became one of the six founders of Cheltenham Ladies College, which banked with the Gloucestershire and so with the Capital and Counties until Vassar-Smith persuaded the College to transfer to Lloyds.

[45] William Gibbins's father, Joseph, was in the Birmingham non-ferrous metal trades and had joined a private banking partnership in Birmingham in 1804. William appears to have served an apprenticeship with a bank at Leighton Buzzard and subsequently became active in promoting joint-stock banks after the 1826 Act. In the third generation W. C. Tunstall served as General Manager in the Gloucestershire Banking Co. Cf. W. F. Crick and J. E. Wadsworth, *A Hundred Years of Joint Stock Banking*, pp. 50–54, and E. Gibbins, *Records of the Gibbins Family*.

Meanwhile Hartland had become one of the leading personalities in the Gloucestershire bank. There was no clear line of demarcation between his duties as General Superintendent and Director,[46] and those of Samuel Baker as Managing Director, and differences of point of view tended to make for strain between them. In particular they differed on the question of relations with the Bank of England, and the strain between the two men was therefore all too apparent in their negotiations with the Bank in the early forties; the reports sent by the Bank of England's Gloucester Agent to his Governors in Threadneedle Street disclose the growing ascendancy of Hartland.[47] Hartland had a good start: having brought to the bank, as personal connexions, highly profitable customers at Evesham and Tewkesbury, he remained uncontrolled manager of these offices and 'always exhibited great jealousy of any interference with what he considered his peculiar jurisdiction'. He had, moreover, displayed 'consistent skill . . . in the general management', and could always claim that he was the man with real banking experience behind him: he was one of the 'practical' men. So Baker was finding himself constantly overborne and, though he broadly favoured an arrangement with the Bank of England, he confided to the Bank's Gloucester Agent that 'more than one of his coadjutors are always lying in wait for every opportunity of bringing forward claims and proposals for alteration, in the Agreement and with the Bank . . .'. And Hartland won this battle: the agreement with the Bank of England was terminated. When the 1844 legislation came along Baker refused to mix himself up with opposition to Peel's principles, but made private representations to Peel against the effect of the measure in discriminating against the Gloucestershire bank.[48] There were also internal sources of friction with Hartland. Some directors called in question the sufficiency of Baker's banking experience, and expressed the view that the Managing Director should give his full time to the work. In the en-

[46] He joined the Board in 1837.

[47] We are indebted to the Governor and Company of the Bank of England for their courtesy in allowing access to and use of this correspondence. For discussion of the general question involved, see Chapter 6 below.

[48] Cf. p. 146 below. In the Peel Papers (British Museum Add. MSS. 40545, ff. 166–7) there is a letter from Baker to 'Sir Christopher' (probably Sir C. W. Codrington) asking him to inform Peel of the facts, and saying that Baker would be 'extremely hurt' if his refusal to join the bankers' opposition to Peel's measure had the effect of placing the Gloucestershire Banking Company in a worse position.

suing reshuffle Baker emerged as Chairman of the Company and Hartland succeeded him as Managing Director.

The reshuffled team proved successful and lasted until Samuel Baker died in office in 1862; Hartland gave up some of his duties shortly before he died in 1866. During the twenty years 1842–62 the bank expanded and flourished: seven branches were added to the four of the late thirties, and to a consistent dividend a generous bonus was added even in the more difficult years. The fact that Hartland was now established at the centre no doubt facilitated the centralization of the branches under closer Head Office control, a development advocated by Baker in a series of lively reports on the bank's organization.

Like many another banker in the nineteenth century, Samuel Baker became a railway director, on the Board of the Birmingham and Gloucester Railway. He became Chairman of the Gloucester and Dean Forest Railway and later joined the Board of the Great Western Railway. In politics he was a strong Conservative, and once stood unsuccessfully for Stroud. Nathaniel Hartland, true to his insistence that he of the two was the practical banker, took as his second wife the heiress of Thomas Dixon, banker at King's Lynn. One of their sons, Frederick Dixon-Hartland, served in the Gloucestershire Banking Company and rose to be manager of the Cirencester branch; later he took a partnership in his grandfather's Norfolk bank and was brought by amalgamations on to the Board of the Midland Bank.[49]

In the great industrial cities the atmosphere of the new joint-stock banks must have been rather different from the semi-rural surroundings in which the Gloucestershire Banking Company flourished, but the bankers themselves were not unlike those we have just been considering. Examples are Robert Spence of Newcastle, James Lister of Liverpool, and Joseph Beattie of Birmingham. All three belonged completely to the nineteenth century: Lister (1803–79) was the eldest, Beattie (1829–89) the youngest, and Spence lived last—into the year of the Baring Crisis. Spence was born into a banking family, while Beattie and Lister were forerunners of a new style in that they rose from the apprentice's stool.

Robert Spence's story begins with the foundation, when he himself

---

[49] Cf. W. F. Crick and J. E. Wadsworth, *A Hundred Years of Joint Stock Banking,* p. 314 n.

was only two years old, of a private bank in Shields by three Quaker tradesmen (Quakers again!) of whom his father was one. The business of Chapman and Co. prospered, and when it spread to Newcastle Robert Spence senior became responsible for the Shields office. In this office the younger Robert began in 1831 (aged 14) his banking career. His exceptional aptitude for figures had been noticed and it was expected that he would in course of time succeed to his father's charge. In fact he found himself in charge surprisingly early, for his father was frequently out on public duties or other business and the elderly clerk used to take the opportunity to slip out to enjoy convivial society and his flute.

So far this is part of the history of English private banking; but in 1836 Newcastle was caught up in the joint-stock banking mania that swept the country. Chapman and Co. of Shields and Newcastle amalgamated with Sir Wm. Chaytor and Co. of Sunderland to form the Newcastle, Shields and Sunderland Joint Stock Bank. By the end of the year it had four joint-stock competitors in Newcastle. The change of form did not, however—perhaps because it was dictated by fashion alone—lead to any revolution in the management. In the 'Union Bank' the former partners in the two constituent banks undertook the management of their respective branches, so our Robert Spence continued at Shields as understudy to his father in the management of that office. It was worked almost as an independent bank, always jealously keeping its own cash reserve and its own portfolio of marketable bills. On his father's death in 1845 Robert Spence (aged 28) succeeded to the management. A year of overwork then broke his health and his recovery was considered hopeless, but a winter in Madeira enabled him to belie the doctors and return to a business career that was to last another forty-three years.

Under his charge the semi-independent business at Shields continued to prosper, and the news in 1847 that the Union Bank at Newcastle had been compelled to close its doors was received with incredulity in Spence's seaport town. The General Director at Newcastle had left the country and Spence was summoned to Newcastle to sort out the affairs of the bank. The shareholders decided to reopen forthwith at North and South Shields with Spence in charge, and when they reopened at Newcastle shortly afterwards Spence moved there to assume the general management of the company. The crisis of 1847 had knocked out three of the other Newcastle joint-stock banks (in one there had been criminal mismanagement), and when the panic of 1857 caused the collapse of the fourth, joint-stock banking in Northumberland and Durham received a blow from which it did not recover for many years. Even the Union Bank's shareholders felt unwilling to carry on, and in 1859 the business was sold to form the private bank of Woods and Co. After twenty years of the new régime private banking had resumed its sway in Newcastle, and Spence moved back to private banking with the tide. He left the Union Bank when it became Woods and Co. and joined the business of Hodgkin, Barnett and Pease (to which his name was added). Under his leadership this private bank opened branches at North and South Shields (where Spence had a clientèle at his beck and call) and eventually in most of the other towns in the area.

Until the late 1870's Spence remained in the lead; thereafter his health gradually declined, though he remained active in the business until his death in 1890. By this time his son had been in the firm for twenty-four years and his grandson had just joined to make the fourth generation in Northumbrian banking. Not, of course, in the same bank all the time: Robert Spence had seen banks flourish and collapse, and he himself had been there to pick up the pieces and rebuild the structure of confidence. He had the unusual experience of seeing private banking almost swept away by the joint-stock fashion and then to stage a magnificent comeback when the joint-stocks (Spence's excepted) had disgraced themselves. He himself had been a broken young man of whom the doctors despaired, but recovered to be for decades one of the greatest names in Northumbrian banking. The vicissitudes of life must have schooled his allegedly impetuous disposition; 'Take things by their smooth handle' was a proverb often in his mouth and (said the *Bankers' Magazine*) 'continually exemplified in practice.'

At Liverpool James Lister had a different start in life, but rose equally quickly to high position in a joint-stock bank. The son of a local Baptist Minister (a Scotsman), Lister went in 1823 as a clerk into the private bank of Lowry, Roscoe and Wardell. After two years with them, followed by four years with Cunliffe Brooks at Manchester, Lister moved into joint-stock banking and became manager of the newly formed Manchester and Liverpool District Bank (the 'District Bank' of today). After a few years with them the stone rolled once more—but for the last time: in 1835 Lister founded and became General Manager of the Liverpool Union Bank, and there he remained for thirty-nine years. He won a great reputation for himself as an authority on banking organization, to whom Lloyds of Birmingham could turn for advice. In 1865, when Lloyds became a joint-stock bank, its methods of book-keeping called for modernization and the Managing Director and Chief Clerk went to Liverpool 'to confer with and consult Mr. James Lister, the Manager of the Liverpool Union Bank, which was considered justly as in the front rank for method and efficiency.... Mr. Lister courteously agreed to lend one of his clerks to assist in the adoption of the new books.' Again a few years later Lloyds sought his advice on the opening of branches: presumably he advised against, for the Liverpool Union itself had no branch until after Lister's retirement.

Unlike Robert Spence, who devoted almost all his energies to the banking business, Lister found time for some outside activities. He held a number of directorships and became Chairman of the Liverpool Gas Company. He did not follow his Baptist father, but became an active member of the Church of England, supporting many church organizations, especially the Church of the Blind. He was an original promoter of the Liverpool Philharmonic Society and remained its staunch supporter for many years. 'He inspired wide attachments, founded not only upon kindliness of heart but . . . also upon an exceptionally well-stored mind and carefully cultured intellect.' Robert Spence was the second of four generations in banking; in contrast, Lister was son of a Baptist Minister and father of a Church of England priest—but a daughter married a London bank manager.

Joseph Beattie of Birmingham was born (at Welshpool) late enough to make his start in joint-stock banking without any preliminary experience in a private bank. From school he was apprenticed to the North and South Wales Bank, entering their Aberystwyth office. Quick recognition of his abilities took him to the Head Office at Liverpool, and then into the London Joint Stock Bank. In the 1850's, however, he did have experience of private banking, in the little Fleet Street bank of Gosling and Sharpe.[50] On the formation of the Birmingham Joint Stock Bank in

[50] This survived as a private bank until 1896 when it went into the Barclays group (see

1861 he was selected from among many applicants to become manager, and for the next twenty-eight years he identified himself with the new bank in its rise to a powerful position in the city. In those twenty-eight years each original share of £10 earned dividends totalling £55. 10s. consistently with the accumulation of strong reserves.

A man of simple habits, Beattie was 'driven down to the bank every morning for more than twenty years by the same coachman in one of Mr. Hunt's cars, and such was his punctuality that he did not once fail to reach his room by the stroke of nine o'clock'. He was more than punctual: he was punctilious, and he expected other people to be the same. Borrowers found that 'no liberties should be allowed beyond those agreed upon', and when speculative fevers had their inevitable aftermath many customers had reason to thank the restraint thus exercised. Not that Beattie was a frigid figure standing aloof from humanity: away from business his manner was 'almost boyish in its freedom and charm'. And, for all his devotion to the business, he had other interests he regarded as of great importance. He was best known as organizer of Hospital Saturday and Hospital Sunday collections, a work to which he was devoted for many years. In the Church of England he interested himself in the building and extension of churches to meet the growing needs of the Birmingham district, and several stained-glass windows in local churches bear witness to his activities. He was noted for his hospitality, which many visitors to the British Association meeting of 1886 enjoyed. In politics his opinions were Conservative, but he kept strictly aloof from party organizations.

In 1884 he moved his residence from Edgbaston to Overley, where he had purchased an estate that made him neighbour to Spencer Phillips of Lloyds Bank.[51] The friendship that ensued was important a few years later when, Beattie's health having failed, the Birmingham Joint Stock Bank sold out to Lloyds, at a price that looked very favourable to Beattie's shareholders. Beattie joined the Board of Lloyds Bank but survived only a few months. He left no children though late in life he had (in keeping with his usual generosity to his relatives) adopted a nephew. The

Tuke and Matthews, *History of Barclays Bank*, pp. 79 et seq.). The London Joint Stock Bank and the North and South Wales Bank were constituents of the Midland Bank.

[51] See p. 36 above.

Birmingham Art Gallery inherited the collection of pictures earlier presented to him by the shareholders of the bank he had so long managed.

The sale of the Birmingham Joint Stock Bank to Lloyds Bank was a sign of the times: the process of amalgamation, leading to the emergence of the 'Big Five', was coming into full tide. Among the men who presided over this consolidation one of the most powerful was Edward Baverstock Merriman, never in Lloyds Bank but a principal architect of the Capital and Counties that was such an accession to Lloyds soon after Merriman's death.

Merriman came from a family well known in Marlborough as solicitors and bankers. Thomas Merriman, son of a cheese-factor, was articled to and became partner of John Ward, a local solicitor, and in 1803 this lawyers' partnership embarked on the business of banking. They continued also to be solicitors, each member of the firm being described as 'solicitor and banker'. Thomas Merriman's son, Thomas Baverstock Merriman, like other members of his family, married a Ward, and their only son, Edward Baverstock Merriman, was born in 1839. Edward is said to have been spoiled, being the only boy among four sisters, but no doubt Winchester did something to counter this influence before he went up to Exeter College, Oxford, in 1857. He rowed in the Oxford boat (a successful one) in 1861, took his degree that year, and then stepped into the family tradition as 'banker and solicitor' in Silverless Street, Marlborough. Shortly afterwards, Merriman being 26 years old, the banking business was bought by the North Wilts Banking Company and Merriman became a director. In 1877 the North Wilts was amalgamated with the Hampshire Banking Company and Merriman joined the Board in London; shortly afterwards the bank's name was changed to 'The Capital and Counties' and it was of this growing institution that Merriman became Chairman in 1885, a position he retained until his death in 1915.

He had thus seen the little family business—never detached from the solicitors' office—merge into a country joint-stock bank that had become part of a much wider business, meriting its new title of The Capital and Counties Bank, Ltd. The 'Counties' concerned were still mainly Wiltshire and Hampshire, but under Merriman's Chairmanship a much wider net was spread. Substantial connexions were acquired in East Anglia and Lincolnshire, mainly by absorption. In Dorset, Devon, and Cornwall the

EDWARD BAVERSTOCK MERRIMAN, 1839–1915

Chairman of the Capital and Counties Bank, 1885–1915

From the cartoon in Mayfair, *25 July 1914*

Capital and Counties spread both by absorption and by opening new offices. Other scattered banks were absorbed in other counties so that Merriman was by 1915 head of a national business. This business of amalgamation and expansion was very much Merriman's own work, directed by his own quill-penned letters from 39 Threadneedle Street where he reigned, a terror to the juniors,[52] for thirty-nine years. No memorandum remains to reveal any general views inspiring this expansionist policy. What we do know is that he could be in a great hurry over the purchase of a country bank. Correspondence with the Northamptonshire Banking Company (1889–90) shows a period of five months elapsing between the first tentative offer and a final clinching of the bargain by a shareholders' meeting in April 1890, but the crucial letters were exchanged in November 1889, when Merriman outbid Lloyds and at the same time indicated that he would like the formal merger to be dated as at the end of the year. By 1903 Merriman, with much experience behind him, was expecting to move even more quickly. Going after Hammonds' Bank at Canterbury, a prosperous little country business for which several of the joint-stocks had been bidding, Merriman opened discussions on 11 June, wrote a firm offer on the 15th without awaiting figures of profits, and proposed to assume the business as on 1 July.

As head for so many years of one of the great branch banks, Merriman naturally became an important personality in the City of London, and was of course among those called into consultation by Whitehall in the 1914 crisis. For banking services performed for the Portuguese Government he received the Portuguese Knighthood of the Royal Military Order of Our Lady of the Conception. What these services were cannot be traced, but it must have been somewhat unusual for an erstwhile country-solicitor-banker to find himself engaged in foreign business normally considered the field of the great merchant-bankers of the City. Neither this mysterious connexion with a foreign Court nor his absorbing work as the creator of a great branch bank were, however, allowed to displace entirely his Wiltshire interests. In 1859, while at Oxford, he had enrolled in the University Volunteer Battalion Duke of Edinburgh's Wiltshire Regiment, of which he was Colonel through the last thirteen of his forty-one

---

[52] In both bank and family circles he is remembered as an exceptionally strong, almost overbearing character. There are endless stories of his Billingsgate gift.

years' service. He was a prominent freemason in Wiltshire and became first Master of the Capital and Counties Lodge. He retained for many years his family interest in the administration of the Savernake Estate and resided at Durley House, Savernake. While there he supported the Tedworth Hounds, and *Mayfair* described him as 'living proof of the adage that the best sportsmen are the best business men'. He married in 1883—shortly before becoming Chairman of the Capital and Counties—a daughter of the then proprietor of the *Marlborough Times*; their son became neither banker nor solicitor but went into the Army.

While banks both small and large, all over the country, were thus producing men who added to the strength and the traditions of the growing Lloyds Bank, the Lloyd family itself continued to produce bankers of note. Among those who followed 'Charles the Banker' one of the most noteworthy was George Braithwaite Lloyd I, who lived 1794–1857 and was a partner in the Birmingham bank from 1821 until the end of his life. He devoted himself to the bank at the cost of all other interests, and had a real flair for taking the more difficult decisions of banking policy. His death in 1857 was one of the weakening factors that led the partnership to give way in 1865 to the new form of organization. But there was already growing up, in another branch of the family, another Lloyd who was destined to put the stamp of his personality on the bank in its new shape.

Apart from the line of Chairmen already mentioned, the outstanding personality of the bank at the close of the nineteenth century was Howard Lloyd, General Manager from 1871 until 1902. During these thirty-one years the bank was transformed from a private bank with a single office into a joint-stock bank of national stature with 267 branches. Nor was it in mere size that Howard Lloyd's ambition for the bank found expression. Lloyds Bank was to be not necessarily, as he used to say, the biggest bank but the best bank, and he strove to make it so by stamping on it his own fine spirit. 'I wish you', he told a solicitor employed by the bank, 'never to let the Bank be a party to sharp practice towards its customers, or do anything mean or dishonourable in the conduct of its business.'

Howard Lloyd was in direct line of descent from the Sampson Lloyd who founded Taylors and Lloyds; his grandfather had been a partner through the first half of the nineteenth century. Howard's father, Isaac

Lloyd, had not been in the family bank but had a brief and unsuccessful career as a banker in other parts of the country.[53] The son's career began in an underwriter's office, followed by some months in the office of his brother in the firm of Lloyd and Lloyd of Birmingham, forerunners of Stewarts and Lloyds of Glasgow, Corby, and elsewhere. At the age of 25 (1862) he joined Lloyds and Co. as 'a sort of Secretary or assistant to the partners' of the bank; two of the partners were his cousins and the other two belonged to the Bingley side of the family. In fact he went through the mill properly, and in later life counted it a great advantage 'to have had actual practice in almost every detail of a bank clerk's work and life, from addressing letters and counting and marking bank notes, up to the careful toil of a ledger keeper and the responsible work of a cashier at the counter'. On the incorporation of Lloyds Banking Company in 1865, Howard Lloyd was appointed its Secretary and in 1871 General Manager. His letters show his activities to have been extraordinarily versatile. In the early days, when expansion was largely by the opening of new offices, he and Joseph Chamberlain (Director of the bank from 1865) used to go round in a hackney cab choosing corner sites. He took a prominent part in the increasingly frequent (not always successful) negotiations for amalgamation. When other banks were absorbed, he made it his special business to settle the delicate questions of fitting General Managers and other senior people into the greater organization. The selection of personnel, whether for a seat on the Board or for a seat on the most junior stool in the office, was always very much Howard Lloyd's own concern. He controlled advances and inspected branches, even interesting himself in the reform of book-keeping methods. Even after his retirement something of these interests remained: his letter written a few days before his death, dealing with regulations for the Widows and Orphans Fund, was characteristic.

A few years ago one of Howard Lloyd's sons, the Reverend Sylvanus Fox Lloyd, wrote an account of their family life in the last years of the century. Howard Lloyd, he wrote,

was of medium height and build, had whiskers close trimmed and inconspicuous, a heavy moustache kept trimmed, dark or black hair.[54] He was

[53] On Isaac Lloyd, see also p. 65 below.

[54] Mr. Walter Barrow, a solicitor, who for a long time acted for the bank, remembered him as 'a man of commanding presence who was regarded with great respect and rever-

always meticulously dressed in pin-striped trousers, black waistcoat with heavy gold Albert watch-chain, a pearl pin in his dark tie below wing collar. Frock-coat and top hat. Everything he bought had to be the best. . . . He lived for the Bank. . . . He personally took on all recruits, never exacting any undertaking of secrecy, he shook hands and said, 'I trust you'. Every day he drove off at 9.45 for Head Office,[55] then in Colmore Row, returning at 5.30 very tired. Once a week he went up to London, Euston, on the evening train, armed with a candle to be put in the carriage window to read by. Mother put a bunch of flowers in his bag for the chambermaid at the Euston Hotel. On New Year's Eve he would set out in a hansom cab at 7 o'clock, with a foot-warmer, rug and heavy ulster, to visit branches within reach, where they were working late, and did not come home till two or three in the morning. He could not laugh out loud, and disliked people who whistled or sang at work.

Even more clearly than in this description by his son, Howard Lloyd lives in his voluminous correspondence, especially in the letters of advice to bankers with whom there was some family connexion,[56] and in daily business correspondence with the London office after the 1884 amalgamations. The correspondence with E. A. Hoare in Lombard Street from 1884 onwards shows Howard Lloyd striving to make himself acquainted with all important business, striving to bring the London office into line with Birmingham arrangements without offence to men set in other ways, and above all interesting himself in the progress and personal welfare of every one on the staff of the bank. The code of the late nineteenth-century banker could be compiled of extracts from his letters. But he himself knew well that the written word was not enough: being recommended to read George Rae's book *The Country Banker* he wrote, '. . . I rather prepare myself to be bored and to have to say Bless the man! everyone knows this on paper. The difficulty is to put it all in practice.' Nor did Howard Lloyd always trust his masters to be putting it all in practice: writing from a sick bed in 1885 he told the City Manager, 'I don't know what mischief the Directors are doing today as I am not with them.'

ence by the whole of the staff'. Another account (The Dark Horse, Oct. 1920) mentions 'a languid exterior, the result of some constitutional delicacy or weakness'.

[55] 'At 9.45 Father started for the Bank. His driving was remarkable, for he started by flapping the reins on Duke's back while holding an open umbrella in the same hand, and putting on his gloves. . . . In the afternoon . . . Father was fetched from the bank. . . .'

[56] e.g. J. Howard Fox, whose mother was sister of Mrs. Howard Lloyd, and who was a partner in Fox Fowler and Co. of Wellington, Somerset.

Bank, Birmingham.
31 August '63

Dear Sir,

Having omitted acknowledging in writing your favour dated 7th July, I beg now to thank you for the terms, &c. expressing my acceptance of the terms proposed namely

1st That I serve you in the capacity of Confidential Clerk at the salary stated, &c.

2nd That the engagement between us is terminable on either side upon a notice of six months being given.

3rd That I undertake to discharge with ability the duties devolving upon me & to abstain from other business engagement which should be ruinous to you.

I am, Dear Sir,

Yours very faithfully,

Howard Lloyd,

Messrs Howard & Co.

LETTER FROM HOWARD LLOYD

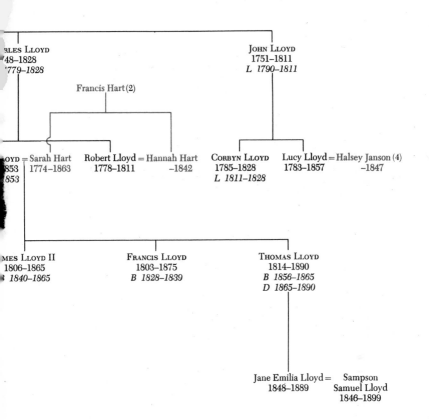

ꜱ Lloyd
ᵗ48–1828
ᵗ779–1828

John Lloyd
1751–1811
L 1790–1811

Francis Hart (2)

ᴏʏᴅ = Sarah Hart
853   1774–1863
853

Robert Lloyd = Hannah Hart
1778–1811   –1842

Corbyn Lloyd
1785–1828
L 1811–1828

Lucy Lloyd = Halsey Janson (4)
1783–1857   –1847

ᴍᴇꜱ Lloyd II
1806–1865
ᵗ 1840–1865

Francis Lloyd
1803–1875
B 1828–1839

Thomas Lloyd
1814–1890
B 1856–1865
D 1865–1890

Jane Emilia Lloyd =   Sampson
1848–1889   Samuel Lloyd
1846–1899

KEY

B Partner in Taylors and Lloyds, bankers, Birmingham.

L Partner in Hanbury, Taylor and Lloyd, bankers, London.

D Director of Lloyds Bank in its joint-stock form after 1865.

Ch Chairman of Lloyds Bank in its joint-stock form after 1865.

(1) Partner in Barclay, Bevan and Bening, bankers, Lombard Street.

(2) Father of a partner in Hart, Fellows & Co., bankers, Nottingham, absorbed in 1891.

(3) Daughter of John Bland, partner in Bland, Barnett, bankers of Lombard Street.

(4) Partner in Brown Janson, bankers of Abchurch Lane, absorbed in 1900.

(5) Manager, Warwick and Leamington Banking Co., absorbed in 1866.

(6) Partner in Truman, Hanbury & Buxton, brewers.

(7) Author of 'The Lloyds of Birmingham'.

(8) Partners in Albright and Wilson, chemical manufacturers, Oldbury.

(9) Partner in Hodgkin, Barnett, Pease and Spence, bankers, Newcastle upon Tyne, absorbed in 1903.

(10) Partners in Fox, Fowler & Co., bankers, Wellington, Somerset, absorbed in 1921.

(11) Secretary to Albright and Wilson.

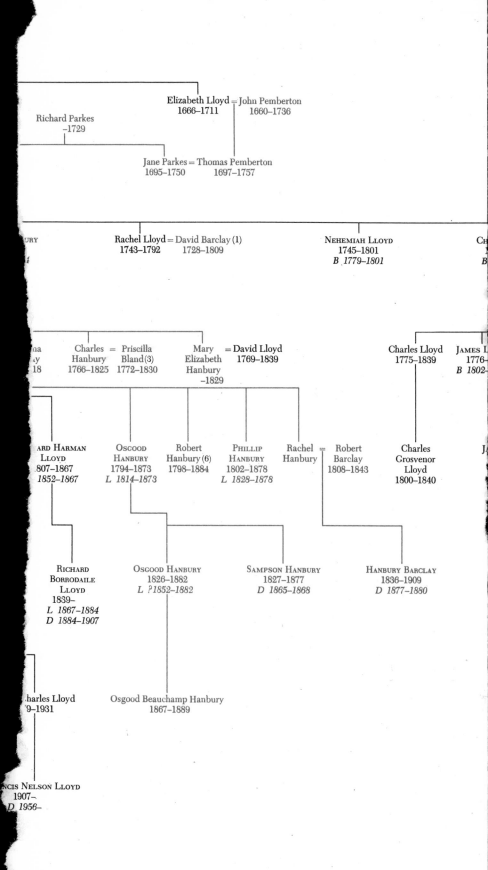

Richard Parkes
–1729

Elizabeth Lloyd = John Pemberton
1666–1711   1660–1736

Jane Parkes = Thomas Pemberton
1695–1750   1697–1757

URY

Rachel Lloyd = David Barclay (1)
1743–1792   1728–1809

NEHEMIAH LLOYD
1745–1801
B 1779–1801

CH
B

na
y
18

Charles = Priscilla
Hanbury   Bland (3)
1766–1825 1772–1830

Mary = David Lloyd
Elizabeth   1769–1839
Hanbury
–1829

Charles Lloyd
1775–1839

JAMES L
1776–
B 1802–

ARD HARMAN
LLOYD
807–1867
1852–1867

OSGOOD
HANBURY
1794–1873
L 1814–1873

Robert
Hanbury (6)
1798–1884

PHILLIP
HANBURY
1802–1878
L 1828–1878

Rachel = Robert
Hanbury   Barclay
1808–1843

Charles
Grosvenor
Lloyd
1800–1840

J

RICHARD
BORRODAILE
LLOYD
1839–
L 1867–1884
D 1884–1907

OSGOOD HANBURY
1826–1882
L ?1852–1882

SAMPSON HANBURY
1827–1877
D 1865–1868

HANBURY BARCLAY
1836–1909
D 1877–1880

harles Lloyd
9–1931

Osgood Beauchamp Hanbury
1867–1889

NCIS NELSON LLOYD
1907–
D 1956–

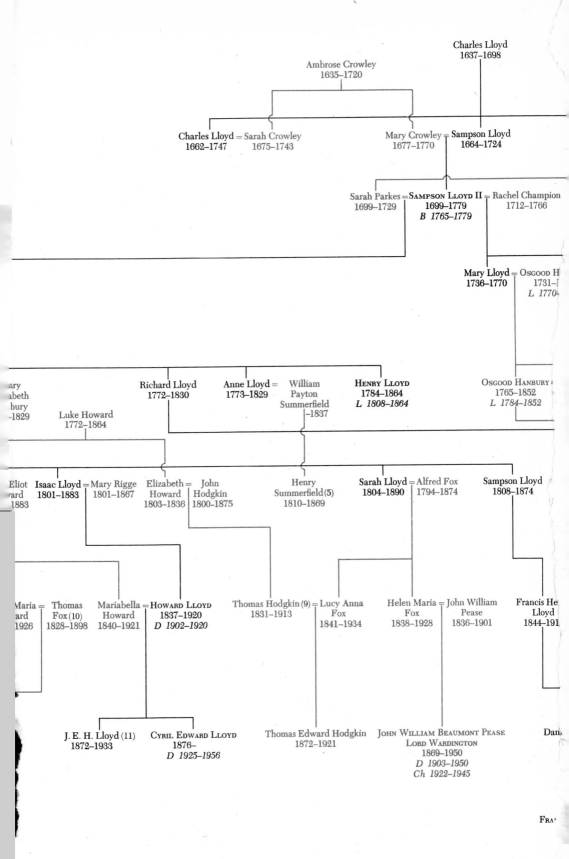

Charles Lloyd
1637–1698

Ambrose Crowley
1635–1720

Charles Lloyd = Sarah Crowley
1662–1747   1675–1743

Mary Crowley = Sampson Lloyd
1677–1770   1664–1724

Sarah Parkes = **SAMPSON LLOYD II** = Rachel Champion
1699–1729   1699–1779   1712–1766
               B 1765–1779

Mary Lloyd = OSGOOD H
1736–1770   1731–
               L 1770–

ary
abeth
bury
–1829

Luke Howard
1772–1864

Richard Lloyd
1772–1830

Anne Lloyd = William
1773–1829   Payton
             Summerfield
             –1837

HENRY LLOYD
1784–1864
L 1808–1864

OSGOOD HANBURY
1765–1852
L 1784–1852

Eliot   Isaac Lloyd = Mary Rigge
ward   1801–1883   1801–1867
1883

Elizabeth = John
Howard | Hodgkin
1803–1836 | 1800–1875

Henry
Summerfield(5)
1810–1869

Sarah Lloyd = Alfred Fox
1804–1890   1794–1874

Sampson Lloyd
1808–1874

Maria =   Thomas
ard   Fox (10)
1926   1828–1898

Mariabella = HOWARD LLOYD
Howard   1837–1920
1840–1921   *D 1902–1920*

Thomas Hodgkin (9) = Lucy Anna
1831–1913   Fox
                     1841–1934

Helen Maria = John William
Fox   Pease
1838–1928   1836–1901

Francis He
Lloyd
1844–191

J. E. H. Lloyd (11)
1872–1933

CYRIL EDWARD LLOYD
1876–
D 1925–1956

Thomas Edward Hodgkin
1872–1921

JOHN WILLIAM BEAUMONT PEASE
LORD WARDINGTON
1869–1950
D 1903–1950
Ch 1922–1945

Dan

FRA

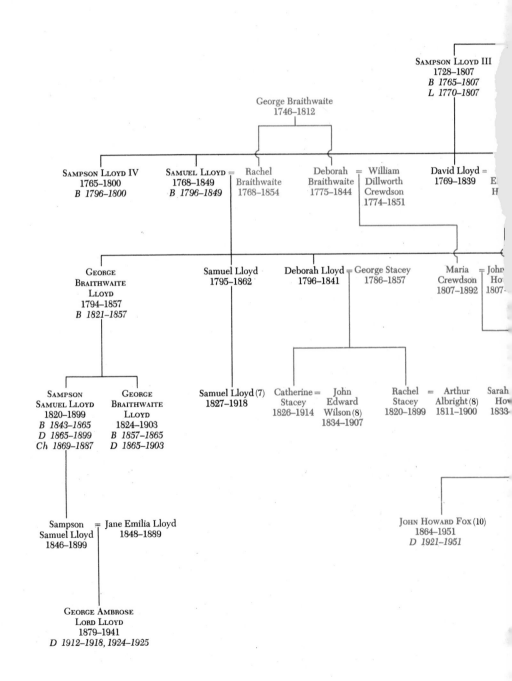

Sampson Lloyd III
1728–1807
B 1765–1807
L 1770–1807

George Braithwaite
1746–1812

Sampson Lloyd IV
1765–1800
B 1796–1800

Samuel Lloyd =
1768–1849
B 1796–1849

Rachel
Braithwaite
1768–1854

Deborah
Braithwaite
1775–1844

= William
Dillworth
Crewdson
1774–1851

David Lloyd =
1769–1839

E
H

George
Braithwaite
Lloyd
1794–1857
B 1821–1857

Samuel Lloyd
1795–1862

Deborah Lloyd = George Stacey
1796–1841   1786–1857

Maria   = John
Crewdson   Ho
1807–1892   1807–

Sampson
Samuel Lloyd
1820–1899
B 1843–1865
D 1865–1899
Ch 1869–1887

George
Braithwaite
Lloyd
1824–1903
B 1857–1865
D 1865–1903

Samuel Lloyd (7)
1827–1918

Catherine =
Stacey
1826–1914

John
Edward
Wilson (8)
1834–1907

Rachel   = Arthur
Stacey   Albright (8)
1820–1899   1811–1900

Sarah
How
1833–

John Howard Fox (10)
1864–1951
D 1921–1951

Sampson   = Jane Emilia Lloyd
Samuel Lloyd   1848–1889
1846–1899

George Ambrose
Lord Lloyd
1879–1941
D 1912–1918, 1924–1925

He lived for the bank, and had few other interests. His son wrote of 'no games or hobbies, except a little tennis, and our Saturday afternoon rides', but this was a boy's view of a father past middle age. Howard Lloyd himself, writing to E. A. Hoare in 1885, had claimed: '... in my elderly degree I still have copious enjoyment in the sea pleasures of boating, sailing, swimming'. He showed also a highly practical interest in the work, in the Birmingham area, of the Church of England. Born a Quaker, he followed the family movement into the Church of England; he was, his son remembered, 'a deeply spiritual man'. After he retired from the General Managership he moved out to Bromsgrove; there he sat on the local Bench and lived for the most part a quiet and comfortable country life until his death in 1920. Through those last eighteen years he had a seat on the Board of the bank and travelled up to London almost every week for its meetings. Back in 1863 he had written to the partners an undertaking 'to discharge with assiduity the duties devolving upon me'; through fifty-seven years he had kept his undertaking—and to spare.

Howard Lloyd's career dominated the bank's growth through the closing phase of the nineteenth century. His twentieth-century successors in the General Managership inherited an institution already very large, and shared importantly in responsibility for its consolidation in the final phase of the amalgamation movement and for its extension into overseas business. Alexander Duff (General Manager 1902–13) had started his banking career by marrying into the Barnett Hoare partnership. After its merger with Lloyds in 1884 Duff quickly rose to high authority. His entire career with the bank was spent in London, and he made it his business to concentrate all Head Office departments in London. His successor, Henry Bell, was by contrast a man who had learned much in commercial centres outside London, and brought to London new ideas that were destined to spread the interests of the bank into altogether new fields.

Bell, who came from a poor family, had started at the age of 17 in the fairly considerable private bank of Leyland and Bullins at Liverpool.[57]

[57] Leyland and Bullins survived into the twentieth century as the last private bank in Liverpool, 'enjoying an unrivalled reputation supported by nearly a century of prosperous and useful life' (W. F. Crick and J. E. Wadsworth, *A Hundred Years of Joint Stock Banking* (London, 1936), p. 158).

Office hours began at 8.30 a.m. and he had a lunch allowance of 6*d.* a day from his father. After five years he moved to the Liverpool Union Bank and there he acquired his important experience of financing cotton, corn, timber, and provisions. On absorption of the Liverpool Union by Lloyds in 1900, Bell was quickly moved, as a man of exceptional promise, to Head Office at Birmingham, and in 1903 he was appointed to manage the City Office in Lombard Street. Here he turned to good account his Liverpool experience of commodity finance, and the office's business expanded rapidly. By the time war broke out in 1914 he had been General Manager for two years and had established a sufficient reputation to be consulted regularly by the Government in its war-time dealings with the banks.[58] In one of the effects of war Bell saw new opportunity for Lloyds: the German banks in London, closed down in 1914, had been doing a considerable foreign exchange and arbitrage business, and Bell determined that Lloyds should jump into the breach and be ready for big development of this business after the war. For this, his own long-standing knowledge of international trade was a tremendous advantage, and he added to the bank's 'know-how' by bringing into his new Foreign Department men from other sources. In short, successful establishment of this side of the bank's business may be ascribed largely to him.

A man of tremendous stamina—he was capped for England's rugby side in 1884—he expected other people to be equally tough, and could generally wear them down in the stifling smoky atmosphere in which he revelled. But his colleagues all learned to enjoy as well as admire: he is remembered as a deeply religious man (a Congregationalist), but having a keen sense of humour and a fund of stories kept alive by an unusually good memory and fed by his wide interests in literature and art. He retired from the General Managership in 1923, but remained on the Board (which he had joined in 1916) until his death in 1935 at the age of 77.

In this chapter we have noticed incidentally a large number of people who have left some mark in the history of the bank, but the central figures

---

[58] After the war he was a delegate to the international financial conferences at Brussels (1920) and Genoa (1922), and was a member of the committee charged with implementing the Dawes Plan.

have been a score of men who for one reason or another stand out above the rest. This is not a random selection; in political history the Cecils, the Pitts and the Churchills appoint themselves for posterity's attention, and so it is in the history of banking. It is perhaps worth looking at these select twenty, and considering what they had in common, and how they fitted into the national institutions of their times. Of the twenty, nine were sons of bankers and three others married bankers' daughters. Nine had sons or sons-in-law who followed them into banking. Seven were born Quakers; these belonged mostly to the earlier generations, and one of them as well as descendants of others turned to the Church of England. Including the one born a Quaker, eight of the twenty belonged to the Church of England; two others (both in Birmingham) were Unitarians. Only three went to a university, two to Oxford and one to Cambridge. Most of them were born with a silver spoon in the mouth, but four quite definitely climbed the ladder. Three were active in politics, all of them Conservative. Such were the men who, if remaining records are any guide, did most to shape Lloyds Bank.

3

THE STAFF OF THE BANK

THE establishment of public confidence in a bank depended in the first instance upon confidence in the banker himself, and the stability and growth of the business depended chiefly upon the discretion and business acumen of the banker. Banking is not, however, a one-man show, and never has been, and the recruitment and permanent employment of staff has always been a major concern of the bankers who built Lloyds Bank. Two centuries ago there were perhaps a few hundred bank clerks and other employees of banks in London, and scarcely any in the provinces; by the middle of the nineteenth century the London bank clerk was well enough established to have crept into the Victorian novel and recruitment for banks in the country had become one of the problems of the industry. By the middle of the twentieth century, despite the economies brought by mechanization, the number employed in banks in England and Wales had grown almost to 100,000. These 100,000 have been recruited almost entirely by gigantic institutions using methods common to other large firms, their terms of employment are highly standardized, their professional conduct is governed by standards the public has come to expect, and their attachment not merely to banking but to one bank throughout their working lives is the almost universal rule. How has this come about? What, in other words, has been the history of the men on the banker's side of the counter?

In a long-established and widespread branch bank such as we know today, men to fill the branch managerships and important posts at Head Office grow naturally—or should do—from within the rank and file of the existing personnel. When the managership of a branch falls vacant, or a new branch is established, the general management has simply to look down the list of its up-and-coming men. When banking as a specialized business was a novelty, especially when new banks or branches were being established here, there, and everywhere, without an existing cadre to draw upon, there was no such obvious way of finding managers and other superior officers. Men had to be attracted from other occupations, their qualities assessed without the convenient record cards that cover the bank's experience of a man over many years. Every kind of question about the responsibilities of the officer had to be faced: whether he might retain other employments or interests; whether he should live on the premises; how much discretion he should have in dealing with customers. Little guidance could be found in earlier experience: the bankers had to feel their way. As might be expected, the records surviving from our constituent banks show great variety in the tackling of these problems and that, although in general the banker's judgement of his man proved sound enough to add soundness to his bank, some mistakes were made. The codes of today, partly embodied in written rules but in larger part so much taken for granted that no one would think of writing them down, are the fruit of generations of experience—some of it dearly bought.

Scarcely any evidence on these matters has come down to us from the eighteenth century. Until 1826 business was, thanks to restrictive legislation protecting the Bank of England, entirely in the hands of small partnerships, and the ordinary bank had much of a family atmosphere. We can picture a country establishment, preferably 'within a few doors of the Market Place', as consisting of an outer office fronted by the counter, and a large parlour in which all the active partners worked. (There is still, in one of the Worcester offices of the bank, a parlour with a single gigantic pedestal table built to accommodate all four partners.) The clerks in the outer office would ordinarily be lifelong servants of the firm, nominated in boyhood by a family or business connexion, firmly attached to the interest of the bank, but having no prospect of eventual promotion to the parlour. This is, no doubt, an unduly simplified picture, and we should certainly not imagine that there was never friction or upheaval in the outer office, or indeed in the parlour itself. But we shall not be far wrong if we suppose that the atmosphere was one of stability, not to say stagnation, from the point of view of the employees, in contrast to the upheaval, even the scramble, that was to accompany the appearance of the joint-stock banks after the legislative changes of 1826 and 1833.

The banks established in those first years—and there were twenty-three that sooner or later found their way into Lloyds Bank—had to look round pretty quickly. For those planning an immediate chain of branches, the problem was a large one. But for each single bank there was one easy way, the way that we, using a word that betrays a later tradition, should call 'poaching'. Some men might be attracted from the private banks, others might not be satisfied with the start they had made in joint-stock rivals still in their infancy; above all, men might be drawn from Scotland and Ireland where there was a longer tradition of joint-stock and branch banking. So we find the West of England and South Wales District Bank, founded at Bristol in 1834, and opening half-a-dozen branches in its first year, deciding to advertise in 'All the Bristol papers, one Edinburgh paper, *The Times*, the *Globe*, the *Standard*, the *Morning Post* and the *Morning Herald*'. The advertisement ran: 'Officers and Clerks are required for this establishment, viz., a Manager, an Accountant, a Cashier and Clerks. Testimonials of character, experience and ability will in each case be submitted to a strict investigation and large security will be required.' Applicants interviewed included men from the Provincial Bank of Ireland, the Royal Bank of Scotland, the British Linen Bank, and the Northern and Central Bank. From this list the bank found its first General Manager: a man who, after ten years in a private bank in Birmingham, had gone to the Provincial Bank of Ireland, first as accountant at Cork then as branch manager at Youghall, and finally as assistant inspector before he left for Bristol. More than a year after the appearance of its advertisement the West of England Bank was still receiving applications from men in other banks, and some of them were appointed as new branches were opened.

When a joint-stock bank was formed on the basis of an established private bank or—as frequently happened—established a branch by absorbing a neighbouring private bank, the staffing problem was naturally much easier. Generally the clerks could be retained. Among the partners the elderly might take the opportunity to retire, but the active partners could often be induced to stay as senior officers. The Coventry and Warwickshire Bank, for example, was able to retain both the partners, Messrs. Beck and Prime, in the private bank on which their Coventry office was based, Beck becoming manager while Prime became cashier.

Sometimes junior members of the banking family were willing to accept mere clerkships, though there may well have been understandings about their advancement. The many private banks that failed in the 1820's left partners looking round for income; an example was Isaac Lloyd, son of one of the Taylors and Lloyds' partners, and father of Howard Lloyd.[1] Isaac Lloyd was a partner of W. M. Christy in a bank at Stockport, which was wound up after heavy losses. Isaac a few years later emerges as manager of the Poole branch of the Wilts and Dorset Bank; thence (possibly after employment at another branch) he went in May 1841 to be cashier of the North Wilts Head Office at Melksham. Only seven months later he resigned, though payment of the removal expenses he had incurred in going to Melksham suggests that his resignation may have been invited: his personal claim to distinction in banking history is as father of a great General Manager of Lloyds.

There was not always such acceptable material at hand and, rather than risk employing complete strangers recruited by advertisement, a bank would sometimes take a chance with inexperienced people available locally. When Nathaniel Hartland, a real country banker of experience, gave up the managership of the Evesham branch of the Gloucestershire Banking Company, the directors appointed John Thomas, whose sole qualification was that he had 'carried on a respectable business at Evesham nearly opposite the bank for upwards of 25 years'. His knowledge of local people and of the trade of the town must have been considerable; but he was soon in difficulties, and resigned after only two months. A private bank, Messrs. Cripps and Co. of Cirencester, had better luck when in 1840 they were looking round for a manager for a branch at Stow-on-the-Wold. A retired sea-captain who happened to be visiting Stow was invited; he accepted and, judging from his long tenure of the post, made a success of it. The County of Gloucester Bank, wanting to open a branch there about the same time, was quite unable to find a suitable manager. No sea-captain looked in on them, and eventually they had to drop the plan of having a branch at Stow. The Warwick and Leamington Bank engaged as manager Henry Summerfield, an old Army man, son of a Coventry brewer and grandson of Sampson Lloyd III.[2]

---

[1] For Howard Lloyd, see p. 56 above.
[2] The Coventry brewer (W. P. Summerfield) had the distinction of marrying two

In recruiting the subordinate staff, even more than in finding new managers, each bank naturally thought of the staffs of other banks as their most reliable source. But of course there was the other side of the story—each bank found itself constantly losing men, often just as they had accumulated useful experience, to its competitors both in the locality and farther afield. The County of Gloucester Bank in 1839 found itself obliged to raise the head clerk's salary as he had been offered a place in a new joint-stock bank in London; in the next year they themselves were the poachers, taking a clerk from their local rivals, the Gloucestershire Banking Company. The Devon and Cornwall Bank in 1836 lost one clerk to the National Provincial at Exeter and two years later an 'apprentice' to Sanders and Co. in the same town. The Liverpool Union in 1840 even lost a cashier to the sub-agency of the Bank of England at Hull. Movements of this kind were naturally most frequent in periods of rapid expansion (notably 1836–7), but reports of them continued to be frequent through the next twenty or thirty years.

The disadvantages of this turnover were more serious for banks than for many other classes of business. Not only was there the waste of experience and the normal friction arising from change of staff; there was also the risk that customers might be annoyed. Efforts to hold men consequently went beyond the bidding up of salaries. Sparkes and Co. at Exeter—a bank eventually merged in the Devon and Cornwall Bank— at a very early date introduced apprenticeship agreements for boy clerks, whereby the apprentice was bound not to engage in any service connected with banking transactions within three years of leaving Sparkes and Co.[3] Twenty years later there was bad feeling at Newcastle and an attempt to get agreement excluding such recruitment. Woods and Co., a private bank, took over a small joint-stock bank, and to cope with their

daughters of Sampson Lloyd III. Rachel died in 1793, and five years later Summerfield and the younger sister, Ann ('Nancy'), flouting the law's attitude to deceased wife's sister, were married at Gretna Green. Henry Summerfield, one of the nine children of this runaway marriage, was noticed by Howard Lloyd as 'a character . . . a man of great stature, about 6 ft. 4 in. high . . . but his health was now broken. He was addicted to drinking the most terrifically strong ale. How such ale can be brewed is a mystery; it was like brandy in quality and strength, and I think it practically killed him, though I never saw him intoxicated.'

[3] Record of this rule has survived because the directors in 1837 considered bringing (though they did not eventually bring) an action against a boy who appeared to have broken his covenant.

expanding business tried to attract a clerk from Lambtons. One of Lamb-tons partners rode over to Alnwick to give the offender a piece of his mind: 'I think it', he wrote to his colleagues, 'a very dirty job of Woods, and have written Cuthbert desiring him to bring the matter before the notice of the Committee.' A letter was then sent to William Woods, say-ing 'that if such a system obtained and was sanctioned among bankers very great inconvenience would arise in running our business more than in any other, and it was desirable that agents or clerks having knowledge of customers' accounts should not move from one bank to another in the same locality'. A written agreement between the local banks was pro-posed, but Woods (the offending bank) declined to accept this and the matter apparently dropped. Although formal arrangements do not appear to have materialized either on this or on any other occasion, the strong feelings expressed no doubt tended to check this poaching of experienced men. The banks also took matters into their own hands by generalizing restrictive agreements with the men they appointed. By the end of the century the Capital and Counties enforced upon the staffs of absorbed banks a clause preventing the employees from joining another bank within 15 miles within one year of leaving a Capital and Counties office.[4] As the bargaining position of the larger banks in the labour market be-came stronger, they came to feel also that they could afford to be more considerate towards other banks. In 1909, for example, when a recently absorbed office in Sunderland wanted a junior, Lloyds declined to take a young man from the North Eastern Bank although he was much the best candidate.

That the banks were becoming stronger in the labour market was due partly to their age and increasing prestige, but mainly to the develop-ment of systematic recruiting and training of boys straight from school. For the banks as a whole recruitment from each other was no solution, inevitable though it often was for an individual bank short of experienced men. The long-term solution of the staff problem was recruitment at the bottom by the offer of an attractive career. In the course of time this began to yield fruit, and after about 1870 it was recognized as the normal way of staffing a bank. There were still examples of movement from bank

[4] Nevertheless, as lately as 1911 the Capital and Counties was recruiting for Head Office posts the employees of Scottish banks.

to bank, especially in the appointment of branch managers,[5] and members of old banking families often jumped the queue,[6] right down to the end of the century. But these came to be regarded as exceptional incidents, needing some explanation to the men who saw themselves superseded after climbing the ladder faithfully in one bank.

The method that was to become the standard practice of English banks —the recruitment of school-leavers—had been practised more or less widely from the early days. As in most other occupations, many applicants had uncles, elder brothers, or other connexions 'to speak for them'. Commonly the boys were apprenticed. The Plymouth and Devonport Bank from its opening year took boys on a five-years' apprenticeship, paying them £10 a year. The Gloucestershire Banking Company had the same period, but paid nothing during the first two years. The age at recruitment appears to have been 14 or 15, sometimes a little more. There had to be assurance that the boy could be maintained by family or friends, but there does not, in these early days, appear to have been quite the rigid insistence on social standing that became common towards the end of the century.[7]

Once he was in, the boy might expect a considerable amount of care. In the 1850's there were still many banks where a family atmosphere prevailed and the apprentice would find something like the medieval status in the master's home. An extreme instance of this may be quoted from Twinings, now the Law Courts branch in the Strand. 'He would', wrote a partner to an applicant's father, 'board and lodge in our house, and an exact conformity to the rules and regulations of the family would be expected from him, as from others.' The story does not go on to tell us that the rising young man married the daughter of the house. He was certainly given every opportunity to learn the business of the outer office, but the barrier between this and the managerial class remained virtually

---

[5] e.g. in Cardigan in 1890 the National Bank of Wales opened a branch, appointing as manager 'a trusted clerk' from another bank.

[6] Howard Lloyd in a letter in 1891 remarked that the arrival of men having family connexions with absorbed banks was sometimes galling to the old and experienced men who had been with the bank for many years.

[7] Independent means could be an advantage to an employee at any stage in his career. In 1861 the Gloucestershire Banking Company appointed a clerk at £150 a year 'upon the understanding that on his marriage he will have at least £100 a year of his wife's'.

impassable in the private banks, and even affected promotion to the highest posts in the joint-stock banks.

If the apprentice did not take properly to the trade, he had to go, and bankers often found themselves writing embarrassed letters to fathers of boys who just would not learn to write up the ledgers tidily. 'Your son', a father was informed in 1848, 'has not acquired that power of hand-writing which our books require. . . . We have formerly urged this upon him, and without saying there has been no improvement I am bound to add our opinion that it falls very short of what we deem of importance to require. This tends much to the effect that we really cannot place him in that higher position which might otherwise have been looked forward to.' In 1867 another father was told, again in exceedingly polite terms, that 'frequent remonstrance both on our part and that of the Senior Clerk' had been unavailing, and the young man had therefore been requested 'to look out for other employment'. But although in these two cases the young men had to go, the letters show—as indeed do many others—how much care was taken to give employees every opportunity to prove their value. In the great majority of cases the man settled down and was in due time considered for higher posts. By 1885 Howard Lloyd was laying it down that 'our better appointments belong of right to the men already in our Staff if they are thoroughly qualified and eligible and exceptions which may and must occasionally occur should be confined to candidates of very real merit or of very special and valid recommendation'.[8]

As service in a bank became more recognizable as a career, and especially as the numbers employed by individual banks rose from dozens to hundreds, salaries became more carefully regulated and probably also more uniform. The only evidence of rates in the eighteenth century is from the Birmingham house Taylors and Lloyds. In 1779 their two chief clerks received £80 each, and this rose fairly steadily to £200 each in 1791. In 1807 their one chief clerk was paid £300. These salaries would not have been thought odd at any time during the nineteenth century, a period of remarkable stability in general standards of pay. At the end of his 'teens —generally after serving four or five years' apprenticeship at £10 or £20

---

[8] There still remained difficulty in filling exceptional posts from within the bank. In 1885 the first London suburban branch was opened at Hampstead: for the post of manager E. B. Hoare did not consider any of the 130 London employees suitable, and Howard Lloyd was equally sceptical about the country staff.

a year—a clerk might expect to be earning £30 or £40 in the country, £60 or £70 in London. As a clerk he might in time expect £100 or even £150, while promotion to cashier or accountant would take him to £150 or £200, or appreciably more in a busy office in, say, Liverpool or Lombard Street. In London of course there was more chance of promotion or special duties, and salaries of between £200 and £400 were relatively numerous in the West End business of Herries Farquhar and Company.

In the early days these salaries were supplemented in various ways. In the very small concerns, with a family atmosphere, gratuities and special payments were the rule rather than the exception. The Cornish Bank in 1805 gave each of its clerks five guineas for working late; in 1843 and 1844 the North Wilts gave its cashier something for extra work in sorting vouchers, mending notes, and handling light gold; in 1851 the Liverpool Union gave each clerk or apprentice £10 to visit the Great Exhibition, and the Gloucestershire Banking Company granted £3 each for the same occasion.[9] The connexion between London agent and country correspondent was particularly important in giving rise to gratuities; it appears to have been the regular practice for each country bank to pay five or ten guineas every Christmas to the clerks of its London agent. This sum was no doubt shared between several clerks concerned, but as some Lombard Street houses had many country correspondents the total supplement to Lombard Street salaries must have been a useful sum for each clerk to take home. In Barnetts Hoares the 'Christmas money' was important enough to be subject to rules imposed by the partners, and in 1868 it became virtually a part of the clerks' regular remuneration.

Amalgamations and the bringing of all payments under the notice of comparatively distant Head Offices inevitably tended to squeeze these comfortable supplements out of independent existence. The problem of increments, for the same reasons, was attracting more systematic treatment. In the old private banks a very small regular increase—as little as £5 a year—was apparently common, anything more depending upon a request from the clerk who would then be considered individually on merits. Even some of the new joint-stock banks in the middle of the nine-

---

[9] Howard Lloyd as a schoolboy went on a day excursion from Bristol to see this exhibition, and was lucky enough to see there 'the military figure, the bowed white head, the aquiline nose, the characteristic dress of blue frock coat and white trousers' of the Duke of Wellington, who had come to see not the exhibition but the crowd.

teenth century followed this practice, or expected the branch manager to take the initiative in an application to Head Office. Others, however, had annual reviews of all salaries and granted increases that discriminated between individuals but also sometimes reflected the profitability of the year's business.[10] The position looked altogether unsatisfactory to Howard Lloyd when he reviewed the whole question after the important amalgamations which brought Lloyds to London in 1884. He objected particularly to the Lombard Street policy of indiscriminate but also insignificant increases: 'I do not believe . . . that it satisfies the men and I am quite sure that it tends to interfere with due discrimination as it appears to be shared by all alike, the inefficient as well as the efficient.' In future the responsibilities of each clerk should be assessed by an inspector and his salary graded accordingly. The London clerks were to be divided into five grades, with these salary scales:

Class 1	. .	£325 onwards
„ 2	. .	£250–£325
„ 3	. .	£175–£250
„ 4	. .	£100–£175
„ 5	. .	£60–100.

These London scales may be compared with those of a typical private country bank, Peacock Willson and Co. of Sleaford. According to a memorandum dated 1900, each branch was expected to have one first-class clerk, one second-class, and the remainder third-class, juniors, or probationers. The scales applicable to these classes were:

Class 1 .	. . . .	£200–£250
„ 2 .	. . .	£120–£190
„ 3 .	. . .	£57/10.–£110
Probationers or juniors .	.	£25–£50.

The young man thus rose almost automatically to £110—which he might expect after about twelve years' service—but thereafter it was a matter of waiting for a rare vacancy to occur.

Opportunities for advancement in a large and progressive business, though outside London, are illustrated by the Lloyds Bank 'Birmingham

---

[10] There were also times when lack of profits (one as lately as 1884) occasioned salary *reductions*.

Salary Book', covering in meticulous detail the period 1876 to 1918, and obviously kept either by or under the close eye of Howard Lloyd himself until his retirement in 1902. In 1876 the lowest salary was £35 a year and the highest, that of Howard Lloyd himself, £1,500. The maximum for inspectors was apparently £500, and there were two others above £350. Seventeen clerks stood between £100 and £250 and seventeen others under £100. In 1890 (when Howard Lloyd's salary was £4,000) the amalgamation with the Worcester City and County Bank brought in a £2,000-a-year man and one at £550. By 1903 the chief inspector was rated at £1,500 and other inspectors ranged from £475 to £650.

All the salaries quoted in these paragraphs were gross, in the sense that the recipient paid any income tax due. This was not universal, and the varying practice of banks created some difficulty following amalgamations. Lloyds traditionally did not pay the tax, whereas Barnetts Hoares, for example, had done so, and delicate adjustments had to be made as Barnetts Hoares were brought into line with the dominant partner. It was not until the major review of 1918–19 that Lloyds adopted the system of paying the income tax due from its employees. Until the 1914 war, however, the amounts of tax had been, by modern standards, trivial, and left the more highly paid bank officials quite well off.[11] An inspector with £500 gross, for example, would pay only about £20 tax if he were a family man, while a Country General Manager at £2,000 still had £1,800 a year net of tax. This left the 'Country General Manager' a long way behind a contemporary Cabinet Minister or a High Court Judge, though he was roughly as well off as their successors in the 1950's. The clerks at the bottom have much higher real incomes than they had half a century ago, though they have lost ground relatively to labourers and artisans.

As employment in a bank came to be a career for which boys were recruited from school, to rise steadily through the lower ranks on regular salary scales, with a chance of selection in due course for higher employment, the banks naturally came to take it for granted that their employees would give their full time to the service of the bank. This had not always been so: in the early days the banks often found it convenient to use for higher posts in the branches men who had considerable interests in other

[11] In 1878 a Maidenhead manager (Stephens Blandy and Co.) expected to be able 'to keep a horse and carriage of some sort'.

lines, and it was by no means exceptional for clerks to be allowed to pick up a little extra money in other employment. Dependence on part-time workers was particularly important in the early phases of branch expansion by the new joint-stock banks in the middle decades of the nineteenth century. The bank would establish itself in a town by opening an agency, which could later be converted into a branch. Under these circumstances there were obvious advantages in employing as agent (and then as branch manager) a man with substantial business contacts in the town, and for such a man there would not be sufficient work in the bank to justify a full-time appointment: he would therefore be engaged on a part-time basis, being allowed to continue his previous occupation. There were equally obvious disadvantages, though these could be minimized by selection of a steady man with a substantial business behind him, or of a professional man. Experience showed, however, that some disadvantage was still liable to appear. The Plymouth and Devonport Bank in 1833 received a protest from tea-dealers and grocers in Kingsbridge complaining that the bank's local manager was intending to engage in the sale of tea; the Directors were cautious in their reply and, though they did not forbid Mr. Fox to deal in tea, they encouraged him to take a branch in the next county. In 1840 a branch manager was requested by the Directors of the Gloucestershire Banking Company to devote more time to the bank's business and less to his practice as a surveyor; but they were prepared to increase his salary in compensation. Similarly we find, at about this time, the North Wilts Banking Company asking their General Manager to relinquish his legal practice; he was not prepared to do this, but agreed to devote more time to visiting the outlying branches.

The clerks also often found time for other employment, generally—as happens in other countries to this day—in helping local tradesmen to keep their books. There are mentions also of agency work for insurance companies. The most enterprising case of which record remains was in the Gloucestershire Banking Company, where the clerks acted as brokers in the sale of shares of the bank itself. In 1841 the money a certain Mr. Green was making in this way attracted the disapprobation of the Directors, but he was not to be deterred. By 1849 he and his fellow clerks had extended their broking activities to stocks and shares generally. In spite of disapproval repeatedly expressed by the Directors, Mr. Green was so flourishing as a stockbroker that in 1860 he offered to retire from the bank if the latter would employ him as their own broker! Without going quite as far as this, the Board did actually give him some encouragement: they paid for their trust when he found his way into Carey Street six years later.

Embarrassments of one kind and another provoked the banks sooner or later to frown upon these ancillary employments, and as the supply of experienced men became more abundant it became customary to prohibit activities of this kind. Often promulgation of the new rule followed close upon the heels of an unfortunate episode. In 1871 the manager who had been supervising five small branches of the Gloucestershire Banking Company was discovered to be employing the bank's funds in his own business; the manager resigned and the bank laid down appropriate rules to preclude recurrence. These rules did not completely exclude trading activities, but made them subject to specific authorization by the central administration of the bank. In general the position seems to have been reached, by the end of the nineteenth century, that paid employment or trading outside the bank was forbidden except for two classes of activity. One of these was agency work for insurance companies.[12] In 1891 Howard Lloyd, with his customary eagle eye upon everything that concerned the staffing of the bank, expressed some anxiety about branch managers 'holding Insurance Agency Appointments and working them unduly', and regretted that he could not do much about it as 'the practice has become one of some standing'. The position remains substantially the same to this day: a local manager may, subject to sanction (which is usually given) by Head Office, hold an insurance agency. The other exceptional pursuit customarily allowed at the end of the nineteenth century, and still allowed today, is farming. There were many early examples of this, especially in the West Country banks where so many of the roots of Lloyds Bank lie. Sometimes the local manager was not the only farmer in the office: in the 1870's the Gloucestershire Banking Company's manager at Stow-on-the-Wold had a farm about 6 miles away, and spent much of his time running it, while the cashier kept an eye on his own farm next door to the bank. The days when such a farmer-banker

---

[12] An early example of this work, at Swansea, has recently been documented in an attractive book, *Box 1299*, issued in 1951 by the Eagle Star Insurance Co. Ltd.

could without hindrance use the bank's funds in his farming business have of course long since gone, but Lloyds Bank has always recognized that rural branches must be to some extent a law unto themselves. If he is to command the respect of his farmer customers, the local manager must know a pig when he sees one.

The process by which employment in a bank became a full-time occupation, subject only to these two exceptions, has not at any time been allowed to interfere with unpaid activities. Honorary treasurerships, especially for charitable organizations, sports associations, and the like have always fallen easily upon the shoulders of the local manager and his colleagues, as they did on the local bankers of earlier days, and it is a matter of pride in every bank to take in this way a share in the responsibilities of the community.[13]

While employment in a bank was thus becoming a regular career, and a full-time one at that, the closer attachment of the man to the institution was enabling the bank to insist upon more rigid standards of conduct both within and without the office. Among the many banks of the nineteenth century there was naturally diversity of ideas in detail, but the general trend was unmistakable. The County of Gloucester Bank, when in 1841 it reprimanded one of the clerks for going to and betting on the races, was no doubt saying what any bank would say. Similarly, the Glamorganshire Banking Company dismissed a clerk who had been fined 5s. for being drunk and disorderly, and its warning against similar behaviour by other clerks can hardly have caused surprise. As the standards of conduct expected in a bank clerk became more generally appreciated, instances such as these became unusual—or at least the way to deal with them was so well understood that no trace was left in the records. In certain less serious matters perhaps the tendency has been towards less strict regimentation. Smoking in the office even after closing time was frowned upon by the Wilts and Dorset Bank—and probably many others —in the 1880's: 'Under no circumstances whatever', the Directors ruled, 'can this be allowed.' The more easy-going twentieth century prohibits

[13] A Margate cashier in the 1890's deserves special mention: C. E. Troughton, who was employed by Messrs. Cobb and Co., first in their brewery, then in their bank, again in the brewery, and finally as cashier in their bank then absorbed in Lloyds, was all the time a member of the Margate lifeboat ('surf-boat') crew. He lost his life when the lifeboat was lost in 1898 (*Bankers Magazine 1898*, vol. lxv, p. 74).

smoking only in 'public parts' of a bank during public banking hours. Time-keeping could also be exceedingly strict: in 1870 the Gloucestershire Banking Company introduced an attendance book for signature, and the manager was at the end of the half-year to count up the number of minutes each clerk had been late. In 1883 a Director of the Glamorganshire Banking Company spotted two clerks walking down the street at 11 o'clock in the morning. To what sign they were going was not recorded, but the Board did decide that these casual ways must stop: in future no one was to leave the premises without the manager's permission. The days that followed were, it seems, austere; nowadays there is a little more flexibility, but the clerks have of course to conform to rules similar to those of other big 'office' organizations.

The Boards of the constituent banks were more often concerned with graver shortcomings of their employees, including managers as well as clerks. There was sometimes careless handling of money, sometimes careless granting of loans, and sometimes downright fraud. In the treatment of such cases (even of the frauds), the banks generally showed an agreeable humanity, and were more concerned to prevent repetition than to penalize the offender, except in the really bad cases. 'W. D.', an apprentice at Plymouth in 1834, had to confess that 'a violent tempest of wind and rain' had caught him in his return from the Bank of England branch. 'Having put the sum of £1,375 of the Notes of the Company in a canvas bag which he placed in his hat, on turning the corner of Princess Square he was blown across the street, his hat was knocked off by the breaking of his umbrella and the Notes issuing from the bag were whirled into the air and dispersed in all directions, ten of which amounting to £50 were not recovered.' Poor W. D. had a bad night, but the Board did not compel him (or his father) to make restitution, and arrangements later made it unnecessary for a clerk to carry bundles of fivers in his hat.

Errors arising in the handling of cash were, as might be expected, a continual source of trouble until banks had settled into a routine by which mistakes, if made at all, are speedily noticed and rectified. In the absence of a protective routine even the most worthy cashiers are liable to get into trouble of this kind. Mr. Jewsbury, eventually to become General Manager of the Gloucestershire Banking Company, in 1845 paid out twenty £5 notes by mistake. The recipient was pursued to Birmingham and the notes recovered; the Board took a serious view and, though it paid for the journey to Birmingham, announced that if such a thing happened again the expenses would be charged to the party committing the error. Recurrence of such errors in fact generally earned severe punishment: in 1885, for example, an elderly cashier in Lombard Street was pensioned when a second shortage appeared in his till, and for three years he suffered deduction from the pension, in partial restitution. A few years earlier the Glamorganshire Banking Company went so far as to dismiss, on a similar occasion, a cashier with thirty-two years' service behind him. The local manager pleaded for him, and even pointed to the risk that he might, as manager of a rival bank, take custom away from his former employers; but all in vain.

There were in the early days many unsatisfactory local managers, and more especially agents who, it will be remembered, were often employed when a bank was first establishing its footing in a town and before it had attracted sufficient business to justify a full-time manager. The North Wilts Banking Company (a major constituent of the Capital and Counties) was particularly unlucky in this respect. They had trouble at Swindon in 1837: the agent persistently made advances contrary to the Board's instructions, and eventually he was dismissed and his sureties were informed that they would be held responsible for any deficiencies arising from the agent's activities. In 1839 they had trouble at Corsham, in 1841 and 1847 at Trowbridge, and in 1849 at Devizes. Other West Country banks had troubles with their local managers, more often than not arising from the undue facility with which advances were made. One instructive example was that of the Cirencester manager of the Gloucestershire Banking Company, a certain Mr. Commeline. When, for a second time, a customer failed after Mr. Commeline had advanced beyond his authorized limit, Mr. Commeline had to pay the £180 loss for which his independence was responsible and the Board rubbed it in with the most solemn warning against further indiscretion. The sequel was twofold: in 1879 the Board informed all its managers that they would be held responsible for bad debts arising out of failure to obey the Board's instructions, and Mr. Commeline rose to become joint General Manager of the bank. Whether his successful career resulted from his having learned discretion in these early experiences, or from the Board's coming to appreciate his courage, is not clear; perhaps it was a little of both. Perhaps, too, Mr. Commeline in his old age helped the desuetude of the Board's rule. Certainly no manager in living memory has been called upon to make good the cost of his mistakes; the Board nowadays relies upon its own judgement in selecting local managers and upon the closeness of contact and understanding between Head Office and local branches.

In course of time—and mostly during the nineteenth century—the banks evolved both a routine whereby technical errors might be minimized and a relationship between local and central management that would ensure proper responsibility for the employment of the banks' resources. The risks of loss by fraud also could be, and of course were, reduced both by the development of routine control and by more satisfactory contact between the centre and the periphery. But risks of this unpleasant class always remained, and remain to this day. From the many stories that can still be traced in the bank's records it is all too plain that Lloyds and its constituent banks have had their fair share of plausible rogues.

There was, for example, Mr. George Burgess at Ramsgate. His family had kept a private bank in Ramsgate since 1808; this business had in 1864 been absorbed into the newly formed South Eastern Banking Company, with George Burgess as manager. When this bank failed, in the 1866 crisis, townspeople petitioned other banks in the area to open a branch in Ramsgate and appoint Burgess as manager. The joint-stock banks first approached were unwilling, owing to their mutual agreements restricting the opening of branches, and Hammonds of Canterbury, a private bank later absorbed by the Capital and Counties, accepted the invitation. Solely on the recommendation of the Ramsgate petitioners—and perhaps influenced by his position as Treasurer to the Town Council—Hammonds appointed Burgess as manager of the new branch.

By 1871 his imprudent lending led his employers to consider dismissing Burgess, though they actually went no further than reducing his salary from £500 to £300. He was then one year old as an embezzler, but it was not until July 1874 that, one of the partners having made a rare inspection, Burgess was given five months' notice, on grounds of mismanagement and recklessness. His offer to purchase the business —doubtless with a view to further milking of customers before either absconding or pulling his Stock Exchange speculations round the corner —was rejected. In the succeeding months investigation revealed total defalcations of some £10,000, the victims having been among the petitioners who had supported Burgess in 1866. In December Burgess was sentenced to ten years' penal servitude.

The complicated story that emerged in the partners' investigations and at the trial show that Burgess had been not a clever criminal but an opportunist who had exploited the trusting ways of the bank's customers and his personal friends—even his late partner's widow. There is no sign that the clerks who handled the books thought his instructions at all suspicious, and even the most cursory audit would have brought the irregularities to light. The episode is, in short, a commentary on the failure of a small banking concern to institute even the most elementary measures of branch control. Whether in 1866 Burgess was already a calculating villain who engineered the petition to Hammonds, we cannot know; probably he was then simply an affable and easy lender who later helped himself in an effort to cover unsuccessful speculation on the Stock Exchange.

There are similarities to Mr. Burgess in Mr. Theodore Evans, another reckless branch manager who had ingratiated himself with the local community. It was in 1855 that the directors of the Gloucestershire Banking Company first complained of Mr. Evans's conduct of their business at Tewkesbury. He was accused of allowing some accounts to be improperly overdrawn and of neglecting the rules laid down by the Board. Special investigation of the branch led the Board to the conclusion that though certain irregularities were admitted by Evans, his personal influence in the district was such that his services ought to be retained in some form even though a new manager, more amenable to central control, should be appointed. Evans was retained as 'the representative of the Bank out-of-doors in any business, whether at Tewkesbury or elsewhere, in which—in the judgment of the Weekly Committee—he be most useful'. A few months later an investigation revealed at Tewkesbury a deficit of £3,250 'of which £1,750 had been explained by Mr. Evans to have been advanced to customers of the Bank without entries in the Bank books'. Evans refused to give any explanation of the other £1,500 and was brought before the magistrates. He was acquitted of felony and the

79

bank did not press a minor charge. Mr. Evans's personal guarantors made good the deficiency; he himself retained sufficient assurance to seek, two years later, to open an account at the Tewkesbury branch that had been the scene of his irregularities.

In terms of figures the biggest fraud of all was that in the Shropshire Banking Company in the early 1850's. This joint-stock bank was formed in the 1836 boom, on the basis of four private banks at Shifnal, Newport, Wellington, and Coalbrookdale.[14] The Head Office was established at Shifnal; the others were within 8 miles but provided important diversity of mineral and agricultural interests. No regular auditing arrangements were made, and in 1848 the General Meeting attributed the great success of the company 'to the strict attention paid to its interests by the gratuitous services of the Directors', to each of whom thenceforward £300 a year was to be paid. Among these directors, whose gratuitous services were thus appreciated, was John Horton. Late in 1854 the local newspapers were agog with rumours of misdeeds in high places in the company, and Horton was obliged to retire. His services had not been as gratuitous as the Proprietors of 1848 had imagined.

Horton himself had got away with a comparatively small sum: he had helped himself to large advances 'without any communication with, or sanction of, the Board, upon securities of a worthless character'. The ultimate deficiency on his account was rather less than £9,000. But his case was linked in some way—all the ins and outs of this case never clearly emerged—with the colossal misappropriations of Allen, the manager at Shifnal, and Gilbert, his cashier. Over a period of years they had been falsifying accounts on a stupendous scale. Gilbert, the cashier, eventually gave information on the understanding that, if he paid back what he had taken, he would not be prosecuted. He did return £53,000 in cash and securities valued at £87,000, but this was not all he had taken: the bank was still £25,000 down on his account. Allen, the manager, had had even more, and the eventual net loss on his account was £159,000.[15] Why

---

[14] The Coalbrookdale business brought in the great iron connexion of the Darbys. One Darby was among the original directors of the Shropshire Banking Company and his relative, Henry Dickinson, became Chairman and was largely responsible for pulling the bank out of the difficult situation created by this fraud.

[15] In the hope of retrieving more of the money the Directors tried to trace what Allen had been doing with it. They found nothing more than vague statements about speculation in railway and mining shares.

Allen at least was not prosecuted never emerged: indignant shareholders were waved aside with the answer that the bank had acted upon the best advice. There were ugly rumours in the local press, and it is difficult to resist the conclusion that the remaining Directors were unwilling to publicize the connexions between the three villains, even if they knew the whole story. The bad feeling engendered between Directors and shareholders is shown by an attempt on the part of the former to lay the blame on the shareholders, in that they had omitted to appoint an auditor.

The most remarkable aspect of the whole story is the bank's quick recovery from losses which had absorbed more than twice its capital and brought it a thoroughly bad press. A mere six months later the shareholders accorded to the Directors 'a most cordial and unanimous vote of thanks . . . with an expression of entire confidence in them' and this was justified by the event. Profits, though never again reaching the fictitious level of the early fifties, showed a steady increase over the next ten years.[16] The secret of this resilience lay in the energetic action of the Directors who, though abstaining from prosecuting the villains, were quick to put large sums into the bank and to bring the accounting under proper control. Dickinson, who took over the Chairmanship at this fateful juncture, himself put £100,000 and four others each put £5,000 in, as loan capital. After this action was made known it became possible to call up more share capital, and under Dickinson's leadership the Board commanded the confidence of the district for many years to come.

The Shropshire Banking Company was a sufferer on an unusual scale, but much smaller frauds by employees could eat quite seriously into the gross profits and even into the capital of small banks. Back in 1801 John Stevenson at Stafford went so far as to write that this was one of the elements making banking altogether too risky a business to be worth while. It therefore became common form for a bank to require each employee to provide some security, the amount depending upon his position in the bank. Occasionally the protection took the form of securities owned by the employee and deposited with the bank; sometimes these securities were shares in the bank itself. Usually, however, the employee was not sufficiently wealthy, and he was then required to pro-

[16] When this bank was absorbed by Lloyds in 1874 (i.e. after another ten years) its position had become prejudiced by the bankruptcy of Abraham Darby which had left the bank with some landed property of disputed value.

duce a guarantee by a personal friend. The sum would be as little as £100 for a porter and was commonly £4,000 or £5,000 for a manager. 'General Managers' of the larger concerns might be required to find guarantors up to a total of £8,000 or even £10,000. Even 'agents' whose remuneration for part-time services might be as little as £100 a year were required by the North Wilts Banking Company to provide as much as £5,000. A clerk would usually have to find £1,000, and this would be increased upon promotion to cashier or accountant.

The difficulty in which a clerk might find himself upon such promotion may well be imagined, and some of the banks were driven to concede some help in the provision of additional security. The Liverpool Union Bank in 1850 promoted two clerks, one to be cashier and the other chief cashier; instead of increasing the security required they arranged to deduct £100 a year from the increased salary to add to each one's security 'fund'. Even this arrangement proved to involve hardship the bank felt obliged to alleviate: only a year later one of the men married and was allowed to draw on his fund and to have his continuing contribution reduced from £100 to £50 a year. As the numbers of clerks increased—and as guarantors found themselves called upon when defalcations came to light—it became practically impossible for banks to continue this system consistently with freedom to promote efficient servants who lacked monied connexions or personal fortune. In the second half of the nineteenth century, therefore, it became common to resort to an insurance society instead of personal guarantors, and various companies came to develop this as a special side of their business. As early as 1854 the Hampshire Banking Company inquired from their London agents which of the Guarantee Societies 'for the faithful services of Bankers' clerks' listed in London they considered the best. In 1865 Lloyds decided that any new clerks appointed must be guaranteed by the Bankers Guarantee and Trust Fund, established in that year. The Liverpool Union, which soon followed, decided to pay the premiums of clerks while extra premiums on promotion should be paid by the employees themselves. It was not long before the insurance system became the general rule, and by 1882 the Gloucestershire Banking Company was refusing to employ an agent who was rejected by the Bankers Guarantee and Trust Fund although he could provide private sureties.

The practice of requiring some outside bond or policy of assurance survived in many of the constituent banks well into the twentieth century, not only in the smaller concerns but also in the Capital and Counties. In Lloyds itself, however, the system was changed in 1899, when the bank ceased to take out new policies with the Bankers Guarantee and Trust Fund and established, for all new risks, its own internal Staff Guarantee Fund. Every junior clerk on appointment had to contribute £10, and a further £10 was transferred to it, from the bank's general expenses account, when a man was promoted to be cashier or manager. During the 1914–18 war Lloyds once again took out policies with the Bankers Guarantee and Trust Fund to cover all temporary clerks at £100 each or £250 on promotion to cashier or certain other posts. Since that time all arrangements of this kind, whether for permanent or temporary staff, have fallen into disuse. An employee who is, in modern conditions of checks and counter-checks, capable of peculation is likely to involve the bank in quite a large amount. It is obviously inappropriate to penalize everyone in the bank on account of the very rare criminal; the bank therefore takes all possible precautions and, if these fail, is in the last resort prepared to take the rap itself.

The Staff in the Twentieth Century

In the previous pages the banks have been seen moving, some more rapidly than others, towards the habits that are the commonplace of today. By the early years of this century employment in a bank had become, almost universally, a full-time occupation, a life-long career, the conditions of which did not vary greatly from one bank to another, though both opportunities and emoluments were better in London than in the country. In the first half of the twentieth century there have been other important developments. The whole business of staff organization has been transformed by the consolidation of hundreds of small banks into the gigantic and nation-wide banks of today: conditions of service have had to be broadly standardized within each bank, and almost every problem arising has to be looked at as a problem affecting not one or a dozen but 2,000 offices spread throughout the country. The salary scales of the early 1900's had to be supplemented when the first war pushed the cost of living up, and the general review necessary after the war and post-war upheaval was the appropriate occasion for bringing all the amalgamated banks completely into line. Consolidation was also necessary in the higgledy-piggledy of retirement pensions. Regular provision for these was a logical step once banks had become the lifelong employers of large numbers; it was also part of a wider change in the nation's ways. Some of the constituent banks—including Lloyds itself—had adopted schemes before the end of the nineteenth century, but in general this has been a development of the present century and it was not until 1922 that provision for all employees—whatever their original banks had arranged —was put on its present basis. Finally, the present century has seen the large-scale employment of women—first the temporary clerks who filled the men's places in the 1914–18 war, and then the more permanent inflow a generation later.

When the war came in 1914 the salary scales were substantially the same as they had been thirty years earlier, though Lloyds in particular had lately raised the ceilings for ordinary clerks, both in London and in the country.[17] Through the early months of war no adjustments were made, though shortage of staff (as younger men volunteered for the Forces) led to the unaccustomed practice of payment for overtime, which no doubt eased the strain of rising prices. When allowance was made, first in July 1915, it was not universal but was aimed at special hardship. The bank inquired into the total incomes of clerks, and granted small allowances where these—not the salaries—fell below £200 for a married man or £150 for an unmarried man with dependants; juniors living away from home could also qualify for an allowance by proving that relatives and friends could not adequately supplement their salaries. In all other cases special personal hardship had to be proved. Today it is difficult to believe that the bank could make these allowances—in intention 'cost of living allowances'—conditional upon a means test; it was of course practicable only in the comparatively small banks of those days.

Anyway, the means test did not last long. In September 1916, when the official cost-of-living index had risen 50 per cent. above the pre-war level, Lloyds increased the allowances and extended them to all clerks and

---

[17] The normal stability of salaries had occasionally been modified long before this date, to allow for quite exceptional rises in the cost of living. Examples are recorded in Glamorgan in 1856 (Crimean War) and Buckingham and Glamorgan in 1873 (the top of a boom marked by an extraordinary rise in prices).

other staff in the lower ranges. The distinction between married and unmarried men remained, but outside income ceased to be taken into account. At the end of 1917 there were further allowances, this time for everybody. The Capital and Counties also discriminated between the single and the married, though the records show no trace of a means test. In the post-war boom the cost of living continued to soar, and further allowances were universal, mostly in the form of percentage additions to salary. When the cost of living fell there were reductions in 1921, 1922, and 1923. Thereafter, salaries were consolidated on new post-war scales, altogether more elaborate in structure and applying to the whole gigantic organization Lloyds Bank had now become.

Retirement pensions were, not so very long ago, a matter of grace. The aged clerk in the private bank might or might not find himself able to retire before he was carried out. There is little doubt that in the family atmosphere of the early nineteenth century many an old man was simply allowed to continue 'working'—sometimes to the intense discomfort of his juniors—far into his seventies. Retirement in those days was usually confined to cases of failing health, when the partners would not have to envisage a long-surviving pensioner and a lump sum gratuity perhaps met the case. Some such instances occurred well into the second half of the century. A Mr. Blay employed by Stephens Blandy at Reading in 1862 wrote to his son in India, worrying that his failing health prevented his proper performance of his duties. The son wrote to the partners, begging them for 'a retiring pension for the short term he may yet live'. Twinings in 1864 took the initiative, but at first failed to persuade a sickly and elderly cashier to retire; two years later they gave him no alternative to retirement on £200 a year for life. This was, judging by other cases, generous treatment. Others were not so fortunate: forty years later there was in a surviving private bank a correspondence clerk who, being refused any pension, died in harness at 78.

The early joint-stock banks, recruiting in the 1830's and 40's young or middle-aged men, scarcely noticed the retirement problem for a generation. By the sixties and seventies cases were cropping up more frequently, but these continued in general to be treated *ad hoc*, sometimes by the grant of a small pension, sometimes by a single gratuity. Lloyds thought about a regular scheme of pensions in 1875, but postponed it in favour of gratuities. About ten years later a pensions scheme was in force, and this was extended to cover the staff of other banks as they were absorbed. The scheme was non-contributory and the pension was proportioned to the salary at retirement. The compulsory retiring age was fixed at 65, though an officer could apply to retire at 60 if he had served the bank for twenty years. On this basis pensions were costing the bank £33,000 in 1905, but the burden grew rapidly as the bank grew and as the age structure tended to rise. (Prospective pension liabilities appear to have been overlooked when banks were absorbed; there was at least one case in which a private bank saw its interest in selling out before its elderly clerks retired.) Partly because of this accruing liability the Superannuation Fund was in 1929 made contributory for all new entrants. It was late in the day to be shutting the stable door—though other banks were even later—and the weight of liabilities to its ageing staff has become a serious matter for the bank.

The employment of women in the bank has of course been mainly associated with the two great wars. Lloyds Bank itself did not employ women at all until the shortages created by the 1914–18 war. Some absorbed banks, however, had engaged women in very inferior positions back in the nineteenth century. One lady, still living, joined Henry S. King and Co. (a private bank in the West End) in 1891. She and another, who had joined in 1887, were employed as typists. They were started at 12s. a week and rose to £1 in ten years. What were the general conditions of their work we do not know; the survivor's memory treasures most clearly the elastic lunch hours of those days when there always seemed to be time 'to go out and have one'.[18] But typists were not as common as shorthand-writers, a capacity in which men had been employed for many years: in 1885 Howard Lloyd expressed to the City Manager his pleasure that the latter had resorted to a 'shorthand clerk' who wrote 'with a good hand'.

A paper among the Lloyds Bank staff records, dated 1910 and headed 'Regulations for Women Clerks', shows that their employment was considered at that time. The reason for this revolutionary suggestion is un-

---

[18] This sense of leisure was by no means universal, even among country banks. A 'Wilts and Dorset' notice to clerks in 1889 complained that the clerks had been exceeding the 20 minutes allowed for lunch, and threatened to make them wait until the bank closed at 3 p.m. if they could not lunch more speedily.

known;[19] certainly it came to nothing and it was not until the stream of volunteers in 1914 and 1915 that reference to lady clerks appeared in the official staff circulars. Eighteen seems to have been the minimum age, and the bank preferred to have them at least 20. The scale of pay was 25s. rising to 35s. a week, and as the cost of living rose the bank became willing to pay the maximum more frequently to women who were living away from their families.[20] They were soon showing their competence: the Institute of Bankers inaugurated special classes for women, and some were promoted, with increased pay, to duties at the counter. In a business in which there were rules for dress for men[21] as well as women right down to 1939, it is not surprising to find this guidance in 1916: 'The dress of every woman detailed for counter duties must be of dark colour and quiet in character. It will probably be found that sleeves loose at or near the wrist are inconvenient.' So the rise of women as bank cashiers encouraged those ugly mannish fashions of succeeding years.

When the men came back most of the women went and they were not replaced. Recruitment for general duties ceased in February 1920: 'In future new women clerks will only be engaged for special work such as shorthand and typewriting, letter opening, filing, machining and similar work.' The shorthand typist, it will be noted, had come to stay; in the larger offices the total number of these remained considerable even after the returning flood of men had been fully absorbed. What 'machining' meant in 1920 nobody can remember—perhaps it was just that someone had a prophetic instinct. In 1924–5 the bank was experimenting with mechanical aids, and their first important use was in connexion with Clearing House work. It was not until 1928 that large branches began the switch to ledger machines. The number of women employed, which had fallen to 1,400 in 1926, now began to creep upwards again—over 2,000 in 1934 and getting on for 4,000 at the outbreak of war. During the war the number of men began to decline and in 1953 it was back at its 1926 level. The percentage of women, after falling from 29 in 1918 to 12 in 1926, rose to over 30 during the second war and to about 43 in 1954.

---

[19] Possibly it was connected with the employment of a telephone operator.

[20] There was also a general increase for women in Aug. 1917.

[21] At Herries Farquhar and Co. (St. James's Street), late in the nineteenth century, every clerk had to wear a top-hat and frock-coat. If he was going away on a Saturday afternoon he could change into less formal clothes, but then had to leave by the back-door.

With this change in techniques and in the labour force the appearance of banks—behind the counter—has been revolutionized. In some large offices 'the machine floor' looks much more like a modern factory than an office—rows of huge machines hum and click while a few girls walk round filling, emptying, and adjusting the semi-automatic monsters. And the change is not in appearance only. The switch to a large proportion of female employees, though in some ways aided by war conditions, was not accomplished without some unnecessary waste here and there. Banks were not used to employing women in large numbers, and it was not surprising that turnover was for a time uncomfortably high. A fairly high turnover among these women, most of whom are employed on more or less mechanical work, has its compensations for the bank—it would be quite impossible to provide attractive careers for more than a small proportion of the women. But there can be too much of a good thing, and the bank has learnt, by developing its welfare services and by other means, to reduce the labour turnover to a reasonable level. Not that welfare services are entirely new in Lloyds Bank: some of its early constituents were outstanding in their kindliness towards clerks in trouble and many Board resolutions witness the attention given to the problems of individuals. But things have moved a long way from the days when Howard Lloyd, as General Manager of the bank, would know the family circumstances of the most junior clerks, and would inquire meticulously into their well-being. A staff of 18,000 has to be handled differently from this: its organization has during the present century been systematized under a formidable body of Staff Controllers, and 1918 saw the establishment of a formal Staff Representative Committee for co-operation between the Board and the 6,000 permanent staff then employed. The 18,000 of today are of course spread over some 1,700 offices, many of them small enough for something like the old office atmosphere. But small and large offices alike are visited and cared for by 'welfare officers' and 'staff controllers', who can do much to combat the loss of personality that so easily accompanies growth.

4

THE BANKERS' CUSTOMERS

WHEN later historians come to write of banking in the second half of the twentieth century, they will probably find it simplest, when investigating the banks' customers, to begin by asking who did *not* have a bank account. Going back into the early nineteenth century, and still more when we attempt to look behind 1800, our investigation must certainly have a more direct approach. To be a banker's customer was something a little out of the ordinary, though it was more common than has sometimes been supposed. A bank might depend largely on the very few large accounts of a handful of local landowners and manufacturers, but the complete list of customers would show a wide variety of occupations and of turnover of business. Particularly the established 'craftsman-trades-man', the emphasis of whose business might be moving either towards manufacturing or in the other direction towards merchanting or retailing, was prominent in the list of customers. Lloyds in 1775 was essentially a town bank,[1] with a manufacturer and merchant background, and the following were the descriptions of the first twenty customers in an alphabetical list:

Publican	Baker
Barber	Butcher
Watch-chain-maker	Victualler
Hinge-maker	Victualler
Plater	Thimble-maker
Victualler	Whip-maker
Factor and chapman	Joiner and carpenter
Thimble-maker	Toy-maker
Malt-mill-maker	Split-ring-maker
Curry-comb-maker	File-cutter.

[1] But for nineteenth-century farming customers, see p. 92 below.

In an older town, Southampton, a list of 1797–1802 shows a wider variety of occupations, but the 'craftsmen-tradesmen' are still much more numerous than those of any other category. Of 44 customers, 6 might be classed as 'gentry'. Another 8 could be called 'professional'—the clergyman, the attorney, the exciseman, the banker himself, Mrs. Holsworthy of the 'Ladies Boarding School', and so on. Two were farmers, one a lodging-house keeper, and one a gardener. All the rest were craftsmen, tradesmen, or small manufacturers: druggist, bookseller, butcher, draper, coachmaker, 'wine-cooper and merchant', stonemason, ironmonger, brewer, plumber, &c. One account in this bank had frequent credits from the Commissioners of the Navy, and a new account in 1800 provided for the 'New London Road'.

Women's names are surprisingly frequent in the early lists. The high proportion at Lloyds in Birmingham is exceptional, but other examples show more than a sprinkling of women among the bankers' customers.[2] At Wirksworth in 1805 Arkwright and Co. had 43 women among the 312 depositors. In 1825 Stephens Harris and Co. at Reading had 52 out of 500—their current account balances ranged from £5 to £3,550. In 1854 the same office had at least 39 women's accounts in a total of 529, and the Maidenhead branch had 22 out of 726. In 1836 Henty's at Worthing had 32 women out of 202. No classification of these female customers is possible but, as we should expect, a large proportion of their accounts were inactive deposits. Some of the accounts may have originated in the legacies or gifts to faithful servants: it is difficult otherwise to account for the appearance of 'maidservant' as a customer in 1806 at Worcester. Fuller information might well reveal that many of the women were widows or daughters of the butchers, bakers, and candlestick-makers who were such active customers of these banks. There may sometimes have been other attractions to bring women into the banks—though perhaps we ought not to be too ready to jump to conclusions about Berwick Lechmeres, where the proportion of lady customers jumped in the last years of the eighteenth century, just when active control of the bank passed into the hands of two elegant young men.

A London bank's customers in these early days would generally be

[2] For Lloyds see p. 10 above. Ladies connected with the bankers' families commonly rallied round a new bank.

JOHN TAYLOR II, 1738–1814

Partner of Taylors and Lloyds, 1765–1814, and of Hanbury Taylor Lloyd and Bowman,
1770–1814

From the painting by (?) T. Gainsborough, R.A.

rather different from those of a country bank. A Lombard Street house—Barnetts Hoares or Hanbury Taylor and Lloyd—would have, besides their country-banker customers, a large proportion of mercantile customers engaged in all sorts of trade in the Port and City of London. Exceptionally there were provincial traders banking in Lombard Street, but the City bankers were inclined to turn these away to their own country connexions, and in the exceptional case insisted on introduction from a country banker before an account was opened for a country customer. Barnetts Hoares—and no doubt other Lombard Street houses as well—had also some accounts of the idle rich: it is remarkable that, though choosy about security of a mercantile nature, they could contemplate a loan on the security of a gentleman's pictures.[3] At Twinings, down the Strand, the 'West End' flavour was much more pronounced. Especially Twinings attached wealthy clerics to themselves. Bishops and Deans were in almost daily correspondence with them, and knew how to try a banker's patience when a loan was outstanding.

For the middle decades of the nineteenth century information about customers can be inferred from lists of shareholders of the new joint-stock banks. In the establishment of these banks great efforts were made to attract business through the shareholders, who were predominantly local people, and it can generally be presumed that these shareholders were customers, and perhaps were at first a large proportion of the customers. The Wilts and Dorset Banking Company when founded in 1835 had about 400 proprietors. Of these 41 were described as 'Gentlemen' and 20 'Gentlewomen and others' (presumably other women) to whom we should add 2 'spinsters'. Forty-one were farmers, 18 'yeomen and millers', 19 grocers, 22 'directors of banks' or 'bankers', 15 solicitors, 13 merchants, and 11 surgeons. These total about half the 400. In the other half there were eighty different descriptions, none of them running to double figures. Among them are 3 coachmen, 3 clergymen, 2 printers, 2 painters, 8 clothiers, a cutler, a brazier, a postmaster, 2 music masters, a glass-cutter, 2 'travellers', a master mariner, a ship-owner, a nurseryman, a varnish-maker, an exciseman, 'Governor of Workhouse', gardeners,

---

[3] 'We cannot see', they wrote in their letter of 21 July 1883, 'how you can make pictures in a private house available security for a loan. If you can do so to the satisfaction of our Solicitors . . . we shall be ready to make the advance you require, for a limited period, although the security can scarcely be considered banker's security.'

dairymen, shop-keepers, craftsmen and petty manufacturers and dealers of all kinds.

The original shareholders of Lloyds Banking Company in 1865 cannot be identified quite so mechanically with the customers, since this was a going concern, but there is some presumption that people interested enough to take up shares would either already be customers or would immediately become customers. The list is not unlike that of the Wilts and Dorset of thirty years earlier, except that the metal industries are more in evidence and the term 'manufacturer' appears more frequently. Twenty-one of the 148 descriptions include this word 'manufacturer', obviously used only in its modern sense of factory-owner and not in the old sense of craftsman; 13 others were 'makers' of various goods, evidently in a big way. The merchants and small tradesmen are there in force, but they are accompanied by a wider variety of middle-class occupations— the doctor, the clerics, and the lawyers are now accompanied by an architect, a journalist, a civil engineer, a rate collector, and a land agent. But Lloyds was by no means purely a townsman's bank: Birmingham was still a market centre for farmers, and Howard Lloyd, writing of the 1860's, recalled the farmers and other country people who gravitated to the end of the counter where Mr. Tatnall could talk of pigs, potatoes, and turnips.[4]

In other banks a Signature Book provides us with a list of *new* customers. That of the Birmingham Joint Stock Bank beginning in 1865 shows a great predominance in that year of merchants and shopkeepers, but there are also doctors, solicitors, two railway inspectors, an accountant, a 'drawing master', an artist, a dentist, and thirteen farmers. In 1866 they were joined by an optician and another railway inspector. Subsequent lists show that this bank remained overwhelmingly a bank for small business men, whether in merchanting, shopkeeping, or manufacturing; but the infiltration of white-collar workers does appear; an 'agent', a secretary, and a poster painter. Classifying the accounts opened in the Liverpool Union Bank by decades, 1835–45, 1845–55, 1855–65, and 1865–75, the widening variety of customers clearly emerges. The bank always

---

[4] The country element may have come largely from the former connexion of Attwood Spooner and Co., which had traditionally been the favourite of the farmers and had failed in 1865.

had a high proportion of merchants of one kind and another—most of them unspecified, but one early 'Brazil merchant' and a later coal-merchant. Brokers were equally numerous—timber, cotton, ship, and general brokers and 22 'commission-agents' (not, of course, of the twentieth-century kind!) A dry-salter and an accountant appear after 1845; after 1855 the list widens to include drapers, tobacco manufacturers, a distiller, a seedsman, an oil miller, a soap manufacturer, an iron manufacturer, and so on. After 1865 four solicitors appear, and seven shipowners, while merchants, cotton brokers, and shipbrokers also multiply, showing that alongside the widening of interest there was great growth in Liverpool's two typical interests, ships and cotton.

Even eighteenth-century bankers had public bodies on their books—the 'Dean and Chapter' of Worcester had a very active account in the 1780's—but the following century saw a great increase in the number of such accounts, mostly for newly established bodies. In 1825 Stephens Harris at Reading had on their books a medical dispensary, three schools, 'Streatley Inclosure', and 'Sonning Inclosure'; also a gas company and 'L. Ansterwick, for Savings Bank'. In 1856 Bradfield Union (Poor Law Guardians) had to have a loan; in 1861 'Burghfield Inclosure' was overdrawn. Vickers Son and Pritchard, of Broseley and Bridgnorth, in 1818 had an account headed 'The Treasurer of a rate levied for the town and liberties of Bridgnorth in lieu of a County Rate'; others were for an Enclosure and for 'The National Society for the Education of the poor in Bridgnorth.' This bank had also a suggestive Election Account, in 1818, in the joint names of Thomas Whitmore and Sir R. J. T. Jones: a remarkable number of even amounts were paid out. Were they bribes?

Banks are necessarily a little more interested in the people who borrow from them than they are in customers who simply deposit money with them, and it has been possible to classify debtor-customers noted from the books of the Gloucestershire Banking Company over many years in the middle decades of the nineteenth century. In a list of about 130, 85 had some business description—haulier, baker, brickmaker, farmer, ship-chandler—making it likely that the loan was needed for ordinary business purposes. But there were eight 'Esquires', borrowing on the security of waterworks bonds, freehold deeds, a letter of guarantee, shares in another bank, and railway stock. Two clergymen borrowed, one on freehold deeds and one on stocks and shares. A stationmaster (1867) borrowed on shares in an American bank. A spinster and her mother borrowed on the assignment of an annuity and a reversionary legacy. A Clerk to the House of Commons, a Captain in the Hussars, a poor-law clerk, a bank clerk, and another clergyman borrowed on life policies. A bank cashier borrowed on shares in the local wagon company and a 'Professor of Music' borrowed on life policies supported by shares in an Irish railway. Some of these loans may well have been for business purposes, but the list at least creates a presumption that the bank was willing to help lower-middle-class people—people with a little property of sorts—over temporary tightness.

'Temporary tightness' is just the contingency from which the banker expects to make his profit, but sometimes the borrower would be in a more lasting difficulty in which his banker would sooner or later become involved. Willis Percival and Co. in Lombard Street had long standing connexions in the West Indian sugar trade; among those in this business was the Culpeper family, owning sugar estates in Barbados. From the 1780's onwards Willis Percival were regularly financing the shipment of the crop, and for some decades all went well—at any rate, 'taking one year with another'. But from 1848 onwards the bad patches in the trade became more and more difficult to survive; proceeds of sale of the sugar ceased to suffice for paying off the season's advances. In 1864 Willis Percival became suspicious that other creditors were getting a prior share of the produce, and a solicitor was consulted. A pathetic letter from Mrs. Culpeper, aged 85, promised sale of the estate if the current year's proceeds did not suffice, and offered a box of plate as security. The prolonged drought which followed settled the fate of this family silver, and Willis Percival soon afterwards had to get what they could out of sale of the estate. Barnetts Hoares in the same period were finding themselves similarly involved in West Indian sugar. They committed themselves to £20,000 in support of the British Honduras Company at a time when this company was making most of its money out of West Indian sugar, with mahogany and other timber as a rather shaky sideline. But over a period of about five years another £27,700 followed the original £20,000, and only after pressing the sale of the sugar estates did the bank manage to pull out—with a heavy loss in its books. Looking back in 1875 one of the

Barnetts Hoares partners remarked that 'the only persons I know of in England who made any profit out of the business were the brokers who sold the produce'.

Old age in a debtor's account might, in such cases as these, foreshadow heavy losses in the banker's books, but there were other accounts where debit balances over many years would mean, more happily, that the banker had involved himself in the rapid growth of a business from small beginnings. Among its most prosperous and largest customers to this day Lloyds Bank numbers firms whose capital was at some stage provided substantially either by Lloyds Bank itself or by one of the banks absorbed by it. The finance would begin as 'temporary finance', but the bank's confidence in the customers would increase and in lean times dependence on bank finance would be allowed to grow far beyond the limits of working capital. As long as the banker could see his customer as 'very respectable and a very good man of business', he was not at all unwilling to stretch a point of banking doctrine, and the successes that have followed are among the most creditable in England's industrial history during the last hundred years.

Among the examples—and the early troubles of businesses now flourishing are not for detailing in this book—it is usual to find that the bank was, despite tradition, helping to build up the capital of a new local industry. But there is one very odd example of the provision of long-term capital, in the correspondence of the Halifax Joint Stock Banking Company between 1885 and 1894. The bank was lending up to £70,000 against mortgages upon the ships of a Sunderland firm. The loan was well covered by the value of the company's fleet—at one time there were as many as nine steamers valued at a total of £231,000—and no loss was suffered by the bank although the company had more than its share of ill-luck at sea and was for a time in financial difficulty. In a seaport bank these transactions would not have been thought at all extraordinary, but it is odd to find the business in Halifax, 70 miles from Sunderland and with no particular connexions to account for it.

There are in the records many other examples of the finance of fixed capital, especially for buildings and public works. In 1901 a loan of £6,000 was made against the security of a public house, and the sum to be paid off in annual instalments was only £200. In 1852 the Coventry and Warwickshire lent £5,000 to the Freehold Land Society to be reduced by £400 a year. In 1891 Hodgkin Barnetts advanced £4,000 to allow a customer to buy a property from the bank, and fixed the interest for five years ahead. Lloyds in 1889 was willing to make a secured advance of £100,000, to a property owner, to be repayable over eight years. More generally loans for these purposes were for shorter periods, pending the arrangement of permanent finance elsewhere. In 1841 the Burton Union Bank was advancing £200 'for the Eccleshall Inclosure'. In 1869 the Coventry and Warwickshire lent to the Coventry Town Council to enable them to buy an estate, on the understanding that the advance would be paid off as soon as suitable arrangements could be made for permanent finance. This could almost be described as common form in lending to public bodies, and was sometimes applied to private industry. But bankers had to look at these propositions with a wary eye: 'large permanent advances did not answer the purpose of the bank' and they had to be careful that, in spanning temporary gaps in outside finance, they did not become, for example, bondholders of the Swansea Harbour Trust or, as a result of helping a schoolmaster, 'simply partners in the school'.

All this may be summarized by saying that, although the bankers were willing to allow a sound business customer to remain in debt for very long periods, in the great majority of cases they were much more interested in the probable period of their commitment than in the object of expenditure by the borrower. The money might be going into fixed capital equipment but, if the borrower could hold out reasonable prospect of repayment in a matter of months, the banker would be glad enough to lend the money. The attraction of loans against stock that was turning over was simply the assurance it gave of quick repayment: an overdraft of £200 to allow a farmer to carry on until the corn was threshed, or to help a customer whose shipment of raw material was delayed by bad weather, or to finance shipments of cotton from New York—this was business the banker really liked to see coming into his office. Even so, he might turn it away if the intending borrower was not an established customer: there are many examples of refusal to open a new account with an overdraft, and as long ago as 1782 Stevenson Salts had laid it down that money should be lent 'to none but those who occasionally lodge cash with you'.

The banker has always preferred, too, that a debit account should be active: a dormant loan on however good security has never been the banker's business. The money should be 'turned over' frequently.

While not objecting to temporary finance of fixed capital, the bankers did object to financing some classes of short-term business. Bankers have always hated the word 'speculation', and although there are necessarily speculative elements in even the soundest business transactions, some transactions more readily attract the word 'speculation' and these have uniformly been frowned upon. A century ago even a purchase of Bank of England Stock fell into this class, for the Liverpool Union Bank refused to discount a six months' bill to enable a customer to buy Bank Stock. In 1886 Williams at Chester were firmly refusing to finance speculative purchases of shares, though in one case they were prepared to accept the stockbroker's guarantee. The damning word 'speculation' was then, as now, most frequently applied to Stock Exchange transactions, but there were other cases: in 1891 finance for the reorganization of some slate quarries was refused as 'in the nature of a speculation'. And Stock Exchange transactions were not, as such, discouraged: a clergyman changing his investments could be allowed an overdraft of £500 to cover the reshuffling period. Willingness to lend on the security of stocks and shares used, of course, to vary a great deal from time to time, according to the state of markets. It is not surprising to find in Board Instructions to branch managers of the Wilts and Dorset in October 1857 (a time of acute financial crisis) the sweeping injunction: 'No loan shall be made on security of any Railway, Mining or other Shares whatsoever; nor on the Stock or Funds of any Foreign Country.'

The attitude towards 'speculation' probably also accounts for curious local variations in the bankers' view of large deals in commodities. In a bank like the Liverpool Union an appreciable proportion of total resources was sometimes tied up in one way or another with transactions in cotton, this being a staple commodity of that port. Yet simultaneously Lombard Street, used as it was to the business of produce markets, could look down its nose at cotton as security for a loan. The loan in question—by Barnetts Hoares in 1875—was, it is true, a big one, about which the bankers were becoming worried. They asked for new security that 'would release the notes relating to the cotton at Liverpool, which is a species of

97

security we are not fond of . . .'. A few years earlier the same Lombard Street bank had been asked to lend for one week against documents covering the shipment of some 'Manchester goods'. But—'This business is not one conducted by London Bankers, and we must decline to undertake it. If Manchester Banks are in the habit of such negotiations, we should recommend you to arrange them there.' It thus appears that the geographical specialization of banks imposed appreciable restriction on the security eligible for bank advances, a restriction eventually removed by the amalgamation movement.

Although there are indications of rules being stretched in order to attract or to hold big accounts, there is scarcely any indication of business being turned away because it was too small. In 1895 Williams of Chester refused an application for a loan of £10 for two months to pay off some small bills, but this was on the ground of the general nature of the transactions rather than on pettiness alone. The same bank, refusing in 1896 to advance £40 to a clergyman who promised repayment out of income, was thinking not that £40 was too little but that it was too much for the poor clergyman to owe. In 1875 a debtor of the Hampshire Banking Company, owing £12, was described as a labouring man out of employment—the bank had evidently been rash, but this was no case of yielding to the pressure of a big customer! Barnetts Hoares in 1878 were more particular; Lombard Street bankers could no doubt afford to look down their noses. 'The trouble involved by opening small discount accounts is so great as a rule we really do not care about taking small bills unless under special circumstances.' London bankers generally appear to have been highly selective in accepting accounts: although the reason rarely emerges, the number of firm but polite letters declining business can only mean that standards were severe. Twinings in the Strand would sometimes go further, and ask a customer to remove his account: thus in 1854—

Messrs. Twinings compliments to Mr. Nutt and have discounted the Bills included in his letter of this day to the amount of £142. 17. 6. They beg to take this opportunity of saying that they would be obliged if Mr. Nutt would make arrangements for removing his account as in its operation it does not accord with their system of business.

There were also isolated examples of country bankers who as a matter of

THE CASHIER'S ALARM SIGNAL

(Reputedly referring to an instruction in the Capital and Counties Bank)

From Punch, 6 May 1914

principle refused small customers. 'St. Barbe's Bank' at Lymington, founded by a grocer in 1786 or 1788, held out almost to the end of the nineteenth century as 'a very high class banking business'. Its consistent refusal to open accounts for small tradesmen was not, however, the way for a bank to hold its own in the competitive world, and the business was declining when it was taken over in 1896 by the Capital and Counties.

Accounts could of course be disagreeable for reasons other than smallness. The strong element of religion in the nineteenth-century bankers was carried into the Board Room, and inevitably coloured the banker's attitude towards some of his customers. A gun-manufacturing firm in the Midlands was in financial difficulties over a period of some years in the last quarter of the century, and the consequential trading in that firm's assets caused acute discomfort in Colmore Row. Howard Lloyd thought the business must be lucrative, but found it 'particularly disagreeable' to have to manufacture 'the means of slaughter' and not always pleasant to employ the agencies through whom contracts with certain foreign governments were secured. The Gurneys and Hoares of Norfolk have traditionally treated guns as very desirable means for shooting birds, but the Lloyds of Birmingham felt differently about arming the forces of contending generals in China or South America. None the less, the account in question was kept.

The banker has to be on his guard every day against people who walk into his office intent on fraud—and against customers in difficulties who resort to fraud in an effort to extricate themselves. From the earliest days there were countless cases such as that recorded in an 1846 Minute of the Gloucestershire Banking Company.

Mr. Green reported the loss of £27 at Gloucester and £25 at Cheltenham thro' an act of swindling of a person calling himself Major Wyndham, lately staying at the King's Head Inn in Gloucester . . . the Weekly Committee were requested to express to Mr. Gittins their opinion of the imprudence of his conduct in giving Major Wyndham a receipt as for Cash, for a cheque on Bankers at Liverpool.

In course of time stricter rules and accumulating experience enabled the banks to protect themselves against the cruder manifestations, but many other sources of trouble remained, always cropping up in some form different from any the banker had encountered before. A farmer's bankruptcy could be followed by a minute that the bank's claim was well covered by securities, only to be followed by another minute recording the discovery of some fraudulent element in the securities. Incidents of this kind might be associated with slackness in the periodic checking of securities, in which case a tightening of inspector's rules would follow. Alternatively, a crop of such cases could easily appear after an outburst of speculative trading. In 1865 the Gloucestershire Banking Company found itself caught up in a phase of 'reckless trading and mad speculations', following which there were heavy losses 'both on ordinary trading, and from direct fraud', the latter involving some inroad into the Guarantee Fund. In another bad year, 1884, the list of failures in Liverpool cost the Liverpool Union Bank surprisingly little, but among the losses the biggest item was due to fraud. The bank had lent, in the course of years, many millions of money to produce brokers, upon whose good faith the prompt dispatch of business in Liverpool commodity markets depended; against these millions the £7,000 loss in the Townshend frauds looked small, but the blow to confidence and the legal repercussions upon trading arrangements were serious. In terms of money alone, however, Mr. T. E. Hooley, promotor of the Dunlop Tyre Company and many others, must have been one of the most expensive customers any English bank had before 1900. The connexion was a brief one: Hooley moved his account to Lloyds in September 1896 and, when in 1898 the bank dishonoured a £30 cheque, Hooley was forced to file the petition in bankruptcy which brought his spectacular career to a temporary halt. The bank had then advanced sums running well into six figures, and Hooley also appears to have been able to tap personal friends of the branch manager concerned. This branch manager had not lent his own money, though after the bank refused to make further advances Hooley had the effrontery to offer this man £35,000 down and £5,000 per annum for five years if he would retire from the bank and become adviser to Hooley. The manager treated the offer with the same disdain as a Hooley present of £600 worth of wine. Fortunately customers of this kind rarely get into the books of the bank.

Unfortunately a banker's losses come not from rogues alone. Hard times sometimes hit the best of debtors, and it is perhaps in years of difficulty that the banker's relations with his customer and his judgement of the latter's permanent qualities count for most. The bank that is too lenient invites bad debts on an unnecessary scale, while undue severity means loss of goodwill and the contraction of business in what may soon become again a flourishing locality. In the nineteenth century agricultural depression must often have posed to the bankers the question, is this a permanent decline or will our district soon recover? The Wilts and Dorset Banking Company, depending largely on agricultural districts, had to think seriously on these lines in 1883–4, for example. A run of bad seasons and the extraordinary fall in cereal prices had affected not only loans to corn merchants and farmers, but also all loans secured by house property. In towns as well as villages, 'House Properties once valuable and much sought after for investment have been submitted for sale by Public Competition and not a single bidding has been obtained.' 'Please look carefully', Head Office instructed branches, 'into all securities you hold consisting of either houses or land and especially all properties situated in country villages. Re-estimate their value and have any deficiency fully made up.' On the other hand, the Directors did not wish 'to curtail further the accommodation which our agricultural friends need, and will consider favourably all legitimate applications made to them for advances, when they can be entertained with perfect safety'. The local managers must have been all too conscious of their dilemma—how to satisfy the 'legitimate applications of agricultural friends' and yet keep within the bounds of 'perfect safety'. Inevitably the wish to preserve a good reputation in the district sometimes reaped a crop of bad debts. And this could happen in industrial districts too, as at Coventry in the late sixties. There, after the failure of another bank, Lloyds were pressed to take over a group of customers whose accounts looked, at first sight, 'very good'. It was not long before the Directors became alarmed and began to look with sceptical eyes at any paper that came out of Coventry. Quite large amounts were in the end written off, but the bank took the knock in such a way as to maintain the goodwill it had built up since the earlier bank's collapse. In dealing with such episodes as these the bankers of the nineteenth century came to balance fear of losses against the claims of goodwill much as their successors balance them nowadays. In the difficult days of 1878 Lloyds Head Office issued these instructions:

(4) Continued pressure on all doubtful or valueless accounts, while refrain-

101

ing from being too urgent with our *first-class* customers, whose requirements must continue to be liberally met.

(5) New loans, and further or additional advances on existing accounts to be firmly refused, where they can be avoided without manifest injury to the business.

Though pointing an unfamiliar tightness of funds, the tilting of the scale in favour of the sound established customer accords closely with the habits of the twentieth century.

Not only in this attitude in times of difficulty but also in advances policy in general, there appears to have been remarkably little change between the early bankers and those of the twentieth century. The preference for the 'self-liquidating' trading transaction, the willingness to give a good customer temporary accommodation for fixed capital investment, the exceptional willingness to give rather longer accommodation to a customer who could be depended upon to reduce his debt steadily year by year—in all these respects there is little to distinguish the bankers of 100 or 150 years ago from their successors in the mid-twentieth century. By contrast, the range of customers has broadened beyond recognition. The highly selective standards applied by some of the London private bankers—particularly those west of Ludgate Circus—had never been reflected in the generality of country banks, and we have seen how the latter often catered for tradesmen and other small customers. The change that came when the joint-stock banks were founded in the 1820's and 1830's was not revolutionary, at any rate outside London; what happened in this phase was rather that the geographical gaps in the country's banking system were filled, the rapid expansion in the country's trade activity was matched, and the opportunities for banking business and the possible customers of the conventional types were more actively cultivated. Even a generation later, bankers saw no possibility of any great enlargement of their custom. Sampson Lloyd, reviewing the position in 1868 (when his bank was still mainly confined to Birmingham), thought that the growth of his bank's business must be largely at the expense of competitors:

New Accounts come to us in one or other of the following ways:—
1. From persons induced to come by holding shares in the Bank.

2. From persons induced to change by some Director, or large Shareholder.
3. From persons never having had a banking account before.
4. From persons differing with their present banks about some temporary difficulty, and requiring special assistance.

The first source of new business has nearly ceased to operate; the second, in our case, does not operate largely; the accounts from the third source are mostly small; the fourth, therefore, is a main source of the increase of a bank's discount business, and a fairly liberal policy is requisite to make it fruitful.

His attitude was typical: what small element of aggressive enterprise the joint-stock banking movement had embodied a generation earlier had evaporated, and banking moved along in a groove which brought, to sound men of business, expanding balance-sheets and expanding profits as British industry and trade expanded. The bankers individually were anxious enough to succeed in competition with their fellow bankers; but they were not looking for new worlds to conquer.

The spur of competition did, however, in the end lead to a tremendous expansion in the number and variety of customers. For some decades after Sampson Lloyd's remarks banks grew not so much by taking business from their competitors as by swallowing the competitors themselves. Once the amalgamation movement had produced a group of giants facing each other, competition between these giants took the form rather of the growth of incidental services and the proliferation of banking offices. Among these services one of the most notable is the work of the Executor and Trustee Department. This service of the bank has a long tradition behind it, in that the private bankers of the eighteenth and nineteenth centuries had commonly been the trusted financial advisers of propertied families, and as such they were sometimes called upon to undertake responsibilities of this kind. But this was in their individual capacities, and it was not until the present century that it became usual for banks, as corporate bodies, to offer to undertake trusts. In 1910 Lloyds Bank decided to come into line with this development, and the necessary resolution was passed at an Extraordinary General Meeting. The Trustee Department was established in Birmingham in April 1910 (it moved to Lombard Street a year later), and branch managers were instructed to bring the new facilities to the notice of 'every suitable customer'. A subsequent circular emphasized that existing relations between customers and their solicitors should not be disturbed: the employment of the bank's solicitor, in preference to a customer's own, must never be recommended for the preparation of wills, nor might any member of the staff undertake such work.

For twenty-three years the department remained in a single office, and the bulk of the work consisted of administration of estates with continuing trusts. By 1933 the department's staff numbered 144 and 3,090 trusts were under administration; in that year 644 new cases fell in for administration and 399 estates were wound up. In May of that year a great expansion was initiated when the first branch of the department was opened in the West End of London. In the next five years 8 branches were opened in the provinces, and further development since the second war has brought the organization to a total of 30 area branches with a Chief Office for control and policy; its staff numbers 84, half men and half women. As compared with the 3,090 at the end of the department's first twenty-three years, nearly 19,000 trusts and estates were under administration at mid-1956; their book value was nearly £200 million.

Among other services greatly developed in this phase were the facilities provided for travellers; one of the West End banks that eventually came into Lloyds Bank was the originator of this service, and its story is told in Chapter 9 below. And there are many other incidental services nowadays, taken almost for granted by the English banker's customer. Competition between the banks has shown itself, in the present century, largely as competition in services, and it is this competition that has been largely responsible for the attraction of millions of small accounts from almost every section of the population. Nevertheless it would be a mistake to picture the old-fashioned banker as a stranger to the ancillary services offered by the giant banks of today. The correspondence of Messrs. Hanbury, Taylor, Lloyd and Bowman (Lombard Street) in the early 1880's shows a variety of instructions received from customers, whereby these sought to use the bankers to facilitate their business and private affairs. The Standing Order to make periodical payments was particularly prominent. Annuities to relatives, especially executors' payments under wills, appear to have been commonly paid by the banker under Standing Order. An Order of 1816 directs the bank to pay eight annuities, ranging from £10 to £250, by quarterly payments, with the proviso, 'In all cases certificates of the Annuitants being alive should be obtained from the Minister of the Parish where they respectively reside, before the quarterly payments are made, unless the Annuitants personally attend'; similar conditions appeared in many other Standing Orders of this kind. Twinings' records also abound in such Orders, especially from 1850 onwards: they refer to payments to clubs, subscriptions to charities, dividends, remittances to relations—all very much as nowadays.

Bankers have always helped with the purchase and sale of their customers' investments, although the early development of organized security markets had the effect of restricting English bankers' activities within narrower limits than those customary in most continental countries. The old private banks used to arrange purchase of Consols and other securities for their customers, just as the local branch of a great bank does today. Our earliest example is dated 1802, when Hanbury, Taylor, Lloyd and Bowman in London had an order from customers to sell £20,000 Bank Stock and Navy Stock and reinvest in 3 per cent. Consolidated Annuities; the interest was to be credited to a specified account. The generality of such transactions in the early days were much smaller than this. We find, for example, Peacock Handley and Co. of Sleaford in 1819 purchasing £200 Consols for a local clergyman; in 1814 purchasing for two customers jointly 'so much Consols as will cost £78–6–2'; in 1819 for another two customers 'so much Irish $3\frac{1}{2}\%$ Stock as will cost £1,750'. This was all treated as part of the work of helping customers in their affairs generally, and in the banker's notebook these orders rubbed shoulders with such notes as this: 'Order Mr. Griffith to send M. J. Peacock 4 gall. rum and 4 gall. gin (not Hollands, but good).' Much later in the century Miss M. called to see her bankers, Bacon Cobbold at Ipswich, 'as to her aunt's Dutch Rhenish Railway shares: also as to her brother' about whom she complained, 'it was a pity young men were allowed to overdraw so heavily'. Twinings—probably like West End bankers generally—gave their customers systematic advice on investments, even printing circular letters of advice. An example in 1879 refers to options offered to shareholders in the East Indian Railway Company; after commenting on the four options in detail, the bankers went so far as to add a general conclusion: 'On the whole, we think Individual Holders, especially if the amount of their holding be not exceptionally large, would do well to

105

decide between Nos. 1 and 3. We shall be happy to take steps for carrying your decision, whatever it may be, into effect. . . .' Here the advice was circularized to customers as the disinterested view of a family financial adviser. In other cases a banker was sometimes thinking of his own profit and loss account in a very direct way; in 1895 a borrowing customer of Messrs. Williams and Co. of Chester reported that his brother-in-law had bought for him some 'Straits Development Shares', on which a call of £1,320 was falling due. 'We queried the desire to benefit him shewn herein, told him it was a dangerous speculative transaction which might ruin him, and that with his liabilities to us it was wrong to have thus committed himself. Desired him to write his brother-in-law begging that the transaction might be taken out of his name.'

An unusual memorandum of the same Chester bank in 1892 shows that even in those days customers engaged in production for export could run into difficulties through their overseas customers expecting longer credit than the Englishman's banker could stomach. An engineering firm, an important customer of the bank, wished to tender for drainage works in the city of Wellington, New Zealand, and it was suggested to the firm that if they would accept payment in 4 per cent. bonds of the city the contract would probably come to them. The engineers referred to their bankers, who explained the disadvantages but proceeded to consult with their London agents, Robarts and Co. The latter were also against the transaction but agreed to find out whether any insurance company would buy the bonds. The market was not easy: Robarts thought that one insurance company might take these 4 per cent. bonds on a $5\frac{1}{2}$ or $5\frac{3}{4}$ per cent. basis, but urged the engineers to insist on cash, leaving the city to raise its own loans. The absence of a recorded sequel suggests that the engineering firm took this advice; what is significant is that neither country bankers nor the London agents appear to have contemplated for one minute underwriting the transaction themselves, though both went to much trouble to help the customer to find some other solution for his problem.

The securities held by bankers against their advances to customers suggest how varied were the investments of the ordinary run of middle-class Englishmen, both in town and in country, during the nineteenth century. Further evidence of this kind is afforded by the safe-deposit lists

106

LLOYDS BANK, COMMERCIAL ROAD, PORTSMOUTH
(Opened 1955)

of bankers; two particularly detailed series survive from Twinings and Bosanquets—the first a 'West-End Bank' with country as well as town customers, the second a typical Lombard Street business. Twinings' customers in the second quarter of the nineteenth century held rather more home than foreign securities; among the former, railway stocks were common, with a sprinkling of canal, dock, gas, waterworks, and other public utility stocks. Among their foreign securities European government bonds headed the list, but Latin Americans were also prominent; Empire stocks (including Australian bank shares, and shares in an Assam company) were few. In successive lists of overseas stocks in later decades of the century, India and other parts of the Empire share much more; railway bonds and bank shares representing a wide range of countries become common; the Near East and Far East appear, and the variety of commercial undertakings increases sharply in the last list (for the 1870's). The Bosanquets list refers to a shorter period—1850–64—and there is some reason to believe that it is heavily weighted by the holdings of the partners themselves. It contains 104 items: of these 38 refer to foreign governments, 15 to home railways, 14 to overseas railways, 12 to banks, 15 to industrial and trading concerns at home and abroad, with the remainder including canals, docks, insurance, mining, and shipping. As in the Twinings list, South America appears more often than the North, though that does not mean that the total money invested was greater.

It would have been interesting to conclude these notes on customers by saying how many people were at various dates banking with the banks which eventually merged into the great business Lloyds Bank has become today. This is not possible: no records remain from which a systematic account could be built up. But there are figures for Lloyds Bank itself; these, summarized in the Table on the next page, show for the end of certain years the number of accounts—and therefore exaggerate, though not very greatly the growth in the number of customers. And it is indeed growth, from the 277 customers Taylors and Lloyds had on their books ten years after they opened their Birmingham bank. It will be remarked that at the end of 1865, when the bank had just become a joint-stock company and there were only five offices and two agencies, deposits outnumbered the current accounts, but that in subsequent decades the current accounts came into the lead. This change appears to have been general, but the run of the figures is affected by the inclusion, especially after 1884, of London offices. In London the deposit account used to be rather exceptional; the Lombard Street office in 1884 had 2,328 current accounts but only 97 deposit accounts, St. James's Street at the same date had 1,322 current accounts but only 33 deposit, and when

Lloyds Bank	Number of accounts			No. of offices
	Current accounts	Deposit accounts	All accounts	
1865 .	2,041	2,483	4,524	7
1875 .	9,350	8,942	18,292	36
1885 .	19,038	14,728	33,766	53
1895 .	67,240	48,388	115,628	199
1905 .	159,441	98,416	257,857	420
1914 .	333,090	229,344	562,434	879
1915 .	. .	. .	592,279	893
1920 .	. .	. .	1,164,711	1,539
1925 .	. .	. .	1,340,843	1,655

the Herries Farquhar business came in (1896) it brought 2,276 current accounts but only 147 deposit. Big jumps in the figures are of course due to the big amalgamations: the Wilts and Dorset in 1914 brought 76,176 current accounts and 41,866 deposit accounts, while in 1918 the Capital and Counties brought in about 330,000, bringing the total of Lloyds Bank accounts close to the million mark.

The average number of accounts in a branch—an average concealing a wide range—tended to fall in the last third of the nineteenth century, reflecting the fact that Lloyds was a big Birmingham bank absorbing some very small local banks elsewhere in the Midlands and West Country. But the fall did not continue, and as the banking habit spread in the second and third decades of the twentieth century the number of accounts to each branch rose above a thousand. With the total of the bank's accounts running well into seven figures, and with the majority of accounts kept in offices where the branch manager has over a thousand customers, the problem of personal contact with his customers has become much more difficult for the banker. The difficulty is acknowledged and faced, and Lloyds insists on its tradition that every customer who comes into the bank is an individual whose requirements are to be considered individually.

5

COUNTRY BANKERS AND
LONDON AGENTS

A LIST or map of independent banks in England and Wales at any time before 1890 would show little sign of London's position as a financial centre. Even after the new joint-stocks gave an impetus to branch-banking, decades passed before the fashion spread beyond three or four banks—and these few did not all centre themselves on London. Yet London was always the financial centre, drawing together the independent banks, private and joint-stock alike, into a single banking system. The unity depended upon the link, as old as the banks themselves, between the country banker and his 'London agent'—or, as the Londoner would see it, between the London banker and his 'country correspondents'. From an economic point of view, this link had direct importance in that it provided the channels through which payments might be made across country and the savings of one district might bear fruit in the investments of another. In the development of the technique of banking, its significance lay in the readiness with which the experience of one bank was handed on to the novice elsewhere. And in the evolution of the highly centralized structure we know today the link between country banker and London agent was often the basis of eventual amalgamation.[1]

The correspondent link appeared from the very beginning of English country banking because the country banker could not otherwise provide the services that his customers expected. London's financial organization already existed, and London's commercial leadership went back into the mists of medieval England. The bill on London was well established, most of the king's taxes had to find their way to London, and London was

[1] For a recent and authoritative account of the functions of the London agent, see L. S. Pressnell, *Country Banking in the Industrial Revolution* (Oxford, 1956), chap. 4.

the centre through which passed most financial transactions with foreign countries. In 'the country' business men looked to London to settle most transactions outside their immediate localities, and wealthy people had become accustomed to placing funds with London bankers. A provincial business man turning banker would therefore look naturally to the bankers in and around Lombard Street for facilities in cross-country and foreign transactions, and as a safe-deposit for surplus cash. Unless the country banker did bring some of the facilities of Lombard Street to the doorstep of the local trader, the big men would often by-pass him and themselves employ the men of Lombard Street.

The function of the London agent therefore developed quite naturally as banking for the country banker. The latter deposited funds with his London agent and he looked upon this deposit as convertible into cash for use in the country at very short notice—it was his second line of defence, almost as good as money in the strong-box. In case of need he might be able to draw beyond this sum; there were instances of loans running on for quite long periods. To facilitate this borrowing the country banker would usually leave with his London agent the title documents of his holding of Consols or other stocks; incidentally, he would often look to his London agent to arrange purchases and sales of such stocks. The London agent could arrange also for the purchase of bills from bill-brokers, or the placing and calling of short loans to the bill-brokers when these became in effect bill-dealers. Bills discounted down in the country, for the local bank's customers, could be sent up to the London agent for rediscount, or occasionally as security for temporary assistance from the London agent himself. There was, too, a great deal of other business relating to the handling of bills—collection, pursuing cases of unpaid bills, sometimes selling the goods, occasionally also accepting—which was taken by Lombard Street in its stride. Above all, there was the clearance of payments between London and the country. This included a substantial proportion of cross-country payments, since cheques and notes on distant places, though sometimes presented directly, would generally be collected through London.

Arising out of all this—and again acting as a banker to his customer—the London agent would be expected to act as guide, philosopher, and friend in all financial business. He would advise his country correspondent on the placing of money in the London market, on investment policy, and on the creditworthiness of other London firms. The country banker would sometimes look to his London agent for advice on staff questions and on the running of his business generally. No doubt he often thought he knew his own business best, just as the banker's customer does nowadays; but at least he had a knowledgeable friend in Lombard Street with whom he was in daily correspondence and whom it was worth running up to see now and again.

The choice of a London agent was generally settled by some previous personal or business connexion of one of the country partners. The extreme case is where the country bank set up its own London house, as did Smith and Payne of Nottingham and Taylors and Lloyds of Birmingham. But these were early examples—Smith and Payne opened in London about 1758 and Taylors and Lloyds in 1770—and at those dates there was no strong competition among London bankers for the agency business of the country banks. The old-established Lombard Street houses did not readily embark on this new line of business, and the 'West End bankers', with their aristocratic clientèle and their abhorrence of the dirty bits of paper that eighteenth-century bills often were, probably looked down their noses at these jumped-up trader-financiers from the country. In the sixties and seventies of the eighteenth century, however, many new banks appeared in the City and these found scope particularly in the agency business.[2] Thus the country bankers looking for a London agent had a bigger choice, but the personal element continued to be important in establishing the connexion. Davison-Bland and Co. (forerunners of Lambton and Co.), founded at Newcastle in 1788, went to a London bank, Masters and Co., that had been founded only a year earlier; the choice appears to have been determined by the chance that Robert Clayton, one of the partners in Masters, had family connexions in the Newcastle area. At Worcester Joseph Berwick employed as his London bankers Messrs. Cocks Biddulph, who therefore became London agents of the Worcester bank of Berwick and Co.; but when in 1791 Joseph Berwick became a founder partner in the new London firm of Robarts Curtis, he took the London agency of his Worcester bank to

[2] Cf. D. M. Joslin, 'London Private Bankers, 1720–1785' in *The Economic History Review*, 2nd series, vol. vii (1954–5), pp. 167–86.

them. The Canterbury Bank, later identified with the Hammonds and Plumptres, employed Stephenson Remingtons from 1803 until 1818; the Canterbury bank then switched to Glyns, with whom there had been an important marriage connexion.[3] James Oakes and Son, of Bury St. Edmunds, took the advice of Gurney and Co., Norwich, who recommended them to employ Barclay and Co. as their London agents. This was no doubt only one of the many occasions on which a country banker took advice from the famous Gurney family, advice that must have helped to build up the great Barclay connexion that formed the basis of Barclays Bank. Not that Gurney advice always tended in that direction: in 1847 the Liverpool Union Bank was looking for an alternative to Cunliffes, the London bankers with whom they had quarrelled, and the manager went to London 'to open a negotiation for the removal of the account to such house as Mr. Samuel Gurney might recommend and introduce him to'. Samuel recommended Barnetts Hoares—with the result that the Liverpool Union eventually came into the Lloyds fold.[4] Hedges Wells of Wallingford, in similar difficulty after Pole Thornton's collapse in 1825, took advice from an even more exalted quarter: 'After great difficulty and perplexity, Providence pointed to the respectable firm of Jones Loyd.'

The advent of 'the joint-stocks' in the 1820's and 30's sharpened competition for the agency work. London bankers, both private and joint-stock, were active in the promotions in the provinces and usually saw to it that the London business came to their firms. Among private firms, Ladbroke, Kingscote and Gillman picked up the agency for the Warwick and Leamington Banking Company, by the local exertions of Mr. Ladbroke in 1834; his partner Mr. Kingscote was similarly busy in Gloucester the next year, and brought the agency of the Gloucester County and City Bank. In the West of England and South Wales Bank a Board minute of 1834 referred to 'Messrs. Glyn, Hallifax, Mills & Co., Bankers of Lombard Street, who had proposed themselves as the London Agents for the

---

[3] Mary Plumptre, daughter of one of the Canterbury bankers, married Sir Richard Carr Glyn in 1785. The reason for the change in 1818 is unknown (R. Fulford, *Glyn's 1753–1953*, Macmillan, 1953, p. 65). On the early London account of the Canterbury bank, cf. p. 121 below.

[4] The connexion between London agent and country banker was often the basis of amalgamation (cf. pp. 247–8 below), but by no means invariably: Oakes of Bury St. Edmunds, just mentioned, banked with Barclays in London, but they were eventually bought by the Capital and Counties and so came into Lloyds.

Bank': the proposal was accepted. Among the new joint-stocks in London, the famous J. W. Gilbart, manager of the London and Westminster Bank, took a very active part in the foundation of the Wilts and Dorset Banking Company, and secured its London business for the London and Westminster.

This competition for new business did have its limits. Private bankers in the country naturally felt a good deal of hostility towards joint-stock rivals springing up in their areas, and a London banker had to take account of these feelings. It is significant, however, that the only trace of such circumstances is dated 1872, by which time the Londoners were not pushing so eagerly for business as they had done in the hurly-burly of the thirties. In that year Barnetts Hoares were asked to become agents for a new joint-stock bank, the London and Yorkshire. Their reaction was to write to all the banks in Yorkshire for whom they already acted, asking them whether they would object to a connexion with this new competitor. 'If you think we should injure your interests in the slightest degree we will refuse the agency, but if not we may take it, as we know that the capital of the bank is sufficient to make us perfectly secure.' This caution cost Barnetts Hoares the business: the London and Yorkshire was anxious to get a London name on their prospectus, and the position was snapped up by the Union Bank of London while Barnetts Hoares awaited replies from their country correspondents.

The strength of the tie between London agent and country correspondent is evident in the strange position which more often than not followed the amalgamation of country banks employing different bankers in London. It might have been supposed that the single firm after the amalgamation would place all the business in the hands of one of the two London firms previously employed, and this is how matters were in fact sometimes arranged. But there were many examples in which the old connexions were left undisturbed, with the result that one country bank, building up a chain of branches by amalgamating with its neighbours, might employ almost as many London agents as it had branches. An extreme case is the Gloucestershire Banking Company, which although it employed Jones Lloyds for its head office at Gloucester and its original branches at Stroud and Newnham, invariably retained for offices absorbed by amalgamation any other agents they had previously employed.

The original adoption of this policy may have been due to a personal element: the three offices of Hartland and Co., absorbed in 1831, remained very much the personal dominion of Mr. Hartland who no doubt insisted on retaining as London agents the firm of Williams and Co. with whom he was used to dealing. Once adopted, the policy continued to be followed, with the result that in 1843 the Company was employing, for various branches, three London private banks, besides having deposit accounts at three of the new London joint-stock banks. In the same way, the Wilts and Dorset by 1860 employed the London and Westminster for eighteen branches, Glyns for four, and Williams and Co. (Williams Deacon and Co.) for two.

An odd position of this kind in the Devon and Cornwall Bank serves to point a change that was coming over the banking world in the middle decades of the nineteenth century. The Plymouth partnership on which this bank was built up had from its earliest days employed Barclays for its London business. In the 1830's it blossomed forth as a minor branch-system, largely by absorption of other private firms. Among the latter, one at Exeter had already an established London connexion (with Hanburys, Taylor and Lloyds) and this Exeter office continued as a Lloyds' correspondent until 1879, when the Devon and Cornwall brought its Exeter office into line by transferring its London business to Barclays. Meanwhile, in 1875 a bank at Brixham was absorbed: Barnetts, Hoares, Hanburys and Lloyd[5] had acted as London agents, but the agency was at once transferred to Barclays. It appears, that is to say, that though in the thirties and for some time later a branch was frequently allowed to maintain its traditional London connexion,[6] by the seventies amalgamating banks thought it best to concentrate all their business into the hands of a single London firm.

Though these oddities of multiple correspondence show how strong was the tendency to leave the business in the channel through which it had long flowed, there were occasional changes besides those arising

[5] The successors of Hanburys, Taylors and Lloyd (see p. 16 above).

[6] When Moilliets of Birmingham (see p. 4 above) were absorbed into the new Lloyds Banking Company in 1865 the new Board decided to retain Robarts Lubbock for the London agency of the new branch. An exceptionally late example was the absorption of Pinckneys, Salisbury, into the Wilts & Dorset in 1897, when the Barclay connexion of Pinckneys was maintained, although the Wilts and Dorset dealt with the London and Westminster and with Glyns.

from amalgamations among country banks. A London bank when merging itself into another institution could not take it for granted that the country correspondents would automatically accept the new régime, particularly when this meant dealing with quite different people and perhaps with quite a different type of organization. When the famous firm of Jones Loyd (Lord Overstone's firm) sold out to the London and Westminster in 1864, the Coventry and Warwickshire accepted assurances that the Westminster Directors 'in times of monetary difficulty . . . would treat [them] with the utmost liberality'; but the Glamorganshire Banking Company declined to fall into line, and instead made an advantageous arrangement with Barclays. The London private banks were evidently still very much in the running for agency business that came into the market. Indeed, Beechings of Tonbridge twice, in 1864 and in 1884, established new connexions with London private banks in order to escape the ravening maw of the joint-stock beast.[7] But there were many changes in which the joint-stocks gained ground: in 1864 Williams Deacons solicited from the Gloucestershire Banking Company the agency of the Cirencester and Stow branches (hitherto with Mastermans), but the Gloucester people replied that they were inclined to a connexion with one of the London joint-stock banks, and they did eventually give the business to the Union Bank of London.

A change of connexion in 1841 not only shows how lively was competition between banks but also paradoxically illustrates the convenience country customers found in the continuity of London agencies. The Wilts and Dorset, which already employed both the London and Westminster and Williams Deacons, had branches in Wimborne and Blandford, towns where they had to compete with Fryer Andrews and Co. Glyns were the London agents of Fryer Andrews, but the latter were now being absorbed by the National Provincial which insisted upon transferring the London business to their usual agents, the London Joint Stock Bank. The Wilts and Dorset thereupon switched the London business of their Wimborne and Blandford offices to Glyns, Fryer Andrews' old agents, and issued the following announcement:

[7] In 1864 Mastermans, the original agent of Beechings, was absorbed in a joint-stock bank; Beechings changed to Barnetts Hoares. When in 1884 the latter joined forces with the joint-stock Lloyds, one partner insisted on another change in order to support a private banker, and the agency accordingly went to Barclays.

This arrangement is made in order to meet the convenience of the numerous residents of the County of Dorset who have granted Powers of Attorney for the receipt of dividends upon their funded property to the eminent House [i.e. Glyns]. Those gentlemen who in consequence of the discontinuance of the Banking House of Messrs Fryer Andrews & Co. may favour the Wilts and Dorset Bank with the future conducting of their accounts will thus be enabled to transact their banking business in its accustomed channel.

Whether the Wilts and Dorset succeeded in attracting many customers is not recorded; certainly they thought the chance good enough to justify the rupture of their own former connexions.

Although in the early days some of the tiny local banks did manage without a London agent, to most country banks the employment of some London firm was absolutely necessary, if only for clearing transactions with other country banks. A note of 1826 reveals the arrangements made by all the banks of Birmingham, dating back through many years:

To send all the Notes of and checks on each other to the [Birmingham] Clearing house every morning at 10 o'clock and pay or receive the difference if under £200 in Bank notes or Sovereigns, but above this sum, it is optional to pay the differences in Bank notes or Sovereigns or to order payment the next day in London. As all our notes of £5, £10, £20 and £100 are payable only in London we do not consider ourselves liable (except as a matter of courtesy) to pay them in Birmingham. . . .

It was common though not universal form for the country bankers' notes to be payable in London, even if there was an option to present at the bank's own office in the country.[8] London redemption naturally made the notes acceptable over a much wider area, and provided a convenience for the local business man or aristocrat—even the bishop—when he visited London. The London agent did not ordinarily have occasion to use the notes again, and would debit them to the country banker's account. Accumulations of paid notes would be sent down to the country from time to time, for cancellation or reissue. It was of course dangerous for the London agent to be too regular in his dispatches to the country,

[8] A Suffolk banker writing to an intending banker in Cornwall in 1824 advised the latter not to make his notes payable in London 'from the great and increasing risk and expense of getting them back'.

116

and correspondence included frequent variations of instructions. Berwick Lechmeres at Worcester in 1801 asked Robarts, their agents in Lombard Street, not to send more than £10,000 notes at one time, as the risk of theft was too great.

There was traffic in the other direction too. The country banker would send up to London, for credit to his account with his London agent, Bank of England notes and notes issued by other country banks (except those cleared locally, as in Birmingham). There were notes of both these kinds, with some bills of exchange, in two parcels, total value £5,000, that were in 1819 stolen from the guard of the Old Fly Coach at the Bull and Mouth, Aldersgate. They had come up from Berwick Lechmeres at Worcester. (Coaches coming Lombard Street way were often mentioned in thieves' kitchens.) In these two parcels there were some bills of exchange; these and ordinary cheques and sometimes dividend coupons formed a very large part of the packages the stage coaches carried up for Lombard Street—and after the stage coaches, the railways. Most bankers entrusted the packages to the Post Office, but Foster and Co. of Cambridge were an exception as lately as 1874. Their habit was to send a messenger right through to Lombard Street, carrying cheques for the clearing: every morning a clerk had to accompany this messenger to the 7.3 train, to see the package safely on its way. The arrival of all these pieces of paper from the country must have demanded serious organization in Lombard Street. A week when there was a rush of dividend payments must have taxed capacity, and it is not surprising to find, even as lately as 1881, Barnetts Hoares complaining to Lloyds at Birmingham how difficult it was to avoid mixing up the coupons sent in by all their various country connexions.

The country banker was of course able to arrange completion of many transactions simply by ordering debits to his account with his agent. In 1798, for example, Oakes of Bury St. Edmunds instructed Ayton and Co. to pay to the Exchequer two amounts of £10,000 and £12,000 in respect of taxes collected by Orbell Oakes in his capacity—not an unusual one for a country banker—as Receiver-General for West Suffolk. In 1810 Peacock Handley and Co., Sleaford, instructed Down and Co. to pay to Hammersley Greenwood, West End bankers and Army agents, a sum 'for Lieut. Peacock for the purchase of a troop in the 9th Light Dragoons'.

In 1843 the Burton Union Bank told their note engravers in London that they would receive payment of their account through Robarts, their London agents. These and similar incidents appearing in correspondence exemplify the variety and facility of these transactions, of which thousands upon thousands appear in the old ledgers: the opening pages of a country banker's ledger would be devoted to his account with his London agent, and it would occupy several times as many pages as the account of his most active local customer.

Business in cheques and bills of exchange was not by any means all routine work for the London banker. Unpaid bills had to be noted, dishonoured cheques returned, forgeries to be detected, even wrongdoers to be detained. In 1855 Lacons Youells (Norwich and Yarmouth) instructed Glyns not to pay drafts without specific advice, as a clerk had absconded with two blank signed drafts. Glyns were asked to detain anyone applying for money on these drafts and were informed that the absconding clerk 'may be immediately identified by his eyebrows which meet on his nose'.

More serious difficulty arose when in 1858 the Country Clearing was established at the London Bankers' Clearing House.[9] Hitherto a country cheque sent up to a London agent had been handled according to individual practices of the London bankers and their country correspondents, which sometimes meant speedy payment of a cheque and sometimes delay. When the Country Clearing was established, it became customary for the country bank to post a cheque on another country bank to his London agent for presentation to the Clearing House, which would then post the cheque to the bank on which it was drawn. As compared with the speed sometimes (not usually) achieved under the old practices, the new regular procedure was slightly more risky for the customer presenting the cheque. In 1861 a customer of Hentys Bank at Worthing was met by the statement that the account on which the cheque was drawn had been stopped by the time the cheque arrived from the Clearing House. He pointed out (correctly in this instance) that under the practice followed by Hentys and their agents before 1858 the cheque would have been presented in time for payment. Hentys spent £600 fighting the case through the Courts, and obtained a judgement that they were entitled to

---

[9] Cf. p. 33 above.

follow the new procedure.[10] It was a test case essential to the continuance of the arrangements established in the Country Clearing.

In the course of the nineteenth century the function of the London agent was often extended to the acceptance, on behalf of the country bank, of bills for customers of the country bank. Arrangements of this kind have been noticed[10a] elsewhere as early as the 1820's, and by the middle of the century the great house of Jones Loyd was often accepting bills for customers of the Gloucestershire Banking Company. Their example was quoted by Lloyds of Birmingham when the latter in 1853 asked their London house (Hanburys and Lloyds) to accept bills for customers of theirs who were importing grain from the Baltic,[11] instead of giving their own (the customers') acceptance. 'In these cases', wrote the Birmingham bank, 'a London banker's acceptance sells abroad so much more freely than a Birmingham merchant's or manufacturer's (however respectable) as to make a difference of full 2 per cent. in the rate of exchange which is almost a profit in itself to a commission merchant.' Naturally the London banker had to reserve the right to limit, even to refuse, these obligations. Barnetts Hoares maintained that it was a privilege they allowed to their country correspondents, and that it formed no part of their regular business obligations. In 1866 and again in 1869 Barnetts complained to Alexanders of Ipswich that one of the latter's customers, a corn merchant, had been exercising the privilege too freely: Alexanders had better take care that Barnetts' interest was adequately covered by bills of lading. In 1883 Barnetts, following standing instructions from the Bradford Old Bank, found that their acceptances for one of the Bradford's customers totalled £140,000, and sought fresh instructions: they did not usually take a standing instruction of this kind, but would continue if Bradford would confirm their satisfaction with their customer's standing. It is apparent from these and other incidents that the London agents themselves did not expect to receive any specific cover; their protection lay in the moral obligation of their country correspondent to underwrite the business. But the London bank would obviously be incurring risk if

[10] *Hare* v. *Henty* (v. *The Bankers' Magazine*, June 1861).   [10a] By Dr. L. S. Pressnell.
[11] At this time Lloyds had only their Birmingham office: the fact that customers of theirs were regular importers of grain from the Baltic throws some light on organization of the grain trade, and on the varied business that could be covered by a single bank office in this Midland city.

the country bank incurred heavy losses, and there was accordingly some point in reminding the country correspondent that the latter's customer should put up adequate cover.

These sterling bills accepted by London agents were important in all foreign trade transactions and, as long as the bill on London was the major medium of exchange in foreign trade, customers' overseas transactions left little other mark in the banks' records. There is, of course, the special case of the foreign business of Herries Farquhars in St. James's Street,[12] and there is an occasional mention of foreign coin required by customers. In 1875 the London and Westminster was asked to advise a Coventry and Warwickshire customer on the terms on which American consignments could be paid for. But in the main, foreign business meant business in 'the bill on London', and in bill transactions the London agent found his work for country correspondents increasing substantially in the nineteenth century.

To meet all the obligations they assumed for their country correspondents the London bankers looked for substantial deposits by those correspondents. 'We shall invariably expect', wrote Robarts in 1826, 'sufficient funds are held in our hands to meet your engagements and to provide for your issue of notes that may be payable with us.' For a substantial country bank the ups and downs of its balance with its London agent were apt to be very considerable, and the agent expected to be well provided against these swings. A letter from Lloyds to their London house in 1845 shows the experience of three days:

Our credit balance with you at the 19th agrees with yours, viz.,

	45,786
On the 20th it was reduced	10,950
	34,836
21 Increase receipts	1,019
	35,855
Decrease 21st payments	14,759
	21,096.

There was nothing exceptional about these figures, which can be

[12] See below, pp. 193–8.

paralleled in hundreds of ledgers; they were the subject of correspondence simply because there was dispute about the state of the account at a certain date; and the figures relate to a bank whose balance-sheet total was around £500,000. Some years later an exchange of correspondence put the understanding between the two houses on record: the minimum was in general to be £20,000 and in no case was the balance to fall below £5,000.

The country banker who was operating daily on his account in London —a high proportion of his bigger transactions must for one reason or another involve a debit or credit to London—naturally came to regard his London balance as part of, and the more important part of, his cash reserve. An early run of balance-sheets of the Canterbury Bank shows that, in a balance-sheet total of £70,000 to £100,000, 'cash in hand' was generally below, and sometimes much below, £5,000, but the 'Balance at Mr. Bollands'[13] was usually much bigger but could vary very widely indeed. At the end of 1789 it stood at £51,958; six months later it was £11,279; in June 1792 it was £37,866, and a year later it was as low as £806. In 1800 the balance-sheet total grew to £150,000 and beyond and the 'Balance at Mr. Bollands' kept at much higher levels, but it still varied very widely and always dwarfed the 'cash in hand'. Another moderately large private bank, that of Stephens Harris and Stephens at Reading, banked with Willis Percival & Co. in Lombard Street. In their 1815 'General Statement', in which assets totalled some £173,000, cash stood at £8,327 and 'Balance in Hands of Willis Percival & Co.' £13,334. Five years later cash stood at £10,561 with £23,739 in Lombard Street. After 1840, when their balance-sheet total had grown to some £300,000, they held rather more cash—£10,000 to £13,000; their Lombard Street figures did not grow in proportion, but were still usually above the 'cash

---

[13] 'Mr. Bolland' never became a pure banker. He was a hop-factor, with whom Mr. Gipps of Canterbury did business when he himself was in the hop business at Canterbury. When Gipps turned banker in 1788 he continued to use Bolland for his London transactions until about 1803 when the London agency was transferred to Stephenson Remingtons. It is notable that in many small ways the relations between Gipps and Bolland were precisely parallel to those between any other country correspondent and London agent: for example, the Canterbury Bank gave Christmas boxes to Bolland's clerks, and when Gipps died, Bolland was one of his executors. Presumably Bolland could not offer the same clearing facilities as a Lombard Street bank would offer, but his services were evidently efficient enough to retain the connexion even after the original Mr. Gipps had been succeeded by other partners.

in hand' figures. A strong joint-stock bank, the Wilts and Dorset, with a balance-sheet total that quickly grew from £400,000 to £500,000, did not reckon to hold proportionately more with its London agent. At the ends of the years 1837, 1838, and 1839 its London balances were £12,028, £20,152, and £6,202, while cash 'on hand' stood at £28,472, £27,627, and £27,996. The different relation between cash and London balance in this case may have been due partly to its relatively extensive network of branches, each of which had to hold an adequate cash balance; but as a new and aggressive institution, out for high profits, it may also have cut its London balances rather finer than a more staid and long-established private banker.

The balance standing in the books of the London agent was by no means always on the credit side; the facility to overdraw the account was one of the advantages the country banker enjoyed from the connexion, just as his own customers had the advantage of being able to overdraw on the country banker. Although the London agent would ordinarily expect to hold a large credit balance, the fact that this could be run down heavily without notice and that in addition the account could be overdrawn gave the country banker very considerable protection against the consequences of illiquid loans to his own customers in the country. 'You will have in mind', a Worcester banker wrote to Lombard Street in 1837, 'that we have no such opportunities here as you have in London of employing our money and therefore are sometimes induced to advance it for certain periods which are not punctually kept.' This banker's firm was from time to time substantially in debt to Robarts, and a letter of 1840 shows that over a long period it was both largely and irregularly overdrawn. This country bank had been well thought of in Lombard Street, though its habits eventually led to remonstrances and a threat to sever the connexion. The case is not untypical of the relations between Lombard Street and the old-established private banks in the provinces, except that persistence of the overdraft gave rise to a lively and forthright correspondence. Letters remaining in other offices show occasional difficulties—as when two offices of an Ipswich bank were independently overdrawing at Glyns, who did not like the combined total—but in general there seems to have been no difficulty about occasional overdrafts up to £10,000 or even £20,000: quite substantial sums for banks whose total assets were generally less than £200,000.[14] Larger banks—like the Bradford Old Bank or Lloyds themselves—might borrow £100,000 or £200,000 in London. On the other hand, the Lombard Street houses were naturally a little cautious in their attitude to the new joint-stock banks of the 1830's and 40's. In 1831 the Plymouth and Devonport Banking Company, in arranging for Barclay, Tritton, Bevan and Co. to be their London agents, told Barclays that they assumed the latter 'would be willing to offer liberal assistance should any emergency require it.' 'It is quite in course with us', Barclays replied, 'to afford temporary accommodation to our friends, and from the nature of your connection such advances will be perfectly free from objection on the score of security, but it would not be in accordance with our habits to come under specific agreement to that effect.'

The availability of these overdrafts gave the Lombard Street men scope, by the conditions they could impose, for influencing the local business undertaken by the country banker. This might take the form of quite general advice, as when Robarts referred Berwick Lechmere's at Worcester to 'the mode in which your neighbours, Messrs. Farley & Co. manage their business'. (Fortunately in this case Berwick Lechmeres did not take the hint, for Farleys collapsed some years later leaving a large deficiency.)[15] Or the country bank might be called more sharply to heel and given instruction in the way to do its business. Alexanders of Ipswich, bankers deeply involved in the corn trade, were drawing heavily on Barnetts, their London agents, in the 1860's and eventually the latter forced Alexanders to obtain the support of other East Anglian bankers to see them through a difficult period. Individual partners in banks in Norwich, Wisbech, Hertford, and Saffron Walden between them found £40,000, part of which was used to purchase Consols for Alexanders, the remainder being placed to their credit at Barnetts. Barnetts themselves put £10,000 into the pool. Nevertheless Alexanders' difficulties con-

---

[14] The balance-sheets of country banks before 1850 are few and far between. Such as there are show wide variation according to the business activity of the town. In small country towns the total may have been nearer £50,000 than £100,000, whereas in expanding industrial towns like Birmingham and Newcastle it might run to several hundreds of thousands.

[15] Farleys suspended payment during the Ante-Christmas Fair, 1857, when the town was thronged. Against liabilities of £90,000 assets of £50,000 were found.

tinued, and Barnetts, in consultation with the other contributing bankers, decided that they must exercise more control over the Ipswich bank. To achieve this, Barnetts found an ex-cashier of an Irish bank who was willing to spend three days a week at Alexanders supervising their business during the next three months. This move was resented by Alexanders, who represented that the presence of a stranger in their bank would cause much local comment and loss of faith.[16] The outcome is not quite clear, but it seems likely that Barnetts did not press this particular plan. They did, however, watch Alexanders' transactions very critically in the future, and were quick to offer advice and to use sharp words. By the end of 1871 Barnetts felt that Alexanders had been pulled into order, and relations continued happily until in 1878 Alexanders amalgamated with Gurneys of Norwich and so eventually passed into the Barclays group.

Pressure to reduce a London overdraft could thus be used to influence the whole course of a country banker's business. It could also be used to check the banker in a particular series of transactions to which Lombard Street took a dislike. (Alexanders was to some extent such a case: the trouble began because Barnetts thought Alexanders were too deep in the corn market.) Bacon Cobbold and Co., another Ipswich firm, in 1855 came under pressure from Glyns to reduce the partners' own overdraft accounts[17]—perhaps because they knew that one of the partners had been speculating in hops. The partners had to set about selling property in order to straighten matters: it was important that they should do so, for an incident soon afterwards showed how a late harvest could necessitate borrowing in London for the ordinary course of their business. Unheeded advice could of course lead to severance of relations: such a case is that of Hill and Sons at Smithfield who, though not 'country' bankers in the ordinary sense, used Glyns for agency work very much as a country banker would. In the 1890's Hills were borrowing from Glyns as much as £130,000; then in 1903 they asked for a further advance of £220,000 to lend to one of their customers, a cold storage company that wanted the

---

[16] This tells us something of the atmosphere of the old country banks: a new face in the office would be noticed and an explanation expected.

[17] It was by no means unusual for the partners of a private country bank to borrow very large sums from the bank: often these sums were employed in their original line of business. The Lloyds, for example, borrowed for their iron business (cf. p. 10 above); and some of the brewer-bankers found from their banks the capital for their breweries.

loan pending an issue of share capital. In 1907 Glyns thought it necessary to warn Hills against allowing their customers' demands upon them to 'become permanently or chronically in excess of your resources thereby entailing our carrying your business'. The warning went unheeded, so in 1910 Glyns said firmly that the overdraft (then £250,000) must be paid off; Hills had better, they said, sell out to one of the joint-stock giants that were eating up the little banks. Hills took the hint and so came into Lloyds in 1911.

While the timing of these pressures would often depend upon the chance circumstances of individual banks, there was inevitably some tendency for the pressure to be associated with the state of the London money market. Because of tightness in that market, and the associated high rates obtainable on ready money, the Lombard Street men would be inclined at such periods to look more critically at their debtors among the country banks. A letter from Robarts to Berwick Lechmere in 1840, reviewing the past, objects to 'your large overdrafts at periods of the most severe and unprecedented pressure': on one of these occasions, in the difficult autumn of 1836, Robarts had told the Worcester bank that owing to the extreme pressure in the money market they would not be able to continue their advance to Berwick Lechmeres. On this occasion and on others they did in fact see Berwick Lechmeres through, but they did it grudgingly, a fact that must have had its effect on the Worcester bank's complaisance towards its own borrowing customers. In 1837 the Liverpool Union Bank, on complaint that they were borrowing too much from their London agents, resolved that 'no exertions should be spared to call in the amount of money absorbed in loans on Current Account'. In 1840 Miles Cave and Co. of Bristol found Barnetts Hoares even more difficult. The Bristol bank wanted £40,000 or £50,000, but Barnetts declined on the ground that the scarcity of money made it inconvenient; they advised Miles Cave to 'borrow on Consols' at about 5 per cent.

Many references to these transactions indicate that the bills pledged with the London agent provided only partial security, but then the London agent's protection would lie in the fact that he usually held in his safe Consols, and sometimes other stocks, belonging to the country banker. The London agent could always tell his correspondent that some of the Consols had better be realized in order to reduce an inconveniently large overdraft, and this was not an anathema to the country banker, who customarily regarded his Consols as his third liquidity line—coming next after cash and balance with London agent.[18] The tendency for country bankers to be sellers of government stocks in times of money market stringency was thus a circumstance pushing long-term interest rates in the same direction as short-term rates were moving.

The lender-and-borrower relation between London agent and country correspondent also helped, when money-rates became flexible in the middle decades of the nineteenth century, to make London rates penetrate to the country. Although full reflection of London changes was not usual, as early as 1839 there is evidence of the rate, for advances to a country bank, being raised from 4 to 5 per cent. 'when the value of money so largely and so inconveniently increased'. By 1849 it was apparently thought natural, in making a new agency arrangement,[19] to suggest that any advances should be 'at the then Bank or market rate of interest'. Other evidence is not conclusive, but suggests that practice varied in detail but was generally based on acceptance of some link with Bank Rate.

The ease with which he could borrow from his London agent and the rate that he would be charged would thus combine to make the country banker sensitive to conditions in the London money market.[20] Similarly many country bankers would be affected by the ease with which, and the rates at which, they could rediscount in London bills which they had discounted for their customers in the country. The country banker who was able to lend locally more money than he collected in local deposits has his parallel today in the busy branch that 'borrows' from Head Office in order to take full advantage of openings for sound lending among its local customers. Although money did not move as easily as it moves nowadays, the independent banker of a hundred years ago could, for the same purpose, draw funds from London. There was more than one way of getting the money from London. We have already seen how the country banker could obtain an advance from his London agent, and how

[18] Cf. John Rae, *The Country Banker* (1885), letter xxix.
[19] The Liverpool Union with Barnetts Hoares.
[20] This broad conclusion and the whole of this passage fully support the conclusions, based on a different class of evidence of Elmer Wood, *English Theories of Central Banking Control, 1819–1858*, esp. chap. 1 (Harvard University Press, 1939).

the latter might sometime expect bills, discounted in the country, to be offered as security for the advance. Alternatively the money could be obtained from the London agent by rediscounting with the latter bills discounted for country customers. Barnetts Hoares did a considerable amount of such rediscounting, even quite late in the nineteenth century. They themselves would never part with a bill once they had taken it; the tradition of London bankers, that to rediscount was a sign of weakness and therefore to be avoided, had already taken root.[21] As between London agent and country banker, however, the more elastic advance was generally preferred: if the country correspondent sent up bills for security, the effect was substantially the same. A third method of raising funds was rather different: the London agent could be employed purely as an agent to arrange the sale of the bills in the discount market. By this method the country banker could tap the general pool of resources in the London money market without obligation to his own banker, who might occasionally find his demands inconvenient. In the early days it was always more satisfactory, from the point of view of the country banker, to get accommodation from the Lombard Street man who knew him, but as the London market became stronger, and it became true that, at a price, a bill could always be discounted in London, rediscounting in the market probably became more common. Certainly by the 1850's it was being greatly overdone in some quarters, with the result that the custom among London bankers, never to let the bank's name appear on paper in the market, spread to country bankers. Lloyds of Birmingham were particularly proud of their record: in 1861 they wrote to a fellow country banker, 'Of course we never require accommodation, not even discount.' They had to eat their words in the difficult days of 1866, when they discounted some bills with Barnetts Hoares, and then again in 1867 when Barnetts Hoares referred them to the National Discount Company. This is believed, on the authority of Howard Lloyd, to have been the last occasion except 1914 on which Lloyds of Birmingham did resort to rediscounting.

While some country banks could lend more than they could raise in local deposits, and therefore tended to draw funds from the London

---

[21] It was very rigidly maintained, with odd effects upon the ways of the London money market, until 1939, when it was relaxed for the convenience of the authorities in their 'smoothing-out' operations.

money market, others were in the reverse position, with deposits to spare.[22] For these 'surplus-deposits' banks London was a repository for funds rather than a source, and the London agent had important functions in relation to these surplus funds. The surplus in question was of course a surplus over and above the large amounts the London agent would expect to hold as a working balance and as a more fixed reserve. When the country banker found that his London balance was much above the level appropriate to his operations on the account and his understanding with his London agent, he looked round for some remunerative way of employing the money. Sometimes the London banker would be prepared to pay his country correspondent a special rate on an extra, more or less fixed, deposit. More often the money would be lent out in some part of the London money market, or used to purchase bills or Stock Exchange securities. In all these transactions the London agent could perform some useful services.

Back in the eighteenth century, when the London discount market was undeveloped and country bankers were very much the country cousins of the sophisticated Lombard Street practitioners, the most usual investments were the 3 per cent. Consols,[23] Exchequer Bills, and other government paper. These were bought through stockbrokers, and the country banker usually expected his agent to employ the stockbroker. Thus we find Lambtons of Newcastle, in 1793, instructing Masters & Co. to purchase £10,000 in the 3 per cent. Consols,[24] because their balance with Masters was unnecessarily high. Such indirect employment of a broker remained the practice not only of the little private banks but also of some quite large concerns: late in the nineteenth century Hodgkin Barnetts at Newcastle were still going through their London agents (by this time, Lloyds) for Stock Exchange business. But the breezier ways adopted by the joint-stock banks, when they appeared in the 1820's and 30's, made for direct contacts with the Stock Exchange.[25] The Plymouth

---

[22] A change in trading conditions could easily swing a bank from one category to the other: thus the slump of 1847 stopped rediscounting by the Liverpool Union Bank and saw them pushing loans out into the market through their London agents.

[23] 'Consols' as such date from 1751.

[24] Maberly Phillips, *Banks, Bankers and Banking in Northumberland, Durham and North Yorkshire* (London, 1894), p. 246.

[25] Some joint-stock banks continued the earlier practice: thus the Coventry and War-

CITY OFFICE, 72 LOMBARD STREET, 1956

and Devonport Bank (soon to become the Devon and Cornwall Bank) and the Gloucestershire Banking Company established from the start direct connexions with London stockbrokers: the London agent had simply to meet their drafts in favour of the stockbroker after the latter had received his instructions directly from the country bank. Oddly enough, the new practice appears to have been encouraged in Lombard Street: in 1834 Glyns agreed to transact the stock business of the West of England and South Wales Bank in its early stages, but on the understanding that when the volume grew larger the business would be handed over to a stockbroker.[26]

As the London money market developed, investment in government paper ceased to be the only important outlet for surplus London funds. There were bills to be bought and bill-brokers, newly developed into bill-dealers, to lend to. Either of these channels had the advantage that it could be used for the employment of funds of whose long-term availability the banker did not feel sure—a point particularly relevant at times when government securities stood high in price, as they often did just when the country banker had most to spare. These developments in the London market were particularly associated with the sharp competition and new habits engendered by the appearance of the new joint-stock banks in London in the thirties and forties. In their search for business the new banks were themselves ready to pay good interest on money deposited by country bankers, and the old-established Lombard Street firms were forced to do the same if the connexions were not to slip from their hands.[27]

Being on the spot, the London agent could be useful in a number of ways in any of these transactions. He could keep his country correspondent posted on the various outlets for funds, the rates offering and other relevant information. He could collect security for loans made to the discount houses or stockbrokers, while allowing these borrowers the convenience of exchanging the security whenever it suited them. Facilities

wickshire (little more, at this time, than an enlarged private bank) continued to send their Stock Exchange orders to Jones Loyd & Co.

[26] At an earlier date (1795) Glyns had strongly protested to a country correspondent who wished to employ a stockbroker independently (Pressnell, op. cit., pp. 86–87).

[27] A clear example is recorded in 1862, when Glyns offered interest to Moore and Robinson (a little joint-stock bank in Nottingham) when they found that the London Joint Stock Bank had been getting Moore and Robinson's surplus.

of this kind carried a risk, of course, and the troubles that beset Barnetts Hoares in 1884 show how a London agent could get into difficulties by making life easy for his country correspondent. A partner in P. W. Thomas and Co., stockbrokers to whom country correspondents were lending money, speculated unwisely and saved his skin by pledging securities held for clients. These securities were at the time being used by Thomas and Co. as cover for loans from the country correspondents of Barnetts Hoares. The latter actually held the share certificates in their vault, but by some means the culprit had used them for raising money from various banks. Thomas's failed for £800,000 and the lending banks lost their money. Miles, Cave and Co. of Bristol, one of these banks, had £145,000 owing to them; they threatened Barnetts Hoares with legal action and eventually country correspondent and London agent shared the loss between them. The heavy losses suffered by Barnetts Hoares in this affair—the £72,500 for Miles Cave was only part of the story—were eventually talked about [28] and, according to Howard Lloyd, encouraged Barnetts Hoares to sell out to Lloyds.

Correspondence between Lloyds, Birmingham, and Hanburys Taylor and Lloyds, their London agent, provides ample illustration of the ways in which Lombard Street was used in the investment of surplus resources. From about the 1820's Lloyds were normally lending money to Overends, the great discount house, and Hichens and Co., the stockbrokers with which the bank continues a connexion to this day. Hanbury Taylors were given frequent instructions to withdraw funds from Overends and Hichens in order to rebuild Lloyds' balance in Lombard Street whenever that balance fell below the customary minimum. Hanburys appear indeed to have had some discretion to withdraw funds from the market for this purpose, for in 1846 and again in 1853 Lloyds were complaining that they had been withdrawing unnecessarily large sums, to the hurt of Lloyds' profits. In the 1870's, when Hanburys had amalgamated with Barnetts Hoares, the London agent appears to have had this discretion in placing money with Alexanders, another discount house. Again there were complaints to which Barnetts replied that it was not always easy to know what big drafts were coming along towards the end of banking hours, whereas the brokers disliked taking new money after

[28] *The Bankers' Magazine*, 1884, p. 376.

about 12 or 1 o'clock.[29] Beyond money market loans, surplus funds were invested in stock exchange securities. Curiously enough, although Lloyds of Birmingham employed stockbrokers directly for transactions in railway securities (which were in those days popular in bankers' portfolios),[30] they always asked Hanburys (later Barnetts) to operate in government securities. They may have chosen to go through Lombard Street for government securities because in the early days the Lombard Street bankers could often get advantageous treatment when government bonds were issued.[31]

As many of the country banks used their London agents when they wanted to deal in Stock Exchange securities, it was natural enough that they should seek from these agents advice on investment opportunities both for themselves and their customers. With the widening, especially from the 1820's, in the scope of popular Stock Exchange securities this advisory service became very important. In 1839 Lloyds asked Hanbury Taylors for advice on which of the American stocks was considered to be the safest and what price should be paid for it. In 1858 the Canterbury Bank wanted to know about the depreciation of Canadian bonds: was it a purely temporary movement or was there some deep-rooted cause? Sometimes the country banker would make a general review of the securities offered by customers as cover for advances; Maddison Atherleys (Southampton) in 1882 submitted to Barnetts Hoares, for confirmation, a list of what they thought were first-class securities. Barnetts added a few more to the list and commented upon the relative liquidity of these securities and on the action the banker might take in appropriate cases.

Advice on investments, important as it could be, was not by any means the only kind of advice that went from London to the country. All sorts of information and counsel went in both directions—the country to London as well as London to the country. A London agent could enjoy

[29] This was in the autumn of 1871, when the market's habits were affected by a very easy year for money. In the spring *The Economist* had reported (15 Apr.) 'there has never been a greater accumulation of money in Lombard Street', and the autumn passed with hardly a trace of the usual seasonal tightness.

[30] George Rae, *The Country Banker*, p. 101.

[31] Lombard Street sometimes enjoyed a start in applying for other bond-issues. In 1860 the Canterbury Bank thanked Glyns for having secured for them £10,000 of a Canadian issue; the Wilts and Dorset applied for £80,000 of this issue through the same channel. Cf. below, pp. 186, 188.

substantial advantage from this traffic in knowledge: according to Lloyds of Birmingham in 1861, Hanburys had 'derived a great many valuable accounts through our recommendation and through the introduction resulting from acting as our agents'. The country banker's knowledge of individuals in his neighbourhood was occasionally of use in Lombard Street. 'The party referred to in yours of yesterday is a man of some property, but he has generally lived beyond his means, and was in consequence obliged to reside in France for a few years . . .' wrote the Wilts and Dorset to Lombard Street in 1860. Again, 'He is a man of gay habits and we should not consider him good for the amount named by you.' But more commonly it was Lombard Street that had the information to pass on. This might be about individuals either in London itself, or in the country: Lloyds of Birmingham, wanting information about a Maidstone man, asked Hanburys who in their turn contacted Mastermans, London agents to the Maidstone bank of Mercer and Co.

Until the end of George III's reign the nation's coinage was in a deplorable state, the resulting difficulties being aggravated by the Mint's traditional refusal to do anything to facilitate distribution of the coin to the places where it was most needed. The work of distribution was actually arranged by traders themselves and by the country bankers with the co-operation of their London agents. Occasional surviving scraps of correspondence reveal this business and show how important was the advice-and-information service provided by Lombard Street. When Davison-Blands (the forerunners of Lambtons) opened at Newcastle in 1788, Masters and Co., the London agents, arranged for gold to be taken to Newcastle in Mr. Hoare's private post-chaise. 'By favour of the Bank [of England] we have already prepared 7 bags of £1,000 each, the greater part of which is new gold, and there are some hundreds of guineas of the last coinage which we were anxious to procure as we thought they would please many of your female customers. All the gold has been carefully weighed so that I trust you will not find a light guinea among them though the friction of travelling may make some slight alteration.' A little later, the war-time disturbance of the circulation was causing all sorts of trouble about coins. Orbell Oakes, one of the partners in the Bury Bank and Receiver-General of Taxes for West Suffolk, sought advice not from the Revenue officials in London but from his bank's London agent, on the status of some dollars the Bank of England had put into circulation. These dollars were poor things, from a technical point of view: Oakes said neither he nor his customers could tell the genuine from the forged: 'most of them have been filed or cut to prove them . . . there is not a person who comes to our Bank will take one of them'.[32] The scarcity of coin during the war period led to relaxation of the Act of 1777[33] under which notes under £5 were prohibited, and the country bankers very commonly issued £1 and £2 notes to fill the void. After the war there was some chopping and changing of government policy in relation to these 'small' notes;[34] finally in 1825 their suppression was decreed: those in circulation were to be withdrawn within three years, and no new ones were to be issued. Robarts in London wrote to Berwick Lechmeres (and presumably also to their other country correspondents) warning them of the possible consequences of this measure:[35] gold would be needed to fill the void, and there might be some irrational distrust of the doomed notes, so the Worcester bank had better stock itself up with gold.

In the latter half of the nineteenth century, after the restrictive legislation on bank notes in 1844 and the influx of Australian and Californian gold, the gold sovereigns and half sovereigns came to occupy a much larger place in the circulation. They were—and had been since the Act of 1816—altogether better coins; indeed, the Victoria sovereign justifiably became the pride of the London Mint and is much treasured in many parts of the world in the middle of the twentieth century. But it was none the less an imperfect coin in one important respect: it wore out quickly. Those that exist today owe their longevity to their long rests in hoarding places in West or East; in circulation few of them would stand up to more than twenty years' wear.[36] Accounts between country correspondents and London agents therefore show a continual traffic in 'light gold', as coins below the legal minimum weight were called. In some cases—particularly in the earlier years—the country banker himself, or

---

[32] For the Mint's story of these coins, see Sir John Craig, *The Mint* (Cambridge, 1953), pp. 261–2; and C. Oman, *The Coinage of England* (Oxford, 1931), pp. 361–2).

[33] 17 Geo. III, c. 30.

[34] See, e.g., J. H. Clapham, *Economic History of Modern Britain*, vol. i, p. 264.

[35] A. W. Isaac, *The Worcester Old Bank*, p. 34.

[36] Sir John Craig, *The Mint*, p. 310.

his cashier, appears to have conducted a separate little business, as a sideline at the bank's counter, in this light gold. When a reasonable amount had been accumulated, it would be sent to London and credited at its bullion value. In later years the public became accustomed to receiving face value for their sovereigns and the banker had to watch sharply for the light coins which—owing to the rapid wear—were still common if individually less under-weight. If the country banker was not sharp to his customers, trouble was likely to arise when he sent surplus gold—as some did at certain seasons—to his London agent. The Brecon Bank, employing Barnetts Hoares as their agents, were used to doing this on a considerable scale. When in 1884 Barnetts and Lloyds became one firm, it seemed economical to arrange for the surplus gold from Brecon to go to Lloyds Head Office at Birmingham instead of travelling all the way to London. Lloyds soon found themselves up against a lax tradition: the gold from Brecon—as much as £160,000 in 1885—was invariably short-weight, as many as sixty or seventy coins in every hundred being below the legal minimum. Birmingham, however, felt their hands tied: 'We have only avoided making a difficulty about it', they wrote to the London people who had been Barnetts Hoares, 'because we regarded their relations with you as your Country Correspondents and did not wish to appear to withhold any ordinary facility.'

When in doubt on a point of banking or fiscal law, the country banker sought the advice of his London agent, who could advise what was being done in London and would be prepared to pass on a professional opinion. The London agent could also be of use when differences arose with other parties in the City of London. Thus in 1883 Williams and Co. of Chester were involved in argument with a firm of stockbrokers, and sought the advice of Robarts Lubbocks. The trouble had arisen from unsuccessful Stock Exchange speculation by one of Williams's managers. The stockbrokers tried to hold the bank responsible for the balance due from the manager, but Robarts advised that this was quite unjustifiable and recommended the bank to go to 'Mr. Daniell the Government Broker, the acknowledged head of the Stock Exchange'. If, advised Robarts, the conduct of the stockbrokers were 'brought under the notice of the Stock Exchange Committee the consequences to them would be serious'.

Sometimes more than advice was useful: London agents could conveniently deal with London produce brokers or warehousemen in disposing of commodities that had fallen to the bank on a customer's default, as when the Liverpool Union Bank sent some hop documents to Cunliffe's 'requesting them to put the hops into the hands of a respectable broker for immediate sale'. An incident in 1860 shows how the country banker could be similarly useful to his London agent—Lacons, Youell and Co. (Yarmouth) made all arrangements and sent to London for sale a vessel called the *Sir Francis Drake* upon which Glyns, their London agents, had a mortgage.

Service by the country banker to the London agent was, however, quite exceptionable, and the balance of advantage weighed very heavily in the other direction. The Londoner was, in fact, the banker to the country firm and looked for some remuneration for his services. One of the earliest recorded discussions as to terms was between Berwick, Wall and Co. of Worcester and Robarts, Curtis, Were and Co. in 1797. Robarts suggested a minimum deposit of £10,000, free of interest; anything above was to earn 4 per cent., while 5 per cent. would be charged on any shortfall. This arrangement was preferred to a rather lower deposit combined with a $\frac{1}{4}$ per cent. turnover charge. In 1826 the interest allowance was dropped when Robarts wrote of 'our conviction of the impropriety and illegitimacy of London banks allowing interest to their country correspondents'. London bankers were dropping the allowance of interest to their ordinary customers and it appears that, in this cheaper-money period which followed Waterloo, they were tending to bring their country correspondents' accounts into line with the new rule. The rise of joint-stock banks in London after 1833 soon destroyed the London no-interest tradition generally, but in their arrangements with the country bankers Lombard Street men held to their refusal to pay interest. At any rate Barnetts Hoares, asked by Wrights of Nottingham in 1844 to allow some interest, contended that 'no respectable banker would do so in these times', and most of the recorded arrangements in the 1840's made no such provision.[37] But competition told, and in 1855 Lambtons of Newcastle wrung a 2 per cent. allowance out of Barclays and in 1864 the

[37] Most of these years were, it is true, 'cheap-money' years, and it cannot be assumed that London bankers would have resisted as firmly in dear-money periods.

Glamorganshire Banking Company, switching to Barclays from Jones Loyds, secured '1½% below Bank Rate'. In 1864, too, Barnetts Hoares were persuaded by the Liverpool Union Bank to allow interest on the balance in excess of £10,000.

Even before interest allowances began to eat into the gain enjoyed by the London banker from the use of his correspondents' balances, annual 'salaries' began to appear. As the interest charges became more common, a salary, related in some way to the turnover of business, became the rule. An early example is provided by the Neath bank of Williams and Rowland, which in 1827 and 1828 was paying an annual salary of £140; when the 1828 figures showed a halving of 1827's turnover of £209,480, the salary was reduced to £100 for the next year. Barclay, Tritton, Bevan and Co. thought the Plymouth and Devonport Banking Company was being very unreasonable in expecting the commission to be fixed irrespective of the turnover of business, and the Director who was negotiating in London reported back to his colleagues, 'I saw it would not do to press it; in fact I believe it is an altogether unknown practice among London bankers. . . .' Even so, the commission proposed was so favourable to the new bank that Mr. Bevan hoped other customers would not hear of it, else they might demand such abatements as might amount to a very serious sum in the whole; 'the less you say about it the better'. Mr. Bevan had 'retired upstairs to consult with Mr. Barclay' who had then come down, also with a long face, and settled for £250 on any turnover up to £1,000,000. Three years later the commission was raised to £350 for a turnover up to £1,250,000, and later this was increased by 9d. per cent. for any excess over £1,250,000. In later years the advantage in negotiation appears to have rested mainly with this country bank, and this may have been due to talk of switching the agency from Barclays to the London and Westminster in 1840.

These figures paid by the Plymouth bank are not untypical. The annual payment, a matter of a few hundreds for a small country bank, generally worked out at about 9d. per cent. The Liverpool Union got off rather cheaply with Cunliffe Brooks in their first contract: they acknowledged this, and in 1837 added to the contractual £500 a gratuity of £250 'in consideration of the liberal manner in which Messrs. Cunliffe and Co. have kept the London account'. Their business grew rapidly, and though the commission was in the forties increased to £1,000, it still worked out at only 6*d*. per cent. But this was for big business, and most country bankers had to pay at a much higher rate. Barnetts Hoares in fact told Cobbs of Margate in 1844 that their 'usual charge' was 1*s*. per cent., though they conceded something on this to Cobbs, for the sake of a long connexion. Perhaps they were mindful also of competition from new joint-stock neighbours in the City. Certainly there seems to have been a general tendency for commissions to be trimmed rather closely in these middle decades of the century, and the competition was also showing itself in arrangements about the size of balances and overdraft facilities.

This atmosphere of competition among country banks themselves, as well as among London agents, showed clearly in correspondence between Lloyds of Birmingham and Hanbury Taylor and Lloyd of Lombard Street in 1861.[38] The question at issue was the salary for the London agency. The Birmingham house was not going to be defeated for lack of information about competitive rates, and wrote round to other country banks—among them the important Liverpool Union Bank—to find how their London agents were treating them. Lloyds discovered that Hanburys' peculiar method of calculating the daily balance led to their being asked for interest on deficiencies[39] although in fact their credit balance was hardly ever less than 25 per cent. *above* the agreed figure. Lloyds of Birmingham thought such methods were behind the times; Hanburys had better be a little more adaptable: 'the whole system of banking charges has been changed since the introduction of joint-stock banking, our scale of commissions being reduced fully one-half and London's charges having succumbed in a similar way'.

Outside these regular commissions the country bankers traditionally reckoned to pay small sums in gratuities to the clerks of their London agents.[40] Typical sums were 10 guineas, paid by Davison-Blands to clerks at Masters in 1789, £20 by the Liverpool Union to clerks at Cunliffes in 1835, and 5 guineas by Williams and Rowlands to clerks at Jones Loyds in each year 1826–9. The new London joint-stocks took a different view; in their agreement with the Coventry and Warwickshire in 1864, the

---

[38] By this date there was no partner common to both Birmingham and London.
[39] i.e. deficiencies below the agreed fixed deposit of £20,000.
[40] Cf. p. 70 above.

London and Westminster stated that such gratuities were prohibited by the Directors.

The London banks themselves, as distinct from their clerks, in total must have derived quite a substantial income from their work for their country correspondents. A run of figures for Barnetts Hoares in the early sixties shows that they were then drawing from the country bankers an average of nearly £3,000 a year, which was an eighth of their total gross income of commissions and interest charged on all customers' accounts. In some Lombard Street banks this proportion must have been higher, for Barnetts, though holding a few very important agencies, had fewer country banks on their books than did some of their neighbours. In addition, it must be remembered that the agency work brought to Lombard Street substantial balances on which little or no interest was paid.

In the twentieth century, with the virtual completion of the amalgamation of country banks with London banks, all this has on the face of it been changed. But readers who know the relationship between the bank's Head Office in London and its branches throughout the country will in the preceding pages have recognized much of what goes on today. Where the country banker in the old days looked to his agent in Lombard Street, the branch manager today looks to Head Office. In the same way, the branch can today serve Head Office as the country correspondent could serve his agent in Lombard Street. And, parallel to the remuneration the country banker used to pay to Lombard Street, every branch is expected to contribute in one way or another to the heavy overheads at Head Office. Only the clerks in Lombard Street do not get their Christmas tips from the country! But this pleasant habit, as we have seen, was already on its way out a hundred years ago.

6

RELATIONS WITH THE BANK OF ENGLAND

———

In the late eighteenth and early nineteenth centuries, when the London money market was emerging from its embryo into something bearing recognizable relationship to the market we know today, the Bank of England narrowly confined its activities to the City of London. It numbered among its customers most of the great banking partnerships in the City, both new firms and old; but from the rise of banking business in the country the Bank held itself completely aloof. In the third decade of the century two circumstances—not entirely independent of each other—led to substantial modification of this aloofness. For twenty or thirty years thereafter the Bank was following a policy of infiltration by which it probably thought to become in a more obvious sense the Bank of England instead of 'The Bank of London' as it had often been called in the past.

The roots of the change lay in the growth of authoritative opinion in favour of two developments—centralization of the issue of bank notes, and a strengthening of the structure of country banking. In the monetary controversies of the early years of the nineteenth century, leading up to the celebrated Bullion Report of 1810, the dominant view had been that the amount of notes issued by the country banks was indirectly subject to control by the Bank of England. This view was based on the convertibility of the country notes into Bank of England notes and on the belief that the balance of payments between London and any part of the country depended upon the relative abundance of bank notes in London and that district.[1] On this basis, sensible regulation of the Bank

[1] This view was a simple application, to interregional relations, of the ruling theory of international payments. It was first clearly expounded by H. Thornton in his *Essay on*

of England's issue sufficed to keep the entire money supply of the country in order. In the second and third decades of the century, however, estimates of the country issues were frequently compared with statements of the Bank of England's own issue, and it appeared that the comfortable theory adopted by the Bullion Committee was, at best, a gross over-simplification of the truth. The country issues could, it seemed, go up when the Bank of England was restricting its own issue, and vice versa. Given the desirability of control, according to principles that were accepted by the Bank of England, of the supply of money in the country, it seemed that the independence of the country banks was leading to their thwarting the Bank of England in its attempts to regulate the supply of money according to sound principle. The extreme remedy was for the right to issue notes to be confined to the Bank of England itself. Although this was not put forward, even in 1844, as an actual proposal, the fact that many experts believed it to be the only really satisfactory arrangement influenced considerably the detailed shape of various reforms over a long period. It did not cause the legislature to prohibit the issue of notes by the new joint-stock banks established (outside the 65-miles' circle) under the legislation of 1826; but when, in 1833, joint-stock banks were allowed inside the London circle, they were not allowed to issue notes. Finally, in 1844, Peel made arrangements that were intended to suppress, over a period, all issues in England other than that of the Bank of England itself. This view that the Bank's control of the monetary situation would be strengthened by suppression of country notes was held within the Bank of England, and it was responsible for a policy, initiated in 1830, of according special privileges to those country banks who withdrew their own notes or, being non-issuing, undertook not to embark on an issue.[2] It was primarily in implementing this policy that the Bank of England was brought into direct contact with some of the country banks with whose history we are concerned.

Alongside the growth of opinion in favour of centralization of the note-issue there was, for closely related reasons, increasing insistence

Paper Credit (1802), pp. 216–21, and was accepted by the Bullion Committee (Report, 1810, p. 28).

[2] J. H. Clapham, *The Bank of England*, vol. ii, pp. 139 et seq., and Elmer Wood, *English Theories of Central Banking Control, 1819–58*, pp. 97–101.

upon the need for strengthening the structure of banking in the country. The instability of the country note-issue—an instability now thought threatening to the maintenance of sound financial conditions —was seen to be in part a reflection of the instability of the country banks themselves. Although the politicians of the nineteenth century— and perhaps historians since—exaggerated the weakness of the old country banks,[3] it was all too true that many of them were too weak to stand up to difficult times, and the numerous suspensions at times of crisis greatly aggravated the commercial convulsions that afflicted the country every few years. In the early 1820's Lord Liverpool's Government was half-inclined to take action on this view; the panic at the end of 1825 completed the conversion, and the Government in 1826 felt compelled to override the remaining opposition. There followed in the two steps of 1826 and 1833 the limitation of the Bank of England's monopoly of joint-stock banking, steps that allowed the foundation of some of the most important among Lloyds' constituent banks.[4] Another step, also taken in 1826, was the decision by the Bank of England to establish Branches of its own—a step that should both directly and indirectly serve to provide the provinces with more reliable banking facilities.[5] The first Branch was established in July 1826 at Gloucester; by the end of 1829 there were ten others. The most active in early years were those at Birmingham[6] and Liverpool; both these and that first one at Gloucester rapidly became important to some of the banks whose stories belong to this book.

Though London bankers—at any rate in Lombard Street—generally had accounts at the Bank of England before 1826, there is little indication of any contact between the Bank of England and country bankers. Any business to be done by a country banker with the Bank of England would normally be done through the London agent. It was by the

---

[3] Cf. pp. 5 and 22 above.   [4] Cf. p. 17 above.

[5] The establishment of branches by the Bank had been talked of for several years. It is said to have been a favourite project of Lord Liverpool, but the Bank was for long reluctant. After the 1825 crisis government encouragement and a declaratory clause in the Act (7 Geo. IV, c. 46; May 1826) settled the question. (For the full story, see Clapham, op. cit., vol. 2, pp. 91–116.)

[6] The Birmingham branch was opened on 1 Jan. 1827 in the premises formerly occupied by Messrs. Gibbins, Smith and Goode, a private bank known as 'Smith's Bank' which had failed in the 1825 crisis (S. Lloyd, *The Lloyds of Birmingham*, pp. 70–71).

establishment of its own Branches that the Bank was opened to direct contact, and through the remainder of the century relations between the branches and the country banks formed an important supplement to the traditional Lombard Street links whereby London and the country had operated as a single banking system. For some reason the Bank of England's new country customers were to be found among the country joint-stock banks rather than the private banks. Possibly this was because the joint-stocks were new and had most to gain from the prestige of a connexion with the Bank, while the private banks would naturally continue to depend upon the older channels. But more than anything else, it was the Bank of England's attitude towards country note-issues that shaped relations with the country banks. Partly on theoretical grounds, partly from the belief that caution in their conduct of their own business had sometimes been nullified by the rashness of other issuing banks, the Bank of England by the end of the twenties was hankering after a complete monopoly of the note-issue.[7] Horsley Palmer, one of the most powerful Governors of the Bank, took this view very decidedly and it was in December 1829, when he was Deputy Governor and about to become Governor, that the Bank secured government approval for discrimination in discounting for non-issuing banks.[8] For the next fifteen years and more the Bank gave favourable treatment to all banks that agreed either to terminate their existing issues or to refrain from establishing new issues. This discrimination was not confined to the discounting privileges formulated in the agreements with the banks; it coloured all relations between the Bank of England and the country banks. An issuing bank was one to which the Old Lady was liable to turn her back.

The first bank to have one of these agreements with the Bank of England was the Birmingham Banking Company in 1830. This bank—which after a troubled career eventually found its way into the Midland group[9]—had been the first fruits for Birmingham of the 1826 Act and was destined to be Lloyds' most important competitor for many years. To persuade this bank to abstain from note-issue was a good start for the

[7] Cf. Clapham, *The Bank of England*, vol. ii, pp. 113, 114.
[8] Ibid., p. 140.
[9] Cf. W. F. Crick and J. Wadsworth, *A Hundred Years of Joint Stock Banking*, pp. 69, 311, and 323.

Bank of England's new policy. It was followed by other banks in the Birmingham region, and the Bank of England's Birmingham Agent (as the Branch managers were and are entitled) must have been in high hopes of establishing in that region a stronghold for the Bank of England note. It must therefore have been disappointing to find that Taylors and Lloyds, standing out against the Bank's new system, insisted on retaining their own note-issue. A Bank of England letter of 1842 refers to some earlier correspondence which has not survived; evidently Lloyds had then rejected the plan. The 1842 letter says that 'the idea was opposed by one of the Lloyds and without giving any reasonable grounds for his opposition'. Whatever their reasons, Taylors and Lloyds were made to feel a loss of convenience. They, like other Birmingham banks, had come to use the Birmingham Branch of the Bank of England extensively, and in January 1846 Lloyds asked for an advance against the security of Bank of England stock.[10] The Bank tersely replied that it was 'contrary to the regulations to discount for Banks of Issue and that the same principle governs the question of Advances'. Lloyds took the hint and removed from the Bank of England to Hanburys some Exchequer Bills 'because we shall then be able to convert them into money quicker than through the medium of the Bank of England'. Rather than convenience an issuing bank, the Bank of England was prepared to miss an opportunity of strengthening its direct hold upon the country banks: it drove Lloyds back to the traditional channel of the London agent.

With some of the new joint-stock banks the Bank of England's plan had meanwhile had an easier passage. Following successful initiation of the system in the Birmingham and Liverpool areas, the Bank's Branches at Swansea and Gloucester negotiated with certain banks in their areas. With the Glamorganshire Banking Company, founded in 1836, the Swansea Agent had a good start, for this bank took advice in such matters from its London agent, and he happened to be Samuel Jones Loyd. This was the famous Jones Loyd, later Lord Overstone, part of whose plan for monetary reform was centralization of bank notes in a single issuer. The new bank decided not to issue its own notes, although

---

[10] Taylors and Lloyds needed purely momentary help in meeting a large demand for Bank of England notes, the very contingency for which they kept Exchequer Bills at the Bank of England branch. The incident was referred to by S. S. Lloyd in his Evidence to the Select Committee on Bank Acts, 16 Apr. 1858, p. 176.

this meant withdrawing the notes of Williams and Rowland, one of the private banks on which the new joint-stock was based. This was a real loss, for around Neath the 'Country Gentlemen and Farmers' were accustomed to holding the Williams and Rowland notes, and scarcely ever touched Bank of England paper. This actual suppression of an existing issue merited, the Glamorgan bankers thought, better terms than the Bank of England offered—a mere discount account for good mercantile bills up to £10,000 at market rate. Their efforts to promote the circulation of Bank of England notes were, they pointed out, already having some success: Bank notes were even displacing National Provincial notes in the district. The Glamorgan bank won the support of the Swansea Agent of the Bank of England, who pressed the Governors to accede to the Glamorgan request, but in vain. Perhaps the Old Lady was beginning to feel time and tide on her side, and that smaller concessions would leave smaller vested interests to be compensated when the great centralizing reform should come.

Although not difficult at first, the Bank of England came to take a firm line also with the Gloucestershire Banking Company, with which, through the Agent at Gloucester, negotiations were opened at the same time as the Glamorgan people were negotiating through Swansea. One of the founders of the Gloucestershire Banking Company appears to have been the same Joseph Gibbins who was a founder of the Birmingham Banking Company in 1829; he was something of a promoter of provincial joint-stock banks, just as Abel Smith of Nottingham had been a sponsor of private banks sixty or seventy years earlier. When the Bank of England settled terms with the Birmingham Banking Company, the plan was new and the Bank of England was keen to popularize it; no doubt Gibbins assumed that Gloucester would likewise get attractive terms. Certainly it was upon his advice that the Gloucester men finally decided to seek an arrangement with the Bank of England and, fore-seeing a financial crisis (this was in 1836) they thought that they had better be quick about it. After some preliminary discussions, terms were formally proposed by the company and accepted by the Bank of England. The Gloucestershire Banking Company was to have a Discount Account at the Gloucester branch at 3 per cent. on a minimum of £100,000 and a maximum of £115,000; above this the Bank of England would have the option of charging 4 per cent. or the 'average market rate of interest'. The company remained free to go elsewhere (e.g. to its London agent) for discount facilities, in addition to those it was to enjoy at the Bank of England. Some compensation was to be allowed for the work of changing into Bank of England notes the notes of other banks and the cheques of country persons coming to the local markets:[11] the work of promoting the Bank of England circulation was going to be taken seriously. The Bank of England was to provide, free of interest, a reserve of notes to be held at the branches of the Gloucestershire bank, amounting to £42,000; Bank Stock, Funded Stock, Exchequer Bills, or India Bonds would be provided as security, with a 10 per cent. margin. The agreement was to be for three, four, or five years at the option of the Bank of England. One unusual feature of this agreement was that it was not for the time being to apply to the company's branch at Evesham 'which is out of this County'. The Gloucestershire Banking Company continued to issue its own notes at Evesham: the fact that this branch was distant from the others and in another county was a mere excuse; the real difficulty was that the Evesham branch was in the hands of the survivor of the old private bank there, who took a strong line and knew that his own notes were well liked locally. A partial continuance of local notes was also tolerated at Stow and Cirencester.

It was not long before the Bank of England was nagging at the Gloucestershire bank to bring Evesham into line. 'It is contrary to the custom of the Bank', they wrote, 'to act partially with any country establishment, and were they to depart from this custom in any instance they feared that they should afford a precedent which might be quoted against them.' So, as from January 1838, the Evesham notes were withdrawn, the Gloucestershire company receiving a corresponding addition to its discount limits at the Branch Bank of England. There were further minor adjustments in 1839 and 1840. But in 1842 the Bank of England, presumably feeling its strength in this matter, informed the Gloucester bank that there could not be renewal on the old terms, and proposed terms more in line with their standard practice, to run until 1844 when all would again be reviewed.

[11] The Gloucestershire company reckoned to effect such exchanges to a total of £12,000–£20,000 a week.

The company did not like this at all; especially they were worried that even worse terms would be proposed when 1844 came round. A deputation, led by Samuel Baker, went to London in May 1842 to wait upon the Governor. The deputation impressed upon the Governor the Gloucestershire bank's anxiety to retain the Bank of England connexion: they were willing to sacrifice £2,000 in yearly profits for its sake. The Governor was not willing to go back to anything like the old terms; in particular, he objected to providing the Gloucestershire bank with bank notes on free loan to constitute reserves at their branches. He offered 1 per cent. commission on notes kept in circulation, if the company would give up its Discount Account. But the Discount Account was valued by the company, and after further efforts to find a basis of agreement, the Gloucestershire bank broke off negotiations and returned to issuing their own notes. The Directors reported to the Annual Meeting that the Bank of England had expected them to forego substantial profits without corresponding advantages. By February 1843 they had got £100,000 of their own notes into circulation, as compared with the £240,000 of Bank of England notes they had put out immediately before the change. When the Bank Charter Act of 1844 came in, the issue authorized for the Gloucestershire Banking Company (on the basis of recent actual circulation) was £155,920, though it had 'required special exertions and the attendance of the Chairman in London' to secure this.

The correspondence between the Bank of England and the Gloucestershire Banking Company shows how the agreements of this kind could vary in detail, and it shows how the Bank of England was pressing towards standardization of the terms.[12] In the records of the Lloyds group there is no indication that any other bank followed the example of the Gloucestershire bank to the length of withdrawing from the Bank's system, and when the Act of 1844 became operative ten such banks were working under agreement with the Bank of England.

[12] Complete standardization was not achieved: in 1844 the East of England Bank had an agreement covering issues at four of their offices, but at the other nine offices the East of England Bank issued its own notes. This case occasioned a drafting error in the original Bill of the Bank Charter Act (letter from the East of England Bank, Norwich, to Sir Robert Peel, 1 June 1844, in British Museum Add. MS. 40546, ff. 62 et seq.; Add. MS. 40545, f. 163 shows rectification by deletion of this bank from Schedule (C) of the Bill).

These were:

> Cunliffe Brooks and Co., Manchester
> Devon and Cornwall Banking Company
> Grant and Gillman, Portsmouth
> Hampshire Banking Company
> Liverpool Union Bank
> Vivian Kitson and Co., Torquay
> I. & I. C. Wright and Co., Nottingham
> Watts, Whidborne and Co., Teignmouth
> Lambton and Co., Newcastle
> Henty, Upperton and Olliver, Worthing.

The Act provided[13] that these agreements were to be terminated with compensation to the banks concerned.

The new statutory regulation of the note-issue did not, however, terminate all agreements between the Bank of England and the country banks. Some of the latter continued regular arrangements for discounting at the Branches of the Bank, particularly those at Liverpool and Birmingham where the banks formed much the weightiest part of the Bank of England's clientèle.[14] One such arrangement was made with the Liverpool Union Bank immediately after the Bank Charter Act had undermined the old basis of agreement. In lieu of compensation the Liverpool Union Bank was to be allowed to discount, at the Bank of England Branch, up to £100,000[15] at 1 per cent. under Bank Rate, subject to a minimum of $2\frac{1}{2}$ per cent. and a maximum of 4 per cent. Some figures for the difficult year 1847 show the bank exercising its privilege for amounts which, though substantial, were a long way below the £100,000 limit. In 1848 five Liverpool banks joined forces for negotiating with the Bank of England the renewal of the arrangements each of them had been enjoying. They jointly asked the Bank for an annual contract, and for a discount rate 1 under Bank Rate, minimum 3, maximum 4 per cent. There was much discussion on the question whether the rate charged should be based on the London Bank Rate or on the published discount rate of the Bank of England's Liverpool Branch. Eventually the wish of the Liverpool banks prevailed: the rate was to be

---

[13] Clause XIV of 7 & 8 Vict., c. 32.   [14] Clapham, op. cit., vol. ii, p. 141.

[15] £100,000 was the notional amount of note-issue, for abstaining from which the Liverpool Union Bank received compensation under the 1844 Act.

$\frac{3}{4}$ under Bank Rate, minimum 3, maximum $4\frac{1}{2}$ per cent. The preference of the Liverpool banks was presumably influenced by the fact that the forties had on the whole been years of cheap money; Liverpool wanted to follow London rates downward. The effect was to spread the influence of London's Bank Rate over country business. The influence of London was also growing through other details of these arrangements: the Bank of England made it clear in 1848 for the first time that the bills discounted must all be of 'approved character'.

The concessionary discount accounts continued until almost the end of the century and appear to have given rise to few problems. There was some friction in the early sixties, but it appears to have been purely temporary; it may have been due to disturbance of the supply of eligible bills by the cotton famine, or it may simply have resulted from smart practice by a Liverpool Union manager. In 1888 the Bank conceded to the Liverpool banks the option of regulating the rate partly by reference to London market rate instead of exclusive reference to the official Bank Rate—again a movement tending to bring Liverpool into line with London practices and London effective rates. But in the easy money days of 1893 the Bank, apparently careless of the consequences, withdrew its latest concession and the Liverpool banks gave up their 'Contract Accounts', reverting to the simple cash compensation to which they were entitled under the Bank Charter Act. The Bank of England's business of rediscounting for country banks was becoming a thing of the past; the spreading tentacles of London's joint-stock banks were beginning to give the nation's banking cohesion in quite a different way.

The Bank Charter Act of 1844, which had given a new aspect to the Bank of England's efforts to replace the issue of other banks, was not by any means universally welcomed among the country banks. The sponsors of the Act (Sir Robert Peel taking the lead) meant the intricate provisions of the Act to have the effect of suppressing the country note in a matter of a dozen years or so; but many country bankers clung to their issues, even at appreciable sacrifice in other directions, and the last country notes did not disappear until 1921. At first the country bankers were not satisfied with merely holding tightly to the vestigial privileges allowed them by Sir Robert Peel; there is evidence that they made deliberate attempts to avert the intended consequences of the Act. Letters from the Bank of England Agent at Gloucester to his chiefs in Threadneedle Street show the Gloucestershire Banking Company as one of the chief offenders in this matter.

The devices to which bankers resorted in these efforts to get round the Act were three. First, the Gloucestershire bank would work right up to the maximum of its permitted circulation and then meet demands above this by paying out not Bank of England notes but notes of their local rivals, the County of Gloucester Bank. This had the effect of making the latter work with a considerable margin to spare and of having to hold, against demands of the holders of their notes, a larger number of Bank of England notes than was their fair share. The fluctuations in local demand for notes were, in short, thrown wholly upon the County of Gloucester Bank, whose *average* circulation was thereby held appreciably below their authorized limit whilst the Gloucestershire bank enjoyed theirs to the full. Although the maxima prescribed in the Act were not exceeded, procedures of this kind were not conducive to the gradual shrinkage of private issues, though they did not directly harm the Bank of England's issue. The harm was suffered by the rival bank, whose manager felt 'much annoyed' with the way the Bank Charter Act was working out for him.

Secondly, the authorized issue could be most fully exploited by pushing at an active branch the notes unused by another branch where there had customarily been a bigger issue. Even country shopkeepers could be persuaded to supplement the efforts of the bank's own offices, to keep the issue up to its maximum.

Thirdly—and this was the genuinely evasive dodge—the bank would issue bills drawn at short date, using the name of the bank's employees, and making the bills resemble notes as closely as was possible. This device was employed particularly by Storey and Thomas at Shaftesbury.[16] By its means they covered the seasonal and other fluctuations in the demand for notes, so contriving to maintain their actual average circulation within £2 of their authorized maximum.

These devices were apparently commonly employed in 1845, with the

[16] This private bank was absorbed by the Wilts and Dorset in 1885, and was thus the basis of the present Lloyds branch in Shaftesbury.

result that those bankers who had not resorted to them were beginning to feel that, if a stop was not put to them, they would have to follow suit if they were to hold their own in a competitive world. The Wilts and Dorset Banking Company's General Manager was already expressing this view in May 1845, and the Bank of England Agent at Gloucester became very worried about it. He knew that the Gloucestershire Banking Company, having felt their authorized circulation to be unduly restricted, would be under temptation to resort to these stratagems, and he feared that local opinion would encourage them.

> The employment of bills for the purposes of a Circulation [he reported] has not thus far been adopted in this district, but . . . should the practice be once adopted here, it would soon become general for such paper would not be unpopular for local purposes, and many persons (especially shareholders and parties needing accommodation from Banks) would give it the preference considering it a sort of duty to prevent, as far as they are able, the operation of a law, which they regard as an improper encroachment on the means which the Country Bankers formerly enjoyed, of assisting their respective customers.

The Gloucester Agent's fears on this score, though not entirely groundless, were soon outdated by the growing popularity of cheques, which soon left the demand for country notes well within, and increasingly within, the limits imposed by the 1844 Act. Stephens Blandy at Reading, for example, with an authorized issue of £43,271, had only £27,000 out ten years later. Berwick Lechmeres at Worcester saw their issue dwindle to £18,000 in 1889, against £87,448 authorized. Even in Suffolk the prosperous private bank of Bacon Cobbold could only get £13,355 out in 1893, against £21,901 authorized; by 1904 it was down to £6,000. Taylors and Lloyds of Birmingham had an authorized issue of £38,816; when they became Lloyds Banking Company Limited in 1865 they had 'no desire to continue the issue of bank notes'. That important joint-stock bank, the Wilts and Dorset, despite its aggressive branch policy, met the same trend, though the precise figures cannot be disentangled. It dropped the note-issue licences it held for its offices at Bristol, Melksham, Ringwood, and Southampton in 1879. But this bank remained a champion of the country bankers' rights in this matter. When in May 1889 there was talk of legislation further restricting the country issues, all their branch managers were circularized:

It is advisable that we should do our utmost to defeat this. One of his [the Chancellor of the Exchequer's] arguments is that country bank circulation is in a chronic state of shrinkage and decay. We do not admit this and think that with the revival of trade our circulation will once more reach our authorised issue. You will please endeavour to your utmost to help on this movement by the circulation of your own notes as much as possible as we are at present far below our limit and I think chiefly so because Bank of England notes are too freely given to the public instead of our own.

There was, after this effort, a small recovery of the Wilts and Dorset issue to £63,199 in 1889, but this was still little more than four-fifths of the authorized figure; by the time the bank came into Lloyds, and so lost its issue rights, in 1914 the issue was down to £39,000.

There may have been some popularizing of Bank of England notes, as the Wilts and Dorset instruction of 1889 indicates, but such evidence as there is in these banks confirms the general view of historians that the rising competitor was not the Bank of England note but the cheque. Analysis of the cash held by a big private bank at Reading in the years 1851–60 shows that Bank of England notes were never more than a quarter of the total held—and this was a period when the decline in the country note circulation was already quite substantial. In later decades—for which unfortunately there is no comparable evidence—the Bank of England note may have gained a little in the provinces, but the cheque was doing more and more of the total work. The gold coins had also, early in Victoria's reign, become more popular than ever before. The prohibition of notes under £5[17] was of course highly relevant to this question. Small notes, country and Bank of England alike, might have held their own against the competition of the cheque; but notes of £5 and upwards gave way, while the growing volume of smaller transactions was reflected in the swelling circulation of sovereigns and half-sovereigns so beloved by our grandfathers.[18]

---

[17] By the Act of 1826 (7 Geo. IV, c. 6) 'to limit, and after a certain period to prohibit, the issuing of Promissory Notes under a limited sum in England'.

[18] For estimates of gold in circulation at various dates, see Tooke and Newmarch, *History of Prices*, vol. vi, pp. 696–701, W. S. Jevons, *Investigations in Currency and Finance*, p. 269, and R. H. I. Palgrave, *Bank Rate and the Money Market*, p. 73. The main figures are:

1844 .	. £46	million
1856 .	. £70	,,
1868 .	. £70–80	,,
1873 .	. £105	,,

So, in one way or another, the country note lost ground, and it continued to do so. More and more banks, in process of amalgamation or other changes of structure, followed the example of Lloyds in 1865, abandoning without a groan the restricted rights allowed them by Peel's Act. By the beginning of the twentieth century the total authorized issue had fallen from the 1844 level of £8,631,647 to £2,618,465, relating to 30 private banks and 25 joint-stocks. In 1911 the total, for the eleven remaining issuers, was a mere £401,719. The last country issue to go was that of Fox Fowlers in Wellington, which disappeared when that firm was absorbed by Lloyds Bank in 1921.

The two subjects of rediscount at Bank of England branches and the country note issue—subjects connected with each other by the policy adopted by the Bank of England in 1829[19]—have been treated here primarily for the light they throw on the business and the attitudes of the country banks that subsequently helped to form the Lloyds Bank of today. But they are of interest also in revealing first how for a time the development of English banking moved towards a more direct influence by the Bank of England throughout the country, and then how the tide retreated. In the second quarter of the nineteenth century the trend was such that the Bank of England might very well have become an important banker directly supporting the finance of business up and down the country, very much as the Bank of France developed. Then the authorities decided on more direct suppression of the country note, and the Bank of England therefore lost interest in using its branch discount facilities as a bribe to persuade the country bankers to refrain from issuing their own notes. Finally—and partly because official policy had made difficulties for note-issuers—the notes themselves lost their old importance; the banking system became a universal provider of a cheque currency while the Old Lady withdrew most of her activities into that City where she reigned supreme.

In the more active phase in their history the Bank of England Branches had, however, established certain useful services to local banks, services

---

Newmarch rejected the estimate 'by competent authorities' that in 1840–4 the gold circulation was only £36 million. The note circulation (Bank of England *plus* private) meanwhile increased only from £28 million to £32 million.

[19] See p. 141 above.

that continued to be used by the local bankers. These services mostly depended upon the Bank of England Branches as reservoirs of cash and as channels through which funds could be moved to and from London. The Plymouth and Devonport Banking Company (later the Devon and Cornwall Bank) as early as 1832 was using the Bank of England Branch at Exeter for remitting funds to their London agents. In 1875 Williams and Co. of Chester were using the Bank of England for transfer of money from one part of the country to another. At first the Bank of England charged 6d. per cent. for transferring money from a Branch to London or from one Branch to another. Later Williams agreed to keep a minimum balance of £4,000 (reduced in 1883 to £2,000) at the Liverpool Branch, in partial consideration of the facilities granted by the Bank of England. The picture is one of a convenient business relationship, the smoothness with which such services were rendered by the Bank leaving little trace in surviving records, and making one appreciate how clumsily financial business was conducted (at least outside London) in earlier days when these services were not available.

There was at times, however, another side to the story. The Bank of England did not look upon its branches as mere conveniences for local bankers; they were there to earn a living, if necessary in competition with the established local bank. Local bankers feared even worse, and an Exeter bank was willing to trim its terms for a Wellington banking customer 'in order to preserve the probability that . . . the [Bank of England's Exeter] Branch will not long continue its very unprofitable career'. The Exeter bankers feared that Threadneedle Street intended 'the extinguishment of the Country Bank system', a grossly exaggerated view. (The Branch closed in 1834.) Contrary to the impression of banking historians,[20] papers surviving in Lloyds Bank do not reveal actual experience of sharp competition in the early life of the Bank of England Branches. Indeed the Bank of England's strict control from Head Office handicapped its branches in competition for the business of ordinary traders.[21] A note of 1835 tells how

[20] Clapham (*Economic History of Modern Britain*, vol. i, p. 276) emphasizes not so much actual competition as the fear of competition which the country bankers expressed.

[21] Clapham (*Bank of England*, vol. ii, p. 138) has referred to the procedure at the Bank's branches. He notes that nevertheless the branches 'did a satisfactory and growing business': in 1830 'the two best patronised branches, Liverpool and Birmingham each had upwards of 200 discounting clients'. Unfortunately no figures of the number of customers in banks in the great towns have survived, but there are various indications that a

the Bristol Bank of England Agent brought to the West of England and South Wales Bank a £2,000 acceptance of Barings, due in twenty days; this had been brought to the Bank of England for discount by a credit-worthy party who, however, had no Discount Account at the branch. The Agent could not discount the bill quickly as he had to apply to Thread-needle Street for permission to open a new Discount Account, and the business therefore came to the West of England Bank which was ready to discount the bill on the spot. Similarly we find Lloyds in 1869 gaining a customer from the Bank of England simply because of 'the inconvenience of their restrictions'. Later in the century competition appears to have sharpened:[22] in 1890 Howard Lloyd was reporting to his Reference Committee that the Birmingham Branch was directly competing 'for certain classes of local business'. In 1894 he read to the Committee a letter from his Smethwick manager, complaining of 'very undue competition of the Bank of England'. This sharpness of competition was still evident in the new century: in 1906 Lambtons at Newcastle found themselves undercut by the Bank of England Branch, which captured the very important account of the Sunderland Shipbuilding Company.[23] This period of rivalry between Bank of England Branches and provincial bankers is still remembered by elderly bankers; there was a strong reaction to it inside the Bank of England in the next generation.[24]

These heartburnings over valuable customers certainly made for strained relations between bankers in the provinces and the local branches of the Bank of England, but they were perhaps—at any rate against the perspective of a century—exceptional. In general the references to the Bank of England's Agents and their offices give the impres-

---

prosperous bank in one of the great towns (e.g. Taylors & Lloyds in Birmingham or the Liverpool Union) had several hundreds of customers at this period.

[22] Clapham (op. cit., vol. ii, p. 368) associates this particularly with the shrinkage of the Bank's income in the cheap-money period of the middle nineties.

[23] As the company took to the Bank of England its best bills for discount, Lambtons were not sorry to drop the connexion. The company took its remaining business (i.e. the part not attractive to the Bank of England) to Lloyds Bank at Sunderland. In October 1911 the account at the Bank of England was closed and Lloyds thenceforward had the whole business for the remainder of the company's life.

[24] In his evidence before the Committee of Finance and Industry (the 'Macmillan Committee') 1929–31, the then Deputy Governor took the view that, although the central bank should have power, for use in exceptional circumstances, to deal directly with the public, it should definitely refrain from competition with the other banks.

sion of cordiality. In the early days the local Bank of England clerks, like the clerks of the London agents,[25] received tips from local banks: the Plymouth and Devonport Bank entered £5 for the clerks at the Plymouth branch in 1838. Later, in 1876, cordiality was expressed in a more modern way: all the Birmingham banks joined to make a presentation to the retiring Bank of England Agent, the contribution from each bank being 'limited to £30'. And so it went on: in 1899 Lloyds, discussing the idea of joining with other banks in the holding of an emergency gold reserve, resolved not to take any step 'which would imperil the friendly relations at present existing between themselves and the Bank of England'. The latter had, in general, settled into the role of a kindly and useful neighbour, not to be lightly offended, even if the Old Lady did sometimes capture a nice little piece of business.

The new atmosphere had to some extent been created by the well-known leadership of Lidderdale, Governor of the Bank of England in the Baring Crisis of 1890. In his successful effort to avert a financial collapse, he brought the various parties in the City together and persuaded them jointly to guarantee the liabilities of Barings, who had got into temporary difficulties.[26] Among the parties brought in were the London joint-stock banks. Lloyds, having lately come among them by the absorption of Barnetts Hoares, was a participating bank though not among the select five who took part in the main discussions. Edward Hoare, the City Manager, had sensed trouble ahead and was ready for a crisis in those gloomy November days:[27] he called Howard Lloyd up to London in a hurry in the week-end of 16–17 November, and it was these two—Edward Hoare and Howard Lloyd—who settled with Lidderdale's Committee the action Lloyds Bank should take.[28] After this incident it was easier for the Bank of England to look to the commercial banks for

[25] See p. 137 above.
[26] The story (it is a good one) is told in Clapham, *The Bank of England*, vol. ii, pp. 326–39; from another angle there are some embellishments in R. Fulford, *Glyn's 1753–1953*, pp. 208–12.
[27] Hoare noticed that an excessive amount of Barings' bills were being presented; he called Lloyd to London and met the latter on a dark November afternoon at Euston Station. Thence they went to the Oriental Club and talked things over. They decided to sell £500,000 of Consols, only to find that no jobber would make a price!
[28] The Chairman (Salt) also came to London and put his signature to a document whereby Lloyds committed themselves up to £250,000.

co-operation in difficulties that fell short of crisis, and in 1906 Mr. Spencer Phillips, as Chairman of Lloyds, shared with other London bankers a novel experience. The story[29] is best told in his own words:

> I should like to mention an incident which took place in December. On the 7th December £14,000,000 of Treasury Bonds were paid off. That released about $4\frac{1}{2}$ to 5 millions of cash on the markets, and the money dealers, who in some ways are rather like butterflies and live only for a day, knocked the rate down for fine bills to $3\frac{5}{16}$ths. The French exchange immediately fell, and there was considerable danger of further withdrawals taking place, which would have depleted the reserve in the Bank of England, which was already much lower than it should have been at that time of the year. Upon this, however, the Bank of England took a new departure. They approached the principal clearing bankers and asked them to co-operate with the Bank to take the surplus money off the market and place it on deposit with the Bank at a low rate of interest. The Bank then charged 5 per cent. on their advances, and the effect was electrical. No bills were discounted under 4 per cent., the French exchange accordingly rose, and the danger of the withdrawal of gold ceased. This precedent has been followed again during the present month by the Bank. I think I may state for ourselves that we welcome, and cordially welcome, this new departure of the Bank; and, although I have no authority for saying so, I am perfectly certain that I am voicing the opinion of the rest of the Bankers in stating that they are equally pleased.

This was a far cry from the Bank of England's unsplendid isolation of the sixties and seventies. Once the difficult year 1907 was passed, there was not again until the 1914 crisis any further occasion for extraordinary action of this kind, but between the Old Lady and the Clearing Banks the new sense of partnership had come to stay. Historically these episodes of 1890 and 1906 do not appear as freakish aberrations; rather they are harbingers of the new ways that are now, at mid-century, part of the accepted order of the City.

---

[29] On the group of operations to which this incident belongs, see J. H. Clapham, *Bank of England*, vol. ii, pp. 383–8, and R. S. Sayers, *Bank of England Operations, 1890–1914*, chap. ii, esp. pp. 36–39.

7

COMPETITION AND
CO-OPERATION WITH
OTHER BANKS

THE few banks that now serve the British public cannot ignore each other's existence; they are competitors, even if the competition is not aggressive enough to be always in the public eye. They also have interests in common, and they believe that the public interest as well as their own is served by a measure of co-operation between the banks in certain matters. This twofold nature of the relations between banks—competition and co-operation side by side—is nothing new. When banks were essentially local, the banker was keenly aware of competition from other banks in the town and country; equally he thought it well to co-operate in some matters with his competitors, and with banks farther afield who could help him to provide better service for his customers. Sometimes the competitive element predominated; at others—especially in difficult days—the protection that could be found in mutual co-operation seemed the more important. But some element of both—of competition and co-operation—was always present in the relations between one bank and another.

In the earliest days the threat of competition by the establishment of another bank in the neighbourhood was always in the banker's mind. Back in 1802 John Stevenson in Stafford wrote to his father in London that caution was necessary in taking new premises, as there were 'some opulent people in this neighbourhood whose fingers itch to give us opposition'. A few days later storm-damage to the bank's existing premises made a removal very urgent, but Stevenson still hesitated to take the proposed new premises because their 'more public situation' might further excite those itching fingers. He thought it safer to get the existing premises repaired and perhaps add the next-door house, a property that included four stables and two pigsties.[1] In these early days the only effective way of precluding competition from a new establishment was personal contact with the rival promoters; no doubt this did sometimes occur, but it is not the kind of negotiation that leaves recognizable trace in the records. In later phases, when competitive establishment was taking the form of the opening of additional branches by other banks, the same privacy would also sometimes obtain, but sometimes there would be formal correspondence which has survived to give the historian his chance. There was an episode of this kind in 1836 in Wiltshire, in the first flush of joint-stock banking. Both the Wilts and Dorset Bank and the North Wilts Bank were new organizations, struggling for a footing in new neighbourhoods. Keen as each was in the effort to attract customers before the other fellow stepped in, both did eventually sense the fact that the opening of rival branches could be overdone. The Wilts and Dorset proposed that if they abstained from conducting business at Melksham, Hungerford, Westbury, Trowbridge, and Bradford-on-Avon, the North Wilts Bank should correspondingly keep off the grass at Warminster, Frome, Wootton Bassett, Malmesbury, Swindon, and Highworth. The North Wilts Bank was ready to negotiate, but finally rejected the proposal as 'inadmissible'. The prize in the competitive struggle was evidently more enticing than the easier profit of co-operation.

An experience of Lloyds in 1864 again showed the bankers disposed to avoid wasteful overlapping, although in the end the competitive spirit proved the stronger. It appears that when Lloyds were preparing to open a branch at Oldbury (their first branch of all) they informed the Staffordshire Joint Stock Bank, whose Head Office was at Bilston and who were also thinking of opening a branch at Oldbury. The Bilston firm agreed to abandon their Oldbury project on the understanding that Lloyds would give up their idea of opening at Wednesbury where the Staffordshire Joint Stock Bank planned to open as an alternative. Nevertheless, in the following year Lloyds established themselves in Wednesbury, by absorbing the private bank of P. & H. Williams; the non-competing agreement was evidently not binding for any considerable length of time. After this,

---

[1] Also, 'We forgot to bargain for the seat in the Church expressly, I do not know whether Bushton considers that a part of the bargain or not.'

Lloyds do not appear to have had any further agreements on these lines, but a book kept at Head Office in 1913–14 shows that there were agreements with certain other banks that warning should be given to the others if any one of the banks intended opening a branch at a listed place. At that date six places were named, in Kent, Hampshire, and Monmouth.

In the important formative period of joint-stock banking—the second quarter of the nineteenth century—the allocation of shares in the company was used as a bait for customers, and this practice remained as a serious element in competition between banks into the next generation. In this context it is important to remember that, despite some resounding failures bank shares were commonly very profitable investments and, especially when the company was based on private firms of acknowledged probity, there was an eager demand for them even at substantial premiums.[2] When Messrs. Moore and Robinson converted themselves, in 1836, into the Nottinghamshire Banking Company, the 30,000 £10 shares were to be allocated as follows:

8,000 shares to the present partners at par.

8,000 shares to the customers of the present bank, at a premium of £1 per share, to be allotted according to their respective accounts. Should any customers decline to take the shares so allotted, the same shall be divided amongst the customers at the same rate and in the same proportions.

8,000 shares to the public at a premium of £2. 10. 0, half of which will form a reserved fund for the benefit of the company.

6,000 shares to be reserved, and left at the disposal of the Directors, for the benefit of the Company.

The customer thus received substantial advantage and the reservation of the last 6,000 shares was designed to enable the Directors to attract new customers. At about the same date the Wilts and Dorset Banking Company, having already allotted 1,689 £15 shares to 72 applicants (who had

[2] The North Wilts Banking Company added a list of market values of bank shares to the end of their prospectus issued in March 1836. Included were the following banks, two of them based on private firms and all three sooner or later absorbed by Lloyds.

	Amount paid per share	Latest Dividend per cent.	Market price of shares
Gloucester Banking Company . . .	£5	10	£16
Halifax Joint Stock Bank	£10	12½	£21
Devon & Cornwall Banking Company . .	£20	6½	£32

incidentally applied for 2,315 shares), became fussy about further applications. Miss Fanny Shaw of Manchester and Mr. James Fletcher of London found their applications declined, on the ground of their distance from the seat of operations; the Provisional Committee resolved to confine future allotments 'to persons residing in the District and who came under a promise to keep accounts with the Bank'. Both these examples are taken from the boom period of 1835–6, and the unhappy experiences of the later thirties and early forties no doubt diminished the attractiveness of the bait. Nevertheless, the practice continued to be common enough, and in the hotly competitive 1860's in Birmingham banking Howard Lloyd observed the success with which banks were by this means tempting customers to transfer their accounts. The Birmingham Joint Stock Bank indignantly complained in 1864 that one of their customers had been offered shares in the Birmingham Banking Company at a very favourable price in return for bringing his account, an account having a turnover of £22,000 a year. But this was a case of the pot calling the kettle black: the Birmingham Joint Stock used similar enticements, and the customer knew this and played one bank off against the other. According to Howard Lloyd, the Birmingham Joint Stock was highly successful in this practice:

The Joint Stock Bank was a rising institution with a visibly strong Board and was paying a good dividend. The bait thus held out was found irresistibly attractive by many firms and customers of good position. . . . I well remember the vexation felt from time to time in our High Street Bank as one and another customer of importance and often of long continued connection thus unworthily passed from us.

As the nineteenth century wore on the issue of new shares became more and more unusual, and the attraction of customers by this method died a natural death. But competition for customers remained very much alive, the old methods giving place to others less unfamiliar to bankers and customers today. In 1891 the manager of Lloyds' branch at Oldbury sent up to Head Office a 'touting' letter a customer had received from a rival bank; this was not unusual in some banks at that time, but early in the twentieth century bankers more generally looked down their noses at anything of the kind. In 1906 another bank's local manager called on his competitor at Lambtons to explain that a customer's move had not

THE BIRMINGHAM JOINT-STOCK BANK, LTD., *c.* 1880
(On the present site of the New Street branch of Lloyds Bank)
Artist unknown

been due to any touting: thereafter the word does not occur in the records. But one bank could still be more obliging than another in lending its money, and this method of attracting customers appears to have become more prominent as the older methods declined. In the last twenty years of the nineteenth century reports of this kind show that Lloyds Bank as well as its competitors was willing to put decidedly poor accounts into its books if this was the price of attracting customers from other banks. Experience in this highly competitive period was showing how dangerous it was to press a borrower to reduce his overdraft: he might all too easily find the accommodation in a rival bank. The risk was not by any means limited to the customer directly in question—banks were at all times ready to exploit any adverse rumours about their local competitors. In early days the absorption of a private bank by a larger branch bank could provide an opportunity for this, as happened in Exeter in 1836. Fifty years later the Worcester City and County Bank was able to attract accounts from the Capital and Counties because the tale went round that the latter intended to conduct their business 'in a narrow way'. Other aspects as well as lending policy could equally give a rival some advantage, as when in 1890 Lloyds attracted a customer who alleged that the rival's clerks were too free in their conversation. In competitive business the moral for the local manager was always to maintain the reputation of his branch in every conceivable way.

Price competition has rarely been of any general importance in English banking, but there have been times when it has been locally important. The rate of interest allowed on deposits has always been more subject to competitive strain than the rate charged for discounts or advances, for the reason that the depositor can more easily take his business to the other bank across the road. In the 1830's and 40's, when the new joint-stock banks in the country and in London were pushing for business, competition in rates on deposit accounts was active. But it was a dangerous weapon for bankers to use against each other: no bank could afford to fall behind in the race, and there was much to be said for a quiet talk with one's competitors and agreement not to go beyond a certain figure. With only two or three banks in a town, it was generally not difficult for the parties to come to some arrangement; so local agreements regulating deposit rates appeared long before anything approaching national agreement was possible. Not that these early local agreements had any continuous life: from time to time one bank or another would feel independent enough to break the ring, though its independence might not outlast many weeks. In 1836 the Glamorganshire Banking Company agreed with its competitors, Messrs. Walters, Voss and Chad, to raise the deposit rate from $2\frac{1}{2}$ to 3 per cent. In 1838, when London rates were falling, the company independently reduced the rate to $2\frac{1}{2}$ per cent.; Walters, Voss and Chad followed suit only after it was clear that the $2\frac{1}{2}$ per cent. rate was accepted by the company's depositors. In the fifties the Glamorgan company was still strong enough—despite joint-stock competition—to take an independent line occasionally, but in 1862 the West of England Bank was thought too serious a competitor, and an intended drop in the deposit rate did not materialize when the competitor declined to move simultaneously.

The broad tendencies of these mid-century decades are clearly exemplified in the West Country where some of the most important roots of Lloyds were growing fast. The new banks began with a presumption in favour of unregulated competition: it was in the spirit of the age, and it looked like the right policy for new institutions pushing their way in an expanding economy. 'The Directors do not approve', a Stroud manager was instructed in 1836, 'of the principle of entering into any arrangements to unite with any bank concerning the rate of discount or allowance of interest on deposits.' These same bankers had inherited the private bankers' tradition in favour of fixity of rates paid on genuinely 'fixed' deposits, and generally no interest at all on fluctuating balances. The inclination of each bank was therefore to fix its deposit rate independently, and preferably at a more attractive level than that ruling in other local banks. The keenness of competition soon broke this attitude, and by 1839 the County of Gloucester Bank, for example, was giving its branch managers discretion to bid 3 per cent. in face of competition from other banks. The next step—in the early forties—was for the various Gloucester banks to come to an agreement ruling rates offered for new deposits, though each bank retained its freedom in dealing with old customers. A little later the intrusion of another bank (the North Wilts) into the area of the Gloucester banks created fresh strains; efforts to get the new competitor into the agreement failed, and deposit rates in the district were held at levels that looked unremunerative in the light of London money market conditions. The pressure towards agreements relating rates to London conditions was germinating.

In London itself the strains of competition were similarly undermining the old ways. Among both West End and Lombard Street bankers, even more than in the country, tradition had favoured fixed rates on really fixed deposits, and nothing on fluctuating balances. By 1857 even Twinings, who always preferred to cling to the old ways, were forced by competition to concede more flexible terms in favour of a big customer. When informing this customer of the concession, Twinings added that 'we should not wish to court business of that kind'—but the water was over the dam.

When, in the later decades of the century, Lloyds Bank itself was spreading its tentacles far beyond its Birmingham home, the Directors had to make up their minds whether to enforce uniform interest rates throughout their system or to allow local determination. The force of local arrangements and local competition was acknowledged, and in 1882 Howard Lloyd as General Manager circularized the branch managers in these terms:

The Board having left the question of our deposit rate to my discretion in a manner which releases me from the obligation of insisting on uniformity over the whole system of the Company and allows me to recognise the exceptional circumstances of any branch, I shall be glad to know from you whether you wish the rate altered at your branch or whether, in consideration of our having allowed $2\frac{1}{2}\%$ so often and so long when our neighbours only allowed 2%, no present alteration is required at your branch. If you think any alteration is requisite I should propose 3%, with leave to allow an extra $\frac{1}{2}\%$ beyond this in cases of a fixed term not exceeding three or four months or a larger amount or longer notice than is usual, and you may consider this authorised accordingly.

Through the remainder of the century this continued to be the general policy, and it had its parallels in other parts of the country. Local agreements remained common, and the Head Offices of branch systems allowed their local managers to adhere to such agreements, although these sometimes implied payment of rates out of line with those ruling elsewhere in the same bank. In these closing decades of the century deposit rates in the country appear to have become much more affected by London rates: local managers were finding that big customers took their deposits to London when London rates rose much beyond the more sticky country rates. It is noteworthy that the lower Bank Rate fell, the more uniform were deposit rates in any locality—the local managers found it easier to agree on maximum rates if London rates were low. A period of high Bank Rates, by contrast, tended to produce discrepancies —local bankers met the competition of high London rates more independently. At the lower end of the scale the banks had one enemy in common: 'Our present rate', wrote Howard Lloyd in 1884, 'is $2\frac{1}{2}$ per cent. at 14 days notice and we have hardly ever gone below this rate as in country districts we are almost held to it by the fact of the Post Office Savings Bank maintaining it. On the other hand we do not follow the upward movements of the Bank Rate except at a respectful distance.' The floor to deposit rates was thus something common to all banks; in the other direction there might be some variance of view as to what was 'a respectful distance' behind Bank Rate.

In the 1900's it became usual for banks in any one town to be offering uniform rates on deposits, and the banking public had come to expect this. Not that competitive bidding had altogether disappeared. The first decade of the new century was a period of wide movements in Bank Rate, and in the spasms of dear money Lloyds circularized branch managers, giving them discretion to go above the usual $2\frac{1}{2}$ per cent., to 3 per cent., where this was necessary in order to meet similar moves by competitors. When Bank Rate went to 6 per cent. in the autumn of 1906 local managers were given more latitude in offering 3 per cent. and were allowed to bid $3\frac{1}{2}$ per cent. in exceptional cases; but at this point Head Office had to watch the risk that one branch of Lloyds would be in effect competing with another branch of Lloyds. The widespread penetration by the great joint-stock banks was creating conditions in which national uniformity of rates was sooner or later inevitable. It was, however, the exigencies of national financial policy in time of war that forced the banks to the final step: at official instigation in 1917 the great banks came to an agreement setting maximum rates for deposits in town and country, subject to exceptional treatment for deposits of foreign origin. After the war the disturbing influence of an extremely high Bank Rate reasserted itself, and in Lloyds Bank there was a return to the discretionary $\frac{1}{2}$ per cent.

margin allowed to managers to counter competition, with an instruction to submit to Head Office requests for rates above this. The broad principle that the 'Town Deposit Rate' fluctuated with Bank Rate while the standard country rate was a stable $2\frac{1}{2}$ per cent. was established; but the pull of a 7 per cent. Bank Rate in 1920 caused the Town Deposit Rate to apply far into the Home Counties and to the south coast. This was only one manifestation of the sharp competition still remaining in the system, and for some years considerable discretion was allowed to local managers. The long period of moderate Bank Rates (generally $4\frac{1}{2}$ to $5\frac{1}{2}$ per cent.) in the middle and later twenties, gave the banks, now great national institutions, more chance to enforce uniformity on mutually agreed lines, but it was not until the long period of cheap money in the thirties that the agreed rates came to be universally enforced.

The competition in deposit rates, and the agreement restraining that competition, find scarcely any reflection on the other side of the account. Interest charged on overdrafts and discounts on bills appear to have been much more stereotyped, much less susceptible to the varying stress of competition between banks. This contrast is no doubt to be explained mainly by the greater difficulty faced by a borrowing customer in transferring his account. But it may also have been a symptom of the thirst of nineteenth-century banks for deposits, and the ease with which most of them could find outlets in lending to business men. The tendency was accordingly for rates of discount and of interest charged on advances to be highly conventionalized, without any negotiation between bankers. The 5 per cent. rate, which had been normal before the Usury Laws were qualified in 1833, gradually gave way to rates varying in some degree with Bank Rate, though away from London the variation was anything but automatic and the round 5 per cent. probably continued to rule most bank lending in the provinces through the greater part of the century. In the long period of extremely cheap money in the 1890's, however, the traditional charges tended to crumble wherever competition was lively. At Maidstone, for example, the London and County Bank were charging 5 per cent. on an account, and Lloyds had the chance of taking it at 4 per cent. At Newcastle Lambtons conceded a rate of $4\frac{1}{2}$ per cent. to a customer, only to hear from him that customers of the rival North Eastern Bank were charged only 4 per cent.—and Lambtons already knew that the National Provincial Bank had just lost two good accounts to the North Eastern. A little later there were allegations that Backhouse and Co. were charging as little as $3\frac{1}{2}$ per cent., and that they had fixed this rate because they believed Lambtons were acting similarly. These examples happen to stand out in surviving correspondence, and it seems likely that, in the exceptional conditions of those mid-nineties, rates did crumble. The evidence disappears as money markets tighten in the latter half of the decade, and in the new century the banks, becoming bigger and more completely tied to London, set their faces more firmly against 'cut-throat competition'. In 1898 Sir Thomas Salt hoped that 'before my banking days are done I may see anything like vulgar competition between large banks given up altogether'. Eleven years later his successor as Chairman still found it necessary to protest: 'I look upon banks cutting each other's throats in the matter of both allowances and charges of interest, as well as the opening of unnecessary branches in places which are already fully banked, as simply suicidal . . . to bid for accounts on terms which can only mean a loss to us is not consonant with the position or dignity of a bank, or with the elementary principles of profit and loss.'

This competition, vulgar or dignified, suicidal or life-preserving, could be expressed not only in allowances and charges of interest, but also in the commission charged for working accounts, and through the second half of the nineteenth century there was continual evidence of the importance of this item in attracting customers from one bank to another. In the old local private banks commission rates for handling business appear to have been extremely varied, as one would expect, and the unusual customer willing to break an old connexion could sometimes get very much cheaper terms. An army doctor in 1853, for example, tired of paying Cox and Co. at Charing Cross their conventional $2\frac{1}{2}$ per cent. for collecting his half-pay, went along Fleet Street and found that Twinings would do the work for a mere $\frac{1}{8}$ per cent. As competition sharpened with the growth of the new joint-stock banks, bankers new and old alike found it wise to watch their commission charges warily. In 1874 Lloyds opened a branch in Coventry and within two months the Coventry and Warwickshire Bank circularized its customers to inform them that the rate of commission would in future be $\frac{1}{8}$ per cent. instead of $\frac{1}{4}$ per cent.; in the following year the lower rate was advertised in the local press. At this

SIR THOMAS SALT, BART., 1830–1904
Chairman, 1886–98
From the painting by Frank Holl

period Lloyds itself was acutely conscious of competition in commission rates in the Midlands generally, feeling safe only to charge a half-yearly fee to cover postage and stationery because this was the practice of the National Provincial and other banks. The competition continued through the next decade; the Oldbury manager failed to get agreement with the Dudley District Bank, precluding a cutting of commission, and more than once he sought authority to reduce the charge from 2s. per cent. to 1s. 6d. per cent. in order to meet specific competition. One Birmingham customer in 1892 even succeeded in wringing from his Lloyds manager repayment of 1s. 3d. per cent. commission charged on the half-year, maintaining that he could do better at another bank.

Similar incidents were constantly occurring in other areas too. At Wrexham the North and South Wales Bank, the National Provincial, and Williams and Co. were in competition with each other, and in 1889, when Williams thought of cutting the standard commission from $\frac{1}{4}$ to $\frac{1}{8}$ per cent., there were discussions between the three. There is no direct evidence that agreement was reached, but two years later Williams were telling a prospective customer from the National Provincial that though they would charge 1 per cent. less on his overdraft, 'as regards commission we did not intend to bid for any account by undercutting the National Provincial'. On Tyneside in 1896 Lambtons, still a private bank but locally very important, met complaints about high commission not only from ordinary customers but also from the London and Westminster for whose customers Lambtons handled Newcastle business. Lambtons denied that other local banks charged less, but conceded a reduction all the same. Against private customers they maintained a tougher front: Lambtons' branch manager at Sunderland took the trouble to check with his competitor (Backhouse and Co.) a customer's allegation about commissions, and called the customer's bluff. 'I always, nearly, find', the manager commented, 'that our customers in quoting other banks' charges make mistakes and so now I always make enquiries before believing them or acting upon them.'

Meanwhile, the other side of relations with other banks was also developing. If the polite jostle of competition between banks tended to the improvement and cheapening of service to the customer, so also did their co-operation in the development of joint services. A nation served, as England is now, by great branch banks spreading themselves across the length and breadth of the country is apt to take for granted—and probably to underestimate—those payment and remittance services which depend upon the connexion between one banking office and another. When banks were small and local, these services were anything but automatic, and their evolution depended upon deliberate efforts of co-operation between banks. We have already seen (in Chapter 5) how the traditional method for the private banks was to operate through London agents; these connexions between country banks and London banks were, however, rather of the banker-and-customer kind—the London agent was banker to the country banker. The stiff competition which the early joint-stock banks faced from the entrenched private banks stimulated them to seek ways of providing better and quicker services for their customers, and for this purpose some of the joint-stock banks made arrangements with similar banks in other districts, whereby the latter would act as agents for handling customers' business.

An 1836 Minute of the infant Liverpool Union Bank states the co-operative policy adopted in this matter: 'As a means of obtaining much information useful to themselves and to their customers and of facilitating at the same time the collection and transmission of money, the Directors found it necessary at the opening of the Bank to enter into correspondence with bankers in almost every town in the kingdom, with many of whom they are now happy in being able to state that they succeeded in establishing it on terms of reciprocal advantage.' Arrangements important in view of Liverpool's trading connexions were made with Boyle, Low, Pim and Co. of Dublin, the Provincial Bank of Ireland, the National Bank of Scotland, and the Gloucestershire Banking Company. Another Irish bank—the Agricultural and Commercial Bank of Ireland—offered its service, but the Liverpool Union decided that association with this bank, 'after the notorious misconduct of their affairs', would be injurious to the Liverpool bank's reputation. Another bank vigorous in establishing agencies was the West of England Bank; within two months of its foundation the management was sounding banks in Manchester, Liverpool, Yorkshire, Birmingham, Gloucester, Ireland, and Scotland. But until about 1880 only a few of the country joint-stock banks appear to have pressed this development in any systematic way, although here and there reciprocal services were established, as between Lloyds at Birmingham and the tiny bank of Wootten and Co. at Oxford.

During the last quarter of the nineteenth century, however, these connexions became commonplace and their development was vigorously pressed by a variety of banks. Often a general arrangement between two banks would grow out of an *ad hoc* service negotiated for the convenience of a particular big customer. In 1882, for example, Lloyds at Birmingham agreed to receive for Gurneys of Norwich credits for a Norwich firm, Messrs. J. and J. Coleman; two years later the arrangement was generalized to cover any of Gurneys' customers. A little later an arrangement with the York City and County Bank to cover Rowntree's business was the prelude to a more general agency. Particular arrangements of this kind —sometimes limited to the cashing of wages cheques or other specified business—carried commissions ranging from a shilling to half-a-crown per cent., but where the arrangements were more general and were reciprocal the tendency was to eliminate commissions. As more and more of the surviving country banks became powerful concerns with many branches, the principle of mutual service without charge became more obviously applicable. At the same time, the competition from the many branch banks spurred the smaller concerns to strengthen their reciprocal services. Williams and Co. of Chester, a sizable local bank with four branches by the eighties, who had established effective agencies covering Manchester, Liverpool, and North Wales, in 1883 agreed with Lambtons of Newcastle 'to do each other's banking business free of charge', and then circularized thirty other banks proposing similar terms. Eighteen of the thirty accepted. The Wilts and Dorset in 1881 superseded its previous Liverpool arrangements by an agreement with the Bank of Liverpool, whereby transactions on both sides should be carried free of charge. Similar arrangements with other areas rapidly followed. 'These arrangements', announced the General Manager of the Wilts and Dorset, 'have been made in order that we might give our customers the same facilities for the transmission of money from one district to another as are afforded by two or three of the larger joint-stock banks which have numerous branches spread over a wide area and thus enable us to compete on more advantageous terms with the banks in question.' With some of the other banks (the Capital and Counties among them) the Wilts and Dorset added a mutual understanding that they would recommend clients moving from one town to another; for example, the Wilts and Dorset might recommend one of their customers to the Capital and Counties in a town where there was no Wilts and Dorset branch.

A logical development of these reciprocal services was the establishment of local clearings for cheques. The manager of the Birmingham Joint Stock Bank had in 1866 worked out a system for clearing in Birmingham though the Birmingham Banking Company did not at first accept the plan. By 1890 there appears to have been some local clearing at Newcastle: Hodgkin Barnetts were instructing their branches that any large cheques or bills on the local bank of Woods and Co., or its branches, should be sent for settlement in Newcastle and not, as hitherto, in London. In the same year the Wilts and Dorset issued instructions that all cheques drawn on Bristol banks or their local branches must be sent to the Bristol office of the Wilts and Dorset; bills, however, had still to go through the London agents.

The development of reciprocal services of this kind depended upon a high degree of mutual confidence; the collection of payments for others could be a tricky business when little banks were liable to put up the shutters, as an incident in 1846 at Dover had shown.[3] There had from early days also been co-operation in more elementary facilities for the public's business. The Royal Mint—in modern times producing coin in London only—had never regarded the distribution of coin as part of its business, and the banks have had to fill the gap. In the eighteenth century, and particularly during the Napoleonic Wars, the Mint's work was so utterly inadequate that there was little new coin to distribute, and all sorts of local efforts by traders and industrialists, were made to provide some means of circulaion.[4] After Waterloo the production of coin was

---

[3] Late on a Saturday evening Hammond and Co. wrote to the Dover Bank that they had placed to the latter's credit in their books a sum of £300 received for William Kingsford. On Monday the Dover Bank stopped payment and litigation ensued, on the question whether the £300 belonged to Kingsford or to the assignees of the Dover Bank. The Gloucestershire Banking Company was similarly caught, in 1851, on the failure of the Monmouth and Glamorganshire Banking Company.

[4] On the work of the Royal Mint, see Sir John Craig, *The Mint* (Cambridge, 1953); on the inadequacy of the circulation and on local efforts to meet requirements, cf. T. S. Ashton, *The Eighteenth Century* (London, 1955), pp. 173 et seq.

taken seriously in hand, but distribution was left by the authorities to the chances of the ordinary channels of business. The tendency was for banks in agricultural districts to collect gold, while the manufacturing towns were always running short of gold.[5] To meet this situation the Coventry and Warwickshire Bank in 1836 made a regular arrangement with Messrs. Beck and Eaton of Shrewsbury, to supply them with 500 sovereigns per week, at a commission of 2s. per cent. Forty years later correspondence between the Neath manager and the Head Office of the Glamorganshire Banking Company (Swansea) reveals difficulties growing beyond a standing arrangement with another bank: the Neath manager was having to scout for coin as far afield as Salisbury and Gloucester. Even a co-operative routine of this kind did of course need watching—things could go wrong, as a Liverpool bank, accustomed to drawing surplus silver from Williams at Chester, found when the latter's manager, having pocketed the key to the silver, was unexpectedly away.

Hours of public business were a matter in which the push and pull of competition and co-operation affected—in a very obvious way—the services provided for the banking public. Presumably in the very earliest days hours of opening were settled by each bank for itself, without any consultation with other banks; but of this phase no clear evidence remains. What is clear is that, when banking offices were in the 1830's and 40's becoming much thicker on the ground, it had become usual for all the bankers in a town to agree upon the hours for public business. The hour for opening was, curiously enough, scarcely ever mentioned in these discussions: opening times of 9 or 9.30 remained usual throughout the nineteenth century. In very early days—going back into the eighteenth century—the day from 9 or 9.30 till 5 was sometimes broken by an hour or more for lunch. This lunch break, where it had not already gone, tended to disappear when closing hours became earlier during the second half of the nineteenth century. The tendency for the hour of closing to become earlier was very slow, and it depended on agreement by all the banks in the town concerned. When the Chairman of the Coventry and Warwickshire Bank wanted, in 1840, to have the bank closed at 4 o'clock

[5] This was remarked upon by Joseph Gibbins in his evidence to the Select Committee on the Joint Stock Banks, 1836 (Minutes of Evidence, p. 67).

instead of 5, on days other than market days, he was told by his colleagues that a step of this kind could be taken only in agreement with the other local banks; when 4 o'clock was established, it was by such an agreement. Banking hours in Cheltenham were the subject of prolonged negotiation in the late sixties and early seventies. The discussions opened with a proposal that the offices be closed at 2 instead of 4 on Saturdays, 4 being then the closing hour on all six days. A counter-suggestion, by the County of Gloucester Bank, was that 3 o'clock should be closing time on every day except Thursday (market day) for which 4 o'clock should continue. This also was rejected, but in 1870 agreement was reached on the basis of 1 o'clock on Saturdays, 4 o'clock on other days. The new rule lasted only a year; on the initiative of the County of Gloucester Bank—which had throughout been against the short Saturday—the Saturday 4 o'clock closing was restored. In Gloucester, not far away and with much the same banks concerned, even 4 o'clock would then (1871) have been considered early closing for a Saturday, and it was not until 1904 that banks in Gloucester agreed to change the Saturday time from 5 o'clock to 4. Another local variation, dating from the earliest times, was for a bank to close at 1 o'clock on early-closing days, but this disappeared as the Saturday afternoon holiday became the rule. At the opening of the twentieth century much local variation remained—with opening hours of 9 o'clock in London and 9, 9.30, and 10 o'clock in the country, no lunch break, and closing hours 3 and 4, or 5 o'clock in some places on Saturdays and market-days. Not until staff shortages forced the problem to a head for all banks at once, in the 1914–18 war, did a common rule become established. London offices then settled on 9 to 3.30, and country offices 10 to 3, with Saturday closing at 12 everywhere, and these hours remained unchanged until the 1939 war.

Upon extraordinary occasions one bank might look to another for help going far beyond these routine matters of distributing coin or fixing hours of business. When a bank in the town was notoriously in difficulties and faced a run by depositors, the natural attitude of competing banks was to stand by and let the crisis take its course, hoping sooner or later to attract the customers of the failed bank. But depositors' suspicions, once roused, were apt to be infectious; a run on a bank could be bad for all the local banks, and there have been occasions when bankers have thought the solvency of a competitor worth preserving. In the long course of its development as a central bank, it became the duty of the Bank of England to intervene in important cases; but for a purely local bank the process of interesting these exalted quarters might well be prolonged or unsuccessful, and purely local aid be more appropriate, or the interest of local bankers might be a step towards aid from Threadneedle Street. In 1869 Alexanders of Ipswich were helped by a combination of Barnetts Hoares with several East Anglian banks, and they then survived for many years as an independent concern.[6] The attempt that Lloyds made in 1878 to rescue the Whitchurch and Ellesmere Banking Company had no such favourable outcome; on the other hand, the anonymity of another bank helped by Lloyds in 1878 suggests that it was successfully tided over. In the Liverpool crisis of 1857 a number of banks (including the Liverpool Union Bank which was willing to stake £100,000) offered a joint guarantee to the Bank of England if it would come to the assistance of the Borough Bank of Liverpool, but Threadneedle Street took a critical view of recent credit expansion in Liverpool and left the Borough Bank to its fate. In the well-known episode of 1890, by contrast, when a great City house was in danger, the Bank of England took the lead and Lloyds as well as other banks participated in a guarantee for Barings' creditors.[7]

In quieter circumstances there were other matters of general interest to bankers and there are traces of sporadic association of large groups of bankers to deal with these common problems. When the devastating financial crisis of 1825 was over, and the politicians and pamphleteers had had their cracks at the country bankers, James Taylor took the chair at 'a Meeting of Bankers' in Birmingham. The spirit of the meeting is evident in the first of the eight resolutions:

> That it is expedient to adopt measures for more effectually protecting the Country Bankers of England and Wales from the injurious consequences of the extraordinary and totally unjustifiable attacks to which they have been subjected.

The meeting approved the hostile attitude towards the establishment of

---

[6] Cf. p. 123 above.
[7] On the Baring Crisis, see p. 155 above.

branches of the Bank of England, adopted by a London meeting on 18 October 1827; and a deputation of three local bankers was appointed to join the London Committee established to defend 'the interests of the Country Bankers generally'. The establishment of joint-stock banks in the next few years was at once followed by meetings between representatives of these companies; the Deed of Settlement of the Northamptonshire Banking Company (1836) explicitly provided that any member of the Board might act as a delegate to any meeting of joint-stock or private banking partners. An association of Joint Stock Banks was formed, as a general purposes watchdog, and one of its first interests was in the Stamp Bill before Parliament immediately afterwards. Nevertheless, arrangements for mutual discussion remained for a long time very informal, the initiative being left to whatever bank felt an urge to bestir itself on any particular question. In 1840, for example, Lloyds at Birmingham (still a private bank) was worried about the trend of the Parliamentary Committees then inquiring into banking questions, and they wrote to Richard Spooner, a partner in Attwood Spooner and Co., suggesting that he should call a General Meeting, in London, of the country bankers. When the 1844 legislation was in process, Mr. Hartland of the Gloucestershire Banking Company was instructed by his Board to confer with Worcester bankers, while Mr. Winterbotham (Hartland's assistant) was instructed to get the views of Stuckeys in Somerset. In 1857 the National Provincial Bank invited others to send representatives to a meeting in London to consider proposed legislation on joint-stock banks, and a Bankers' Parliamentary Committee was formed in the following year. Through the remainder of the century—and afterwards—bankers were in conference with each other whenever legislation was touching their affairs.

Towards the end of the century the Association of English Country Bankers—it had become a permanent association of private banks—was busy trying to get agreement on publicity for accounts. Public opinion had come to expect bankers to demonstrate the soundness of their business, and the publicity which many joint-stock banks gave to their balance-sheets was believed to give strength to the joint-stocks in their efforts to supplant the private bankers. At a meeting in 1887—four years before Goschen's famous speeches on this subject—there was a long discussion, which revealed sharp divisions of opinion. Evidently there was

THE RT. HON. LORD BALFOUR OF BURLEIGH, D.C.L., D.L.

Chairman, 1946–54

From the painting by James Gunn, A.R.A.

already decided pressure from outside, and some of the private bankers wanted to 'stop the mouths of people', if not by publication of balance-sheets then by some other method. Up in the north, too, where private bankers under the leadership of Lambtons preferred to keep themselves apart from southerners, similar discussions went on. The discussions trailed on without issue, until the Chancellor of the Exchequer's attack in 1891 drove the bankers' associations into agreed steps on the publication of quarterly and (in London) monthly 'statements'.

The continuous associations of the banks in London and in the country respectively lasted into the twentieth century, but the amalgamation movement, culminating in the emergence of the 'Big Five' towards the end of the 1914–18 war, made reorganization appropriate. The Association of English Country Bankers—the lineal descendant of those informal discussions in Midland and West Country towns seventy, eighty, and ninety years earlier—was merged into the Central Association of Bankers, and the latter was in 1919 reorganized as the British Bankers' Association. This Association remains as the only comprehensive body watching the common interests of all the banks operating in Britain; but the more important matters are usually discussed in the Committees (at two levels) of the London Clearing Banks. The tightness of this organization allows a standard of co-operation, in important matters of policy, such as could not have been attained in the informal and sporadic meetings of nineteenth-century bankers, while much routine business that was formerly a matter for inter-bank arrangement is now covered by the normal contacts between branches and Head Office in the nation-wide banks of today. Co-operation in small matters is less necessary now that each bank has hundreds of branches scattered over a wide area. And the other side of relations—the competition between banks—has changed too. Among large and powerful banks the competitive methods in practice a hundred years ago have, as Thomas Salt and Spencer Phillips hoped, become outdated. But there are other ways of attracting customers, and the tradition of competition between independent institutions remains firmly embedded in Lloyds Bank and (as we may still call them) its rivals.

8

THE EMPLOYMENT OF FUNDS

TRADITIONALLY no banker has thought of himself as his customer's accountant, nor has he thought of his business as in any sense an investment trust, although both these elements enter importantly into the nature of contemporary English banking. In the banker's own view his business has consisted essentially of taking care of his customers' money and employing a safe proportion of it in loans of one kind and another to his customers. In conducting his business from day to day the banker had at his disposal his own capital and his customers' deposits; of this total, he had to keep some in the till and in the vault, or readily at his command elsewhere, in order to meet the daily requirements of his customers. Beyond this liquid reserve which obviously had first claim on his resources, the needs of his customers for business or personal loans, whether in the form of overdraft, loan, or discount, came next. Consideration of other employment for the funds at his disposal traditionally was called for only in relation to any surplus of funds after the prior claims of the liquid reserve and the requirements of borrowing customers had been met.

This historical attitude of regarding assets other than liquid reserves and loans to customers as outlets only for residual or surplus funds contrasts with the banking conventions evolved during the first half of the twentieth century. Nowadays we expect the balance-sheets of the great banks to conform to some logical pattern in which the ratios of various classes of assets are prominent. If we look into a banker's business of a hundred years ago and expect to find parallel conventions we shall be disappointed: there were no established fashions, much less rules, about the size of liquid reserves, and the bankers' investments had a residual nature that allowed diversity of practice infinitely greater than would be thought proper today. Consequently, the only safe generalization to be made about the balance-sheets of early banking is that no generalization is possible.

The balance-sheets available for study are unfortunately far fewer than could be wished, and the circumstances of their composition reduce their comparability to narrow limits. Of those surviving, some were the statutory published documents of joint-stock companies while others were the purely internal accounting papers of private partnerships. Those prepared for publication were subject to window-dressing in infinitely varying degrees; even those for internal use might be unrepresentative through some accident of dating. The analysis of assets was generally only of the broadest kind, whether the balance-sheet was for private or public inspection. In country banks it was, for example, normal to group cash with balances at London agents, while some London banks until a late date showed cash and money-market loans as a single item. Taking these figures of 'cash-plus-callable-money' in relation to deposit-plus-note-circulation liabilities, the liquidity of various banks at various dates can be compared: the method has justification in that the bankers did look primarily to their cash-plus-callable-money rather than to cash alone in assessing their liquidity.

The result is a bewildering variety of figures. The earliest, for the Canterbury Bank from 1789 to 1801, show the ratio ranging between 73 and 18 per cent. for December 1789 and December 1799; it may be surmised that the extraordinarily high figure for 1789 merely indicates that the bank had not yet got into its stride. In this early period the only comparison possible with another bank is with Berwicks at Worcester in December 1797: their ratio was then 21 as compared with 22·2 per cent. at Canterbury. Stephens Harris at Reading show ratios of 13, 21, and 13 for May 1815, 1820, and 1825 respectively, the end of the period during which the private bankers had the country business to themselves. After joint-stock banking began this same private bank appears to have worked to rather higher ratios: it was still 13·7 in 1830, but mostly over 20 in the forties and fifties, with a peak of 28·5 in 1840. Among the new joint-stock banks the Halifax Joint Stock Banking Co. at December 1830 (within six months of foundation) had 21·7; the Gloucestershire Banking Company in 1836, 23. The Wilts and Dorset, founded in 1835, was always a low-liquidity bank: in 1837 it showed 13·3, but two years later it was down to 8·3 and in 1842 to 4·9. In the forties and fifties it was often below 10 and never above 12·4 (reached in the crisis year 1847); in the second half of the century this bank appears to have settled down to a published figure of 11 or a little higher. A later joint-stock bank, the Bucks and Oxon Union, began in 1853 with 52 per cent., but soon worked down to about 20 and went below 10 in the early seventies. The wide range of practice in the private banks in this period is seen in the figures of Cripps and Co. at Cirencester, down to 4·1 in 1841, Stephens Blandy at Reading working from 26 in 1856 to 13·5 in 1859, and Lambtons at Newcastle, who ran their ratio down from 21·6 in 1855 to 12·6 in the crisis year 1857. It is significant that Cripps, whose figure was at the bottom end of the range, ended their independent existence in 1841, and that Berwicks at Worcester, whose liquidity was similarly low at this time, were threatened with sanctions by their London agents.

In the eighties the wide range of ratios was still there. Among private banks, Haydons at Guildford had only 7·3 in 1884, Berwicks at Worcester had 22·5 in 1889, and Garfit Claypon at Boston 24·5 in 1888. Among the joint-stocks the differences were even greater: 4·8 in the Halifax and Huddersfield Union, 9·2 in the Birmingham Joint Stock, 18·6 in the Gloucestershire, and 32 in the Capital and Counties, with many other figures between 10 and 20. After that the range tended to narrow: as they became bigger, banks became more like each other, although in the opening decade of the twentieth century banks at the top end of the range still had liquidity ratios double those at the lower end. Both Lloyds and the Capital and Counties still maintained high ratios; whatever else was the basis of their success, it was not economy of liquid assets. In their early joint-stock days Lloyds had been as low as 10·2 (June 1867) though also as high as 24·4. In the seventies the range narrowed, but was still far above that of their local competitor, the Birmingham Joint Stock Bank, and there was adverse comment at Lloyds' annual meeting in 1877. Thereafter, although there may have been economy in cash, the cash-plus-call-money ratio was maintained generally above 20, reaching 25 in 1899 and nearly 30 in 1914. The Capital and Counties had over 30 in the eighties, but appear to have run this down somewhat in later years. Lloyds certainly, and probably also the Capital and Counties, felt the need for high liquidity once they had established themselves as a large London bank. It did not follow that their actual cash ratios were high: a high proportion was probably at call in the money market. Nor does it follow that Lombard Street bankers had in the past regarded high liquidity ratios as necessary, though Barnetts Hoares in the early sixties had cash ratios (including balance at the Bank) ranging from 8·3 to as high as 24.

Looking at all the figures together there is little to support any view of the early private bankers as normally illiquid. On the other hand there is some evidence that among the early joint-stock banks were some who were ready to sail close to the wind, and that their competition made for lower liquidity generally: the lowest ratios noted for private banks refer to 1841. But all such views must be qualified by a reminder that the ratios mentioned above refer to cash-plus-callable-money and not to cash alone. They must be qualified also by emphasis that the evidence relates only to the survivors: the practices of those who went under may well have justified the stronger terms occasionally used by critics both of the private banks and of the early joint-stock banks. What remains without qualification is the extreme diversity of the figures throughout the nineteenth century. Only at the close of the century and in the opening years of the twentieth century did publicity and the dominance of a few large banks make for a recognizable standard with which almost every bank thought it necessary to conform.

Included with cash in the liquid reserves referred to in the above paragraphs there would normally be, for country banks, substantial balances with the banks' London agents.[1] Most banks—and this was especially true of London banks and the larger country banks—would also include substantial balances available at call or short notice in London or, occasionally, elsewhere. The precise uses to which these temporarily employed funds were put changed substantially during the nineteenth century, the change reflecting the development of the London money market as well as the growth of the banks themselves. At first, in the eighteenth century, the principal if not the only employment for funds was in the actual purchase of bills of exchange. Then, with the

---

[1] Cf. Chapter 5 above.

transformation of the bill-brokers into bill-dealers holding, with the help of borrowed money, bills on their own account, the short loan to the bill market substantially replaced the purchase of bills. In the second quarter of the nineteenth century the growth of business in the London Stock Exchange brought members of the Stock Exchange into the field as big borrowers of short money. In the thirties and forties, or rather in the depressed years in those decades, the rapid development of banks created a quite extraordinary pressure to open new employments for funds in London. This pressure accelerated the growth of loans to the Stock Exchange; it was largely responsible for the hothouse growth of Overend and Gurneys; and it encouraged country bankers to push their tentacles out beyond their established geographical range. The greater flexibility of money rates in the second and third quarters of the nineteenth century was both a symptom of and an incentive to the elaboration of the channels through which short money was pushed out by the country's growing banks. London was becoming the nation's financial centre more completely and more efficiently with every decade that passed.

The first phase of country banking was bound up with the great development of trade in inland bills of exchange, but it preceded the further specialization that gave the London bill market its well-known nineteenth-century character. London indeed provided a market for bills, but it was a market in which bill-brokers were still in the strict sense 'brokers' and not the dealers they in fact became after 1810. The country banker—the London banker too—found an outlet for his funds not yet in lending to the bill market, but only in the outright purchase of bills. These bills were, in Taylors and Lloyds at Birmingham, regarded for accounting purposes as no different from bills discounted for local customers, so that although they might physically be left in the charge of the London house, no entry in the Birmingham books distinguished them. There is, however, sufficient evidence to show that the purchase of bills in London represented a substantial part of the business: in the last twenty or thirty years of the eighteenth century something like a quarter of the Birmingham bank's total resources appears to have been used in this way. If other Birmingham banks were working in the same way the amount of Birmingham money so placed in London may well have been over £100,000. That a rapidly growing industrial town should be putting so much into the London market, beyond what was invested in government and other London stocks, shows how powerful was the attraction the London money market already exercised upon those who had to take close care of liquidity.

The straight loan to a bill-broker, whereby the latter was enabled to hold bills on his own account, appears in the Taylors and Lloyds papers first in 1812, when £12,000 with Sanderson and Co. was noted at the end of a list of investments.[2] In the following year the entry stood at £3,000, then disappeared until 1818, from which date the business was continuous. In 1818 Richardson, Overend and Co. appear as borrowers of £7,000; this firm became Overend, Gurney and Co. in 1827 and was of course the famous Overend and Gurneys that dominated the money market until its inglorious 1866.[3] Other banks were soon following suit: Stephens Harris of Reading put £34,000 with Overends in 1834, Henty's of Worthing £14,000 in 1836. In the thirties there were the new joint-stock banks coming into the market with funds to place: in 1836 the West of England and South Wales Bank, which had discounted bills at Overends in 1835, placed money with Overends—up to £40,000 without security. In 1838 the Plymouth and Devonport had £30,000 with Alexanders and £10,000 with Sandersons; in 1843 the Coventry and Warwickshire decided to put £15,000 to £20,000 with Overends.

The development of the new technique did not mean that the old business of buying bills in London was entirely superseded. From 1828 onwards—that is to say, after Lloyds had begun placing money with the bill-brokers—Williams and Rowlands of Neath were using Alexanders to buy bills for them in the London market.[4] A letter of 1841 mentions £10,000 Lloyds had available in London for the purchase of bills from Overends, and in the following year Lloyds, in writing to Overends, claimed that they had been 'steady lenders of money on Loan and dis-

---

[2] This places the independent establishment of Sandersons rather earlier than is indicated by W. T. C. King (*History of the London Discount Market*, p. 119); it is also an unexpectedly early date to find call-money placed with a bill-broker.

[3] In 1855 Samuel Gurney wrote that he believed Lloyds were one of their earliest connexions. The Gurneys had actually been in the firm since 1807, although their name was not incorporated until twenty years later. For the earlier history of the firm, see King, op. cit., pp. 17–26.

[4] Again, the money was flowing from an industrial area to the London market.

counts with you for a long time'.[5] The country bankers were in fact using the discount houses (as we can by this time call the bill-brokers) much in the same way as the banks use the discount houses today—as both a source of bills to go into the banks' portfolios and as an outlet for call money. The bill-broker was expected to guarantee the bill he sold to a bank[6] and, in the generality of cases, to deposit with the country bank's London agents sufficient bills to cover the call money placed by the country bank.

Business of this kind received fresh impetus from the slack money conditions of the early forties. In the years of depression—1841 and 1842 were about the bottom—country banks generally were finding that prudence dictated the contraction rather than the expansion of local lending, and many of them, unwilling to increase indefinitely the sums placed through their usual London channels, sought to cast their nets more widely in the London market. The Gloucestershire Banking Company, previously using Overends alone, began placing money also with Bruce Buxtons, and then with Alexanders too. Lloyds also opened business with Bruce Buxtons, putting £12,000 with them in 1844, and Lambtons of Newcastle opened an account there in the following year. In spite, however, of the opening of new accounts, the bulk of the business appears to have been in Overends' hands, and this concentration of business was encouraged by the Lombard Street bankers who acted as agents for the country bankers. The Liverpool Union Bank was for long content to leave its surplus balance with its London agent, receiving interest thereon; but when in 1849 they asked their new agents to continue this practice, Barnetts Hoares replied: 'With many of our country friends we have arranged, whenever their balances exceed a stipulated amount, to hand the surplus to Messrs. Overend & Co.' Glyns apparently adopted the same attitude. Country bankers were not always happy that so much money was going into the one firm: as early as 1855 Lloyds of Birmingham and Hammonds of Canterbury were asking questions, and in 1860–1 there were doubts expressed in Newcastle and Liverpool. The Liverpool

[5] The terms then proposed for 'loans' were '3 per cent subject to a recall at 1 day's notice'.

[6] Precisely when this became the general rule is unknown; Richardson in Evidence to the Bullion Committee (1810) had said that the brokers never guaranteed the bills they sold to bankers. Cf. King, op. cit., p. 11.

Union, refusing to accept the comforting words offered by London bankers, went so far as to withdraw all their money from Overends in 1861. Lombard Street continued to breathe reassurance about Overends' safety: only down the Strand at Twinings were there sceptics who took their money away in time. It is strange indeed that, while Overends were quietly going to rot behind their counters, distance and not proximity was the prerequisite of suspicion.

After the 1866 crash the country bank money going into the bill market was much more widely spread. Brightwen Gillett, Harwood Knight and Allen, and the National Discount Company appeared in the list of houses with which the Gloucestershire Banking Company placed funds. In 1872 Green Tompkinson and Co. managed to interest Lloyds. Ten years later Lloyds (still in Birmingham) so arranged their money market business that they had short loans maturing on different days of the week with Gilletts, Alexanders, the United Discount Corporation,[7] and Anderson and Co. Then, becoming a London bank by the 1884 amalgamations, Lloyds found their money market business becoming altogether more important to them, and their connexions gradually spread to include most of the firms in the money market.

It was apparently in the second quarter of the nineteenth century that the country banks found another outlet for short funds among London stockbrokers. In December 1826 Lloyds had £5,000 with Hichens and Co., a firm that remains one of the bank's stockbrokers; ten years later the figure had become £27,000. The stockbrokers paid Bank Rate on the money[8] and deposited Stock Exchange securities as cover. When Lloyds found in 1841 that these were mostly American stocks which had taken a bad fall, they asked for additional cover. Even Exchequer Bills could be a worry, though Lloyds were relieved to find that those lodged with them were not among the forged bills Hichens discovered a little later. The Gloucestershire Banking Company appears to have taken up this kind of business after a partner in an absorbed bank left local banking to go into the Stock Exchange: the firm of Hutchinsons, to which he went,

[7] The United was one of the two constituents of the Union Discount Company, formed in 1885.

[8] In 1866, when Bank Rate stood for three months at 10, stockbrokers bid 1 per cent. above Bank Rate and so obtained some money previously lodged in the bill market.

held £30,000 of the Gloucester bank's money a few years later, the money being fixed for three or six months at $5\frac{1}{2}$ per cent. against railway securities. The stockbrokers deposited securities in London, first at Williams Deacons and then at the Union Bank. The business continued right down to the amalgamation with the Capital and Counties in 1884, the amount outstanding at any one time reaching in later years as much as £80,000. The general presumption seems to have been that the period of loan was three months and that interest ran at $\frac{1}{2}$ per cent. above Bank Rate, subject to a minimum of $3\frac{1}{2}$.[9] From 1862 onwards this same bank began lending to other stockbrokers, and the total outstanding rose to £200,000 in 1881. The terms for these other firms were similar to those ruling the loans to Hutchinsons.

Other country banks making loans to stockbrokers included the Birmingham Joint Stock Bank, Wells Hogge and Co. of Biggleswade, and Miles, Cave, Baillie and Co. of Bristol. The last named had an unfortunate experience with the stockbrokers: securities deposited with Barnetts Hoares (the bank's London agents) proved to be worthless certificates, substituted by one of the stockbrokers who abstracted the true documents in order to cover his unsuccessful speculations in North American railway stocks. Miles Cave held Barnetts Hoares responsible, and Barnetts compromised in order to avoid the publicity of litigation. The event did of course become known in banking circles and some years later shareholders of Lloyds were seeking reassurance that business of this kind was being carefully watched. Hodgkin Barnetts at Newcastle at this same time (around 1890) lent substantial sums to the Stock Exchange but did the business entirely through their London agents (Lloyds) who for a commission of 5s. per cent. guaranteed the money: nonetheless, the Newcastle bank insisted upon checking the securities deposited by the stockbrokers. When the Bank of England, searching about for ways of adding to its income after Gladstone's hard bargaining, sought some of the Newcastle bank's business in London, Hodgkin Barnetts required that the Old Lady should, like Lloyds, guarantee loans they arranged to the Stock Exchange. The Bank would not itself give a written guarantee, but they agreed that their brokers, Mullens and Marshall, should handle

---

[9] In the dear-money period of the early sixties the rate charged did not always move with the extreme upward movements of Bank Rate.

the business and should give the required guarantee. This novel arrangement did not last long: for some reason, Mullens and Marshall never obtained such a good rate on the money as did Lloyds, and Hodgkin Barnetts very soon reverted to their custom of leaving Lloyds to place all the money.

A minor though not always negligible outlet for funds was found in other banks—other country banks or London banks not operating as the London agents of the depositing banks. There may well have been business of this kind between smaller and larger private banks in the very early days, though no trace remains. Traces first appear when the joint-stock banks were rising in the 1830's. The Evesham branch (operating with substantial independence)[10] of the Gloucestershire Banking Company in 1835 had placed money with the Birmingham Banking Company, and in 1839 also with the Royal Bank of Liverpool; in 1835 and 1836 interest receipts indicate that these deposits were equal to about one-quarter of the amount lent in the London money market. The business was not continuous: it ceased in 1839 but reappeared in the slack-money forties, and later when the London and Westminster and the London Joint Stock were added to the recipients of deposits. In 1855 Lloyds explained to Overend and Gurney that they were similarly using banking outlets in the country: 'One or two of the first-class Banking Companys having offered to take our money at call at rates fully equal (and sometimes better) than you allow we have occasionally availed ourselves of this source of employing our spare funds.' The Liverpool Union was probably one of these banks; certainly Lloyds did over a long period normally keep a substantial deposit there, without any security. Lloyds and the Liverpool Union were old friends, and the Liverpool Union had in its two main offices an unusually good lending ground. Not that Lloyds were always a bank to be at the depositing end in transactions of this kind: in the nineties they were taking deposits from the little Biggleswade bank of Wells Hogge and Co.

At the long (investment) end of the portfolios there was again wide variety and no parallel to the modern predominance of government paper. Back in the closing years of the eighteenth century, Berwick and

[10] Cf. p. 145 above.

Co. at Worcester had rather more than 12 per cent. of their resources in 'Investments'. Of the £17,700 rather less than half was a recent purchase of Consols (bought at 49½), the rest was unspecified, and may conceivably have included some lottery tickets their stockbroker had been instructed to purchase. James Oakes and Co., at Bury St. Edmunds were also about this time in the market for Consols, but left their brokers wide discretion as to purchases of these or other securities; they also seem to have been investing, as other private banks did now and later, in life assurance policies. At Birmingham, Taylors and Lloyds in their earliest days were holding South Sea Annuities and East India Bonds. In 1781, when the War of American Independence had occasioned some years of government deficit, Lloyds were holding Navy Victualling Bills, Long Annuities, and Exchequer Bills. They were still holding their East India Bonds, while a new fashion in investment showed itself in mention of 'Navigation Shares' from 1774, these probably being shares in the Birmingham Canal. By 1800 their total investment in canal shares had risen to £8,000, and through the next thirty years these formed a weighty part of the investment portfolios. Other banks were doing the same: as small a bank as Stephens Simmonds and Harris at Reading in 1802 put £300 into Thames and Medway Canal shares. It was a speculative business for bankers: there were losses long before the railway broke the canal companies' monopoly, as Taylors and Lloyds found when they revalued their investment portfolios in 1827. As far back as 1801 the Cornish Bank had refused to take Grand Junction Canal shares, as an improperly speculative investment for a bank, and other banks besides Taylors and Lloyds had reason to regret that they had been more sanguine.

A twentieth-century banker would also hold up his hands in horror at the popularity of foreign bonds among the country bankers. Hentys at Worthing, between 1827 and 1833, were holding Bank of England Stock, Consols, Exchequer Bills, and Annuities, and local government bonds, but fully one-third of the investment total consisted of foreign bonds—Brazilian, Danish, and Russian. Taylors and Lloyds had gone into American bonds as early as 1817; this may have resulted from the presence in Pennsylvania of an emigrant branch of the Lloyd family.[11] By 1821 they

---

[11] Thomas Lloyd, great-uncle of the founder of the bank, played a prominent part in the colonization and government of Pennsylvania in the late seventeenth century.

had added Prussian, Russian, and French stocks. A few years later a strangely speculative element crept into the bank's business. After Francis Lloyd (grandson of 'Charles the banker') had visited America,[12] the bank was in 1827 persuaded by Rathbones of Liverpool to sell, in America, some of their U.S. Government bonds and to invest the proceeds in raw cotton. They began with a mere $10,000, but at least thought of putting another $100,000 into the speculation a little later. They used Rathbones as agents throughout and, Lloyds not wishing their venture to be known, the cotton arrived in Lancashire consigned to Rathbones. The bank appears to have been satisfied with the outcome, for Lloyds intended to repeat it the following season. Rathbones, however, advised them to wait and see, and that was the end of the story. No memory of the family flutter seems to have been passed down in the traditions of the bank: perhaps its success made it too tempting a precedent to be embodied in the banking lore that successive generations handed down.

When the joint-stocks came on the scene, they dabbled in no such speculations but went straight for Consols. The County of Gloucester Bank purchased £100,000 of 3½ per cents. within a month of foundation. The Gloucestershire Banking Company five years after its foundation held £25,000 in British Government securities, Bank Stock, and India Stock, and only £5,500 in stocks and shares of other public companies. When, in 1838, they were experiencing a pressure of surplus funds, they thought of buying some U.S. Government bonds, but discovered that the lawyers officiating at the bank's birth had precluded investments of this kind. Within a few years an alternative outlet at home became voracious: the railways were crying out for money from private banks and joint-stocks alike. Stephens Blandy (Reading) became indirectly involved in 1842 and in 1843 they bought shares in the Brighton Railway. The North Wilts in 1842 invested £10,000 in South Eastern Railway Company debentures. In 1843 Taylors and Lloyds refused to take 4 per cent. Loan Notes of the Great Western but wrote to stockbrokers asking for advice on 'the best and most important lines of Railway as an investment' for the surplus funds they were finding so difficult to employ. This and other

---

[12] The bank voted to Francis Lloyd 100 guineas 'for his great exertion in his voyage to America and in consequence of the expenses of his outfit and private expenses'. He was not then a partner but succeeded his grandfather two years later.

evidence plainly shows how the great railway boom was fostered by the pressure of investible funds; banks new and old experienced this money-glut and served as channels through which some of the money passed into the hands of the railway-builders.

In the second half of the nineteenth century railway investments continued to be important. Debentures of the well-established home lines were regarded as 'not only safe but convertible', and preference shares were also normally included in Lloyds' portfolio and probably in bankers' portfolios generally. From the sixties Indian railway stocks were held, and a decade later foreign railway stocks too. In 1888 Howard Lloyd sought the sanction of his Board for the investment of £250,000 'in best Stock Exchange securities of the second class'; this meant a doubling of this section of the portfolio, in total investments of the order of £5 million. Subsequent lists of Lloyds, as of other banks, included more and more of colonial government, foreign government, and English local government bonds. The Bucks and Oxon Bank's portfolio of foreign bonds back in 1869 had included Russia, Turkey, Brazil, Argentine, Chile, Peru, Portugal, and the U.S.A.; this was exceptional but does indicate how wide a choice of foreign bonds a bank could contemplate. Widely scattered private banks appear to have regarded variety of investments—and a wide geographical spread—as much more important than a high proportion of British Government stocks. Among joint-stocks, the County of Gloucester Bank in 1880 had about one-third of its investment portfolios in British Governments, the remainder being in railways, colonial governments, and municipal bonds; in 1892 this bank was buying Jamaica Railway Mortgage Bonds, Cape of Good Hope Inscribed Stock, and Ceylon Inscribed Stock.

In noticing this variety of investments it is necessary to remember that bankers had not in those days a wide range of British Government stocks from which to choose. There were not available successive maturities at reasonably near dates, such as would have allowed a banker to hold maturities for almost every year through the following ten or fifteen years. If he wanted to hold British Government stocks alone, there were very few maturities and the weight of his investment necessarily went into the undated Consols. When interest rates went down to very low levels Goschen came along and reduced the rate on Consols; when interest rates rose, Consols depreciated. The shortcomings of Consols as bank investments became all too plain at the end of the century, and their weakening effect was, as we shall see,[13] a factor in driving some of the smaller banks to throw in their hands. The wider range of colonial and foreign government and English municipal bonds at least gave the banker the chance to space his maturities sensibly, and the higher yields obtainable on these and on railway stocks seemed in Victorian England ample compensation for the risks they carried. At least these securities did not appear, like Consols, to be in the 'heads you win, tails I lose' class. And if it came to borrowing in a crisis, experience showed that Consols were no more useful than any other Stock Exchange securities.[14] Given these general conditions, there was room for the exercise of individual judgement between a very wide range of securities a banker might reasonably hold, and it was inevitable that there should be wide variety in the composition of portfolios.

All this was changed by the 1914–18 war. The British Government offered a rapid succession of new and dated securities, many of them with quite short lives. Self-interest coincided with patriotism, and the banks took up such large amounts that it soon became natural to expect a bank's investment portfolio to consist very largely of British Government securities. The change appears sharply in the successive balance-sheets of Lloyds Bank: at the end of 1914 'Consols and other British and Indian Government Securities' stood at £7,825,343 and were slightly exceeded by 'Other securities' at £8,308,173; four years later the 'Other securities' had actually dwindled to £1,380,324 while the 'Governments' had leapt to £53,630,322. This transformation, a transformation on which there has been no going back, was typical of all the banks. Investment policy ceased to be a matter of holding a relatively small block of Consols and spreading the bulk of the money over a wide range of 'second-class' securities. It became instead the much simpler business of spreading huge funds over a time-scale of government stocks. Some of the fun had gone out of banking for ever—and some of the profit and loss.

[13] Cf. p. 256 below.
[14] Cf. p. 213 below.

9

WEST END BANKING TRADITIONS

═══

THE days when banking was a mere sideline to the business of a great merchant, manufacturer, goldsmith, or tax-collector belong to the century before the last. Specialization has become the order of the day, and the banker, like most other specialists, expects to concentrate his energies very largely in his chosen line of business. But there is one instance in Lloyds Bank where the traditional ancillary business has persisted: the Army agency of 'Cox's branch' in Pall Mall, a colourful heritage from the eighteenth century, has remained to give a peculiar character to the work of this large office. In another of the 'West End' forerunners of contemporary branches of Lloyds, Herries Farquhar in St. James's Street, the eighteenth century saw the birth of the travellers' cheques that have now become a part of every bank's business. Like other ancillary services provided for the convenience of customers, this business has been stimulated by the direction taken by competition between banks in the twentieth century, to such an extent that it has become almost improper to regard it as a sideline. But there was a time when it was the novel speciality of a West End bank, and this bank, like Cox's, has a special place in the traditions of Lloyds Bank.

The work of the Pall Mall branch as Army agent has its origin in the organization of the Army from the time of its formation, in the seventeenth century, into regiments each commanded, under authority of the Army's Commander-in-Chief, by a Colonel. In the words of an official memorandum of 1841,[1] every part of the Regiments'

---

[1] This memorandum is in the possession of the Pall Mall branch of Lloyds Bank. An early official account of the Army agent's function is to be found in the Report from the Select Committee appointed to consider the state of His Majesty's Land Forces and Marines, BPP. 1st series, vol. ii.

internal economy, their discipline, their clothing, their arms and appointments, should be conducted through the medium of their respective Colonels, who for the due and effective performance of all the details indispensable to the complete efficiency of each corps, should be held responsible.... To enable the Colonel to transact all the manifold business necessarily arising out of these various duties, he is allowed the assistance of a Secretary, who being especially appointed for this purpose by a Power of Attorney from the Colonel, becomes *de facto* the Regimental Agent, and thus empowered communicates when necessary and in the Colonel's name (for he has no other authority) with the Public Offices of the State, and with every individual of the Regiment under the Colonel's immediate command, thus becoming the medium through which all the business of the Regiment is transacted through every part of its detail.

In 1758 (during the Seven Years' War) Lord Ligonier, Colonel of the 1st Foot Guards (after Waterloo known as the Grenadier Guards) appointed his secretary, Mr. Richard Cox, to be the regimental agent. With two clerks in his house in Albemarle Street, Cox undertook the business with such success that the agency for most other regiments had come into the firm's hands before Waterloo. The tremendous enlargement of the work during the French Wars gave rise to parliamentary inquiry in 1798, and a Select Committee reported in favour of continuance of the system. Reforming brooms were again busy in the long peace between Waterloo and the Crimea, but in 1828 and again in 1841 the system survived all assaults, Palmerston himself taking up the cudgels in its defence. The weight of authoritative evidence, both administrative and military, was clearly on its side, and an alternative plan had short shrift as partaking 'largely of the defects of the times, namely, a mania for the creation of new offices'.

At the time of these inquiries the functions of the Army agents were at their maximum. The responsibility of the Colonel for the clothing and equipment of the Regiment involved purchase, collection, and forwarding of numerous items, and various financial adjustments with the men under his command. Then there was the

managing and settling all pecuniary matters relating to the sale and purchase of Military Commissions. . . . The Mess and Band Funds, investing in and receiving back monies from the Savings Banks, becoming joint Trustees for officers labouring under Mental Delusion, for sums invested in the Public

191

Funds for non-commissioned officers and privates who may be abroad, occasionally taking out . . . Letters of Administration for Officers and Men dying
abroad . . ., receiving Prize Money . . . recovery of lodging money for Officers,
travelling expenses, losses of baggage . . . Remittances are made by Officers
of Corps abroad and particularly in India, for the use of their families or
friends, and also by soldiers on the same account. . . .

For all these services and the transmission of pay, the agent received,
for a regiment of 740 rank and file, £232 a year; this had to cover all office
costs and losses due to bad debts, frauds and mistakes. Even when
organized on a large scale this would hardly have been remunerative
business by itself; in fact Cox's made it pay by developing a very extensive general banking business for military men and their families who
were brought into contact by the Army's arrangements.

In 1854 the agent's duties were substantially lessened, all clothing
business being removed from the Colonel's responsibility. In 1881 the
appointment of agent itself ceased to be the Colonel's business, but the
War Office continued the system; the commission paid, having been
reduced in 1858, was about $1\frac{1}{2}$ per cent. on disbursements. Even this
reduced remuneration was terminated in 1892, the agent being left to
make his income out of the banking profits that could be made to grow
out of the link with Service officers. These are now not confined to the
Army, for in the twentieth century the Royal Air Force followed the
Army in the employment of Cox's as agents for the management of
officers' pay and allowances. Expansion of the business had meanwhile
meant successive changes of premises: from Albemarle Street to Craig's
Court in the 1760's, from Craig's Court to Charing Cross in 1888, and
finally to Pall Mall in 1923.

Its association with the red coat has always made for picturesqueness
in the business of this office. Royalty and the famous families of the
aristocracy have provided many a customer—many a borrower, indeed,
since it was a recognized privilege of officers to keep a small balance on
the debit side and the banker had sometimes advanced the capital required for the purchase of a commission or promotion. When the Duke
of York introduced his banker to King George III, it was as 'the gentleman who keeps my money'. 'I think it is rather his Royal Highness who
keeps mine', the banker corrected; this of course was how Mr. Cox and

his successors made their living. The ways of an office have to be adapted to the predominant type of customer, and well into the present century officers of the Guards retained the privilege of going to a special counter where they could call for the ledger in order to inspect their accounts. This friendly privilege had long died out in banking generally, but at Cox's it lasted until subalterns became too curious about those other pages that told tales of the Colonel's habits.

Now that red coats have given way to khaki and the War Office has taken away many of the former duties of the agent, the business has become less unlike that of any other bank. But in the years of national peril, when many other offices found business rather quieter than usual, Cox's necessarily experienced spectacular expansion. In 1914 Cox's had a staff of 180 and in 1918 4,500. Through that war the office was manned day and night; cheques were cashed twenty-four hours a day, Sundays and Bank Holidays included, for officers arriving from or returning to the Front. In the second war, when Cox's had become the Pall Mall branch of Lloyds Bank, mechanization allowed business to expand without such an increase of personnel. The face of business was different too: the 'Leave Train' had dominated London in 1914–18 in a way it never did in the second war, and 'Cox's' (as Army men still called it) observed ordinary banking hours, though a ring at the bell would bring down a resident cashier in his dressing-gown. After 1945 the work shrank again, when many of the accounts went to other branches; but Pall Mall remains, with its staff of well over 1,000, one of the biggest bank offices in the country, and still one with a character all its own.

When they were already well established as bankers to Army families Cox's naturally enough became important also in the arrangement of foreign credits for travellers. This special line of business had been developed in the eighteenth century by another West End banking house that eventually found its way into Lloyds Bank: Herries Farquhar and Co. in St. James's Street. The founder of this firm, and the originator of the travellers' cheque, was Robert Herries, son of an impoverished Scottish laird who put his boy into a merchant's business in Rotterdam. Robert had soon moved into the great firm of Hope and Co. at Amsterdam (their wide European connexions were destined to be of great importance to

Herries) and thence, at the age of 23, to set up business on his own account in Barcelona. There he prospered and soon added partnerships in businesses at Valencia and Montpellier. In his Rotterdam days he had known John Coutts of Edinburgh, and when the Coutts family was looking for fresh blood for their banking and merchanting business in Edinburgh and London, Herries had the obvious qualifications.

The Coutts family at this time had two London establishments, the counting-house in Jeffrey's Square, St. Mary Axe, which was essentially the London correspondent of the Edinburgh house, and Messrs. Coutts, bankers in the Strand, which derived from the earlier firm of Middleton and Campbell through the marriage of a young Coutts into the Campbell family. At the beginning of the 1760's the thriving branch of the Coutts family was ruling the Strand business, while the Edinburgh and Jeffrey's Square partnerships had run thin. It was to strengthen these last two firms that the Strand brothers brought in Robert Herries and others in 1762. The Edinburgh partnership was henceforth to become a purely banking house (to include 'dealing in exchanges on London, Holland, and France'); this firm was to have the title John Coutts and Co. The house in London, at Jeffrey's Square, was to confine itself 'chiefly . . . to the sale and purchase of goods on commission and the business of exchanges'; it was called Herries, Cochrane and Co., Robert Herries being one of the active partners. Through the next twelve years Robert Herries was clearly in the ascendant, and the Coutts interest in the two houses was finally broken in 1774.

Coutts remained (as their name remains to this day) bankers in the Strand and, although the connexion had come to lack cordiality, the Herries partnerships in London and Edinburgh continued to do business with Coutts. It was therefore natural enough that it was to Coutts that Robert Herries in 1769 or 1770 took an idea for supplying travellers with money on the Continent. The story is told by Forbes, who had for some years been in the Edinburgh partnership.[2]

In the course of his [Herries] own journeys on the continent, and in the transacting of business, he had remarked that travellers were not unfrequently exposed to inconvenience and disappointment while abroad, by having their

[2] *Memoirs of a Banking-House*, by the late Sir William Forbes of Pitsligo, Bart., 2nd ed., Edinburgh, 1860, pp. 28 et seq.

letters of credit limited to particular places, while they might wish, perhaps, to change their route, but from which they were prevented until they wrote home to have their credits altered, and, perhaps, before those new credits reached them, they had again changed their plans and wished to follow a still different route. Mr. Herries bethought him, therefore, of issuing what should serve as an universal letter of credit in the form of promissory-notes, which should be payable at all the principal places in Europe where travellers were likely to be. For this purpose it became necessary to establish correspondents in all those various places who would give money to the travellers for these promissory-notes, at the current exchange of the place on London, without any charge or deduction whatsoever. The convenience to the traveller of this device was obvious; and Mr. Herries was to find his profit from the use of the money, which of course was to be paid to him on his issuing the notes, till they again came round to London, after having been paid by his agents abroad.

Finding Coutts not interested in implementing the plan, Herries with others took a house in St. James's Street, entered into partnership as The London Exchange Banking Company, and opened for business on 1 January 1772.[3] The ostensible business of the firm was to issue promissory notes to travellers, payable on the Continent; one at least of Herries's partners had no ulterior motive. But customers who came for travellers' notes were willing enough to do their other banking business under the same roof, and the energetic Robert Herries was not one to let his chances pass him by. The situation in the West End had been chosen with a view to an aristocratic clientèle, in an age that regarded the continental Grand Tour as more important than a university education. The customers who called in at St. James's Street were thus drawn from the same circles as those who frequented Coutts's in the Strand, and although there was no soliciting of Coutts's customers, relations between the two houses went from bad to worse. Mr. Herries was not the man to be worried by that.

The arrangements he made were comparatively simple, and were made posible by the widespread business connexions Herries and his associates carried from their previous mercantile business on the Continent.

The Circular Exchange Notes [a notice explained] are given for any even sum from Twenty Pounds upwards, payable at any one of various places on the Continent of Europe, at the option of the possessor, who is furnished with

[3] Specimen documents indicate that plans had reached an advanced stage, and were perhaps being implemented, before the end of 1769.

a Letter of order for that purpose addressed to the Agents of the Company at those different places. Those Agents are alone instructed to distinguish the Authenticity of the Notes, and are also instructed to take two receipts serving for one sole purpose, one by way of discharge, the other separately to prove the payment in case any of the Notes, which therefore are not negotiable to indifferent persons, should be lost, in sending them back discharged. Their value is reduced into foreign money at the current usance course of Exchange on London at the time and place of payment.

The notice concluded with the following list of places where the notes could be encashed:

Amsterdam	Genoa	Prague
Aix la Chapelle	Ghendt	Rheims
Aix in Provence	Gibraltar	Riga
Alicante	Gothenburg	Rochelle
Angers	The Hague	Rome
Antwerp	Hamburgh	Seville
Auxsberg	Hanover	Spa
Avignon	Konisberg	Stockholm
Barcelona	Leghorn	Strasburg
Bayonne	Leipzig	Toulouse
Berlin	Liege	Tours
Berne	Lille	Turin
Besancon	Lisbon	Valencia
Bilbao	Lyons	Venice
Blois	Madrid	Vienna
Bordeaux	Malaga	Warsaw
Bologna	Mannheim	
Boulogne Sur Mer	Marseilles	*Additional Names*
Brussels	Middleburg	Amiens
Brunswick	Milan	Basle
Cadiz	Montpellier	Bruges
Caen	Moscow	Dunkirk
Carthagena	Munich	Lausanne
Cologne	Nancy	Ostend
Copenhagen	Nants	Rouen
Dantzig	Naples	St. Omer
Dijon	Nice	Trieste
Dresden	Orleans	Rotterdam
Florence	Paris	Rattisbon
Franckfort on the Mayn	Parma	Narva
Geneva	Petersburg	L'Quentin

196

The notes were paid without the deduction of any commission; Herries made his profit by having the use of the travellers' money (between the purchase of the notes in London and their encashment abroad) and by the attraction of general banking business.

This general banking business flourished and acquired additional prestige when, after the knighting of Robert Herries, it took the description 'Sir Robert Herries & Company'. But the issue of travellers' notes for long remained the business by which the firm was most generally known. By 1790 the list of continental towns at which the notes were payable had grown much longer, and places as distant as Smyrna and St. Petersburg were included. The long explanations that had characterized earlier notices had given way to the terse statement: 'This business is now so generally known as not to require any other explanation than is contained in the Notes, etc., themselves.' In 1815 or thereabouts the system was extended to cover the British West Indies and came into general use by Service men and civilians travelling to those islands. At the same time Herries Farquhar and Co., as the bankers had now become, saw in the termination of the French wars opportunity for development of the business on the Continent. The following circular, prepared in the brief peace when Napoleon was at Elba, was actually circulated a few months after Waterloo, to 250 of the principal country bankers:

Sirs,

As, in consequence of the restoration of general Peace, many persons of all classes will doubtless take excursions to the continent, either for health, business or pleasure; and, as enquiries may probably often be made of you with regard to the mode by which travellers can best be supplied with money during such excursions, we take the liberty to enclose a few copies of our plan of Circular Notes, which we are persuaded will be found superior in every respect to ordinary Letters of Credit, and, if you would have the goodness to communicate the same to any of your Friends who may require information on the subject, we shall feel particularly obliged to you.

Signed—Herries, Farquhar & Co.

Experience had long shown that other bankers were compelled to oblige their customers by applying to Herries Farquhar for Circular Letters of Credit, and it is not surprising that St. James's Street thought it worth while to advertise their facilities to country bankers. They were

by this time having to face important competition from West End neighbours. Among early partners of Sir Robert Herries was Thomas Hammersley, who left the firm in 1782 and was soon afterwards in a banking
partnership with Charles Greenwood (whose sister he had married) and
others. The Greenwoods were cousins of the Cox family; from 1783
onwards there was always a Greenwood partner in Cox and Co., and into
that firm the Hammersley and Greenwood business appears to have been
merged. Probably by 1814, and certainly by 1821, Cox's had assumed the
style of Hammersley, Greenwood, Cox and Co., with a partner from each
of those three related families. The Army agency work remained the
primary business of this partnership, but the fact that Army men were
frequent travellers naturally encouraged the development of this bank's
services to travellers generally, and the Hammersleys brought the tradition from Herries. So, when David Ricardo went on his continental tour
in 1822, it was notes 'of Hammersley's' that he took with him.[4] He changed
a £50 note at 'Mr. Ferrier's counting-house' in Rotterdam, and at Frank-
fort a fortnight later called for the same purpose on Messrs. Gogel, Koch
and Co., a firm famous as exporters of hock to England but also doing
an extensive remittance business. At Basle he changed another £50; at
Zurich a few days later, not wanting to be in town during business hours,
he asked his landlord to apply to 'Hammersley's correspondent' and
thereby involved himself in an argument about the rate of exchange. The
fault was none of Hammersley's, nor of their correspondent's, for the
landlord had been his own exchange market. Ten weeks later, on his
homeward journey, Ricardo's stock of 'Hammersley's notes' had run out,
and he was made to feel the difference.

I entered Lyon [he wrote] without money and with an exhausted exchequer
in bills. I was without credit and unknown. I endeavoured to get money from a
banker here by a display of my Passport, which gave me my most distinguishing title; a letter with some complimentary expressions of their confidence in
me from Messrs. Delessert; and lastly certificates of a large sum of French
Stock being in my name; but without success—they would not give me a
shilling.—My good-natured landlord came to my relief in my difficulties and
advanced me 2,000 francs, which I am to repay in Paris.

[4] *The Works and Correspondence of David Ricardo*, ed. P. Sraffa (Cambridge, 1955),
vol. x, pp. 195, 223, 244, and 341.

While their original line of business had thus ceased to be a monopoly and was destined in the next century to become a commonplace of every bank in the country, Herries Farquhar were going from strength to strength as West End bankers to the aristocracy and landed gentry. As such they continued the West End tradition, in contrast to that of Lombard Street, that they were uninterested in discounting mercantile paper but very much interested in government bonds and other investments of that class. During the Napoleonic Wars they were particularly active when new issues of bonds were being made by the Treasury. The system remained that of a few finance houses contracting with the Treasury, while the general run of subscribers had to depend upon getting into the lists of the contractors.[5] Among the contractors were the famous names of Baring, Ricardo, and Goldsmid. Herries Farquhar would have themselves entered, for substantial sums, sometimes on the lists of one or other of these famous houses, but more frequently they were on the lists of Trower and Battye or Reid Irving and Co. Herries Farquhar in turn would have their own lists, in which would be entered sums for the partners as individuals and for customers. There would also be sums in the names of their clerks and, more surprisingly, the clerks of other banks; these clerks would be tendering, in effect, for customers or other acquaintances, and no doubt made some useful pocket-money out of the transaction. In a loan contracted for on 14 June 1815, for example, Herries Farquhar appear to have had £540,000 on Trower's list; in the event they took up £270,000. Out of £270,000, £22,500 was listed for Sir W. Farquhar and £6,000 for J. C. Herries. Other individuals took a total of £18,000. Eight groups of bank clerks took a total of £8,000, and eight of their own clerks £1,000 each, leaving £207,500 for Herries Farquhar themselves to take up. In the 1820 loan they had £340,000 on the three connected lists of Battye's, Ward's, and Reid Irving's; out of this total £45,000 was for partners and other individuals while twelve of 'our own clerks' had £1,000 each, a figure that appears to have been the conventional privilege of the Herries Farquhar clerks.

Papers relating to the 1835 issue open a window through which may be seen something of the to and fro involved in these bond issues. At this

---

[5] The system has been described in the *Works and Correspondence of David Ricardo*, op. cit., vol. x, pp. 75–91.

time the partner in charge of this side of Herries Farquhar's activities was Sir Thomas Farquhar, and he appears to have acted mainly through Reid Irving's as contractors; Lord Melbourne and Spring-Rice were those concerned at the Treasury. The story begins with a statement dated 25 July 1835:

> Notice has been given to the Stock Exchange that Lord Melbourne and T. Rice will be ready to state the amount of Loan required, the time and manner of bidding to any parties who may attend at the Treasury on Wednesday next at 11 o'clock.

Two days later (on the Monday) Farquhar seems to have been on the Treasury's doorstep:

> While Sir T. H. F.'s carriage was waiting at Lord Melbourne's door, Mr. Irving left word he wished to see Sir Thos. Farquhar. Mr. Irving stated that his House and Barings, supported by Jones Loyd and other influential Firms, had determined to bid for the Loan. He did not know any of the particulars— it is supposed it will be either 12, 15 or 20,000,000 in 3 per cents—the biddings in $3\frac{1}{2}$ per cents. Mr. Irving offered to insert our names in Reid, Irving & Company's list if we should wish it.

On Tuesday Farquhar, in the firm's name, wrote, 'In consequence of the conversation I had with you yesterday, I should wish that, if convenient to you, my name may be included in the list you are making for the ensuing Loan for Two hundred Thousand Pounds and you will oblige.' But when Irving went along to the Treasury on Wednesday, he evidently did not like the terms, for on Thursday he wrote informing Herries Farquhar, 'it is not our intention to make any Bidding for the Loan announced yesterday morning, at the meeting held at the Treasury'. On this occasion, therefore, the Herries clerks did not enjoy their customary opportunity of placing £1,000 of the new loan.

With all their foreign connexions, it is not surprising that Herries Farquhars participated in the great development of English lending abroad in the decades that followed Waterloo. Through Rothschilds in Paris they took up £200,000 of French Government bonds in 1830 and another £200,000 through Delepert and Co. of Paris. At a time when the restored Bourbons were just about to fall, this was a little rash, and a few weeks later Herries Farquhars thought of selling. Rothschilds advised them to hold: they refused to believe that a constitutional upheaval was imminent, and Herries apparently held on.

The rise of joint-stock banks in London meant intensified competition, even for such an aristocratic business as this St. James's Street bank had always maintained, but Herries Farquhar stood up to the strain. They continued to attract the typically West End custom—a saddler in Ryder Street, the Clerk of the Kitchen at Buckingham Palace, the Oxford and Cambridge Club, the Bishop of Winchester's son, and the wife of H. R. Baring. And once they secured a customer they held on: few accounts were closed otherwise than by death. Thus deposits, from £226,000 in 1815, reached half a million ten years later and held close to that level through the competitive quarter of a century. After 1850 they rose further, and after the purchase of the little Bond Street bank of Call Marten and Co. the deposits soon reached the million mark. The Circular Notes of Credit reached their peak, £120,000 in 1839; they remained between £50,000 and £100,000 for decades afterwards, though the unsettlement of Europe in 1848 seems to have scared the travellers and sent the total for 1849 down to £36,473. Bad debts, even in the Circular Notes business, were generally low. Profits, after averaging four or five thousand a year at the beginning of the century, were £7,228 in 1843, £36,629 in 1873, and about £40,000 just before the business was merged into Lloyds. The business was then, in 1893, presided over by Sir Walter Farquhar who had earned, by service running well over half a century, the title of 'the grand old man of the bank'. But his day, like the day of independent banks, was obviously coming to an end, and Lloyds Bank bought the business. They had earlier opened an office in St. James's Street at No. 54; the business of this branch was brought up to No. 16 in 1896, with Alexander Duff continuing as manager for a brief period before he assumed the General Managership of Lloyds Bank. The building that now stands on the original Herries site was erected in 1910 to house the greatly enlarged business. It is an imposing building architecturally, more successful than many other offices of that period. Robert Herries would probably have approved of this monument to his foundation, but his true memorial lies rather in the travellers' cheques in the pockets of every British traveller as he leaves these islands. In 1955 Lloyds Bank issued more than one and a half million of these cheques to a total value of £14 million or so and out of Herries' list of places for encashment had grown negotiability in countries throughout the world.[6]

The Herries business was thus merged into Lloyds and its distinctive contribution to English banking has become a commonplace shared by every bank in the country. By contrast, Hammersley, Greenwood, Cox and Co. retained their independence down into the 1920's, and their peculiar business became almost their monopoly. The title of the firm had reverted to its earlier form, Cox and Co., although the Hammersley connexion was maintained. This bank was also notable for its overseas extension, almost unique in English domestic banking before 1914. The extension arose from its business for Army families: the importance of India in the life of Army men was continually increased during the nineteenth century, and it was primarily to improve facilities for its Army customers that Cox and Co. opened a branch at Bombay in 1905. Another was opened at Rawalpindi in 1906; then a sub-branch at a hot-weather station and new branches at Karachi and Srinagar in 1907. The establishment at Calcutta in 1911 marked a further departure, for this was intended primarily for commercial customers, and business of this kind was also now developed at Bombay and Karachi. After the first war the spirit of expansion bit more deeply into Cox's and branches were opened at Rangoon, Cairo, and Alexandria; several agencies were established in Upper and Lower Egypt and two ginning factories were acquired. To cope with the new class of business arising from these Eastern branches Cox's opened an office in Gracechurch Street in 1922.

In this overseas business Cox and Co. had a rival both in Pall Mall and in the City: the bank of Henry S. King and Co. This little firm had a long history as booksellers, stationers, East India agents, shippers, and bankers, a business that had in 1868 become concentrated on banking and agency work relating to Indian trade. It had a Cornhill office as well as the West End office, and connected businesses in Bombay and Calcutta, to which Port Said, Delhi, and Simla were added later. Throughout these developments the firm remained a purely family partnership and it was failure of the family succession that put an end to its independence at the end of 1922. The ageing senior partner arranged an amalgamation

---

[6] There is a lawyer's difference between the circular note and the modern travellers' cheque.

with the rivals across the street; but 'Cox and Kings' had scarcely any independent life as bankers, though the ancillary business has continued under that name. The bank of Cox and Kings was almost immediately taken over by Lloyds Bank. The story of this amalgamation must await a later generation; its sequel was the organization of the Eastern Department of Lloyds Bank with its Head Office now in Threadneedle Street. The offices founded both by Cox's and by King's in Egypt were soon afterwards sold to the National Bank of Egypt; the Indian business of both these old firms was reorganized and became the basis of the present sixteen main branches spread over India, Pakistan, and Burma. The business of Cox and Co. as Army agents remained at Pall Mall, giving still a distinctive flavour to that very large branch. Its unique business is almost all that is left as a reminder of the days when the West End bankers were sturdy firms, doing specialist business for an aristocratic clientèle and rather looking down their noses at those mercantile fellows down in Lombard Street.

10

DAYS OF CRISIS

———

THE people who can remember a banking crash in England must by this time (1957) be a minority of the population: some of us can remember newspaper photographs of angry depositors crowding outside the shuttered offices of Farrow's Bank, and there are a few who can say that their fathers lost money in that collapse. There are memories, too, of 1914, when the delicate mechanism of the City of London was thrown out of gear by the international political crisis. But these events are fading into the background of living memories, and the banking system appears to have become immune to the troubles that used to lead to suspension of business. This immunity has its origin in many of the developments discussed elsewhere in this book; in part the immunity is, like immunities the human body develops, the system's own response to the afflictions of earlier days. One curious result is that fiction writers of our generation portray our banking offices as the dens of sleepy unadventurous fellows whose only task is to follow the even tenor of their way. Things were not always like this; the nineteenth-century novelists could always give the story a fresh turn by bringing the local bank crashing down. And there was substance in their fiction, as the records of Lloyds and its constituent banks can show.

Sometimes the crisis that upset the local banker was part of a widespread storm centred upon the City of London: the 'commercial convulsions' that afflicted English economic life every ten years or so through the nineteenth century took their toll in the banking system. Others could be purely local, unconnected with events in the City, and causing hardly a ripple—if that—in the quiet waters of Lombard Street. One of these purely local storms burst upon Lloyds and Co. in 1856, when the firm was still a family business working in the one Birmingham office. A trivial local occurrence started it off: for some reason certain railway stations suddenly refused to accept payment in the notes of local private banks. Would-be passengers from Solihull and Coleshill stations quickly alarmed the neighbourhood with their story that Lloyds' notes (those circulating in this area) were being refused; the obvious inference was that the railways suspected the solvency of Lloyds. Not only the noteholders but also the depositors naturally hurried to the bank to demand gold.

Lloyds were in fact in no difficulty—until the unexpected demand for gold descended upon them. Their first step was to go to the Birmingham branch of the Bank of England, through which they were by now accustomed to draw on London funds. The branch came to their aid with that newfangled device the telegraph, in order to mobilize Lloyds' resources in London, against which the Bank of England could hand over gold in Birmingham. They called part of their balances with Alexanders, the discount house, and instructed Hanburys (their London agents) to sell £8,000 Exchequer Bonds and £3,500 Exchequer Bills. £12,000 was at two days' notice with Hichens, the stockbrokers; due notice was given to withdraw this sum, but Hichens waived the second day's notice. All this was put to the credit of Lloyds at the branch Bank of England. Two days later they believed the worst over but, as the weekly wage day of the local manufacturers might involve further exceptional demands, they telegraphed to Hichens to sell the remainder (£16,000) of their Exchequer Bills, and took preliminary steps towards mobilizing further resources, including some Bank of England Stock. The partners were, however, right in their belief that the storm was passing and when, two days later, a wealthy local family offered assistance, Lloyds were able to say that all was well. There had been the annoyance, of course, and the expense involved in realizing securities. Reflecting on the episode, the partners appreciated the speed the new telegraph had given to their efforts to mobilize their resources. They did reflect also that telegraph clerks might gossip and so add to the panic; certain abbreviations and inverted signatures were therefore included in standing instructions for the future.

In 1874 just such another local storm burst upon the Lincolnshire bank of Messrs. Garfit Claypon and Co. At Spilsby, Boston, and other places where the bank was in business, a malicious and unfounded rumour was circulated. The run was comparatively slight, but sufficiently threatening to induce the partners to take prompt measures. At Boston 'they called in several solicitors and some of the largest tradesmen and submitted to them indubitable proof that their resources were very far in excess of the sum total of the claims that could be made upon them. We are glad to learn', the local newspaper added, 'that, so far as Boston is concerned, the effect of the rumour has been very slight, the withdrawals being limited to a few deposit accounts.' (As in the great American banking crisis fifty-eight years later, it was the 'time deposits' that proved the most volatile.) Efforts were made to track down the origin of 'the villainous report' but, as no slander or libel suit followed, presumably the villain escaped. The purport of the rumour was evidently too libellous to be reported in the newspaper; it failed to put the bank's shutters up, but the bank had to incur 'serious expense in fighting the shadow'.

To the economic historian of nineteenth-century England certain years of financial crisis are as familiar as the stations down the line: 1825, the Christmas that wrought such havoc among the country banks; the three mid-century crises of 1847, 1857, and 1866; 1878, when a Glasgow bank went down with a crash that shook every banker in Britain; and 1890, a shudder rather than a crash. There were other years too, when banks were in special difficulty—most notably 1837, followed by only one quiet year before 1839 proved another difficult year. In each of these years the crisis was felt, to some degree, in these banks, and their experiences in the successive episodes illustrate their growing strength and resilience. As time went on the repercussions of general economic disturbance upon the banks were less devastating: for the banks the significance of 1890 and 1907, for example, is not so much that they were years of crisis as that they ushered in years of depression. At the other end of the century smaller fluctuations in economic activity could occasion days of actual danger for local groups of banks. In 1815 the months after Waterloo were, for the system as a whole, 'deceptively encouraging' and at the Bank of England there was 'complacency from the Governor's Chair'.[1] Yet locally these months appeared full of hazard.[2] Several Durham banks failed in July: Mowbray, Hollingsworth and Co., Lumley, Smith and Co., and Hammond, Hirst and Close. This was enough to

---

[1] Clapham, *The Bank of England*, vol. ii, p. 50.
[2] Cf. L. S. Pressnell, *Country Banking in the Industrial Revolution*, p. 471.

shake a large area, and a meeting of local landowners came to the support of the Newcastle banks, declaring their willingness to take the notes of those whose doors were still open. Merchants and tradesmen shortly afterwards joined in similar declarations, and further trouble was avoided. A few weeks later a trail of bankruptcies (not of bankers themselves) in Cornwall was spreading alarm, and Praeds and Co. decided that they had been lending too easily for business that effectively locked up their money. Besides taking such immediate steps as they could by way of restricting advances and calling for additional security, the partners resolved on certain long-term rules of policy. Against their issue of notes they would henceforward hold government securities (never to be less than £100,000) and short-dated bills amounting to not less than two-thirds of the notes outstanding. Together these incidents of 1815 illustrate the typical response of early nineteenth-century bankers to the storms into which they ran—their reliance on the declarations of local men of substance, and the exercise of greater caution in lending to customers.

For the generality of banks up and down the country, the great financial crises of the century appeared as having originated in London. Thus it was the freezing of their London funds that caused Hartland and Co. at Evesham, Tewkesbury, and Cheltenham to stop payment on 20 December 1825, and the news of this suspension led to a brief run on Lechmere, Wall and Isaac at Tewkesbury. Like many other country banks that suspended payment it was only temporary suspension for Hartlands. Sometimes the country bankers managed to move a little ahead of the metropolitan crisis, as in the autumn of 1836, when things were getting tight but not positively critical in London and the Liverpool Union Bank decided that the times—and not their own reserve position—necessitated reduction of advances to customers. By the end of November the London money market had developed 'extreme pressure', and at this stage Robarts Curtis (London agents) warned Berwick Lechmere (Worcester bankers) that the latter's outstanding debt could not be continued. Eleven years later Taylors and Lloyds at Birmingham could hardly believe the news of the restrictive action taken by the Bank of England in the first phase of the 1847 crisis; they stiffened their attitude to local customers at once. In 1866 the Overend Gurney crash was not entirely unforeseen in the country—the Canterbury Bank was suspicious as early as 1855—but when the crisis did come it was one more example of trouble beginning in London. Widespread runs on country banks would have been surprising; in fact the days passed quietly enough, and the country bankers had time to consider how they could protect themselves in the dark days that obviously lay ahead. 1878, which began not in London but in Glasgow, caused altogether more nervousness among bank customers in many parts of the country. The City of Glasgow Bank collapsed in October, and when this was followed in December by the somewhat similar failure of the West of England and South Wales District Bank, tension was high enough to bring grave trouble upon any banks that were exposed to fortuitous suspicion. Tweedy Williams at Truro happened to circulate an announcement of the death of the last surviving partner from the Williams family; the tension was so high that an enemy of the bank (a discontented former partner) was able by scurrilous pamphlets to provoke a run on the bank to the extent of forcing it to close its doors despite its actual solvency. The Baring Crisis of 1890, on the other hand, was like the Overend Gurney crisis in being a London-brewed storm. Some country bankers had a pretty shrewd idea that trouble was coming; the County of Gloucester Bank was drawing in its horns in mid-October, three weeks before the famous Sunday when the Governor of the Bank of England took his son to the Zoo.[3] Howard Lloyd himself had word from Edward Hoare, the City Manager of Lloyds, who noticed the excessive amount of Barings bills being presented and met Lloyd in November gloom at Euston to discuss what they should do about it.

While banks were small and purely local, there is no doubt that the quickest way of precluding panic was to secure a declaration by local men of substance. On 2 January 1826, after Hartlands' suspension in Gloucestershire, five independent persons issued a notice to the effect that they had investigated the bank's accounts and assured the public that 20s. in the £ could be paid and £97,000 left over for the proprietors. Confidence in local banks (Turners as well as Hartlands) was soon re-established; a hatter's shop in Cheltenham proclaimed

> John Church's will, as others do,
> Take Hartlands' notes and Turners' too.

[3] The story of this Sunday is told by Clapham (*The Bank of England*, vol. ii, p. 328), cf. p. 155 above.

208

The Mayor and Aldermen of Worcester, this same month, publicly declared their confidence in the bankers of Worcester, and soon all was quiet again in the West Country. In Berkshire that same crisis threatened to bring down the Wallingford Bank. Their London agents (Pole Thornton) had put up the shutters, and in the light of this event the retirement (through illness) of a Wallingford partner was assumed to be due to dissatisfaction with the bank's affairs. Hedges himself (the retiring partner) issued a circular, and this was backed by two declarations, each signed by about ninety people, expressing confidence and willingness to accept the notes of the bank. In 1857 the Mayor of Worcester followed his predecessor's example; he convened a public meeting to make a declaration of confidence in all the local banks. There were isolated examples of such steps in later years elsewhere; but as banks became bigger and more widely spread, they outgrew the possibility of defence by the wealthy townsmen, and had to rely on prompt steps to mobilize their resources, and on the public's lengthening experience of the banks' ability to do this.

If down in the country the banker was to demonstrate his strength, he had to reinforce his cash position, and this meant first strengthening his London funds. Thus in mid-October 1857 Lloyds wrote to Alexanders, the bill-brokers, asking for a loan on the security of bills. Lloyds were not going to rediscount if they could help it, but they offered to deposit with Alexanders a parcel of bills not endorsed but supported by a letter of guarantee. Alexanders obliged, though Lloyds had to pay full 10 per cent. (the crisis level of Bank Rate) for the accommodation in December. The Glamorganshire Banking Company, looking back on this same crisis, boasted that they had not rediscounted a single bill during the crisis: one wonders whether they escaped by the technical device Lloyds had used in getting money in the London market. In the next bout, 1866, the Coventry and Warwickshire Banking Company ran their overdraft in London up to a figure at which their London agents raised their eyebrows; liberal accommodation was continued, but special security was expected. The tightness in London and precautionary steps by country bankers on this occasion continued an unusually long time: as late as April 1867 Barnetts Hoares were refusing to commit themselves to £100,000 for Lloyds. In 1878, after the City of Glasgow crash, country

209

bankers drew heavily on London and late-comers to Barnetts Hoares were told that further money was hardly obtainable on any terms. Nevertheless, the York City and County thought it necessary to press for a large sum, while Miles Cave at Bristol, after thinking that the trouble had blown over, had to ask for another £20,000 to be put at their disposal at the Bank of England. By the time of the Baring Crisis Lloyds had themselves become London bankers and Howard Lloyd was able to see the reverse side of the medal: at their City Office the agency balances (i.e. the balances of the country bankers for whom they acted as London agents) were depleted 'almost to insignificance'.

By thus drawing on the London market, bankers all over the country could open their doors each morning with some confidence that the till would not be completely emptied. Even in London itself precautions were necessary: at quite an early stage in 1847 Twinings in the Strand responded to rumours by getting a substantial stock of gold into the office. Looking back over 1857 the County of Gloucester Bank told shareholders that the low profits were due partly to the necessity of keeping idle gold and bank notes in the tills through the weeks of danger; the same bank in 1878 reiterated strict instructions to branch managers that one-third of deposits must be kept on hand to meet all possible demands. When the Glasgow failure was followed by a major failure in the Bristol area it was inevitable that every bank in the West Country should take precautions, at the expense of profits. But banks all over the country trembled: even a little bank in Nottingham went through the same story of higher cash, lower profits, to induce sounder sleep for the banker.

Meanwhile the banker would be reacting to the situation by showing less willingness to lend money locally. The crisis had sometimes cast its shadow before, inducing greater caution in lending even before the storm burst, as in the Liverpool Union Bank in 1836. In the spring phase of the 1847 crisis the extraordinarily restrictive action of the Bank of England frightened Lloyds into similar severity towards its own customers: some were called upon to pay off their overdrafts, while others were told that the overdraft permissions previously agreed no longer stood, 'for we cannot be guilty of the presumption of undertaking what the Bank of England has judged it unsafe to undertake'. To one customer (an M.P.) Lloyds wrote asking him to repay a loan, that 'it may possibly give your Bankers an opportunity of rendering aid to some trader, with whom the Loan may afford a wider field of usefulness in keeping hands at work at factories'— a formula bank managers enforcing the credit squeeze of 1955–7 may well envy. The tightness of that 1847 spring passed off, however, without a panic, only to recur in more acute form in the autumn. Perhaps the difficulties of the spring made bankers unusually cautious in the months between; certainly both the Gloucestershire Banking Company and the County of Gloucester Bank were reluctant lenders at the end of the summer. The Liverpool Union Bank that autumn stopped all 'discounts over the counter', a literal phrase that vividly presents a bygone phase of English banking. An 1866 County of Gloucester instruction, just after 'Black Friday' when Overends failed, has a less old-fashioned ring: the managers were 'to use the utmost possible caution in advancing money on accounts current, discount or otherwise, and to exercise a due discretion in getting in the overdrawn accounts due from their customers'.

The 1878 crisis was in some ways the most disturbing of all; certainly it seems to have shaken banks all over the country more than any other event since 1825.[4] There was, complained the Chairman of Lloyds in January 1879, 'a feeling of unreasoning and general distrust about the country, perhaps not specially of that bank but the banking fraternity in general, arising out of very unreasonable unfounded and exaggerated rumours of various kinds'. Lloyds had, despite their substantial strength, experienced a drain of cash so persistent that they were thereby forced to make further reductions in loans and overdrafts. Over the six winter months the balance-sheets showed a drop of £400,000 (8 per cent.) in the deposit liabilities, and Howard Lloyd hinted at a much bigger figure as the maximum. The bank simply had to reduce its investments—not an easy matter in crisis markets, and inevitably expensive. (The County of Gloucester Bank had lost £16,000 when forced to sell government stock in the autumn of 1847.)

After the crisis itself had passed the days continued to remain gloomy enough for the banker: the trail of bankruptcies could stretch out with seeming endlessness for a year or two. Looking back over the panic days

[4] Nearly eighty years later, one of Howard Lloyd's sons remembered, as one of the few impressions of childhood, 'the sense of anxiety and depression' occasioned by this crisis.

of 1857, when one of the worst Newcastle banking failures occurred, a partner in Lambtons bewailed the 'very gloomy appearance. . . . Up to this time there have been very few failures of any significance, but as soon as ever the screw is put on to get in the large overdrawn accounts of the bank, people go down like mushrooms [? ninepins]. For the next six or nine months we shall have to keep our eyes open but after that time I see everything clear before us.' Among the things that became clear were the bad debts that had to be written off. In 1847 Lloyds faced, besides its local business losses, a bad debt of £1,900 due to the failure of a London bill-broker—a sizable item in a £400,000 bank. That year the County of Gloucester Bank reckoned that the crisis one way and another cost them £20,000; ten years later they thought they escaped lightly, when 1857 cost them only £3,000. Their local competitors, the Gloucestershire Banking Company, reported that in the latter year they were virtually untouched; in 1866 they thought so again, but prematurely, for losses that year wiped out their trading profits. The Liverpool Union also found that 1866 was much worse than 1857: in the later year they recorded eighteen bad debts totalling £55,000 against only five totalling £8,400 in 1857.

Experience of crises naturally encouraged bankers to shun long-term commitments, and each successive upheaval would be followed by extreme caution and avoidance of anything that looked like a 'lock-up' of the banker's money. This implied a preference for discount rather than overdraft business, since in mid-century the more obviously liquid business tended to be handled by the discount method. In 1848, reflecting on the difficulties of the previous year, Lloyds told a customer that, if he wanted help, it must be 'confined to the discount of your bills. . . . We think it best rather to contract overdrafts than to increase them.' This 'for the present': evidently they might let him have an overdraft later. The objection to overdrafts was repeated to another customer, to whom Lloyds explained that they had 'strong objections to locking up money in loans for longer periods than 2 or 3 months'. Nor was it only overdrafts that were to be avoided. The pressure to sell investments virtually broke the market on these occasions, and this was particularly troublesome in 1866 when the London markets were affected for an unusually long period. After that episode Lloyds decided that neither Consols nor railway stocks could really be regarded as a 'crisis reserve'; gossip with City friends revealed that during the critical period good bills had been more readily negotiable than Consols and that railway bonds had sometimes been scarcely more valuable than the paper on which they were inscribed.

If the London market was so difficult, ought not the country banker to provide his own reserve against this periodic crisis? The question was squarely faced by the Liverpool Union Bank in 1847. This was, of course, the first crisis after the Bank Charter Act of 1844, and a fair inference from Peel's legislation was that banks must not rely on emergency help from the centre. The Liverpool Union Bank was thus being perfectly logical when it considered establishing a 'Reserved Money Fund'—a special cash reserve—to be held sacred except under extreme emergency; consideration was given to a special call upon shareholders for the purpose. In the event nothing was done: perhaps the Directors made up their minds that the Bank of England would always, when extreme emergency developed, relieve the market. If so, they were right, although another generation was to pass before the responsibility of the Bank of England was finally established. With that development of the central banking tradition and of the banks themselves into great nation-wide institutions hingeing on the London money market and a fully-fledged central bank, the black days of the Victorian financial crisis gradually slipped back into the memories of old men.

When the Baring Crisis came in 1890 this twofold process was already far gone, and the episode lacked all element of panic in the streets. But there were black moments enough in the inner sanctums of the City. When his suspicions had first been aroused, Howard Lloyd agreed with Edward Hoare (manager at the City Office) that they should try to sell £500,000 Consols. Things had, however, gone too far for that: no jobber would make a price. The next Sunday Howard Lloyd travelled up to Euston, by which time the main part of the Barings guarantee fund had been made up. On the Monday Thomas Salt as Chairman signed a preliminary document committing Lloyds to £250,000 in the guarantee fund; his Board had been reluctant, stressing that Lloyds held only £9,000 of Barings' acceptances, but all eventually agreed that Lloyds was too important to stand out of a concerted City operation of this nature. In the further week that elapsed before the final documents were completed

213

in Threadneedle Street, Howard Lloyd and Edward Hoare were a little put out because they were not invited to the discussions at the Bank of England; their sensitiveness on this score serves to underline the fact that worse anxieties had by now been allayed. For Lloyds there was really very little trouble through the entire episode. When it was found that Lord Revelstoke owed £4,000 to a tradesman there was hesitation about allowing the tradesman an overdraft, so minimal were the troubles of this crisis for the general banking business of Lloyds Bank.

The real importance of the Baring Crisis in English monetary history lies rather in its long-term repercussions through the reformist discussions to which it gave impetus, and this is well illustrated in the traces that survive in the Lloyds records. Goschen, a Chancellor of the Exchequer who had made, much earlier, a mark in the City, made the crisis the occasion for an attack on the banks, particularly for the inadequacy of their cash reserves and the uninformativeness of their published accounts. The Lloyds people were critical of Goschen's ideas. The Chairman, in February 1891, was telling the Annual General Meeting that he did 'not believe that a Chancellor of the Exchequer or any other government officer can manage our business half as well as we can manage it ourselves'. Howard Lloyd inside the Board conducted a fighting retreat in face of the general movement towards more publicity; in September 1891 he was jibbing at other banks' custom of issuing the monthly figures to the press, and in November he made a last effort to get a modification of the whole business. But the weight of opinion was against him; he saw that he must turn his mind to the practical questions of monthly valuation of the bank's investments and manipulation of the end-of-the-month cash.[5] Actually, Howard Lloyd had not needed Goschen to push him into window-dressing, but he was perturbed at the effects on profits of the higher cash ratios now being called for, and it is quite clear that he was determined to protect the profits by increased window-dressing. In so doing he was only doing as others did, and Goschen's objects were thus defeated in substance if not in appearance, as Goschen himself complained some years later.

[5] The papers on this matter show that bank notes (i.e. Bank of England notes) were used in huge amounts for adjustments between banks and the money market, in contrast to the ease with which cheques and mere book entries settle the transactions in the middle of the twentieth century.

JOHN WILLIAM BEAUMONT PEASE, 1869–1950
Created Baron Wardington of Alnmouth, 1936
Chairman, 1922–45
From the painting by Sir William Nicholson, R.A.

When Lloyds felt that they were being rather left out of the high-level discussions of November 1890, they may have thought with some justice that this was because, with their Head Office in Birmingham, they were still regarded as essentially country bankers. Before the next crisis, at the outbreak of war in 1914, they were thoroughly established as one of the biggest banks not only in the country but in the City itself, and there could be no question of their being treated as the little brothers who were let into the secrets only at second hand. On the contrary, Beaumont Pease (the Deputy Chairman) found himself rushed off his feet. 'These are exciting if interesting times', he wrote on 6 August, 'I never thought I should have so many Bank holidays together or that there should be so much Bank about them and so little holiday! I have spent them from morning till late at night in meetings and conferences.' At first international and not at all domestic, the crisis in the very last days of July began to have its effects on ordinary business over the counter, and on the 31st the General Manager circularized all branches:

Timid people who have lost their heads have, in some cases to-day, sought to obtain gold for hoarding purposes.

If any of your customers, in withdrawing moneys, ask for an undue proportion of gold, you should refuse to give it. Bank Notes, of course, are legal tender.

It is as well to meet moderate requirements as liberally as possible, but any amounts in the least unusual should be paid, say, as to 80 or 90 per cent., in Notes.

Down in the West Country local banks had special reason to tremble. The Naval Bank at Plymouth had been under suspicion for some time, and it became known to bankers that its suspension would be announced immediately after the Bank Holiday.[6] Mr. Fox of Wellington feared that this would provoke a run on neighbouring branches of Fox Fowlers at Tavistock and elsewhere. He himself therefore travelled to London, called on Barclays, and took down to the west £100,000 in gold and fivers, the money being packed in three wooden boxes which accompanied the banker in his railway compartment on his return journey: probably the

---

[6] Thanks to the moratorium and special arrangements by the government for the Naval Bank, the feared upheaval did not occur. The Naval Bank was wound up during succeeding months.

last occasion on which a banker took gold from London to meet an expected run.

In Lloyds Bank further instructions on 3 August told managers to retain all old notes at branches and reissue them when necessary, to send a return of cash held to Head Office every evening, and to cash cheques in notes of as large a denomination as possible. The managers were also told on the same day that as far as the London City and Midland or the National Provincial were concerned 'any possible help may be mutually given or requested'. This could also apply to 'any of your banking neighbours with whom we ordinarily work in friendly accord'. There is no indication that help on any appreciable scale was actually given to (or received from) any other bank, though a note of thanks shows that something was done to help the Blackburn Savings Bank on 7 and 8 August.

Meanwhile the Government had been taking action. On 6 August a circular to branches referred to the moratorium, which covered bank deposits as well as other debts. Managers were instructed to exercise the right thereby conferred to refuse repayment of deposits only 'where it appears that withdrawals are being made for the purpose of hoarding or exporting currency'; as an indication, proportions of customers' balances that might be repaid were laid down, subject to an overall limit of '£2/3,000'. Steps were also taken by the authorities to secure the unfreezing of the London money market. Lloyds themselves had £50,000 in German acceptances bought from Mendelssohn and Co., falling due in August, and other houses in the City had much more of such frozen assets; extraordinary action was clearly called for if the markets were to get to work again and cope with special new business developing. On 13 August the Bank of England, backed by Treasury guarantee, announced itself willing to discount at Bank Rate, without recourse to holders, all approved bills accepted before 4 August: a bold step beyond anything the banks had sought. Lloyds Bank themselves took advantage to the extent of discounting at the Bank of England over £2,000,000 of bills.

With such vigorous, indeed almost excessive, relief measures, the authorities put an end to the 'liquidity panic' and the London money market sailed into an easy money period that lasted well into 1915. The last (we may guess) of the great banking crises was over and branch managers up and down the country were soon turning their thoughts to the employment of women to replace men going off to the wars. Some in coastal towns, anticipating the more elaborate precautions of 1939–40, were removing bearer securities to inland towns; before very long some were writing to Head Office reporting Zeppelin raids. But there was no more fear of a run for cash. England, in that first great war, was settling to a greyer life: the golden sovereigns disappeared from circulation and the excitements of Victorian financial panics likewise slipped back into the past. The term 'financial crisis' was destined to find another meaning in the twentieth-century history of England.

11

THE ORGANIZATION OF BANKS

THE corporate form of Lloyds Bank today is simple enough: a joint-stock company with limited liability, with capital and published reserves totalling £35,565,000, the capital being divided into 18,565,000 fully paid £1 shares, and the reserves amounting to £17,000,000. Equally if we go back a hundred and thirty years, we find the corporate organization of the constituent banks simple enough—they were all private partnerships, with not more than six partners, these partners being liable for all the debts of their banks. But between 1826 and the end of the nineteenth century there was bewildering variety. In addition to several minor changes, there were important legal changes in 1826, 1833, 1844, 1857, 1858, 1862, and 1879. Banks founded between these various dates were subject to different rules, and some of the earlier banks did, while others did not, change their corporate organization as new legislation gave opportunity. The legislation has been explained fully by Clapham,[1] Gregory,[2] and other authorities, and details need not be repeated here. Broadly, the changes were these: the 1826 Act allowed unlimited joint-stock banks beyond a 65-miles' radius of London; that of 1833 allowed such banks, if non-note-issuing, within the 65-miles' radius; the Act of 1844 forbade foundation of further joint-stock banks, except under certain rules; the Act of 1857 repealed the restrictive Act of 1844; the Acts of 1858 and 1862 allowed joint-stock banks to limit the liability of their shareholders; and the Act of 1879 provided for 'reserved' liability of shareholders. The foundation of new private banks continued to be permissible, and in 1857 the limit of six partners was raised to ten; but such foundations were already rare: the youngest among those coming into the Lloyds group was Jenner and Co., founded at Sandgate in 1872.

[1] *An Economic History of Modern Britain* (Cambridge, 1952), vol. ii, pp. 350–2.
[2] *The Westminster Bank* (London, 1936), vol. i, chaps. 1, 2, and 5.

Classification of the constituent banks of Lloyds Bank, in relation to these steps in banking legislation, serves to emphasize how strong was the private element and how, when joint-stock banking came, it was in the provinces rather than in London that new developments important to Lloyds appeared. Before 1826, 122 of these banks (necessarily private) had been founded; many of them have been referred to in Chapter 1. Sixty-eight of these 122 retained their independent existence as lately as 1865, when Lloyds was refounded as a joint-stock company. Some of the other 54 had fallen by the wayside, but many had provided some basis for joint-stock foundations under the Acts of 1826 and 1844. During the period 1826–44 when joint-stock banks with unlimited liability, and with the right of note-issue, could be established outside the 65-miles' circle, 24 such banks, destined to find their way into Lloyds, were founded. Most of these 24 were in the West Country and the Midlands: they proved to be strong plants, and 20 of them remained in independent existence in 1865. The 1833 Act, which permitted the establishment of non-issuing joint-stock banks inside the London circle, was very important to the Westminster Bank, but not a single one of the Lloyds banks was founded under this law: the roots of Lloyds in London have been exclusively in private firms, among them Hanbury Taylor and Lloyds itself, Barnetts Hoares, Bosanquet Salts, Brown Jansons, Herries Farquhar, Twinings and Praeds. Under Peel's restrictive legislation of 1844 the only Lloyds foundations were the Bucks and Oxon Union Bank (based on three private banks) and The Three Towns Banking Company (Plymouth, Devonport, and Stonehouse). Following the important reform of banking law in 1857–8, there was only one new foundation of importance to Lloyds: the Birmingham Joint Stock Bank, opened in 1862. The full tide of joint-stock organization showed itself rather in the reorganization of some of the older banks, both private (Lloyds itself was one of these) and joint-stock foundations under the earlier law. There was also an odd throw-back up in Newcastle, where an unhappy record of joint-stock banking led to the establishment in 1859 of the powerful private bank of Hodgkin Barnett Pease and Spence.[3]

The Birmingham Joint Stock Bank opened its doors on 1 January 1862, just too early to enjoy the rather less restrictive Act of 1862. The Acts of

[3] See p. 51.

1857–8, however, allowed it the important advantage of limited liability for its shareholders, and it was in fact the first of our constituent banks to have this privilege. Its share capital was fixed at £500,000, divided into £100 shares. Only £25 per share was called, thus leaving an uncalled capital of £375,000 as security for the depositors. It was also provided that the company should be dissolved if the Guarantee Fund (to be constituted out of profits) plus one-quarter of the capital had been lost. The stress laid on these measures is an indication of the importance previously attached, as a protection for depositors, to the unlimited liability of shareholders. The promoters also felt that the reserve of uncalled capital would establish confidence so strongly as to eliminate all risk from the periodical publication of balance-sheets, which was compulsory for banks registered under the recent legislation.

The reorganization of Lloyds itself came after the 1862 Act, which allowed shares to be of less than £100 each. After the withdrawal of the Taylor family the Birmingham house had replaced its original name 'Taylors and Lloyds' by 'Lloyds and Co., the Birmingham Old Bank', in 1853. Now, in 1865, Lloyds and Co., joined by Moilliet and Sons, was incorporated as *Lloyds Banking Company Limited*.[4] The prospectus, dated 29 March 1865, stated that

The recent alterations in the law affecting Banking Partnerships, and the growing requirements of the Trade in this District, have determined Messrs. Lloyds and Company and Messrs. Moilliet and Sons to extend the basis of their present Partnerships by converting them into a Joint-Stock Company with limited liability.

The Authorized Capital was £2,000,000 in 40,000 shares of £50 each; 25,000 were to be issued forthwith, the remainder being 'reserved for issue at such premiums, at such times, and to such persons, as the Directors shall consider most conducive to the Interests of the Company'. 12,500 shares were to be allotted to the partners in the two firms, and they were also to receive, in payment for the goodwill, the cash premiums of £5 a share which the public were to pay on the other 12,500 shares issued immediately. On all issued shares, calls were not to exceed £12. 10s. a share except on winding-up of the company—a 'reserved liability' as it

---

[4] For some discussion of the circumstances leading to this reorganization, see Chapter 1 above.

came later to be called. Actually only £7. 10s. a share was called in the first years, so that outside shareholders put down £12. 10s. and assumed a liability of £42. 10s. a share. A further issue in 1866 brought the total number of shares up to 40,413, and by 1875 the full 50,000 had been issued, and the £7. 10s. paid was raised to £8 by the declaration (and retention) of a bonus of 10s. per share for the year 1874.

Although the joint-stock company fever that now took hold of English business had no great immediate effects on the structure of English banking,[5] Lloyds was not entirely alone in taking advantage of the new company law. Moore and Robinson's Nottinghamshire Banking Company, an unlimited company formed in 1836 on an earlier private concern, became a limited company in 1866. The Bucks and Oxon Union Bank, one of the few banks established under Peel's legislation of 1844, had not widened the ownership of share capital beyond partners in the constituent private banks; in 1866 it became a limited company and increased its paid-up capital from £55,000 to £80,000. The former shareholders (originally partners) took half the shares, the other half being sold mainly to customers. The 16,000 shares, £5 paid, carried an uncalled liability of £20 a share. The Halifax Joint Stock Banking Company, another of 'the 1826 banks', registered itself as a limited liability company in 1875. Early in 1878 the Directors of the County of Gloucester Bank made proposals, but before agreement could be reached the upheaval of 1878 and the new Act of 1879 overtook them.

The 1878–9 episode has been fully treated elsewhere[6] and the story need not be repeated here. Until this date opinion among bankers, shareholders, and customers alike had been divided on the issue of limiting the liability of a bank's shareholders. The tradition of private banking had created a prejudice in favour of entrusting deposits to 'gentlemen of known wealth and standing who were themselves responsible to their last farthing [rather] than to directors whose only stake in the institution they manage might be comparatively inconsiderable'.[7] The joint-stock

[5] The joint-stock fever manifested itself rather in the establishment of overseas banks in London. Cf. A. S. J. Baster, *The Imperial Banks* (London, 1929) and *The International Banks* (London, 1935).

[6] Gregory, op. cit., vol. i, pp. 203–14.

[7] Extract from the Directors' Report, Liverpool Union Bank, published in the *Liverpool Daily Post*, 6 Feb. 1880.

banks, perforce unlimited liability companies and struggling in the face of this tradition, tended to emphasize the security afforded to their depositors by the absence of any limit to the shareholders' liability. Consequently, the permissive powers opened to banks by the Acts of 1858 and 1862 were not at all fully exploited: though some reconstructions were effected, as we have seen, the majority of joint-stock banks in the seventies were still unlimited liability companies. The question was much debated, and every now and again another bank would become a convert to the new faith. The controversy was brought to a head by a shocking failure in Glasgow in October 1878, demonstrating that even the bankrupting of scores of shareholders might not provide adequate protection for depositors. Though support of unlimited liability did not disappear at once, the trickle of converts became a flood, and the Government was called upon to facilitate by legislation the corresponding capital reorganization of the banks. The bankers themselves were prominent in pressing the change; indeed, according to one story, a Director of the Capital and Counties was 'mainly instrumental' in getting the Bill introduced and passed.[8] The resulting Companies Act, 1879, allowed banking companies registered under earlier law, whether as limited or as unlimited companies, to re-register as limited companies with capital structures altered to provide a 'reserved liability' callable only on the winding-up of the company. Lloyds Banking Company Ltd. had already such provision, under its original registration: at the annual meeting in 1880 the Chairman was able to boast of 'the radical constitution of this bank from its beginning' which had in effect anticipated the legislators of 1879.

Despite some persistence of the traditional view, those banks who were not in the position of Lloyds at once began to take advantage of the new Act, and soon there was a headlong rush into reorganization. The first to act was the Capital and Counties Bank, the renamed Hampshire and North Wilts Banking Co. Ltd., formed in 1877 by the amalgamation of two important branch banks. The Capital and Counties having given the

---

[8] E. B. Merriman, the great Chairman of the Capital and Counties, claimed this achievement for Gabriel Goldney, M.P. for Chippenham who, according to the Parliamentary Reports, made only two short and insignificant speeches in support of the Bill. Speeches in the House are, of course, not the only way of engineering a legislative change.

lead,[9] 'bankers, being very like ordinary individuals, as soon as one institution had the fortitude to accept the altered principles, all the others followed its example like a flock of sheep'.[10] The Glamorganshire Banking Company was considering the question even before the Bill reached the House of Commons, though it was not until November 1882 that the company was registered, with a new reserved liability of £30 added to the existing £10 shares. The Liverpool Union Bank hesitated, watching the movement of other banks and contending that they were already in an entirely satisfactory position. The Directors nursed a hope that the 1879 Act might be amended, but in 1882 they gave way and joined the 'flock of sheep'. The Devon and Cornwall Bank—a powerful branch system of the nineteenth-century kind—also hung back at first. In 1882 a Directors' questionnaire elicited the fact that a majority of the shareholders favoured the change, but for the moment they deferred to an influential minority; in 1883 the majority prevailed and the capital structure was reorganized to include substantial reserved liability.

Thereafter the legal framework remained unchanged. As it absorbed more and more banks, Lloyds Banking Company Ltd., changed its name and greatly enlarged its capital. When the two Lombard Street banks joined with Lloyds of Birmingham in 1884, the company became Lloyds Barnetts and Bosanquets Bank Ltd., a cumbrous title assumed in deference to the London recruits. Five years later further important amalgamations provided the opportunity for reverting to a simpler form, and the present designation of *Lloyds Bank Limited* was adopted. The 1884 amalgamations almost doubled the share capital of the bank, but this was little as compared with what was to come. By 1900 the Authorized Capital had reached £13,750,000, and by 1914 £40,000,000, still in £50 shares on which £8 was paid. The merger with the Capital and Counties involved another huge increase. In 1920 the capital was rearranged, the £72,500,000 of Authorized Capital being divided into 14,500,000 shares of £5 each, £1 paid; the issued capital totalled £14,137,796—almost as great as it is in 1957.[11]

[9] The Capital and Counties had, in company with other banks, been represented at a meeting called by the Manchester and Liverpool District Bank, which was mobilizing opinion in favour of the Act (cf. Gregory, op. cit., vol. i, p. 206).

[10] The quotation is from E. B. Merriman, looking back from 1897.

[11] The uncalled liability was cancelled when the capital structure was simplified in 1956.

The adoption of limited liability as the usual system of corporate organization gave important impetus to the movement in favour of publication of balance-sheets. The Joint-Stock Companies Act of 1844 had prescribed the twice-yearly publication of a statement of assets and liabilities, for all banks registered under it; being an almost ineffective Act in its main purpose, little came of the publicity clause. The Act of 1858 was much more important: this, permitting for the first time the limitation of the liability of bank shareholders, imposed the condition that banks taking advantage of this permission should publish a statement of assets and liabilities twice yearly. This went against the grain with bankers, and is believed to have been a circumstance checking any inclination of banks to register under the new system. Public confidence was still believed to depend upon the substance of a bank's proprietors; the collapse, in disgraceful circumstances, of the largest bank established under Peel's 1844 legislation had shown that publication of crude balance-sheets afforded no protection. When the Birmingham Joint Stock Bank was founded in 1862 it commanded confidence by fixing its nominal capital at such a high level that the liabilities shown in its early balance-sheets were overshadowed. Nevertheless, the tide was running in favour of publicity, the growing strength of important joint-stock banks which voluntarily published their balance-sheets helping to turn the fashion. Even a private bank found it worth while to publish a balance-sheet upon occasion: in its last days as a private firm, Lloyds and Co., hearing that another Birmingham firm had failed, published, on the front pages of the local newspapers, a statement of their position. A 'very straightforward though, for a private bank, somewhat unusual course', commented one of the newspapers.[12]

For a private bank this course remained unusual, while the spread of limited liability incorporation, especially after the 1879 Act, made the twice-yearly balance-sheet almost universal among the joint-stock banks. The publicity of the joint-stocks was contrasted with the secrecy of the private banks, to the disadvantage of the latter at a time when confidence in their future was sapped by the remarks of eminent authorities.[13] The

[12] Aris's *Birmingham Gazette*, 11 Mar. 1865.
[13] The public comments of Bagehot (*Lombard Street* (1873), chap. x) were expressions of an opinion which became widely held in the last quarter of the nineteenth century;

concern felt by the private bankers at this development found vigorous expression at a meeting of the Association of English Country Bankers in November 1887. There were weighty arguments against falling in with the practice of the joint-stocks: the Capital and Reserve Funds of private banks would look so puny against the Reserved Liability of many of the joint-stocks, while the true reserve capital of the private banks—the private properties of the partners—would not lend itself to inclusion in published statements. The consensus of opinion remained against publication. Two years later one of the oldest private banks in the provinces, Berwick Lechmeres of Worcester, set an example by publishing their balance-sheet for 31 December 1889; it appears in *The Bankers' Magazine* 1890, introduced by a terse note:

Sir,

We enclose a copy of our balance-sheet, now published for the first time. We are a private bank.

Yours faithfully,
Berwick & Co.

The movement for greater publicity was soon to be given its sharpest push: after the Baring Crisis in November 1890 the Chancellor of the Exchequer, Goschen, in a series of speeches complained of the inadequacy of bank reserves, and called for frequent publication of balance-sheets as a precaution against undue depletion of cash ratios.[14] As the reserve in danger of exhaustion in November 1890 was London's international reserve, and not the internal cash reserve of the domestic banking system, there was little logic in Goschen's attack, or in the prolonged agitation in City circles to which Goschen had given point. But logic or no logic, a powerful Chancellor of the Exchequer—one, moreover, who had been a Director of the Bank of England—had attacked the banks for concealing the inadequacy of their cash reserves, and had called for monthly publication of balance-sheets. The ensuing negotiations between the banks led to the determination of the London joint-stock banks to publish monthly statements, and of the country joint-stock banks to

Goschen in 1891 (*Essays and Addresses on Economic Questions*, London, 1905, pp. 111 et seq.) mentioned the private banks particularly in his criticism of the inadequate reserves of the banks.

[14] Goschen, op. cit., pp. 111–17.

publish quarterly statements. This still went against the grain with many leading bankers—Howard Lloyd in March 1891 still doubted the expediency of monthly publication—with the result that no effort was made to secure either uniformity or any really informative detail. The resulting series of English banking statistics, running from 1891 to 1915, can have no place in a statistician's paradise. The private banks were naturally affected by the new practice, though they felt themselves in rather a different position from the joint-stocks. Hodgkin Barnetts in Newcastle began publication of their balance-sheet in 1891; a letter from Fosters at Cambridge, to whom they had sent a copy, expresses the general attitude of the private bankers: 'Like yourselves, we feel very forcibly the strong objections to this publicity but fear we must follow the fashion though we cannot approve it.' Lambtons, Hodgkin Barnetts' local competitors, followed suit in the same year. Others followed in the next few years; among these were Bacon Cobbolds at Ipswich and R. and R. Williams at Dorchester, both of whom appended to their balance-sheets the following statement:

The publication of an Annual Balance Sheet in no way alters the private character of the Bank, or the responsibility of the Partners to the full extent of their property.

In the twentieth century, when the private banks finally lost their independence, these concise reminders of the earlier foundations of English banking have necessarily disappeared. Before 1914 English banking statistics were rapidly falling into the shape set by the practices of the dominant joint-stock banks. The Cunliffe Committee of 1918 recommended a more detailed statement for use by all the banks when the monthly statements were resumed after the war;[15] when the Macmillan Committee reported in 1931, Lloyds Bank was named as the only bank to have adopted the Cunliffe changes in full.[16]

The great changes in the legal status of banks during the nineteenth century were of the first importance in enabling banks to become large

---

[15] *First Interim Report of the Committee on Currency and Foreign Exchanges after the War* (Aug. 1918), para. 34 and Appendix 1. (Reprinted in Gregory, *British Banking Statutes and Reports*, vol. ii, pp. 355 and 365.)

[16] *Report of the Committee on Finance and Industry* (June 1931), para. 370 (p. 157).

enough to include an extensive network of branches. The old private bankers had normally confined themselves to a single office, possibly with a branch or two in the neighbouring towns or villages. In 1826, when joint-stock banks were just about to appear, Pitt, Bowley, Croome and Wood of Cirencester had four branches;[17] Lacon, Youell and Co. of Yarmouth were also at Lowestoft and North Walsham; Williams and Co. at Chester had one branch at Caernarvon and another at Bangor; Hartlands of Evesham had an office at Tewkesbury and had just ventured into Cheltenham; and Garfit Claypons at Boston were also just opening a second branch. No others, among the roots of Lloyds Bank, had more than one branch, and most had not even that. Lloyds itself had no branch until 1864. Towards the end of the century, when the private banks were having to struggle for a place against the omnivorous joint-stocks, and when they had learned something from the methods of the joint-stock branch networks, a few of them became more venturesome. Hodgkin Barnetts, that rather exceptional North Country pillar raised against the joint-stock tide, had as many as thirty branches before its absorption in 1903, and there were others with a dozen or so branches. But even these remained small-world giants, their networks being still essentially local.

From the first, the joint-stock banks had bigger ideas. Their use of salaried managers even at Head Office meant that their system of working could easily be extended to comparatively distant branches, and many of them were in any case determined to be big from the start: it was indeed largely in order to get branch-banking that there had been agitation in favour of joint-stock organization. Nevertheless for almost half a century the really big widespread net of branches remained exceptional, and none of these large networks found their way into the Lloyds group. The more typical early joint-stock branch bank was in fact rather like the late-style big private bank, with perhaps half a dozen branches within a radius of 20 or 30 miles of its Head Office. When returns were called for by a Select Committee in 1836, at the one extreme was the Halifax Joint Stock Banking Company with no branches at all (it disapproved in principle); at the other, the Wilts and Dorset already had twenty-four branches. The latter was indeed venturesome, for one of its

[17] Tetbury, Faringdon, Cheltenham, and Burford, all of them 10–15 miles from the Head Office.

branches was 66 miles from Head Office; the Devon and Cornwall (so named after the Plymouth and Devonport went beyond the Plymouth area) soon had a branch 54 miles away. More typical than any of these three was the Gloucestershire Banking Company. It started life with just its Gloucester office. In 1831 it acquired three branches by absorbing Hartlands of Cheltenham, Tewkesbury, and Evesham. Evesham worried the Directors because it was as much as 22 miles from Gloucester; but they had confidence in Nathaniel Hartland, who remained in charge there as manager. Hartland indeed continued to regard the Evesham office as his own little kingdom, and a considerable measure of branch independence was signalized by the frequent use of the term 'District bank' instead of the more subservient 'branch'. Of Hartland's previous agencies, Stroud, with its important industrial business, became a branch in 1834 and Alcester by 1840. The bank also opened an agency at Newnham, a spare-time occupation for a local surveyor. That was all for a few years; the Board's aim, shareholders were told in the Report for 1836, was 'to confine their operations within moderate limits and to move with great caution in extending them'. In 1842 two branches were added by the absorption of Cripps and Co. at Cirencester and Stow. In 1853 a branch was opened at Moreton-in-Marsh, where the opening of the railway created new prospects. In fact this office failed to attract much new business, although the railway had brought a cattle-market; but the bank thought it 'prudent to occupy the ground to prevent other banks from trespassing upon a valuable district'. A proposal for a branch at Malvern was rejected. Then in 1858, 'for the purpose of maintaining and extending the agricultural connection of the Bank', the tiny private bank of W. Hall at Ross was absorbed. An invitation to open in Coleford had come from local people in 1840, but it was not until 1861 that a renewed invitation was accepted.

The story of the advent of the Gloucestershire Banking Company to Hereford reveals the tangle of local and temporary circumstances that might influence branch extension. The Directors were discussing possibilities in November 1861 and decided to open in Hereford in the following April. In February, however, came reports of a serious fraud on Morgan and Adams, a private bank in the town, and in view of the weakened position of this bank (which the company declined to purchase) the

Directors decided to bring forward the opening by a few weeks. They appointed as cashier—with the prospect of managership—a man from the National Provincial's Hereford branch. Evidently he was an immediate success, for a few months later increased business necessitated the acquisition of the 'Nag's Head' public-house to provide more commodious premises. Meanwhile Morgan and Adams were persistently in need of help, and equally persistently trying to persuade the Gloucestershire Banking Company to buy them out. The company in the end preferred to leave Morgan and Adams to stop payment, and were justified in the event by the transference of many important accounts to themselves. Other private banking troubles in Hereford brought more accounts, although one of the collapsing banks eventually sold its goodwill elsewhere. In the next few years the expansive mood continued to prevail in the Gloucestershire Banking Company: in 1866 a branch was opened at Redditch on completion of the railway, and a year later the agency at Lydney became a branch.

In other banks, both private and joint-stock, the same reasons were behind the opening of the majority of branches—snapping up the business of a failed bank, getting a foot into a town before a competitor who was rumoured to be coming, responding to a call from influential residents, or—in the more venturesome joint-stock banks—breaking into quite a new district. The County of Gloucester Bank, for example, which had previously established branches only by absorbing other banks, opened at Wotton-under-Edge in 1863 in response to the wishes of people in the neighbourhood. Twenty years later it decided to spread itself into South Wales; beginning at Cardiff in 1888, success encouraged it to add a Newport branch in 1889. But some of the joint-stock foundations were more aggressive from the start. The Plymouth and Devonport Banking Company lost no time in spreading itself into the Devon and Cornwall Banking Company, often finding a local tradesman to become first their agent and then manager of a branch. Outside the Plymouth area they went first, in 1833, to St. Austell, as 'being situate in the centre of an agricultural and mining district surrounded by several inland and seaport towns and populous villages, exhibiting evident marks of prosperity, and of which it appeared to be the commercial metropolis, all of which being destitute of a regular Bank . . .'. In the next year a branch was opened at Dartmouth with a local banker as manager, after letters from local inhabitants promised support, and in 1835 at Newton Abbot where a coal trader, who had a discount account with the bank, was put in charge. Then to Exeter, where they soon swallowed a private bank, and to Crediton, because another joint-stock bank was said to be thinking about it. A shareholder recommended Launceston, and the bank was not deterred by the existence of two others already in the town. After that, the epidemic of cold feet in the joint-stock banking world seems to have called a halt, for in 1839 the Directors recorded their intention not to increase the number—it was then fifteen—of their establishments. Not until 1847 did they venture again—then during the remainder of the century the familiar reasons recurred, and by 1880 there were twenty-six branches in all.

The West of England and South Wales District Bank, founded at Bristol in 1834, believed in branch expansion at the outset—and the quicker the better. Less than a month after the Provisional Committee had first met, two members of it were sent to tour Bath, Taunton, Exeter, Plymouth, Swansea, and Gloucester, where they were to make contact with influential people who might bring business. Within a year branches were open at Barnstaple, Bridgwater, Swansea, Taunton, Exeter, and Bath. Then there was a lull—the quiet years in banking development generally; from 1844 expansion was renewed, in Somerset and, especially after 1850, into Wales. In these first twenty years the bank continued to follow its original determination to get first footing in a town whenever it could, but not to bother with places where one of the other joint-stock banks was already established: Brixham was ruled out as being 'too much within the limits of the operations of the Devon and Cornwall Banking Company'. From 1859, however, this inhibition disappeared; the 'Devon and Cornwall' found itself facing a competitor on its home ground at Plymouth, and in 1860 a branch at Gloucester challenged two well-established joint-stock banks. Thereafter new branches quickly followed throughout Devon and Somerset and in the towns just across the Bristol Channel—a consolidation rather than an extension of territory.

Wiltshire had from 1835 two typically small branch systems, aggressive within their districts but not venturing beyond. The smaller was the North Wilts Banking Company, which began with a Head Office at

Melksham and agencies, soon converted into branches, at Devizes, Calne, Corsham, and Trowbridge. At Chippenham the Directors tried to buy a private bank; when their offer was declined they set themselves up in competition. They rejected overtures from the Wilts and Dorset Bank which wanted to share the towns out between the two banks, and soon had another half-dozen offices open. (Their plan was to begin with an agency and convert it into a branch with a full-time manager when the business had grown.) It remained a Wiltshire bank until its amalgamation in 1877 with the Hampshire Banking Company, soon to become the Capital and Counties. Their neighbours, the Wilts and Dorset Banking Company, were willing to go farther afield, perhaps because that great joint-stock banker J. W. Gilbart was one of its organizers. He and other members of the Provisional Committee went scouting round for premises, and within a year or so there were twenty-four branches, at distances ranging from 12 to 66 miles from Head Office. For this bank also the race to occupy the ground gave a zest to the early days. Rumour said that a competitor from Bath was going to open in Westbury, so the bank's solicitor was instructed to secure an office at once. He won the race: 'I have taken a respectable house. . . . The rent is only £15 per annum, and the other outgoings about £2. . . . The Bath Provincial Banking Company have publicly announced their determination of going to Westbury immediately, but have taken no house. I therefore wrote a notice and placed it in the window of the house that "The Wilts & Dorset Banking Company will commence business in Westbury early in December". We have now the most ostensible footing.' After this early race new branch establishments were rare until the early sixties, when the bank expanded into the Bournemouth area. In 1865 the Directors believed that another race—one that would speedily supply all towns not hitherto occupied—was imminent, and a spate of new branches in Somerset resulted. A contraction of other banks at Southampton led to an invitation to open there, and the success of this branch encouraged the invasion of Bristol shortly afterwards. There was widespread development in 1878, when the Wilts & Dorset took premises over from the failed 'West of England' in several Somerset and Devon towns; and the bank continued to add to its offices right down to 1914, when it took a chain of 100 branches into Lloyds.

Not all joint-stock banks were as venturesome as this. The Worcester City and County, founded in 1840, had only the one office until 1857, and not until the sixties did it set foot outside Worcestershire. Even the branches established—in a slow succession—in neighbouring counties did not change its local character. When it came into Lloyds all its offices were within about 30 miles of the Head Office at Worcester. By this time (1889) the two great private banks of Newcastle—Lambtons and Hodgkin Barnetts—were comparable in their coverage of a compact area; though both these banks continued to open branches, they remained compact as the Worcester City and County had been. Another important joint-stock bank that held to compactness was the Liverpool Union. Founded in 1835, it opened no branch at all until 1877. Between 1884 and 1899 it opened fourteen others, most of these being in Liverpool and Birkenhead. All of these were regarded as collectors of deposits that could be profitably used in the two main offices in Liverpool itself; the lending business, bringing the profits, was heavily concentrated in the commerce of Liverpool itself, and the bank showed no inclination to venture beyond.

Apart from the races of 1833–6 and the early sixties, when many banks were opening new branches at a relatively high rate, the growth of branch networks proceeded at a pace allowing comfortable development of the organization appropriate to these more or less compact local systems. Of the largest systems—the Devon and Cornwall and the West of England and South Wales District—no useful evidence of organization remains, but the story of the Gloucestershire Banking Company does throw some light on the relationship between Head Office and branches. The first branches had a great measure of independence. They were told not to make large advances for permanent capital; otherwise they could use the money at discretion, even in the conduct of business with London agents. Dishonoured bills and any overdrawn accounts about which the branch manager was unhappy had to be referred to Head Office; and a quarterly account for the branch was presented and checked by a Committee of three Directors. In 1836 Nathaniel Hartland, previously manager at Evesham, was appointed General Superintendent, and his duties included periodic visits to every branch. Some of the local managers no doubt enjoyed their independence: the man at Newnham certainly lost no time in drawing on the London agent. Others, like John Payne at Stroud, felt isolated and wished for more counsel from the centre.

The tightening of control by Head Office in the next phase seems to have come not so much as the result of any conscious need for centralization, but rather as a corollary of the strengthening of the professional management at Head Office. The first Directors of this as of other joint-stock banks were local business men whose main interests were in their own trades and might incidentally conflict with those of customers at the bank. In 1837 the Board decided to appoint a Managing Director, whose duty it should be to keep a close eye on individual accounts and to bring cases before the whole Board, as far as possible without revealing the customer's identity. The appointment of a Weekly Committee consisting of Chairman, Deputy Chairman, and Managing Director further tended to strengthen the central power. These changes were followed by new definition of the duties of the Managing Director and the Superintendent *vis-à-vis* the branches, including particularly all arrangements for investments of funds in London and negotiations with the Bank of England. In 1840 the branch managers were told that they must keep within over-draft limits set by the Board, and that they would be held personally responsible for any unauthorized excesses. The depressed state of trade in the early forties reinforced the interest of Head Office in checking the branches; Lindsey Winterbotham was brought in to assist Hartland, and to have special responsibility for branch action to prevent the occurrence of bad debts, 'leaving what may be considered more strictly banking with the Manager of each place and the Managing Director': an odd division of labour!

These early developments in control necessarily depended greatly on the personalities of the few men who were feeling their way in a new world of experience. Outbursts of criticism were inevitable, and were healthy enough. When Samuel Baker became Chairman, he instituted the system of annually reporting to the Directors his views on each branch. In his first such report he let himself go, not so much on the branch concerned as on the central control:

The Weekly Committee sit for several hours every Thursday somewhat unprofitably—their labour is almost wholly directed to a system of checking the acts of the Manager, and not infrequently in resorting to remarks and resolutions tending to deprecate the course which he thinks it necessary to pursue. I think that their time should be otherwise occupied. . . . In a department so important the Manager should adopt a system of management (and carry it out by his own personal authority) so well regulated as to render himself in a great measure free from those fetters which the Weekly Committee now feel it necessary to adopt.

But a few years later Baker was more satisfied: 'It is your Chairman's opinion', he reported in 1846, 'that the Managers of Branches who are willing to follow and carry out the instructions given them are most successful.' Faithful to the latter opinion, in these years the Board brought more and more matters under the direct surveillance of itself, of the Weekly Committee, or at least of the management at Head Office. In 1845 the Board reserved to itself the right to engage or remove clerks, and instituted an annual review of the staff and the salaries paid to them. In 1852 rules were laid down, including the rate of interest chargeable on inter-branch borrowing, hitherto a matter for bargaining between the branch managers concerned; each branch was to maintain a 20 per cent. reserve against its own liabilities. A few years later surplus funds were centralized at Head Office. Each branch was to hold a local reserve of 10 per cent. against its liabilities and to share in the interest earned by the bank on the surplus funds which were now to be centralized in Head Office; correspondingly, a branch drawing on Head Office to make up its 10 per cent. reserve was to be charged 4 per cent. by Head Office. About this time, too, Baker was getting worried about the absence of any systematic checking of the securities held by the bank against loans to customers, and the first steps were taken towards the modern system of constant scrutiny. A book of rules was printed and distributed to managers in 1882; these rules soon called for qualification but, having been revised, were to be strictly enforced. 'It having been brought to the notice of the Board', ran a Minute of 1884, 'that the rules recently printed and distributed among the Managers of the several Branches for their guidance had been frequently disregarded—it was resolved that the Weekly Committee be authorised to dismiss any Manager who after this notice wilfully fails in their observance.' The old days of casual supervision by a visitor from Head Office had gone. Accountants, auditors, inspectors, all became more prominent; the structure was becoming a prototype of modern banking organization—and the share of Head Office in the total cost of administration was rising.

In other banks the same trends appear. At first the branches appear to have been almost independent banks, and Head Office control of a very loose kind crept in by the development of inspection, first by directors and then by full-time inspectors. The Plymouth and Devonport Banking Company (the Devon & Cornwall) was among the most progressive in the development of regular inspection, its first inspector being appointed as early as 1839. Accompanied by one of the Directors, he was to visit each branch once a quarter, 'to inspect the accounts, revise the limits of credit and generally to examine into the transactions of its business'. The County of Gloucester Bank appointed an inspector in 1837. His commission was in very general terms, probably because the Directors had exceptional confidence in the man. But when this first inspector left in 1860 his post was abolished as being too expensive; the economy proved itself false when the auditors uncovered a long-period fraud at Faringdon some years later. The North Wilts Bank first discussed branch inspection in 1838, and put the work into the hands of a committee. Its neighbour, the Wilts and Dorset, was more casual, making no provision at all in the early years. The Hampshire Banking Company does not appear to have had a regular system until the seventies, when it had more than twenty branches.

One of an inspector's most important duties was to ensure that Board instructions on discounts and loans were strictly observed. In a few of the banks the limits imposed on managers were so narrow that managers must have been continually in touch with Head Office on questions of individual accounts. More latitude seems to have been allowed in the discounting of bills than in other lending, although even when discounting the manager's limit was as low as £200 in the West of England and South Wales District Bank in 1834. In the Plymouth and Devonport Bank all other advances were at first dependent on reference to Head Office, and in the Wilts and Dorset the limit was only £100 as lately as 1857. The discretion of a branch manager in lending appears in general to have been so limited that there is little justification for the modern view that the nineteenth-century English customer could negotiate his borrowing on the spot; this would be true only of customers who kept their accounts at Head Offices, while customers at the branches had to kick their heels while the local manager referred to his superiors 30 or 40 miles away.

The system as it had evolved by the 1870's was, in short, one of considerable centralization of lending power and dispersion of general office control subject to increasingly tight inspection. When Lloyds itself began to grow rapidly from the sixties, it jumped from the organization of a family business in a single office to the kind of branch organization that had been evolved in the joint-stock banks in the previous thirty or forty years. Immediately before its incorporation as a joint-stock company, Lloyds and Co., the 'Birmingham Old Bank', had been in the hands of four partners, all Lloyds, running a single office in the High Street.[18] Now control passed to a Board of thirteen Directors, and the body to be controlled was soon to push out branches in increasing number.

The first hesitant steps towards a branch network were actually taken during the last year of Lloyds as a private bank, and may indeed have influenced the decision to assume the form of organization more appropriate to a branch system. First of all was Oldbury, whence Albright and Wilson, the phosphorus manufacturers, had every week to hire a coach to drive to the Birmingham bank to collect the money for wages.[19] The firm was connected by marriages with the Lloyds,[20] and the exceptional step of opening a branch was a concession within the family as well as a convenience granted to outstanding customers. The opening in the next year of a branch at Tamworth was defended by reference to its importance for the collection of deposits and its service to a large number of customers. When the Birmingham Banking Company failed in 1866 Lloyds stepped into its shoes at Walsall and Dudley, but distrust of branches remained. 'It would be better', a Birmingham Alderman maintained at a shareholders' meeting, 'to pay attention to the business in Birmingham and develop and extend that. The business in Birmingham was much more profitable; and must necessarily have more supervision

[18] Even in 1871, six years after the reorganization, Head Office and branches together employed only 115 clerks.

[19] R. E. Threlfall, *100 Years of Phosphorus Making* (Oldbury, 1951), p. 79.

[20] Arthur Albright and John Edward Wilson had married two sisters, grand-daughters of Samuel Lloyd (see facing p. 362).

LLOYDS BANK, OLDBURY
The first branch of Lloyds and Co., 1864

than so many branch establishments'. The Chairman replied by pointing to the experience of the National Provincial, successfully running a long chain of branches; and unless new branches were opened to attract deposits, discounts in Birmingham would have to be reduced. It was with this pressing need of deposits, and sometimes in response to definite requests from the local business people, that Lloyds opened eleven branches in two years; besides those already named, Longton, Warwick, Leamington, Stratford, Stafford, and Lichfield were invaded. Rugby was added in 1868 and Wolverhampton in 1872. Then, after looking at the experience of others in Manchester and Liverpool, the Directors decided to open more offices in Birmingham itself: Deritend, Edgbaston, Aston, and Halesowen. The Shropshire Banking Company brought, in 1875, four branches to the north-west; others at Burton and in the Potteries were added in these years, and in 1882 a branch was opened at West Bromwich 'in compliance with frequent suggestions and to meet the increasing requirements of that important and populous town'. By 1884 Lloyds had a total of thirty-three branches, thirteen of them established by absorption of other banks. All were within a radius of about 50 miles from Birmingham; even in that circle there was a gap in the south-west, where Lloyds did not venture into the ground strongly held by the Gloucester and Worcester joint-stock banks.

When Lloyds became a joint-stock bank and—with many searchings of heart—embarked on the course that was to make it an important country network of branches by 1884, there was readiness for the revolution of administration that was to come. Howard Lloyd has described the confusion in which the book-keepers tried to cope with the new business that poured in. 'From the Managing Director down to junior clerks no one had the slightest idea how to work the new ledgers on the progressive system or how to start or carry on proper entries in the new suit (*sic*) of books ordered, and brought into use on the first day of the new Company's business.' Help was sought from one of the Liverpool banks[21] which lent a clerk (he later became an inspector in Lloyds) and from Liverpool accountants who sent Mr. Alexander down to Birmingham. Even a leading Birmingham customer, Messrs. Rabone Bros. and Co., sent a man along 'to witness and join in the confusion that befell'. For a

[21] Cf. p. 52 above.

fortnight no daily balance would come right; neither the ledgers nor the London account could be checked. By the end of the month, however, 'the machine was in fair working order'. Even so, the year-end balance-sheet was beyond everyone in the building, until Howard Lloyd took down from the shelves of the private room the two volumes of Gilbart's *Banking*, and with much sweating of the brow put the figures together.

These long-remembered toils in the first year were sufficient to get a reasonable book-keeping system established, but the adjustment of managerial functions and relations with the branches evolved much more slowly. At first the supervision of business was arranged almost as though only a single office—and a small one at that—was in question. Sampson Samuel Lloyd became Managing Director with chief executive responsibility, and the Board appointed a Committee of Reference 'Whom the Managing Director is authorised to consult at any time upon the subjects of customers' accommodation and discounts and whose duty it shall also be to look over the overdrafts and bills once a week before the meeting of the Board.' The managers of the early branches appear to have consulted this Committee or the Managing Director on quite trivial matters: from Oldbury the Managing Director's sanction was sought for advances as low as £50, and the branch manager frequently took customers along to see him before business was settled. As more branches were opened and business expanded this became an impossible arrangement, and in 1868 the Managing Director, contemplating resignation, drew up an indictment. Although the Head Office manager had recently been relieving him of some of the interviews with customers, he himself was still far too fully occupied in personal interviews, conducting correspondence, and attending through two whole days a week the tiresome Reference Committee. This Committee, he complained, gave decisions 'which have restricted and embarrassed the Managing Director in the discharge of his responsibilities (frequently greatly against his own judgement) and rendered him unable to decide with promptitude questions of business which daily arise.' After this criticism the Reference Committee appears to have become rather an investigating and advisory body, giving preliminary consideration to matters in which a Board decision was really necessary. Another of S. S. Lloyd's recommendations, that a General Manager be appointed to relieve the Managing Director of some of his burdens, was followed in 1871, when Howard Lloyd assumed this post in addition, for the present, to the Secretaryship. The General Manager's duties were thus defined:

(a) To attend all Meetings of the Board and Committees.
(b) To have the charge of the Finances of the Bank.
(c) To inspect all the Bills that come into the Bank.
(d) To inspect from time to time all the Branches and examine all the securities.
(e) To appoint all the clerks and fix the salaries.
(f) To advise and consult with the Managers but without relieving them from their responsibility to the Board.

When Howard Lloyd undertook these duties there were sixteen branches besides sub-branches and agencies. Although an immensely industrious man, with quite extraordinary mastery of detail and memory for it, he could hardly hope to take all these duties in his stride, even had the bank not continued to grow. As it was, the further growth (to thirty-three branches in 1884 and 266 when Howard Lloyd retired in 1902) made the burden altogether too heavy and the history of the administration during the ensuing 30 years is largely the switching of the more routine elements to new specialist branches of Head Office.

An important duty among those so devolved upon newly established officers was that of inspection. In the early days the Directors (and behind them the shareholders) had largely depended upon the auditors. The firm of Edwin Laundy and Co., the leading accountants in Birmingham, were appointed auditors in 1865; Mr. Laundy was 'a very exact elderly Quaker' who with the aid of his partner conducted the audit with due care and severity. They visited every branch at least twice a year, checking cash and ledgers as well as securities. This was a manageable task at the outset, and when coupled with the peregrinations of the Managing Director it was thought adequate; S. S. Lloyd in 1868 thought it excellent. But in 1871 several frauds were uncovered and the auditors were asked to consider intensification of their examination. They, however, thought that their duties should be restricted to verifying the accounts at the half-years, and suggested that inspection should become a managerial duty. Inspection was, as we have seen, listed among Howard Lloyd's duties as General Manager; in due course branches were notified that a special inspecting clerk, Mr. Crosbie, had been appointed. Branch managers were asked to give any necessary assistance, and were also told that, while the inspecting clerk would be responsible to the General Manager, he had been instructed to act with the greatest deference to every branch manager. Crosbie continued in charge of this work until his retirement in 1896; long before this he had become, as chief of a team of inspectors, one of the institutions of the bank, evidence enough of his success in establishing the desired relations with the branches.

Five years after the Inspectors' Department had made its one-man start Howard Lloyd divested himself of his office as Secretary of the bank; the new Secretary remained responsible to him as General Manager. In 1879, continuing increase in the General Manager's work led to the establishment of the Advance Department at Head Office, with Mr. J. M. Richardson in charge. Howard Lloyd as General Manager maintained his general responsibility, and with increasing experience found himself more able to anticipate Board decisions. The lightening of some of his routine difficulties also gave him more time to conduct the increasingly frequent negotiations for amalgamations, an activity he made peculiarly his own. And when an amalgamation was completed, Howard Lloyd gave much attention, as we shall see in the next chapter, to the delicate tasks of welding together the formerly independent units. He continued to hold tightly in his own hand some of his original functions—to the last those employed in the bank had his individual attention—but Howard Lloyd was becoming much more than a bank manager: he was establishing himself as the architect-in-chief of an institution transformed beyond all recognition.

12

AMALGAMATION AND EXPANSION

IF Howard Lloyd had been asked in 1920 to say in a word what had happened to English banks in the previous fifty years, the first word to come to his lips would almost certainly have been 'Amalgamation'. For the amalgamation movement had dominated the story of English banking for as long as living bankers could remember. A trickle in the middle decades of the nineteenth century, it had become a headlong rush as the century neared its end. In the new century amalgamations continued to follow one upon another, and they were now amalgamations between banks already greatly enlarged by earlier absorptions. Finally, during the 1914–18 war the movement culminated in the formation of the 'Big Five', of which Lloyds was one. At the same time the banks taking the lead were expanding by the opening of new offices, generally filling 'gaps' so that the double process of amalgamation and branch establishment gave to each of the Big Five a network that could with little exaggeration be described as nation-wide. The bankers continued to call themselves the London Clearing Banks, but they had become the English banks.

For the amalgamation movement, by which this transformation largely came about, there is no starting date: there had been amalgamations practically as long as there had been banks. Even before 1826, in the days when joint-stock organization was ruled out by the Bank of England's privileges, one private bank would join forces with another private bank, especially if one of the partnerships was too narrowly based to provide a continuous line of reasonable ability or family wealth. The earliest example recorded in Lloyds banks was about 1796 in Caernarvon; there the business was sold by the founder's son to a Chester bank, the vendor staying on as manager. Another case, in 1829, exemplifies situations which must have been common enough in the previous thirty or forty years. In Bury St. Edmunds the bank of Oakes and Son (as a separate banking business it had existed since about 1795) was weakened by the death of James Oakes; Robert Bevan of the Bevan Bank had long considered his business insecure, though not unprofitable, and he grasped the opportunity to join with the next generations of the Oakes family. This would, thought Bevan—against the sceptical view of his wife's trustees—'make my business more safe as well as lucrative'. The event justified Bevan's confidence, for Oakes, Bevan and Co.[1] survived as a private bank into the twentieth century before being absorbed into the Capital and Counties and eventually becoming the Bury St. Edmund's branch of Lloyds Bank.

In the second quarter of the nineteenth century amalgamations between one private bank and another continued, but many more were directed to the establishment or enlargement of joint-stock banks. Indeed many of the earliest joint-stock banks in the country were formed on the basis of two, three, or four private banks which decided that the future lay with the new system, though here again, as in the earlier amalgamations, the primary motive in one or other of the partnerships might be the desire to escape from a position weakened by recent death or trading losses. The Glamorganshire Banking Company, for example, emerged in 1836 from Eaton, Knight and Stroud of Swansea, and Williams and Rowland of Neath; the former was a reconstruction of Eaton and Gibbins which had been in trouble in 1825 and probably still felt in need of strength. Another such case was the formation in 1836 of the Shropshire Banking Company by the amalgamation of four partnerships: Reynolds Charlton and Co. of Wellington, Biddle, Mountford, Pidcock and Cope of Shifnal, Darby and Co. of Coalbrookdale, and Hordern and Hill of Newport, all of them well-established banks but converts to the view that joint-stock organization of the four together was the right way to face the future. In 1839 two private banks in Burton-on-Trent amalgamated, to form the Burton, Uttoxeter and Staffordshire Union Bank. Several years later, after the slump and then Peel's legislation had put the brake upon joint-stock establishments, the Bucks and Oxon Union Bank was formed by the merging of three private banks. Preliminary dis-

---

[1] After 1895 the enlarged partnership traded as Oakes, Bevan, Tollemache and Co., the Bury and Suffolk Bank.

cussions had begun in 1850 between Zacharias Hunt of Aylesbury and Thomas Hearne of the Buckingham Old Bank, but Hunt thought that joint-stocks were not 'much in favour with the public at present'. The possibility of interlocking partnerships—of which there were examples elsewhere—was next considered, but Hunt thought partnership in two banks would cause embarrassments. When a third partnership—Cobbs of Banbury—was brought into the negotiations, doubts were expressed in that quarter also about a joint-stock organization. By this time, however, one of the Buckingham partners accepted the inevitability of joint-stock organization sooner or later, and in 1852 steps were taken to secure the Board of Trade's approval, necessary under the Act of 1844. The Board's lawyers made many difficulties—Peel's conditions proved no empty formality—but at last the Letters Patent were forthcoming and the three partnerships gave way, in July 1853, to the one joint-stock company. The change involved, under the Bank Charter Act, loss of rights of note-issue, a matter of regret at least to Aylesbury.

Once joint-stock banks were founded, whether in this or some other way, they might run for many years—as did the Bucks and Oxon—without further amalgamation. Others—and particularly those founded in the thirties by apostles of the joint-stock form—enlarged themselves continually by the purchase of private partnerships. The motives behind these amalgamations were by no means uniform: one odd case was the absorption, by the new-born Coventry and Warwickshire Banking Company, of Messrs. Beck and Prime because the company wished to secure the services of James Beck as General Manager. The absorption, by the County of Gloucester Bank in 1842, of Messrs. Strange and Co. at Swindon and Highworth appears to have been similarly inspired. Two partners in the Swindon bank were retained as joint managers, and when the Gloucester bank wanted to open a branch at Stow, they regretted that they could not, by a procedure similar to that followed at Swindon, find a qualified manager. The Plymouth and Devonport in 1832 made a clean sweep in Kingsbridge: the cholera struck down Mr. Nicholson senior, and the Plymouth and Devonport thereupon absorbed both Nicholson and Son and Mr. George Fox's bank 'so as to form one effective bank for Kingsbridge and its vicinity'. Nicholson junior and his clerk and Fox were all retained, and all the business was brought into Fox's premises.

Few amalgamations in this early period have left any detailed record; one of the few surviving accounts is of the prolonged negotiations leading to the absorption in 1842 by the Gloucestershire Banking Company of the Cripps family banking business at Cirencester and Stow-on-the-Wold. The initiative came from the Cripps family, possibly in consequence of the failing health of the senior partner. The balance-sheet was not encouraging: there was an overdraft with London agents; such bills of exchange as could be reckoned liquid amounted to only £32,000; and no less than £65,000 was tied up in the acceptances of a single railway company. The family asked, and eventually received, a price of two years' net profits, on condition that the family assumed responsibility for any accounts the Gloucestershire Banking Company should decide to reject. (A clause of this kind became common form in bank amalgamations.) A younger Cripps was retained as manager, and another as local Director. The implementation of this agreement proved no simple matter. The new manager fell below standard, and though deference to the feelings of the family (who remained important customers) gave young Cripps a long run, patience was finally exhausted and after five years he had to go. The outstanding debts dragged on even longer: a total of £116,000 was involved and in 1847 £55,000 remained outstanding. In 1848 securities deposited by the family were realized and all but £7,000 repaid; by this time the company decided that the family had done enough, and the £7,000 was written off. The two branches were doing pretty well for the bank—Cirencester alone yielding some £3,400 in annual profit—and the Directors felt justified in doing the handsome thing to terminate a wearisome business.

Although amalgamation was already becoming a method by which the joint-stock system would supersede private banking, many private bankers and many of their customers maintained their faith in the old system. To these, amalgamation among themselves appeared a source of strength whereby they might maintain the old ways; amalgamations of one private bank with another therefore continued to occur right through the nineteenth century. Among the more important of these combinations of private bankers was that of Hanbury, Taylor and Lloyds with their neighbours in Lombard Street, Barnett Hoares. The occasion of their coming together in 1864 seems to have been the need of Barnett Hoares for larger premises; at any rate, the initiative came from their side at a time when their expanding business had caused them to think hard about the accommodation problem. The secrecy with which discussion between banks had to be conducted is illustrated by the fact that the critical talks between Gurney Hoare and Robert Hanbury were held at the brewery in which Hanbury was a partner. The profit record of the previous ten years was taken into account, and Barnetts were able to enforce their position as the dominant partners: their share of the new capital was to be £104,000 out of £143,000. Barnetts did, however, concede that four of the others' partners, with five from Barnetts, should be partners in the new firm. One of the four was a Lloyd, a relative of the Birmingham Lloyds,[2] and the agency of the Birmingham bank was an important part of the business they brought. As the name of the London agent necessarily appeared on certain drafts and notes issued at Birmingham, the Birmingham Lloyds asked their London cousins to press for retention of their name in the new title and the new London partnership was eventually called Barnetts, Hoares, Hanbury and Lloyd.

1867 saw another such amalgamation in Lombard Street, Bosanquet, Whatman, Harman and Bosanquet merging with Stevenson Salt and Sons, to become Bosanquet Salt and Co. There was a personal link between this firm and Lloyds at Birmingham, for the latter had in 1866 absorbed Stevenson Salt of Stafford which had partners in common with the Lombard Street firm. The interest of Thomas Salt, Director of Lloyds Banking Company, was later to be important in bringing Bosanquet Salt and Co. into Lloyds. In the West End Herries Farquhar absorbed in 1865 Call Marten and Co. In Southampton Atherley Falls joined with Maddison Pearce in 1869. In the eighties Fox Fowlers of Wellington were already becoming West Country giants among private bankers, absorbing Marshall and Harding at Barnstaple and then Gill and Morshead at Tavistock. In Shrewsbury the two private banks of Rocke Eyton and Co. and Burton Lloyds and Co. joined forces. In 1893, on the other side of the country, Bacon Cobbolds of Ipswich merged with Cox Cobbolds at Harwich; the two had had a common line of partners with a name destined to be heard again in English banking history.

[2] This was R. H. Lloyd (see facing p. 362).

Among the amalgamations in which joint-stock banks were engaged, two stand apart in that the motive in each case was the desire of a country bank to gain a seat in the London Bankers' Clearing House. The importance attached to this by Lloyds Banking Company and by the Capital and Counties Bank underlines at once the efficiency of the Clearing House and the growing importance to these banks of business with areas (including London) beyond their established range of branches.

The Capital and Counties was the first to make the attempt. In 1877 (or late 1876), having lately become by amalgamation the Hampshire and North Wilts Banking Company, and having opened an office in Threadneedle Street, the bank applied for admission to the Clearing House. This was refused: the Lombard Street bankers who ruled the Clearing House decided that a country bank with practically all its business in the country did not become a London bank simply by putting its name on a door within the Square Mile; no doubt Lombard Street had an eye on the profits of its agency work for the country banks. The Hampshire and North Wilts next tried (in 1878) to force the Clearing House Committee's hand by buying up the ancient Lombard Street bank of Willis Percival, which had just failed with liabilities over half a million. The preliminary agreement for absorption fell through when the Clearing House Committee refused to be bounced into allowing the Clearing House seat of Willis Percival to be bought as part of the business: the Committee resolved 'that in the opinion of this Committee the Hampshire and North Wilts Banking Company is at present essentially a country Bank, but that if in virtue of the arrangement referred to in Mr. Willis' letter or otherwise their business in London should become important the Committee would be willing to consider any application from them for admission to the Clearing'. Nevertheless the purchase of Willis Percival went forward. The Hampshire and North Wilts paid £9,000 and paid out £238,000 in cash (subsequently recouped by liquidation of the Willis Percival assets) to settle the creditors at 9s. in the £. The bank emphasized its London acquisition by renaming itself The Capital and Counties Bank, and a few years later, after repeated applications, succeeded in persuading the Clearing House Committee that its London business now justified admission. So one of the main stems of the Lloyds tree became recognized as belonging to the select circle of London banks, absorbing in the process the ruins of one of the oldest banking firms in the City.

It was not long before Lloyds of Birmingham followed the example, and Howard Lloyd, looking back from twenty years later, described it as 'the most important forward step of the bank's history'. A country bank without a London office was like an image with feet of clay. Scottish bankers who had recently come to London were boasting of the profits that had resulted: one of them told Howard Lloyd that he was making an additional £20,000 a year on his London balances. It was high time, the Board of Lloyds Banking Company decided, for them to have their own footing in the City. The London agency of the Birmingham Head Office and of several branches was in the hands of Barnetts Hoares by reason of their amalgamation with Hanbury Taylor and Lloyds which had been the family connexion since 1770, while the remaining branches of Lloyds employed Bosanquet Salt and Co. The greater weight as well as the long tradition of the Barnett connexion seemed to point to an approach to them, but Howard Lloyd was a little shy of such a big fish. An approach to Bosanquets looked easier, Thomas Salt being both Director of Lloyds and partner in Bosanquets, and through him negotiations were opened. Lloyds made no secret of the fact that it was the seat in the Clearing House that particularly interested them, and made their offer conditional upon entrance to the Clearing House without necessarily moving the Head Office to London. Subject to this condition, Lloyds were very keen to buy, and Bosanquets made the most of their situation; an extraordinarily high price was paid for the goodwill. Howard Lloyd had no doubt that it was worth it; in fact, he was encouraged to look more seriously at the bigger fish. To his surprise and pleasure, 'a brief reply came in the handwriting of Mr. (afterwards Sir Samuel) Hoare intimating that they would not refuse discussion and consideration of such advances and proposals if made'. Circumstances had been disposing Barnetts Hoares that way; they, with some of their country correspondents, had recently suffered discomfort and embarrassment from frauds by a Stock Exchange firm, and Samuel Hoare himself was more interested in politics than in banking. To the surprise of the City, no less than that of the Directors at Birmingham, the thing was done. The two Lombard Street partnerships were absorbed simultaneously. Barnetts received £150,000 in cash and

7,000 shares, £8 per share paid. The market price of the shares was about £24, and on this basis the consideration represented about seven years' profits, greatly exceeding the 'four or five years of preceding annual profit' which Howard Lloyd regarded as setting 'a fair or maximum standard'.[3] Bosanquets' partners received 5,000 shares and, it is almost certain, no cash. This, too, Howard Lloyd thought 'inordinately costly', though the double purchase was abundantly justified by subsequent development. Three partners of Bosanquets and four of Barnetts joined the Board of what now became, cumbrously and ephemerally, Lloyds Barnetts and Bosanquets Bank.

By the time the Capital and Counties and Lloyds established themselves as London Clearing Bankers, the tide of absorption of private banks by the joint-stocks was running strongly, and had become—in Bagehot's *Lombard Street* for example—almost an accepted step in Victorian progress. The circumstances prompting individual absorptions of private banks were very much as Bagehot pictured them: loss of family interest or ability in the business, financial weakness, or even simply loss of faith in the ability of private banks to survive in a world of joint-stock banks. In the 1860's and 1870's most of those absorbed by Lloyds were firms in which the families were losing the enthusiasm or the ability of the older generation of bankers. At Wednesbury death reduced Messrs. P. and H. Williams to a single owner, a wealthy man whose real interest was in his iron and coal business. Having no taste for banking, he sold the firm to Lloyds in 1865 for £15,000 in cash, representing three years' profits. He was not even interested enough to accept shares in the bank, though he was eventually persuaded to qualify as a Director, bringing to the Board useful knowledge of the local iron and coal trades. Butlins at Rugby was just such another case: the partners were tired of business, they were wealthy, and no younger generation was ready to carry on. So in 1868 Lloyds bought them out, like Williams's, for £15,000 cash representing three years' profits. Howard Lloyd thought it a good bargain, the business being in such a healthy state. A higher price was paid for Fryers at Wolverhampton, where the surviving partner had become an

---

[3] He allowed that 'more may rightly be given in the shape of premium value of shares allotted'. At this time it was not uncommon for small banks to be bought for three years' profits, paid in cash.

M.P. and had no great faith in his nephew's capacity to cope with the worrying borrowers in Cannock Chase. In 1900 Cunliffe Brooks of Manchester failed, after three successful generations, to maintain the family line; the bank came into Lloyds. In 1912 a family bank in Lincolnshire (Peacock Willsons) was bought by Lloyds following the death of the last family partner. In the previous generation the family had had the distinction of providing the leader of Fane's Horse in the Indian Mutiny; he was for many years a partner in the bank but left no descendants to carry on the bank. In Pagets and Kirby at Leicester, Thomas Tertius Paget died in 1892, leaving no Thomas the fourth to carry on: he had provided for the situation by the preliminary negotiations leading to absorption by Lloyds in 1895. The Capital and Counties similarly in 1883 took over Haydon and Co. at Guildford when one of the two partners became too ill to continue in business.

In most of these cases the basis of purchase was a cash price reckoned to be so many years' profits. The purchaser had to look carefully at both sides of the balance-sheet. Sometimes potential bad debts were specified and excluded from the bargain, while on the other side of the account liabilities on old notes had to be taken into account. Dormant balances, those small but welcome perquisites the silent law allows to bankers, sometimes entered into the bargaining; retention by the vendor could complicate bank accounts for long afterwards. Merriman knew the drill on this—he had been on the other side of the table when the North Wilts bought the family bank to which he belonged. Negotiating now with Haydons, he insisted that an agreed balance-sheet be drawn up so that any subsequent claims not listed in the balance-sheet should be unmistakably the responsibility of the vendors. Although the amalgamation was agreed and was effective as at 1 October 1883, it was not until 1888 that Merriman settled with the partners precisely what was and what was not taken over.

Reservations as to particular accounts were far more important when the private bank was being absorbed primarily because its financial situation was weak. The absorbing bank would in any event think twice about engaging in such a transaction at all, and the Directors of Lloyds often remarked that they declined many opportunities. But there were occasional instances where an expanding bank could think some price worth paying in order to secure quickly a foothold in a new district. Sometimes Lloyds or the Capital and Counties would actually take over after the private bank had shut its doors, the purchase being scarcely more than acquisition of premises; in other cases the bigger bank might step in soon enough to prevent a smash, and so secure appreciable good-will as well as an office, office stool, and ageing clerk. Thus the Capital and Counties in 1886 thought James Knight and Son, Farnham, worth £9,000. Knights had deposits of only £27,000 and were £42,000 in debt to their London agents; their considerable capital was largely tied up in £159,000 of overdrafts, probably mainly on partners' accounts. Despite this odd balance-sheet, the bank stood quite well in the district, and the Capital and Counties thought one of its partners worth employing as £400-a-year manager. Slocock Matthews at Newbury got themselves into trouble by financing a local man's invention for smoke-abatement. The inventor found nobody to buy his appliance, so the bankers thought it wise to find someone to buy the bank before worse befell: they sold to the Capital and Counties for £24,000 in 1895. Beechings of Tonbridge, Tunbridge Wells, Hastings, and Bexhill, was once a prosperous little bank, but in the eighties one of the partners speculated unsuccessfully on the Stock Exchange and his debt to the firm ran into six figures. To make good the loss, his partners sold their estates and the goodwill of the bank: Lloyds paid a price representing four years' profits, and retained three of the Beeching family as branch managers.

The weakness of Wells, Hogge and Co., Biggleswade and Baldock, arose not from any particular misadventure but from general slackness over a long period, due perhaps to the partners' preference for activity in the brewing business which was closely linked with the bank. When the brewery itself went downhill, the partners approached Thomas Salt, then Chairman of Lloyds. He gave advice but made no offer to purchase; four years later they approached the Capital and Counties who paid £8,000 cash on the understanding that debts amounting to £46,000 were taken over by a partner.

When banks had actually collapsed before absorption the purchasing bank usually sought to salvage some goodwill by helping in a composition with the firm's creditors. Messrs. Eliot Pearce and Co., of Weymouth, with branches at Dorchester, Portland, Bournemouth, and Boscombe, had been weak for many years, trading since 1884 with no partners' capital at all. They looked for salvation in speculation in land at Dorchester, but it was ill-judged, and even the cheap-money period of the mid-nineties did not save them. When dearer money returned in 1896 their portfolio of stocks and shares dropped sharply in value and their Dorchester speculation looked worse than ever. They approached Lloyds with a view to sale, but Howard Lloyd decided to let them take their fall. When they suspended payment in 1897 the event 'was taken very quietly and hurt no-one but themselves and customers. Hardly a dog barked or a cock crew.' The Capital and Counties conditionally agreed on £12,000 for the goodwill, for the sake of immediate entry into the premises, and they consoled depositors by offering immediate advances up to 5s. in the £ against their claims on Eliot Pearce. The price paid for the goodwill was to be proportionately reduced if the deposits at the offices should be lower after one year, and under this clause the sum paid by the Capital and Counties was in the event reduced from £12,000 to £3,700. Lloyds acted similarly twenty years later, in taking over what remained of the Naval Bank at Plymouth, owned by Messrs. Harris Bulteel and Co. This business had been tottering for a very long time, and back in the seventies had made its first approach to Lloyds. Again in 1909 they sounded Howard Lloyd; he thought 'if solvent, locked up' described them. Unless strengthened by new partnership capital the Naval Bank would, thought Howard Lloyd, have to sell out to another bank: 'But I don't want Lloyds to be the one though our Chairman is half inclined.' The partners decided to carry on, and their business became the one bank in the kingdom to be broken by the financial crisis of August 1914. On their putting up the shutters Lloyds stepped in with an agreement to advance 5s. in the £ to depositors and to allow overdraft facilities for customers of the Naval Bank. The final transfer of business was caught in unusual legal complications, and it was not until 1917 that Lloyds finally settled on payment of £4,000 for the goodwill.

In both these cases in the south-west the purchasing bank eventually paid a small sum for immediate access to premises and what little goodwill could be salvaged from a decrepit business. Head's Bank at East Grinstead and Edenbridge, when it failed in 1892, seemed worth even less. Nevertheless Lloyds walked into the premises at once, made its own arrangement with the London and Westminster Bank (the London agents who held the title deeds as security), and offered the creditors' trustees the problematical sum of three times the first year's profits.

A rather different case, illustrating other aspects of the amalgamation movement, was that of Hill and Sons of Smithfield. As might be guessed from the location of its Head Office, this little bank was wrapped up in the cattle trade: its branch list—Islington, Deptford, Romford, and Liverpool—has its own tale to tell of the history of London's meat supplies during the nineteenth century. Towards the end of that century cattle traders and butchers supplying the London market were becoming very big men, too big for Hills to manage. So Hills began looking to their Lombard Street agents, Glyn Mills, for loans to enable them to lend the big sums their customers were now seeking. Many other London bankers by this time would, in similar circumstances, have been quick to swallow the little bank, but Glyns were unambitious and though, as they wrote to Hills in 1906, 'always happy to grant you any facilities in our power', preferred to advise sale of the business elsewhere. In 1908 there were negotiations, all unsuccessful, with Parrs and with the London Joint Stock Bank. Then in 1910 Lloyds Bank took over the agency and lent Hills the money with which Glyns could be paid off. In 1911 the process was completed by amalgamation of the bank with Lloyds, whose resources allowed the branch manager at Smithfield to lend, without turning a hair, the sums wanted by the big men of the meat trade.

From about 1890 onwards the process gathered speed. Goschen's attack in 1891 on the inadequacy of cash reserves[4] was among the causes of this acceleration. The suggestion that their cash reserves ought to be of the order of 15 per cent. set them thinking hard: it would at best mean a sharp reduction in profits, and might be achieved only by putting more capital into the business. In one case—that of Hart Fellows at Nottingham—the effect came directly and quickly: rather than publish a balance-sheet, they transferred the business to Lloyds in return for shares issued at £16 (against the market price of £28). More generally

[4] Cf. above, pp. 214 and 225.

252

Goschen's campaign merely served to sharpen in the minds of the private bankers the fear that their day was coming to an end. Twinings in the Strand, a remarkably strong bank with a long family tradition, in 1891 resisted the argument from a joint-stock bidder that 'the public mind has pronounced decidedly against private banks', but they were in fact already half convinced. If they did not amalgamate they would have to bring in more capital and publish their accounts. 'Of course', commented Richard Twining, '*both can* be done if there should be no help for it.' But they preferred to accept an offer—a good price, in the shape of 2,000 shares on special terms—from Lloyds. The senior partner wrote personally to many customers to advise them of the change; one of them replied by removing his account to another private bank.

Farther up the Strand, Praeds and Co. now accepted proposals they had disdained six years earlier. Cobb and Co. at Margate joined the procession in the same year (1891). In Lincolnshire the Capital and Counties bought (by issue of shares) Garfit Claypon and Co., and at Teignmouth, Watts Whidborne and Co. Both these transactions were the work of Mr. Merriman, who had become a leading figure in the amalgamation movement. Spencer Philips, who became Chairman of Lloyds in 1898, was just such another. While these two men were guiding the destinies of Lloyds and the Capital and Counties, other joint-stock banks were engaging in the same business; the 'movement' had in fact become something of a race, a race in which personalities counted for much. In the earlier days the joint-stock banks could establish themselves and expand not only by eating up the private banks but also by moving into towns where for one reason or another little banking service had previously been available. By the end of the nineteenth century gaps in the banking map had become very rare, and a bank bent on expansion had to achieve its aim by invading someone else's territory. Much the quickest and most effective way of invading a town already provided with banks was to swallow one of these banks. And these end-of-the-century bankers were expansionist-minded —stagnation was alien to the air of late Victorian business.

In the final phase of the amalgamation movement the remaining small banks therefore found that they did not have to take the initiative: the big banks were after them, and were indeed sometimes making competitive bids against each other. The Canterbury Bank of Messrs. Hammond and

Co. was one of the prosperous little concerns that bided their time and eventually found themselves able to pick and choose between the bids of the big fellows who were competing for their goodwill. Both Barclays and the London and County Banking Company (later in the Westminster) approached Hammonds in 1897, the latter's offer having the unusual attraction of being entirely in cash. Mr. Furley, one of the senior partners, advised his colleagues to hold fast: the bank had never been in a more prosperous state, though the time might come when feeling against private banks would become too strong. Lloyds made a tentative approach in 1898; their overtures were immediately rejected. In 1902 the Dover manager of the Capital and Counties came along with a suggestion of eight to ten years' purchase on the basis of profits over the last five years. (How Howard Lloyd's standards were being left behind!) The partners would not even agree to meeting Mr. Merriman. A few months later Prescotts tried; they did get as far as a meeting but a slip by a Prescotts' manager put an end to negotiations.[5] Then in May 1903 the death of Mr. Hammond, one of the senior partners, brought matters to a head. No less than six London banks were immediately on the doorstep: Barclays, the London and County, Lloyds, and the Capital and Counties all renewed their suits, almost in the ante-chamber of death, and the National Provincial and the Union of London and Smiths joined in the bidding. Lloyds reached discussion of specific terms and broke on the period over which profits should be calculated: Hammonds had been doing better in the last two years and insisted on this as the standard period. The Union of London and Smiths were willing to take this two years' period, if Hammonds would agree on eight years' purchase. Merriman, for the Capital and Counties, was ready to go higher, and eventually settled at twelve years' purchase on the two-years base, without waiting to know what this figure would be. The price finally worked out at £189,672, in addition to the price paid for premises at Canterbury, Ramsgate, and Whitstable. This did not put an end to the competition, for a few months later the Union of London and Smiths opened a branch at Canterbury with one of

---

[5] The manager of Prescotts' branch at Faversham, addressing an envelope to go through the post to the Canterbury bank, unthinkingly wrote 'Messrs. Prescotts', which he crossed out and corrected. But Hammonds, on receiving the envelope, were afraid of public association of the two names, judged the envelope a grave indiscretion, and broke off negotiations.

254

the old bank's family connexions as local director. The former partners of Hammonds felt that this broke the spirit of their sale to the Capital and Counties and tried, without success, to persuade Mr. Plumptre to withdraw from his directorship.

The tide engulfing the private banks was almost equally powerful against the smaller joint-stock banks. The Warwick and Leamington Banking Company in 1866 found its position very like that of a private bank: a small body of shareholders could find no likely successors to the elderly Directors, and a bargain was concluded with Lloyds. This odd case is perhaps the exception which proves the rule that the joint-stock method of organization provides continuity lacking in a private business; in general the joint-stock banks did not sell out to their big brothers for this reason. But other sources of weakness could affect the smaller joint-stock banks equally with private banks, and many of the absorptions, particularly the earlier ones, were occasioned by some important weakness in the smaller business. Notable examples were the English and Jersey Union Bank taken over by the Hampshire Banking Company in 1873, the Shropshire Banking Company bought by Lloyds in 1874, the Bucks and Oxon Union Bank absorbed by Lloyds in 1902, the Cornish Bank by the Capital and Counties in 1902, and Grant and Maddison's Union Banking Company by Lloyds in 1903.

The Jersey amalgamation in 1873 was the sequel to a severe banking crisis in the Channel Isles, beginning in February of that year. When a second bank failed in July, the General Manager of the Hampshire Banking Company sent his Portsmouth manager over to Jersey to see what could be salvaged.[6] On arrival he found a third bank, the English and Jersey Union, in difficulties consequent upon the earlier failures, and within a few weeks he had persuaded the shareholders to accept an offer of absorption by the Hampshire bank. He proceeded to assist in the orderly liquidation of one of the other banks, and so established the Hampshire's goodwill on such a firm footing that no other English bank ventured competition in the Islands until 1897.

The decision of the Shropshire Banking Company to sell out arose not

[6] The Portsmouth manager, Mr. F. J. Hooper, travelled at short notice and expected to be back within a week, but he became Jersey manager and stayed thirty-five years. His records include the copy of his letter to the railway company seeking refund on the unused return half of his ticket.

from any sudden collapse but on reflection upon difficulties long drawn out. In 1856 fraud had occasioned a loss of £184,000,[7] and the personal contributions of the Directors lessened but did not avoid the consequent call on shareholders. Then in 1867 Mr. Abraham Darby, an important customer in the iron trade, went bankrupt and the realization of some security for his borrowings proved difficult and costly. After struggling on for some years the company decided to throw in its lot with a more powerful concern that would be less vulnerable to the inroads made by a few big customers.

The absorption of the Bucks and Oxon Union Bank by Lloyds in 1902 was occasioned directly by the fall in the price of Consols. The Bucks and Oxon had had a good reputation through its fifty years, and its operations had in the main justified this reputation. But, as the Chairman of Lloyds told his shareholders, the Directors of the little bank had 'divided up their profits a little too closely', with the result that their reserve fund was scarcely sufficient to cover the depreciation of their investment portfolio when the cheap money of the mid-nineties gave way to the rising interest rates that characterized the succeeding period. £27,000 depreciation looked uncomfortably large against capital and reserves totalling £120,000. Had the Directors confined their lending to commerce and industry on their usual conservative lines they might well have had a longer life as an independent bank. Having put money into long-term government securities, their shareholders were left reflecting that in accepting the terms of purchase by Lloyds—terms signalizing a big drop against the previous market value of their shares—they were making 'the best of a bad bargain'. Bankers making up their balance-sheets in 1955 would no doubt sympathize.

The same circumstances of depreciating Consols helped to drive the Cornish Bank into the arms of the Capital and Counties in that same year 1902. Their loss on this account was not as heavy as that experienced by the Bucks and Oxon, but it came at a time when the bank was weakened by a curious repercussion of the South African War. Many Cornishmen, with their metal-mining tradition, had emigrated in the nineties to the South African mines and had been in the habit of sending home thousands of pounds—partly to remain on deposit and partly for the support

[7] Cf. p. 80 above.

of their families. When the outbreak of war disrupted business in South Africa this flow of money dried up and was even reversed, drafts on the deposits being necessary to support Cornishmen out there. Like the Bucks and Oxon, this little joint-stock bank might well have survived these temporary sources of weakness, but given the fashion for bigger banks they probably did well to sell out to the ambitious bankers from Birmingham and Threadneedle Street.

Others among the smaller joint-stock banks were affected in some degree by the fall in Consols, but as the years went on the decisive factor seems to have been the feeling that the future lay with bigger banks. The movement was inevitably cumulative: as firms became accustomed to finding the familiar banking names in new localities to which their own business was extending, they dropped into the habit of continuing their business with the big branch systems to the exclusion of the surviving local banks. Even before the end of the nineteenth century the Glamorganshire Bank was remarking upon this:

There is a movement on the part of Midland manufacturers now to transfer their establishments to the seaboard and where that is impracticable to open offices at the shipping ports. A firm coming to Swansea would know little of the Glamorganshire Bank and they would quite naturally do their business with one of the greater firms [banks]. Thus handicapped the Glamorganshire Bank would as time went on find an increasing difficulty in even maintaining its business; much greater in extending it.

Succeeding years brought no reason to reverse this view; in 1898, therefore, the Glamorganshire Banking Company was absorbed into the Capital and Counties, bringing to the latter a useful extension and consolidation of the South Wales territory it had entered thirteen years earlier.

Whether the bank involved in a proposed merger was small or large, the utmost secrecy enshrouded the negotiations. This secrecy was no doubt inspired partly—especially where sizeable joint-stock banks were concerned—by a desire to avoid giving a handle to speculators in a company's shares. To the smaller banks it was important that there should be no suspicion that the bank was having to seek the help of a stronger institution; otherwise its deposits might melt away and the value of its goodwill dwindle before negotiations could be brought to finality. And even if customers were not frightened, they might take offence; at any rate, the retiring private banker preferred his customers to have the first word from himself. Bankers had also to consider their position in dealing with competing bids: if amalgamation were rumoured, shareholders and depositors might demand more information which could be disclosed only at the risk of compromising a negotiation or affecting the terms that might be obtained elsewhere. So, for one reason or another, the parties tried to keep negotiations a very close secret. In the abortive negotiations between the Wilts and Dorset and Grant and Maddison's Union Banking Company (Portsmouth) in 1902—another case prompted by the depreciation of Consols—the Wilts and Dorset Directors visiting the Portsmouth bank were told not to enter the bank's office but to go through a private door straight into the drawing-room of the resident Director. The rupture of the negotiations between Prescotts and the Canterbury Bank, referred to above,[8] also illustrates the sensitiveness of the smaller banks about the risk of rumours. In Lloyds Bank little went on the record about any discussions with other banks: Board Minutes relating thereto, terse as they are, were generally confined to the Private Minute Book, and even in this book the secretary had to leave a blank for the name of the bank concerned, the blank being filled in by the Chairman in his own handwriting.

We have seen how the merger generally took the form of a purchase by the larger bank on the basis of so many years' purchase of the profits of the smaller, and we have seen how the competition between the racing giants of the twentieth century raised this number of years' purchase from the three or four that Howard Lloyd had thought right to the eight, ten, or even twelve to which Merriman would go. The purchasing bank preferred to pay its price by the issue of shares, an enlarged capital being appropriate to its enlarged responsibilities. But an odd amount, not readily adjustable by an exchange of shares, might be settled by part payment in cash, as when Lloyds paid 7 shares (£8 paid) for every 5 Burton Union shares (£10 paid) together with a bonus of £1 cash per share. In taking over the very small banks from family hands the more powerful joint-stocks could sometimes be persuaded to pay a large proportion, exceptionally the whole, in cash.

[8] p. 254, footnote.

Negotiations could also stick upon the question of compensation, in status or in cash, for individuals whose controlling functions were in effect being taken away. This question appears to have been a major stumbling-block in successive attempts of Grant and Maddisons to find a buyer. In 1902 the Directors of this Portsmouth bank were asking for £11,500 in addition to two annuities of £300 and £390. This handsome compensation was based on actuarial valuation of the Directors' emoluments continuing for their lives and increasing somewhat. When the Wilts and Dorset, the prospective buyer, demurred, one of the Portsmouth gentlemen agreed to substantial reduction of his proposed annuity provided that he should be given a directorship in the Wilts and Dorset. Further manœuvres of this kind suggest that the individual Portsmouth Directors were thinking more of these personal advantages than of the value of the bank as a whole: there was even complaint that one was grabbing all he could get for his son, if necessary at the expense of his other colleagues. Negotiations not surprisingly broke down. When the Portsmouth bank subsequently thought of selling to Lloyds, these personal questions again loomed large: a Portsmouth Director thought it unlikely that Lloyds

would accord them such a position as Local Directors, District Managers or anything of that kind—they would probably have to come down to mere ordinary Managers of a branch bank in a provincial town, liable to be hectored by some vulgar Inspector, reprimanded and ordered by the Board, bound to long and regular hours, made to sign their name when arriving at or leaving the Bank, and, finally, it would be exceedingly likely that they would be discharged altogether after Lloyds had got a firm hold of the business as the latter might think it more to their interest to have a more common type of Manager who would procure business by going out to supper with a tradesman.

In face of this attitude it is perhaps remarkable that Lloyds were ever able to offer satisfactory terms; but the depreciation of their investments was so weakening the Portsmouth bank that they felt compelled to give way sufficiently. In the end Lloyds agreed to constitute three of the Portsmouth gentlemen a Local Committee at Portsmouth while a fourth was similarly appointed at Southampton, the change being further sweetened by £5,000 cash compensation.

When the Grants at Portsmouth were engaged in these efforts to salvage their personal eminence, they were encouraged by news from a friend in the north that Lloyds had given local directorships to the partners of Hodgkin Barnett and Co. This was indeed the case, but there Lloyds were picking up some outstanding men. J. W. Beaumont Pease, later Lord Wardington and Chairman of Lloyds 1922–45, was one of the partners who became Directors of Lloyds by this amalgamation. Another was T. E. Hodgkin who came from a family of scholar-bankers (he himself took a double first in Natural Sciences at Cambridge) and was eventually worthy of appointment as Assistant General Manager with charge of Lloyds' entire Northern District. Several other absorptions of small banks were like this in bringing men of high capacity into the big banks. We have already seen how Vassar-Smith, later Sir Richard and Chairman of Lloyds from 1909 to 1922, came in from the Board of the Worcester City and County.[9] Before him two other Chairmen of Lloyds, Sir Thomas Salt and John Spencer Phillips, had come in as partners in Stevenson Salt and Co. and Beck and Co. respectively.[10] E. B. Merriman joined the Board of the North Wilts when they absorbed his family bank, and so found his way to the Chairmanship of the Capital and Counties.[11] Edward Brodie Hoare, eventually Deputy Chairman of Lloyds, had been a partner in Barnetts Hoares when they were amalgamated with Lloyds in 1884. William Garfit, Chairman of the Capital and Counties at the time of their amalgamation with Lloyds, had entered banking to become partner in a Lincolnshire family bank. The little Banbury bank of Cobb and Co. included T. E. Cobb who became a Director of the Bucks and Oxon Union Bank, and put his son out to learn banking in Lloyds at Birmingham. This son in turn became Director of the Bucks and Oxon, and on their amalgamation with Lloyds became General Manager's Assistant, later distinguishing himself as Treasurer of the bank and as Chairman of its Sports Club.

Besides partners or directors and their families, some among the employees of the private and smaller joint-stock banks subsequently distinguished themselves in the service of the bigger bank into which their original employers were merged. Two outstanding examples, Alex-

---

[9] For Sir Richard Vassar-Smith, see pp. 38, 39 above.
[10] For Salt, see pp. 33–37 above, and for Spencer Phillips, see pp. 36–38 above.
[11] For Merriman, see pp. 54–56 above.

ander Duff and Henry Bell, entered upon their banking careers in the same year, 1875. Duff was the elder, having been up to Cambridge some years before joining the staff of Barnetts Hoares in Lombard Street. When the great amalgamation came he had already established himself sufficiently to be appointed manager at No. 73; after holding other offices, all in London, he became General Manager of Lloyds Bank in 1902, and was elected to the Board on his retirement in 1913. Henry Bell came into Lloyds with the Liverpool Union Bank in 1900. He was quickly promoted and became General Manager in 1912 and a Director in 1916; his great abilities brought him frequently into the service of the State.[12] The absorption of the Birmingham Joint Stock Bank in 1889 brought Alexander Fyshe, Country General Manager in Lloyds until 1912. When Brown Jansons came in 1900, W. S. Draper had been with them twenty years; he rose to be Joint General Manager from 1918 to 1929. E. D. Vaisey began his banking career in the Gloucestershire Banking Company back in 1870; in 1875 he moved to the North Wilts Banking Company and so eventually into the Capital and Counties, where he became General Manager and then Director, joining the Board of Lloyds on amalgamation. And there were many lesser lights. Altogether, the process of amalgamation brought into the Capital and Counties and Lloyds a galaxy of talented men from whom the general managers and directors of tomorrow were to be drawn. The purchasing banks could afford to be generous to the minority of passengers who came in with them.

By the beginning of the twentieth century the process of amalgamation had already gone so far that Lloyds had lost its character as a local bank. It was now not even confined to the Midlands, but was fast becoming the national bank that it is today. On the first day of 1900 it entered Lancashire on a big scale by absorbing the Liverpool Union Bank. This required some courage, for Lancashire men valued their independence of London—and of Birmingham, as was to appear to much effect three years later. In June 1903 secret negotiations were opened between Lloyds and the Manchester and Liverpool District Bank, by this time a powerful institution with ninety-five offices and a balance-sheet total close to £20 million. The moving spirit was Mr. Andrew Walker, a

---

[12] For further details about Henry Bell, see p. 59 above.

shareholder in both banks. After an interview with Mr. Spencer Phillips of Lloyds, Walker wrote that there was 'no eagerness on either side, no indifference on either side, an open mind on both and high appreciation of each other'. Correspondence reached the point of equating the shares of the two companies, the basis reached being 175,000 Lloyds shares (market value £33 each) plus £250,000 cash for the 125,000 District shares (market value £49. 10s. each).[13] In the autumn, pensioning and retention of senior staff were under discussion, and the negotiators reached the point of fixing dates for their respective Annual Meetings at which the amalgamation would be announced.

Then the balloon went up. News of the projected amalgamation leaked into the Manchester newspapers on 3 December. A storm of protest developed in the *Manchester Guardian* both in letters to the editor and in editorial comment. The leader on the 3rd regretted that a peculiarly Lancashire bank of very high reputation should be merged into a still larger concern: that 'even the strongest, best conducted and most prosperous of the so-called "country banks"' should lose their identity was a most unwelcome prospect. Letters to the editor emphasized the affront to local pride and the distinction that ought to be drawn between little country banks and the powerful District Bank. A Director of Lloyds Bank in an interview strove to allay the fears of Lancashire men: the fullest possible control would be left with the local managers. But this would not do; 'Lancashire business men should be able to undertake the more delicate negotiations with Lancashire bankers' and similar assurances in an earlier case had been all too quickly followed by the disappearance of the personal element 'in that business formerly dealt with here is referred for decision to headquarters'. Oddly enough, the *Liverpool Daily Post* had nothing to say on the question, but Manchester certainly knew its mind and was not going to have its own leading bank 'effaced'. There was nothing for the negotiators to do but drop the project. The Directors of the District telegraphed for Spencer Phillips 'and they told me', he reported to his shareholders, 'that they were not sure of the complete concurrence of their shareholders or of the loyalty of their customers'. (He must have known, from his own mail-bag as well as the

[13] In this correspondence Spencer Phillips commented that market quotations often over-valued local bank shares; holders of the latter were 'very tenacious', so that the market was somewhat unreal, whereas Lloyds shares were 'very freely dealt in'.

columns of the *Manchester Guardian*, that this was putting it mildly.) 'It did not take many minutes to decide what was the right thing to do, and what had taken five months to build up was knocked down in five minutes.' 'The Idea Abandoned' was the Manchester headline on the 9th.

Manchester's independent frame of mind was based partly on the belief that there was no advantage in the merger of two banks each of which was already strong. Only one of the letters to the newspaper mentioned the advantage of reducing dependence upon the fortunes of local industries; to most of the correspondents the idea that Manchester business problems should be taken to London or Birmingham was an insult not to be tolerated. In their uncompromising attitude the Lancashire men were by now standing alone, or almost alone. Elsewhere the powerful bank of one area was joining forces with the powerful bank of another area. As far back as 1877 the amalgamation of the Hampshire Banking Company with the North Wilts had been a union, if not of really powerful banks, at least of equal partners each of weight in its own area. Each had a good branch system, and the two did not overlap. It was a true amalgamation, and all the Directors of both companies took seats on the new Board. Similarly when in 1886 the Gloucestershire Banking Company amalgamated with the Capital and Counties, it could hardly be said that one bank was absorbing the other. Though the more general title of the latter was retained for the united bank, the Gloucestershire Banking Company had thought of the amalgamation mainly as its own way of establishing itself in Bristol and London. For the Capital and Counties the merger represented an important extension of its territory, without the trouble of opening new branches in a well-banked area.

In 1889 it was the turn of Lloyds Bank to become party to an amalgamation with a bank that could be regarded, if not as an equal partner, at least as comparatively powerful in its former role of competitor in the heart of the Lloyds territory. The initiative taken by the Birmingham Joint Stock Bank came as a surprise to Lloyds: a pleasant surprise, for Howard Lloyd regarded the Joint Stock Bank as 'a very powerful and trying competitor'. To clinch the bargain it was worth paying a good price, and Howard Lloyd thought that he was 'giving 21/- or 22/- at least for a sovereign'. The merger increased the paid-up capital of Lloyds

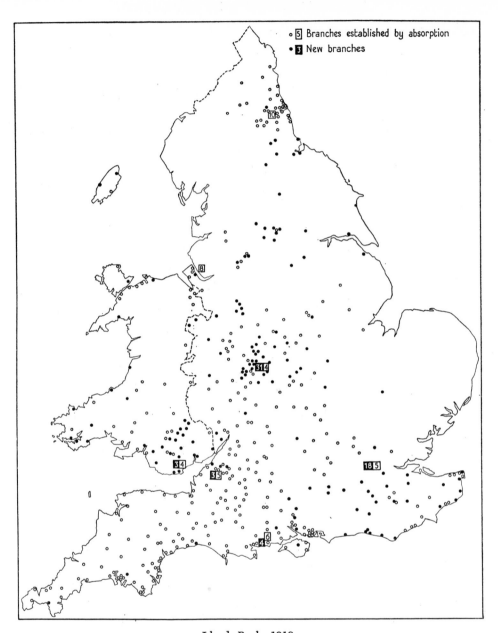

Lloyds Bank. 1918

264

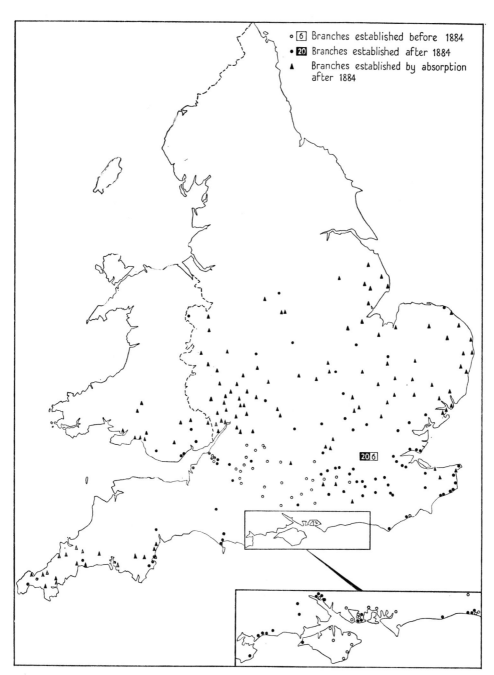

Capital and Counties Bank. 1918

by about 50 per cent., though only two of the Joint Stock Bank's Directors came on to Lloyds' Board. In the same year Lloyds had absorbed the Worcester City and County Bank; after this double accession of strength Lloyds did not engage in major amalgamations for some years. The absorption of the Bristol and West of England Bank (the old 'West of England and South Wales District Bank' reorganized after 1878), of the County of Gloucester, and of Williams and Co., all in the nineties, implied important extensions of area, but not amalgamation with equal partners. Collectively (with smaller banks thrown in from time to time) they so much increased the size of Lloyds that at the beginning of the twentieth century, especially after its invasion of Lancashire in 1900, it was properly regarded as a banking giant. Thus when it absorbed the powerful banks of Hodgkin Barnett in 1903 and the Devon and Cornwall (with 55 branches) in 1906, it was very much the big firm talking to the smaller firm, important as the latter was, in each case, in its own area.

The amalgamation movement was in fact reaching its culminating phase. In 1914 Lloyds absorbed the Wilts and Dorset Banking Company, which had a hundred branches in territory already well sprinkled with offices of Lloyds Bank. In 1918 came the merger of giant with giant, Lloyds with its £174,000,000 of deposits and 888 offices merging with the Capital and Counties with £60,000,000 of deposits and 473 offices. The 473 offices of the Capital and Counties overlapped quite substantially with the 888 of Lloyds but, as appears by comparison of the two maps facing this page, Lloyds was virtually unrepresented in East Anglia where the Capital and Counties was strong, while in the north the recent expansion of Lloyds contrasted with complete absence of branches of the other bank. In Surrey, Kent, and Sussex both banks had been opening new offices and here, as in Cornwall, there was much overlap. In the Birmingham area itself the Capital and Counties had hardly any representation, but in the south-west Midlands this amalgamation meant that two powerful competitors were joining forces. In the north-west of England neither bank had offices, apart from the few Lloyds offices in Liverpool and east Lancashire; this part of the country stood out alone resistant to the new combine, and even today the bank has few offices in north Lancashire, Westmorland, and Cumberland.

In announcing the proposals to shareholders, the Chairman of the

Capital and Counties mentioned the attraction of the business Lloyds had acquired in the north of England; the other advantage mentioned was the 'considerably larger Continental, Colonial and Foreign connexion than that possessed by ourselves'. These foreign connexions included particularly participation in a bank in France, and agencies for banks in Canada, Mauritius, and Brazil; there were already afoot important proposals for participations in banks in India, South America, and Scotland. The Capital and Counties had kept closer to the nineteenth-century traditions of English banking; its foreign exchange business was all handled by one man who posted up his own books three times a day. But times were changing and like other London banks it had become conscious of the desirability of having more direct channels for the conduct of foreign business for its customers. Its connexions with New York banks were not enough for a giant bank of the new age; but they formed an important complement to those of Lloyds in other parts of the world.

Proposals were under discussion between the two banks in the early weeks of 1918 and were before the Board of Lloyds Bank on 1 March. A week later the negotiations seemed likely to break down: either at this or a slightly later stage, the Lloyds representatives were critical of the relatively low liquidity of the Capital and Counties. By the end of June the Capital and Counties had, as requested, 'converted as large an amount of their assets as possible into liquid form', and the merger went forward, its formal date being 17 July 1918. The terms of capital adjustment remained as had been suggested five months previously: one Lloyds share (£8 paid) and a bonus of £2 cash were given for each of the 175,000 Capital and Counties shares (£10 paid). As the market values of the shares were £26 for Capital and Counties and £25. 10s. for Lloyds, the shareholders of the smaller bank secured a good bargain, quite apart from the advantages, in wider ramifications at home and abroad, that might be expected to enlarge their prospects for the future. From the point of view of Lloyds, the terms represented a price paid essentially in order to bring the bank by a single step much closer to being the nation-wide institution it now aspired to become.

Immediately before the amalgamation the Capital and Counties had 15 Directors. Of these, 2 were General Managers, and at least 6 of the other 13 had roots in the old private banking families. The Board of the

266

amalgamated bank—the title remaining Lloyds Bank Limited—consisted of the 19 former members of the Lloyds Board and 7 from the old Capital and Counties Board. Of these 7, 2 were the General Managers, Harvey and Vaisey, 2 (including Garfit, who was Chairman) from the old private banking families, and 3 who were not. The 7 were to form a Capital and Counties Committee, to supervise the Capital and Counties Section which, as we shall see, remained in many ways a separate entity for some time. The agreement continued the remuneration of the 7 at the total of £10,750 free of income tax. Other conditions assimilating their terms to those of the Directors of Lloyds throw light on principles becoming standard in English banking: they were forbidden to engage in the conduct, direction, or supervision of any other bank (though with specific consent they might become Directors of any foreign or colonial joint-stock banks) and their shareholdings in banks were unrestricted.

The last amalgamation to add any considerable number of offices to the branch network was that with Fox Fowler & Co., an amalgamation having a special place in banking history because it occasioned the extinction (under the Bank Charter Act of 1844) of the last country bank note issue. This family bank had grown, in the eighteenth-century way, out of a business in wool manufactures, notes being issued without a break from 1778 until 1921. For nearly a century it operated in Wellington only; then at Howard Lloyd's suggestion the Wellington bank had stepped into part of the void left by the failure of the West of England and South Wales District Bank, and opened branches in Somerset and Devon. Only at this stage was the banking business separated from the woollen business, and the banking partnership was widened by admission of Mr. W. H. and Mr. Gerald Fowler, the sons of Sir Robert Nicholas Fowler, whose name is thereby joined with Fox in all later references to the bank. Through the expansionist period following these events, the Fox brothers remained the mainstay of the business. They were constantly advised by Howard Lloyd with whom they had become connected by marriage;[14] two of the family received their training in Lloyds at Birmingham. Howard Lloyd sensed the logical consequences but did not seek to hasten the march of events: in 1890, informing his nephew

[14] See facing p. 362.

(J. Howard Fox) of a Lloyds amalgamation, he noted that there would 'still be the width of a county and a channel between us'; two years later, 'I am obliged to put my long arms round you (for protection not embrace!)'. After the 1914–18 war—which had taken its toll in the Fox family—the partnership was ready to accept the new fashion in English banking. Successful management and a run of good years had made the firm an attractive proposition for Lloyds. The partners, on their side, were conscious of their other business commitments, and they realized that they would be faced with quite exceptional difficulties in steering the bank through the increasingly difficult period which was developing as an inevitable outcome of the post-war boom. Sir Gilbert Garnsey, head of Messrs. Price, Waterhouse and Co. Ltd., auditors both to Lloyds Bank and Fox Fowler and Co., sounded the partners in January 1921, and they decided to accept the quite generous terms. Thereby, Lloyds Bank gained a useful network of fifty-five branches and agencies in Somerset, Devon, and Cornwall. Lloyds had become a bank with 1,600 offices and £342 million of deposits.

Negotiation of an amalgamation was generally a complicated and delicate business, the burden of which was necessarily concentrated upon a few men on either side. The weight of this burden was occasionally given formal recognition, as in 1903 when the Chairman was voted additional remuneration and in 1918 when the Board formally recorded and communicated to the shareholders 'their sense of the great services rendered' by the Chairman and the Deputy Chairman in the important negotiations recently completed. But agreement upon terms of amalgamation was from one point of view only the beginning of a process: there remained the less confidential but even more delicate business of welding two firms into one. And the succession of amalgamations meant that one welding problem followed hard on the heels of another. In the sixty years before 1922 Lloyds had grown from one office to some 1,600 offices, and the majority of these had come in by amalgamation. Even the Board of Directors had grown to a membership of 33; the functions of these Directors and their relationship with the management had to be evolved from the varied ways, indeed varied outlooks, of family bankers and joint-stock bankers from the provinces and men bred in the traditions of

Lombard Street itself. Recruitment and employment of staff had to be forced into tolerably uniform terms. The book-keeping and office routine had to be brought into a single framework. Above all, the men in the bank—especially those in the more responsible positions—had to shake down into new status (and new personal relationships) in an essentially new institution.

These problems of adjustment were most difficult—and their solution most important—when one powerful bank merged with another. When Lloyds, Barnetts Hoares, and Bosanquet Salts were amalgamated in 1884, a strong Birmingham bank was absorbing two Lombard Street firms; the men in Birmingham knew how to lend to the local metal industries, but who were they to order Lombard Street men in the running of a London bank? The Head Office remained for many years in Birmingham with Howard Lloyd as its executive chief. If the contrasting parts of the enlarged bank were to become a single organization—and this fusion alone could justify the amalgamation—Howard Lloyd had to exert his authority and all his diplomacy to bring together the best of Lombard Street and the best of Birmingham. His letters, especially those to Edward Hoare who served as manager in Lombard Street, show Howard Lloyd's devotion to this task.

A main attraction of joining with Lombard Street had been the prospect of securing fuller and more remunerative employment of surplus cash, and active steps had to be taken if this advantage was to be fully exploited. It meant even a change in Birmingham habits of thought: there, the distinction between cash in hand and cash at call had not been important, for cash at call was virtually as good as cash in hand. In Lombard Street the banker had to think in terms of big differences in the Clearing; subject to this, a Lombard Street office could maximise the interest to be earned on the bank's resources. Discretion to employ surplus balances from hour to hour must therefore rest with the Lombard Street management, Birmingham's part being confined to watching, and advising Lombard Street well ahead of its own needs. For a time Howard Lloyd devoted detailed attention to ensuring that the men in Lombard Street used the bank's resources up to the hilt, but he recognized that the daily business must be controlled on the spot. Similarly, though he would on occasion express views upon the general level of the bank's investments, Howard Lloyd regarded the day-to-day management of investments as a proper function of the London office.

As I have repeatedly said [he wrote in 1885] I think the particular question of the proportion of cash balances held in London and of liquid assets and of the use or conversion of the latter is one which as a consequence of the amalgamation and with ready acquiescence on my part must rest upon the shoulders of the London management and the London Committee, at all events, subject to any interposition of mine or over-ruling of the Board. I considered this practically settled when the power of purchase and sale of investments was especially devolved by the Board upon the London Committee.

If the absence of further correspondence on this matter is any guide, we may conclude that from 1886 onwards the division of powers worked smoothly enough. There were also problems of internal accounting, unusual in degree because the Lombard Street houses had been accustomed to earning commission from Lloyds and other country banks, for whom they served as London agents. The normal Lloyds Bank rule, at this time, was for Head Office to allow branches 4 per cent. on surplus balances transferred from branches and to charge Bank Rate (subject to a maximum of 5 per cent.) on branch borrowing from Head Office, in addition to which there was periodic overall settlement related to the results of using funds in the London market. The former commissions earned by Lombard Street could not easily be fitted into this framework and, because the Lombard Street office through its first years proved unremunerative (in a narrow sense), the division of earnings and costs between London and Birmingham was long disputed; feelings could run high and years went by without mutual satisfaction.

Some attempt had also to be made to bring reasonably into line the practices of Birmingham and Lombard Street in dealing with their customers. On deposit accounts Birmingham paid the steady $2\frac{1}{2}$ per cent. that was becoming standard country practice, while Lombard Street paid the variable Town Deposit Rate. When the latter rose above 4 per cent. (as in November 1884), customers were tempted to move balances from the country to London; this had been known to happen before the amalgamation, but the customer was more likely to take the step if, as was now possible, he could make the change without changing his banker. To adopt a uniform Deposit Rate throughout the bank would, however, have thrown out of line either the Birmingham rate in relation to rates paid by other banks, or that of London in relation to the rate prevailing there. Lloyds, like other banks, preferred to maintain the two-price tariff. This implied acceptance of the customer's freedom to switch his deposit, though the bank could try to persuade a customer 'to follow Bank Rate down as well as up'. Only long after all the big banks had become national institutions did they join in solving this problem by establishing a single deposit rate for Town and Country.[15]

On the other side of the ledger varying ideas of lending in town and country proved to be a source of friction. In the provinces English bankers, joint-stock as well as private, had sometimes been elastic in their attitude to industrial borrowers, but their lending for mercantile business ran in narrower grooves, thanks to the traditions associated with bills of exchange. In the City of London, on the other hand, the private bankers of Lombard Street, to whom anything savouring of 'industrial banking' would have been anathema, could be less rigorous in the conditions of lending to merchants who were their neighbours within that closely knit community, and sometimes of their family connexions. This difference of attitude appeared particularly when certain of the Bosanquet accounts passed under the surveillance of bankers from outside: the country bankers were shocked at the idea of warehouse warrants as security for a large loan to a family connexion of one of the Bosanquet partners. The amalgamated bank eventually took a stiff line, perhaps a foretaste of that narrowing of bank lending that became, in the early decades of the twentieth century, a stock subject of complaint by commentators on the mammoth banks. Thomas Salt, who straddled the banking worlds of both town and country, was unhappy about the bank's stiffness in this case, and perhaps he was right. The only satisfactory way of achieving assimilation without establishing unduly restrictive rules was for country bankers and Lombard Street men to get to know each others' business at first hand. Howard Lloyd, realizing how ignorant he was of the ways of Lombard Street, encouraged interchange of personnel. One of the first London men to come up to Birmingham was Alexander Duff, who was destined to be a power in the bank for many years ahead. Even Edward Hoare, the City Manager, was eventually pressed into a

[15] Cf. pp. 161–5 above.

visit, though Howard Lloyd had virtually to issue an order before Hoare would come. Lloyd himself took to visiting Lombard Street every week. In course of time the bank's centre of gravity inevitably shifted to London; from 1899 the Board met alternately in London and Birmingham, and by the end of 1910 all Head Office business had been transferred to London and the Board ceased to meet anywhere else.

In the later days the amalgamation with the Wilts and Dorset Bank in 1914 presented Lloyds with one of their major problems of absorption. This was a strong country bank with nearly two hundred offices, and it had felt able to refuse earlier advances from ambitious banks, waiting until a really big bank made a good offer. When Lloyds at last made a high enough bid, every precaution was taken to avoid offence to customers or staff of the absorbed bank. All customers received (the more important of them by personal communication) assurance that the conduct of their accounts would be unaffected as the entire staff would be retained and two Wilts and Dorset Directors would be joining the Board of Lloyds Bank. Actually continuity was provided by constituting the entire former Board of the Wilts and Dorset as a local committee at Salisbury, while the former General Managers became District Managers; the local committee was given a discretionary limit of £15,000 for advances. But this continuity in the management did not affect the need for assimilation of the machines. The Wilts and Dorset staff had to forego holidays until the work was completed and Lloyds found from branches all over the country a team of men to check, in each of the absorbed offices, the advances and securities and to give instruction in the Lloyds' methods of working. Then there was the problem of assimilating employment conditions: the two salary scales looked quite different, and holiday arrangements also required adjustment.

A major problem on this occasion, and one to be repeated in the amalgamation of giants four years later, related to the overlap of offices. In 48 places both the banks had offices, and inquiries were at once received from other banks who were looking for premises in which they might establish branches. Lloyds, however, made haste slowly: at only a quarter of the places was one or other of the overlapping branches closed within a year, while a further 10, making 22 in all, were closed in 1916, when Army requirements were encouraging the banks to eliminate redundancy. The merging of 44 branches into 22 did mean, despite war conditions, that some managers became anxious about their positions. The bank adopted the general principle, in these cases, that the two managers should become joint managers; the men were told, '. . . it is hoped that these Managers will show good sense, good humour and tact in sitting together in the same room and carrying on the business progressively and successfully as heretofore'. Joint managers were, the bank's letter added, common enough in London, and worked well; they might have added that in traditional country banking two or more partners had commonly shared the parlour and administered the business jointly.

When the Capital and Counties joined Lloyds later in the war, problems of the same kind arose: again there was quite a substantial overlap of branches, though among the 200 places involved were some where the two offices were catering for quite different groups of customers. At Cambridge, for example, the Capital and Counties had a huntin', shootin', and fishin' type of manager with an extensive country connexion; a branch of this kind could not easily be merged in another local office. More generally important, the end of the war, coming not long after the amalgamation, ushered in a phase of branch expansion: just as the conditions of 1915–16 had encouraged the closing of offices after the Wilts and Dorset amalgamation, so now the tendency was to open rather than close offices. The merging of overlapping offices was therefore a much slower process and affected a much smaller proportion of branches. The process of merging the two great banks was also impeded by the systems of book-keeping; the Capital and Counties worked on single entry, and this could not give way over-night to the double-entry system of Lloyds. Partly because of this obstacle for the accountants, the Capital and Counties continued for some time to operate more or less as a separate entity. The Capital and Counties Committee of Directors only gradually ceased to operate as an effective governing Board.[16] The recruitment of staff continued quite independently until consideration of the special post-war problems of staffing underlined the need for a common policy; even so, it was five years before 'Lloyds men' and 'Capital and Counties men' were regarded as interchangeable when appointments to managerships were

[16] Until the death of Mr. H. W. Jervis in 1934 the Committee continued to conduct some business; in 1956 Lord Bledisloe survives as the only member.

in question. Only in the handling of money market and investment business did the merger have full effect at once.

After amalgamation with such large concerns as the Wilts and Dorset and the Capital and Counties, the absorption of the thirty-four offices of the West Yorkshire and the fifty-five offices of Fox Fowler and Co. must have been comparatively easy tasks for hands now well-tried in the art of welding. And the repetition of the task on the largest scale was now ruled out by government policy. The run of amalgamations among the banking giants themselves had excited public anxiety lest banking monopolists should provide a less satisfactory service, and a Departmental Committee[17] had examined and reported upon the movement. This Committee concluded that the possible dangers were material enough to outweigh the general arguments against government interference, and recommended legislation establishing machinery for some check upon further amalgamations. Though the Bill introduced into Parliament was dropped, its substance passed into the unwritten law of the land: since 1918 there has been an understanding between the banks and the government, implementing the spirit of the Committee's recommendation. The understanding is that every proposal for amalgamation will be submitted for Treasury approval. The Treasury has apparently acquiesced in all proposals for the absorption of small banks by bigger, if not the biggest, brothers, while it is generally understood that the amalgamation of two giants would not be permitted. Under this régime the West Yorkshire and Fox Fowler amalgamations were permitted, and in 1923 Lloyds acquired an important footing in the Indian sub-continent by absorbing the historic West End businesses of Cox and Co. and Henry S. King and Co. Apart from these amalgamations, the further expansion of Lloyds Bank has necessarily depended on the opening of new offices and the growth of business at those previously established. The emphasis has in fact been on the last: since 1920 the number of offices in England and Wales has grown from 1,539 to 1,655 in 1925 and 1,760 in 1957,[18] while the number

[17] The Treasury Committee on Bank Amalgamations, 1918, whose *Report* is reprinted in T. E. Gregory, *British Banking Statutes and Reports*, vol. ii, pp. 323–33. Cf. T. E. Gregory, *The Westminster Bank*, vol. ii, p. 16.

[18] These 1,760 offices include sub-branches and agencies as well as the branches listed in Appendix 2.

SIR RICHARD VASSAR VASSAR-SMITH, 1843–1922

Chairman, 1909–22

From the painting by Sir William Orpen, R.A.

of accounts has jumped from 1,164,711 in 1920 to about $2\frac{1}{2}$ million in 1956. Spectacular expansion but not, from the point of view of organization, a difficult growth: the sensations, the upheavals and the frictions of the amalgamation movement have slipped back into the past.

Thus from the 1920's onwards it has been proper to describe Lloyds Bank as a nation-wide institution. Under Sir Richard Vassar-Smith, followed as Chairman by Mr. Beaumont Pease (Lord Wardington), Mr. Henry Bell as General Manager, and Mr. F. A. Beane and Mr. A. Davidson after him, the absorbed banks and newly established offices were welded together into one gigantic business. The principles on which the business is based differ little from those of Sampson Lloyd and John Taylor in 1765, or from those of Howard Lloyd and others a century later, but the size and shape of the business make it almost incredible that it has sprung from that single Birmingham office of a century ago.

Appendix 1

CONSTITUENT BANKS

In this list will be found the name of every bank which has contributed to the present structure of Lloyds Bank. The title given against a foundation date is the earliest title known and changes are given only where necessary to show the connexion between the original firm and that ultimately absorbed by Lloyds Bank. The title shown in capitals is that by which the firm was known when it was absorbed.

The place-name beside a private bank indicates where it was founded, and does not imply that this was the only office of the bank.

Italics indicate banks which had suspended payment before being taken over.

Foundation date	Title at Foundation	Changes in Title and Amalgamation				Absorbed by Lloyds
1765	TAYLORS & LLOYDS, Dale End, Birmingham	1853	Became LLOYDS & COMPANY	1865	Amalgamated to form LLOYDS BANKING COMPANY LIMITED	
1766	Robert Coales, Birmingham	1840	Became J. L. MOILLIET & SONS	1884	Title changed to LLOYDS, BARNETTS & BOSANQUETS BANK LIMITED	
				1889	Title changed to LLOYDS BANK LIMITED	
1809	S. & W. Addison, Wednesbury	1851	Taken over by P. & H. WILLIAMS			1865
1737	John Stevenson, Stafford	c. 1800	Became STEVENSON, SALT & CO.			1866
1834	WARWICK & LEAMINGTON BANKING COMPANY					1866
1791	Dawes, Tomes & Russell, Warwick	1834	Absorbed by WARWICK & LEAMINGTON BANKING COMPANY			
c. 1791	Finch & Co, Dudley	1807	Became *Dixon, Dalton & Amphlett*	1844	Taken over by BIRMINGHAM BANKING COMPANY	1866 (Dudley branch only)
1791	A. BUTLIN & SON, Rugby					1868
1807	R. & W. F. FRYER, Wolverhampton					1872
1791	Hordern & Co, Newport					
1805	Reynolds, Charlton & Co, Wellington	1836	Amalgamated to form SHROPSHIRE BANKING COMPANY			1874
1810	Darby & Co, Coalbrookdale					
1824	Biddle, Mountford, Pidcock & Cope, Shifnal					

Foundation date	Title at Foundation	Changes in Title and Amalgamation				Absorbed by Lloyds
1835	COVENTRY & WARWICKSHIRE BANKING COMPANY					1879
1790	Wyatt, Inge & Lant, Coventry	1829	Became Beck & Prime	1835	Absorbed by COVENTRY & WARWICKSHIRE BANKING COMPANY	
1810	Eagle, Goodall & Co, Coventry	1829	Became Goodall, Gulson & Co.	1839	Absorbed by COVENTRY & WARWICKSHIRE BANKING COMPANY	
1800	BECK & CO, Shrewsbury					1880
1840	WHITCHURCH & ELLESMERE BANKING CO.					1881
c. 1665	Humphrey Stokes, the Black Horse, Lombard Street	1728	Became John Bland at 54 Lombard Street	1864	Amalgamated to form BARNETTS, HOARES, HANBURY & LLOYD	1884
1771	Hanbury, Taylor, Lloyd & Bowman, later at 60 Lombard Street	1772	Became Bland, Barnett & Hoare at 62 Lombard Street			
1796	Bowles, Beachcroft, Brown, Reeves, Collins & Co, 18 Exchange Alley, Cornhill	1854	Became Bosanquet, Whatman, Harman & Bosanquet at 73 Lombard Street	1867	Amalgamated to form BOSANQUET, SALT & COMPANY	1884
1787	William Stevenson, 58 Queen Street	c. 1800	Became Stevenson, Salt & Co, at 80 Lombard Street			
1799	Vickers Son & Pritchard, Broseley & Bridgnorth	1884	Became PRITCHARD GORDON & CO.			1888
1861	BIRMINGHAM JOINT STOCK BANK LIMITED					1889

Foundation date	Title at Foundation	Date	Changes in Title and Amalgamation	Date		Absorbed by Lloyds
1790	Attwood, Spooner & Co., Birmingham.	1865	Failed. Premises taken over by BIRMINGHAM JOINT STOCK BANK LTD.			1889
1840	WORCESTER CITY AND COUNTY BANKING COMPANY					1890
1840	Ludlow & Tenbury Bank	1864	Absorbed by WORCESTER CITY & COUNTY BANKING CO.			
1837	Parsons & Co, Presteigne	1876	"			
1778	WILKINS & CO., Brecon					1890
1815	BEECHINGS & CO., Tunbridge Wells					1891
1802	PRAEDS & CO., Fleet Street					1891
1785	COBB & CO., Margate					1891
1808	Fellows & Co., Nottingham	1824	Became HART, FELLOWS & CO.			1892
1824	TWINING & CO., Strand					1892
c. 1846	HEAD & CO., East Grinstead					
1834	West of England & South Wales District Bank	1878	Failed	1879	Some branches re-opened as BRISTOL AND WEST OF ENGLAND BANK LIMITED	1892
1819	Towgood & Co., Cardiff (1836–43 part of Monmouth & Glamorganshire Banking Co.)			1855	Absorbed by West of England & South Wales District Bank	
1841	Kingsbridge Joint Stock Bank			1862	Absorbed by West of England & South Wales District Bank	
1807	Pritchards & Co., Ross-on-Wye	1853	Became Allaway & Macdougall	1863	"	

Foundation date	Title at Foundation	Changes in Title and Amalgamation				Absorbed by Lloyds
1862	Harwood & Harwood, Clevedon					
1790	Curteis & Co, Rye	1866	Became CURTEIS, POMFRET & CO.	1877	Absorbed by West of England & South Wales District Bank	1893
1772	London Exchange Banking Company, 16 St. James's Street	1775	Reconstituted as Sir Robert Herries & Co.	1797	Became HERRIES, FARQUHAR & CO.	1893
1773	Call Marten & Co, Bond Street	1865	Absorbed by HERRIES, FARQUHAR & CO.			1894
1819	BROMAGE & CO, Monmouth					1895
1825	PAGETS & KIRBY, Leicester					
1836	COUNTY OF GLOUCESTER BANK					1897
1790	Pitt, Croome, Bowley & Brown, Cirencester			1836	Absorbed by COUNTY OF GLOUCESTER BANK	
1834	Gloucester County & City Bank			1836	,,	
1803	Vizard & Co, Dursley			1836	,,	
1830	Watts, Wyatt & Co., Stroud			1838	,,	
1798	Grazebrook & Co., Stroud	1837	Absorbed by Watts, Wyatt & Co.			
1807	T. & R. Strange, Swindon			1842	,,	
1836	Cheltenham & Gloucestershire Banking Co.			1856	,,	
1792	WILLIAMS & CO., Chester					1897
1792	Roberts & Co., Caernarvon	1796	Absorbed by WILLIAMS & CO.			
1872	JENNER & CO, Sandgate & Shorncliffe					1898

Foundation date	Title at Foundation	Changes in Title and Amalgamation		Absorbed by Lloyds
1806	Meek, Mousley & Co., Burton	1812 Became Blurton, Webb & Peel	1839 Amalgamated to form Burton, Uttoxeter & Staffordshire Union Bank	1899
1790	Wilson, Dalrymple & Co., Burton	1811 Became Henry Clay & Co.	1843 Title changed to Burton, Uttoxeter & Ashbourne Union Bank; 1893 Title changed to BURTON UNION BANK LTD.	1899
1790	Micklem, Stephens, Simonds & Harris, Reading	1841 Became STEPHENS, BLANDY & CO.		1900
1833	VIVIAN, KITSON & CO., Torquay			1900
1835	LIVERPOOL UNION BANK			1900
1792	CUNLIFFE, BROOKS & CO., Blackburn			1900
c. 1824	Cunliffe, Brooks, 29 Lombard Street	1864 Reconstituted as BROOKS & CO., 81 Lombard Street		1900
1813	Nicholson, Brown & Co., Leeds	1824 Became WILLIAM WILLIAMS BROWN & CO.		1900
1813	Nicholson, Janson & Co., 75 Threadneedle St.	1823 Became BROWN, JANSON & Co., 32 Abchurch Lane		1900
1783	Cobb, Wheatley & Cobb, Banbury			
1783	Philip Box & Co., Buckingham	1811 Became Bartlett & Nelson	1853 Amalgamated to form BUCKS & OXON UNION BANK LTD.	1902
1795	W. Rickford & Son, Aylesbury			
1791	Jemmett, Whitfield & Jemmett, Ashford, Kent	1875 Became POMFRET & CO.		1902

281

Foundation date	Title at Foundation		Changes in Title and Amalgamation			Absorbed by Lloyds
1859	HODGKIN, BARNETT, PEASE, SPENCE & CO., Newcastle-upon-Tyne					1903
1770	Sadleir, Hilgrove, Lowder & Durell (later Atherley, Fall & Co.), Southampton	1869	Amalgamated to form Maddison, Atherley, Hankinson & Darwin	1888	Amalgamated to form GRANT & MADDISON'S UNION BANKING CO. LTD.	1903
1785	Edwards, Harrison, Simpson & Maddison, Southampton					
1787	Grant & Burbey, Portsmouth					
1797	Wells, Allnatt, Wells & Wells, Wallingford	1858	Became HEDGES, WELLS & CO.			1905
1832	Plymouth & Devonport Banking Co.	1833	Title changed to DEVON & CORNWALL BANKING CO.			1906
1809	Symons, Saltau & Co, Plymouth	1814	Became Hingston & Prideaux	1832	Formed basis of Plymouth & Devonport Banking Co.	
1829	Nicholson & Co., Kingsbridge			1832	Absorbed by Plymouth & Devonport Banking Co.	
1832	George Fox & Co., Kingsbridge			1832	„	
1809	Prideaux & Bentall, Totnes			1833	Absorbed by DEVON & CORNWALL BANKING CO.	
1832	Prout & Stapleton, Dartmouth			1834	„	
1810	Skinner, Brown & Co., Cullompton	1828	Became Hurley & Co.	1836	„	
1818	Sparkes & Co., Exeter			1836	„	

Foundation date	Title at Foundation		Changes in Title and Amalgamation			Absorbed by Lloyds
1807	Turner, Eddy & Co., Truro	1836	*Western District Banking Co.*	1847	Absorbed by DEVON & CORNWALL BANKING CO.	
1830	Brooking & Browse, Brixham	1844	Business taken over by Ricketts, Enthoven & Co., Truro	1875	,, ,,	
1863	Three Towns Banking Co., Plymouth	1839	Became Green & Vittery	1890	,, ,,	
1788	Davison-Bland & Co., Newcastle upon Tyne	1790	Title changed to LAMBTON & CO.			1908
1799	DAVID JONES & CO., Llandovery					1909
1831	Jones, Evans & Co, Lampeter	1839	Merged with DAVID JONES & CO.			
1825	HILL, & SONS, West Smithfield					1911
1792	Peacock, Handley & Kirton, Sleaford	1861	Became PEACOCK, WILLSON & CO.			1912
1835	WILTS & DORSET BANKING COMPANY					1914
1812	Robins, Young, Smith, Ody & Hanks, Malmesbury	1835	Known as Luce & Co.	1836	Absorbed by WILTS & DORSET BANKING CO.	
1809	Gundry & Co., Chippenham			1837	,,	
1800	John West, Lymington			1848	,, ,,	
1837	Tice & Welch, Christchurch			1849	,, ,,	
1816	Storey & Thomas, Shaftesbury			1855	,,	
1821	Ledgard & Sons, Poole			1861	,, ,,	
1807	Warner, Newman & Footner, Romsey	1846	Became William Footner & Sons	1873	,, ,,	
1790	Sealy & Prior, Bridgwater			1875	,,	

Foundation date	Title at Foundation	Changes in Title and Amalgamation				Absorbed by Lloyds
1803	W. Hancock & Son, Wiveliscombe					
1811	Everett & Co, Salisbury	c. 1859	Became Pinckney Bros.	1890	Absorbed by WILTS & DORSET BANKING CO.	
1786	Cox & Co., Dorchester	1878	Became R. & R. Williams & Co.	1897	" "	
1774	*HARRIS, BULTEEL & CO. (The Naval Bank),* Plymouth			1897	" "	1914
1834	Hampshire Banking Company					
1836	*Southern District Banking Co.*	1840	Absorbed by Hampshire Banking Co.			
1807	Wickham & Co, Winchester	1854	"			
1790	Gilbert & Co. (later Heath & Co.), Andover	1861	"			
1818	Atkins & Sons, Portsmouth	1863	"			
1806	Raggett, Seymour & Co., Basingstoke and Odiham	1864	"			
1862	*Le Neveu, Sorel & Co. (English & Jersey Union Bank)*	1873	"			
1846	*De Carteret & Co. (Jersey Joint Stock Bank)*	1873	"	1877	Amalgamated to form the Hampshire and North Wilts Banking Company	
1835	North Wilts Banking Company			1878	Title changed to CAPITAL AND COUNTIES BANK	1918
1792	Moule & Co., Melksham	1835	Absorbed by North Wilts Banking Co.			
1777	Horlock, Everett, Mortimer, Everett & Co, Warminster	1860	"			
1803	Ward, Brown & Co. (in 1813 Ward, Brown, Merriman & Halcomb), Marlborough	1866	"			

Foundation date	Title at Foundation		Changes in Title and Amalgamation		Absorbed by Lloyds
1670	Willis, Percival & Co., 76 Lombard Street	1878	Absorbed by Hampshire & North Wilts Banking Company		
1775	Sutton, Leach, Bevan & Read, Devizes	1803	Became Locke & Co.	1883	Absorbed by CAPITAL AND COUNTIES BANK
1765	Haydon & Smallpiece, Guildford			1883	„
1831	Gloucestershire Banking Company			1886	„
1809	Hartland & Co., Tewkesbury	1831	Absorbed by Gloucestershire Banking Company		
1819	Russell & Skey, Gloucester	1832	„		
1796	Cripps & Co., Cirencester	1842	„		
1836	J. W. R. Hall, Ross	1858	„		
1790	Hankins & Co. (in 1815 Webb & Co.), Ledbury	1883	„		
1806	Stevens & Co, Farnham	1828	Became Knight, Jenner & Co.	1886	„
1836	Northamptonshire Banking Company			1890	„
1783	Watkins & Co., Daventry	1836	Absorbed by Northamptonshire Banking Co.		
1864	Clymo, Treffry, Hawke, West & Co., Liskeard	1885	Formed into Western Counties Bank Ltd.	1890	„
1754	Garfit, Claypon & Co., Boston			1891	„
1840	Watts & Co., Teignmouth			1891	„
1808	Mellersh, Moline & Weale, Godalming	1814	Became Mellersh & Co.	1893	„
1807 / 1810	Williamson & Co., Baldock / G. & W. Hogge, Biggleswade	1830	Amalgamated to form Wells, Hogge & Lindsell	1893	„

Foundation date	Title at Foundation		Changes in Title and Amalgamation		Absorbed by CAPITAL AND COUNTIES BANK	Absorbed by Lloyds
1791	Toomer, Bunney, Slocock & King, Newbury			1895	Absorbed by CAPITAL AND COUNTIES BANK	
1788	St. Barbe & Co., Lymington			1896	,,	
1808	Margesson, Henty, Henty & Hopkins, Worthing			1896	,,	
1812	Thomas Wheeler & Co., High Wycombe			1896	,,	
1791	Eliot, Pearce & Co., Weymouth			1897	,,	
1821	Williams & Rowland, Neath	1836	Amalgamated to form Glamorganshire Banking Company			
1828	Eaton & Co., Swansea			1898	,,	
1821	Walters, Voss & Walters, Swansea	1841	Absorbed by Glamorganshire Banking Company			
1760	Wright & Co., Nottingham			1898	,,	
1795	James Oakes & Son, Bury St. Edmunds	1830	Amalgamated to form Oakes, Bevan & Co., later Oakes, Bevan, Tollemache & Co.			
1801	Crowe, Sparrow & Brown, Bury St. Edmunds			1900	,,	
1795	Fenn & Addison (later Sparrow, Brown, Fenn & Co.), Sudbury					
1791	Lacon & Co., Yarmouth	1870	Some offices taken over by Lacons, Youell & Co.	1901	,,	
c. 1783	Harveys & Hudsons, Norwich			1901	,,	
1802	Moore, Maltby, Evans & Middlemore, Nottingham	1836	Formed into Moore & Robinson's Nottinghamshire Banking Co.			

Foundation date	Title at Foundation	Changes in Title and Amalgamation				Absorbed by Lloyds
1780	John Toplis (in 1804 Arkwright, Toplis & Co.), Wirksworth	1875	Absorbed by Moore & Robinson's Nottinghamshire Banking Co.	1902	Absorbed by CAPITAL AND COUNTIES BANK	
1771	Sir John Molesworth & Co. (in 1800 Praeds & Co.), Truro	1830	Became Tweedy, Williams & Co.			
		1879	Reconstituted as The Cornish Bank Ltd.			
1881	Commercial Bank of Cornwall	1891	Absorbed by The Cornish Bank Ltd.			
1788	Gipps, Simmons & Gipps, Canterbury	1800	Became Payler, Hammond, Simmons & Gipps	1903	„	
1804	Foster & Co., Cambridge			1904	„	
1786	Crickett, Truelove & Kerridge, Ipswich	1825	Became Bacon, Cobbold & Co.	1905	„	
1807	Cox, Cobbold & Co., Harwich	1893	Absorbed by Bacon, Cobbold & Co.			
1772	Berwick & Co., Worcester			1906	„	
1790	Lechmere & Co., Tewkesbury	1831	Amalgamated with Berwick & Co.			
1792	Eyton, Reynolds & Bishop, Shrewsbury	1884	Amalgamated to form Eyton, Burton & Co.	1907	„	
1812	Scott, Burton, Pemberton, Lloyd & Coupland, Shrewsbury					
1829	Halifax Joint Stock Banking Co.	1911	Title changed to WEST YORKSHIRE BANK LTD.			1919
1807	Rawson & Co., Halifax	1836	Formed into Halifax & Huddersfield Union Banking Co.	1910	Absorbed by Halifax Joint Stock Banking Co.	
1787	Fox & Co., Wellington, Somerset	1879	Title changed to FOX BROS. FOWLER & CO.			1921

(Eyton, Reynolds & Bishop, Shrewsbury and Scott, Burton, Pemberton, Lloyd & Coupland, Shrewsbury are bracketed together as "Amalgamated to form Eyton, Burton & Co." in 1884.)

Foundation date	Title at Foundation	Changes in Title and Amalgamation				Absorbed by Lloyds
1791	Cutliffe, Roch & Gribble, Barnstaple	1888	Became Marshall, Harding & Hiern	1888	Absorbed by FOX BROS. FOWLER & CO.	
1791	Gill, Morshead & Co., Tavistock			1889	" "	
1758	COX & CO., Albemarle Street					1923
1816	Smith, Elder & Co., 65 Cornhill	1868	Became Henry S. King & Co.	1923	Absorbed by COX & CO.	

Appendix 2

BRANCHES OF LLOYDS BANK

THE following is a list of present-day (May, 1957) branches or clerk-in-charge branches of Lloyds Bank. Against each is shown the date when an office or agency was opened in that place by Lloyds Bank, if a date only is given, or by the bank named. Banks which failed are shown in italics.

The sources of information for this list, apart from original documents in the possession of the bank, are the Banking Almanac 1845–1956, Pigot's Directories, Holden's Triennial Directory, the Post Office Directory 1801–45, and local directories, newspapers, and histories which have been checked by the individual branches.

HEAD OFFICE	1765	Dale End, Birmingham.
	1842	High Street, Birmingham.
	1871	Anne Street, renamed Colmore Row.
	1902	Jointly Colmore Row and 71 Lombard Street.
	1912	71 Lombard Street.

LONDON BRANCHES

ACTON	1926	
ALDWYCH	1907	Capital & Counties Bank.
BAKER STREET	1930	
BALHAM	1926	
BATTERSEA	1922	
BAYSWATER	1914	
BELGRAVE ROAD	1886	(Known as Pimlico until 1890.)
BELGRAVIA	1925	
BERKELEY SQUARE	1939	
BERMONDSEY	1920	
BLACKHEATH	1928	
BRIXTON	1921	
BROOK STREET	1923	
CAMBERWELL GREEN	1926	
CAMDEN TOWN	1926	
CHEAPSIDE	1901	(Took over the business of Brown, Janson & Co. of 32 Abchurch Lane.)
	1913	Capital & Counties Bank.
	1919	Business merged in Lloyds office.

CHELSEA	1926	
CHISWICK	1928	
CHURCH END, FINCHLEY	1924	
CITY OFFICE,		
72 Lombard Street	c. 1665	Humphrey Stokes at 54 Lombard Street.
	1728	Known as John Bland.
	1749	Business, now Bland & Co., moved to 62 Lombard Street.
	1761	Known as Bland, Barnett & Co.
	1770	Hanbury, Taylor, Lloyd & Bowman at 14 Lombard Street.
	1778	Moved to 60 Lombard Street.
	1796	Bosanquet Salt at 73 Lombard Street.
CLAPHAM	1922	
COMMERCIAL ROAD, E.1	1899	Capital & Counties Bank. (Known as St. George's-in-the-East.)
COVENT GARDEN	1881	Capital & Counties Bank. (Known as 1 Long Acre.)
CRICKLEWOOD	1923	
CROUCH END	1926	
EALING	1921	
EARLS COURT	1928	
EASTCHEAP	1936	
EAST DULWICH	1930	
EASTERN	1914	(Known as 127 Whitechapel High Street until 1915.)
EASTERN DEPARTMENT	1924	
EAST HAM	1927	
EDGWARE ROAD	1898	
FENCHURCH STREET	1899	(At 96 Leadenhall Street until 1902.)
FINCHLEY ROAD	1895	
FINSBURY CIRCUS	1905	Capital & Counties Bank.
FINSBURY PARK	1927	
FINSBURY SQUARE	1957	
GOLDERS GREEN	1914	
GREAT PORTLAND STREET	1915	Capital & Counties Bank.
GREENWICH	1927	
HAMMERSMITH	1926	
HAMPSTEAD	1885	
HANOVER SQUARE	1934	
HANWELL	1926	
HARLESDEN	1927	
HENDON	1924	
HENDON CENTRAL	1927	
HERNE HILL	1926	

Highbury Corner	1930	
Highgate Hill	1927	
Highgate Village	1929	
High Holborn	1909	Capital & Counties Bank.
Holborn Circus	1897	
Horseferry Road	1937	
Islington	1889	Capital & Counties Bank.
Kensington High Street	1908	Capital & Counties Bank.
Kentish Town	1930	
Kilburn & Brondesbury	1922	
King's Cross	1904	Capital & Counties Bank.
	1916	
Kingsway	1914	
Knightsbridge	1911	(At 16 Brompton Road.)
	1913	Capital & Counties Bank at 171 Brompton Road.
	1953	Businesses merged at 79/81 Brompton Road.
Langham Place	1956	
Law Courts	1802	Praeds & Co. at 189 Fleet Street.
	1824	Twinings & Co. of Devereux Court, later 215 Strand.
	1895	Businesses merged at 222/225 Strand.
Leadenhall Street	1934	
Lewisham	1926	
Leytonstone	1927	
Ludgate Hill	1878	Capital & Counties Bank.
Maida Vale	1928	
Mill Hill	1925	
Mincing Lane	1907	Capital & Counties Bank (at 22 Fenchurch Street).
Minories	1928	
Moorgate	1931	
Muswell Hill	1927	
Newington Causeway	1889	Capital & Counties Bank. (Known as Newington Butts until 1898.)
Norbury	1925	
North Finchley	1926	
Notting Hill Gate	1929	
Old Bond Street	1920	
Old Street, E.C.	1919	(This office closed in 1941 and re-opened in 1944 as a sub-branch to Shoreditch at 13 Old Street.)
Oxford Street (125) (C. & C. branch)	1876	Hampshire Banking Company.

OXFORD STREET (399)	1912	
PADDINGTON	1878	Capital & Counties Bank.
PALL MALL	1758	Cox & Co.
	1816	Smith, Elder & Co. (Later Henry S. King & Co.)
PALMERS GREEN	1926	
PARK LANE	1928	
PARK ROYAL	1938	
PECKHAM	1922	
PICCADILLY	1889	Capital & Counties Bank.
PUTNEY	1926	
RAYNES PARK AND WEST WIMBLEDON	1926	
REGENT STREET	1930	
ST. JAMES'S STREET	1772	London Exchange Banking Co. (Later Herries, Farquhar & Co.)
	1885	
	1896	The two businesses merged at 16 St. James's Street.
SHOREDITCH	1898	Capital & Counties Bank.
SLOANE SQUARE	1929	
SOUTHAMPTON ROW	1928	
SOUTH KENSINGTON	1931	
SOUTHWARK	1929	
SOUTH WOODFORD	1928	
STAMFORD HILL	1926	
STEPNEY	1924	
STOCK EXCHANGE	1921	
STOKE NEWINGTON	1927	
STRATFORD	1924	
STREATHAM	1921	
SYDENHAM	1926	
TEMPLE FORTUNE AND HAMPSTEAD GARDEN SUBURB	1922	
THREADNEEDLE STREET	1876	Hampshire Banking Company.
TOOTING BROADWAY	1927	
TOTTENHAM	1929	
TOTTENHAM COURT ROAD	1913	
UPPER NORWOOD	1928	
VICTORIA STREET	1897	Capital & Counties Bank. (Known as Westminster branch. Moved to 38 Victoria Street in 1900.)
WALHAM GREEN	1921	
WALTHAMSTOW	1923	
WANDSWORTH	1927	

BRANCHES OF LLOYDS BANK

WEST DULWICH	1926	
WEST KENSINGTON	1886	
WESTMINSTER HOUSE	1915	
WEST SMITHFIELD	1825	Hill & Sons.
WIGMORE STREET	1909	Capital & Counties Bank.
WILLESDEN GREEN	1927	
WIMBLEDON	1925	
WIMBLEDON COMMON	1924	
WOOD GREEN	1927	
WOOLWICH	1876	Hampshire Banking Company.

COUNTRY BRANCHES

ABERAVON	1861	Glamorganshire Banking Co.
ABERDARE	1854	Wilkins & Co.
ABERGAVENNY	1872	Gloucestershire Banking Co.
	1890	
ABERTILLERY	1889	Capital & Counties Bank.
	1910	
ABERYSTWYTH	1912	
ACCRINGTON	1922	
ALCESTER	1826	Hartland & Co.
ALDERSHOT	1875	Hampshire Banking Co.
	1916	
ALFORD	1887	Garfit, Claypon & Co.
ALLENDALE	1901	Lambton & Co.
ALNWICK	1832	Lambton & Co.
	1866	Hodgkin, Barnett & Co.
ALRESFORD	1859	Hampshire Banking Co.
ALTON	1858	Hampshire Banking Co.
ALTRINCHAM	1856	Cunliffe, Brooks & Co.
AMERSHAM	1889	Wheeler & Co.
AMERSHAM-ON-THE-HILL	1919	
AMESBURY	1897	Wilts & Dorset Banking Co.
	1915	Capital & Counties Bank.
AMMANFORD	1891	Glamorganshire Banking Co.
	1902	David Jones & Co.
ANDOVER	1790	Gilbert & Co.
	1851	Hampshire Banking Co.
	1914	
ANNFIELD PLAIN	1892	Hodgkin, Barnett & Co.
ARUNDEL	1808	Henty & Co.
ASCOT	1922	
ASHBOURNE	1843	Burton, Uttoxeter & Ashbourne Union Bank.

ASHBURTON	1863	Watts & Co.
	1889	Devon & Cornwall Banking Co. (Also from 1834–c. 1844.)
ASHBY-DE-LA-ZOUCH	1900	
ASHFORD, Kent	1791	Jemmett, Whitfield & Jemmett.
	1904	Capital & Counties Bank.
ASHFORD, Middlesex	1928	
ASHINGTON	1896	Hodgkin, Barnett & Co.
ASHTON-UNDER-LYNE	1956	
ASTWOOD BANK	1875	Gloucestershire Banking Co.
	1877	Worcester City & County Banking Co.
ATHERSTONE	1875	Worcester City & County Banking Co.
ATTLEBOROUGH	1919	
AXBRIDGE	1836	*West of England & South Wales District Bank.*
	1878	Premises taken over by Wilts & Dorset Banking Co.
AXMINSTER	1834	Williams, Cox & Co.
	1836	Wilts & Dorset Banking Co.
	1897	Devon & Cornwall Banking Co.
AYLESBURY	1795	Rickford & Son.
	1912	Capital & Counties Bank.
BALDOCK	1807	Williamson & Co.
BANBURY	1783	Cobb, Wheatley & Co.
BANGOR	1823	Williams & Co.
BANSTEAD	1927	
BARGOED	1892	
BARKING	1928	
BARNET	1929	
BARNSTAPLE	1791	Cutliffe, Roch & Gribble.
	1835	*West of England & South Wales District Bank.*
	1878/9	Premises taken over by Devon & Cornwall Banking Co.
	1880	Fox Fowler & Co.
	1899	Wilts & Dorset Banking Co.
BARROW-IN-FURNESS	1922	
BARRY DOCKS	1890	
	1890	County of Gloucester Bank.
BASINGSTOKE	1806	Raggett, Seymour & Co.
	1914	
BATH	1867	Wilts & Dorset Banking Co.
	1890	Bristol & West of England Bank.
BATH (C. & C.)	1898	Capital & Counties Bank.
BATH, LOWER WESTON	1901	Wilts & Dorset Banking Co.

BATLEY	1911	Halifax Joint Stock Banking Co.
BEACONSFIELD	1889	Wheeler & Co.
BEACONSFIELD, PENN ROAD	1908	Capital & Counties Bank.
BEAMINSTER	1834	Williams, Cox & Co.
	1861	Wilts & Dorset Banking Co.
BEAUMARIS	1899	
BECCLES	1824	Lacons, Youell & Co.
BECKENHAM	1927	
BEDFORD	1915	Capital & Counties Bank.
BEDWORTH	1920	
BELLINGHAM	1891	Hodgkin, Barnett & Co.
	1904	Lambton & Co.
BEMBRIDGE, Isle of Wight	1896	Capital & Counties Bank.
BERKHAMSTED	1920	
BEVERLEY, YORKS	1957	
BEXHILL-ON-SEA	1885	Beechings & Co.
BEXLEYHEATH	1930	
BICESTER	1919	
BIDEFORD	1865	*West of England & South Wales District Bank.* (Also *c.* 1836.)
	1878	Premises taken over by Devon & Cornwall Banking Co.
	1879	Fox Fowler & Co.
	1899	Wilts & Dorset Banking Co.
BIGGLESWADE	1810	G. & W. Hogge.
BILLERICAY	1953	
BILLINGHAM	1920	
BILSTON	1923	
BIRCHINGTON-ON-SEA	1884	Cobb & Co.
BIRKENHEAD, BEBINGTON & ROCK FERRY	1931	
BIRKENHEAD, CHARING CROSS	1899	Liverpool Union Bank.
BIRKENHEAD, HAMILTON SQUARE	1957	
BIRKENHEAD, WEST END	1892	Liverpool Union Bank.

Birmingham Branches

ACOCKS GREEN	1907
ASTON ROAD	1875
BLACKHEATH	1923
BLOOMSBURY	1888
BOURNBROOK	1931
BOURNVILLE	1909
BRISTOL STREET	1887
CAPE HILL	1908
COLESHILL	1865

Birmingham Branches (contd.)

COLMORE ROW	1766	Robert Coales Bank.
	1872	Worcester City & County Banking Co.
CORPORATION STREET	1889	Capital & Counties Bank.
COTTERIDGE	1914	
DERITEND	1874	
EDGBASTON	1874	
ERDINGTON	1895	
GOOCH STREET	1882	Worcester City & County Banking Co.
GRAVELLY HILL	1913	
GREAT HAMPTON STREET	1874	
	1874	Birmingham Joint Stock Bank.
HALL GREEN	1913	
HANDSWORTH	1885	
HARBORNE	1884	
HIGHGATE	1900	
HOLYHEAD ROAD	1903	
JAMAICA ROW	1893	
KING'S HEATH	1913	
KING'S NORTON	1890	
KNOWLE	1949	
LADYWOOD	1894	
MOSELEY	1883	
NEW STREET	1865	Birmingham Joint Stock Bank. (On failure of *Attwood, Spooner & Co.*)
	1872	Worcester City & County Banking Co.
NORTHFIELD	1926	
OLD SQUARE	1922	
OLTON	1930	
PARADE	1898	
PERRY BAR	1947	
QUINTON	1957	
SELLY OAK	1889	
SHIRLEY	1901	
SMALL HEATH	1895	
SOUTH YARDLEY	1921	
SPARKBROOK	1889	
SPARKHILL	1903	
STIRCHLEY	1895	
SUMMERFIELD	1894	
TEMPLE ROW	1861	Birmingham Joint Stock Bank.
TYSELEY	1919	
WASHWOOD HEATH	1930	(Known as Alum Rock until 1949.)
WYLDE GREEN	1925	(Known as Erdington until 1935.)
BIRTLEY	1898	Hodgkin, Barnett & Co.

BISHOP AUCKLAND	1911	
BISHOP'S STORTFORD	1874	Foster & Co.
BISHOP'S WALTHAM	1899	Capital & Counties Bank.
BLACKBURN	1792	Cunliffe, Brooks & Co.
BLACKPOOL	1927	
BLACKPOOL, SOUTH SHORE	1928	
BLACKWOOD	1890	
BLANDFORD	1836	Wilts & Dorset Banking Co.
BLAYDON-ON-TYNE	1883	Lambton & Co.
	1900	Hodgkin, Barnett & Co.
BLETCHLEY	1921	
BLOXWICH	1874	
BLYTH	1862	Lambton & Co.
	1893	Hodgkin, Barnett & Co.
BODMIN	1865	Clymo, Treffry & Co.
	1890	Devon & Cornwall Banking Co. (Also 1834–50.)
BOGNOR REGIS	1921	
BOGNOR REGIS, ALDWICK ROAD	1921	
BOLTON	1924	
BOREHAM WOOD	1954	
BOSTON	1754	Garfit, Claypon & Co.
BOURNE	1810	Peacock & Co.
BOURNE END	1898	Capital & Counties Bank.
	1898	Stephens, Blandy & Co.

Bournemouth Branches

BOURNEMOUTH	1861	Wilts & Dorset Banking Co.
	1897	Capital & Counties Bank. (On failure of *Eliot, Pearce & Co.*)
	1884	R. & R. Williams & Co.
	1900	
BOSCOMBE	1884	Wilts & Dorset Banking Co.
	1890	R. & R. Williams & Co.
	1897	Capital & Counties Bank. (On failure of *Eliot, Pearce & Co.*)
	1909	
CANFORD CLIFFS	1908	Wilts & Dorset Banking Co.
CHARMINSTER ROAD	1901	Wilts & Dorset Banking Co.
EAST BOSCOMBE	1897	Wilts & Dorset Banking Co. (Known as Pokesdown until 1917.)
IFORD	1931	
LANSDOWNE	1897	Wilts & Dorset Banking Co.
MALMESBURY PARK	1898	Wilts & Dorset Banking Co.
MOORDOWN	1924	

Bournemouth Branches (contd.)

WESTBOURNE	1886	Wilts & Dorset Banking Co.
	1909	
	1912	Capital & Counties Bank.
WEST CLIFF	1903	Wilts & Dorset Banking Co.
WEST SOUTHBOURNE	1902	Wilts & Dorset Banking Co. (Known as Boscombe Park until 1906.)
	1911	
WINTON	1895	Wilts & Dorset Banking Co.
BOURTON-ON-THE-WATER	1888	County of Gloucester Bank.
	1888	Capital & Counties Bank.
BOVEY TRACEY	1883	Devon & Cornwall Banking Co.
	1891	Capital & Counties Bank.
	1898	Wilts & Dorset Banking Co.
BRACKLEY	*c.* 1841	Bartlett, Parrott & Co.
BRACKNELL	1872	Stephens, Blandy & Co.
BRADFORD	1883	Halifax Joint Stock Banking Co.
	1895	Halifax & Huddersfield Union Banking Co.
	1907	
BRADFORD, BARKEREND ROAD	1915	West Yorkshire Bank.
BRADFORD, WEST BOWLING	1913	West Yorkshire Bank.
BRADFORD-ON-AVON	1836	North Wilts Banking Co.
	1861	Wilts & Dorset Banking Co. (Also an agency 1835–*c.* 1838.)
BRAINTREE	1920	
BRAUNTON	1891	Devon & Cornwall Banking Co.
BRECON	1778	Wilkins & Co.
BRENTWOOD	1938	
BRIDGEND	1902	
	1914	Capital & Counties Bank.
BRIDGNORTH	1799	Vickers Son & Pritchard.
	1866	Worcester City & County Banking Co.
	1892	Eyton, Burton & Co.
BRIDGWATER	1790	Sealy & Prior.
	1836	*West of England & South Wales District Bank.*
	1878	Business taken over by Fox, Fowler & Co.
	1899	Devon & Cornwall Banking Co.
BRIDLINGTON	1927	
BRIDPORT	1813	Williams & Co. (Later R. & R. Williams.)
	1836	Wilts & Dorset Banking Co. (Closed *c.* 1840–56.)
	1898	Devon & Cornwall Banking Co.
BRIERLEY HILL	1914	

BRIGG	1920	
BRIGHOUSE	1883	Halifax Joint Stock Banking Co.
	1894	Halifax & Huddersfield Union Banking Co.

Brighton Branches

BRIGHTON	1860	Hampshire Banking Co.
	1896	
DYKE ROAD	1900	Capital & Counties Bank. (Known as Prestonville Road until 1906.)
KEMP TOWN	1893	Capital & Counties Bank.
PRESTON CIRCUS	1911	Capital & Counties Bank. (Known as London Road until 1924.)
WESTERN ROAD	1864	Hampshire Banking Co.

Bristol Branches

BRISTOL	1834	*West of England & South Wales District Bank.*
	1879	Bristol & West of England Bank.
	1872	Wilts & Dorset Banking Co.
AVONMOUTH	1892	Capital & Counties Bank.
	1903	Wilts & Dorset Banking Co.
	1906	
BEDMINSTER	1902	
BRISLINGTON	1908	Wilts & Dorset Banking Co.
CHELTENHAM ROAD	1889	Capital & Counties Bank.
	1901	Wilts & Dorset Banking Co.
	1904	
CLIFTON	1890	Bristol & West of England Bank.
	1901	Wilts & Dorset Banking Co.
CLIFTON, REGENT STREET	1862	*West of England & South Wales District Bank.*
	1878	Premises taken over by Wilts & Dorset Banking Co.
	1897	Capital & Counties Bank.
DURDHAM DOWN	1906	Wilts & Dorset Banking Co.
EASTVILLE	1899	Capital & Counties Bank.
FILTON	1937	
FISHPONDS	1896	
HENLEAZE	1924	
HORFIELD	1902	Wilts & Dorset Banking Co.
KEYNSHAM	1911	Wilts & Dorset Banking Co.
KINGSWOOD	1885	Bristol & West of England Bank.
MERCHANT STREET	1957	
PORTISHEAD	1908	Wilts & Dorset Banking Co.

Bristol Branches (contd.)

REDLAND	1894	Wilts & Dorset Banking Co.
	1903	
	1880	Capital & Counties Bank (Whiteladies Gate).
ST. GEORGE	1889	Bristol & West of England Bank.
ST. PHILIP'S	1881	Bristol & West of England Bank.
STAPLE HILL	1892	Bristol & West of England Bank.
STOKES CROFT	1881	Bristol & West of England Bank.
TEMPLE GATE	1888	Bristol & West of England Bank.
TOTTERDOWN	1899	
WESTBURY-ON-TRYM	1901	Wilts & Dorset Banking Co.
BRITON FERRY	1889	Glamorganshire Banking Co.
BRIXHAM	1830	Brooking & Browse.
BROADHEATH (Altrincham)	1903	
BROADSTAIRS	1887	Cobb & Co.
	1904	Capital & Counties Bank.
BROADSTONE	1905	Wilts & Dorset Banking Co.
BROADWAY	1889	Capital & Counties Bank.
BROCKENHURST	1898	Wilts & Dorset Banking Co.
	1898	Capital & Counties Bank.
BROMLEY	1913	
BROMSGROVE	1864	Worcester City & County Banking Co.
BROMYARD	1879	Berwick & Co.
BROSELEY	1799	Vickers Son & Pritchard.
BRYNMAWR	1874	Gloucestershire Banking Co.
BUCKFASTLEIGH	1887	Devon & Cornwall Banking Co.
	1891	Capital & Counties Bank.
BUCKINGHAM	1785	Philip Box & Co.
BUCKLEY	1891	Williams & Co.
BUDE	1890	Fox, Fowler & Co.
	1894	Devon & Cornwall Banking Co.
BUDLEIGH SALTERTON	1872	*West of England & South Wales District Bank.*
	1878	Premises taken over by Wilts & Dorset Banking Co.
	1895	Devon & Cornwall Banking Co.
BURFORD	1825	Pitt & Co.
BURGESS HILL	1875	Hampshire Banking Co.
BURNHAM-ON-SEA	1876	Wilts & Dorset Banking Co.
BURNLEY	1951	
BURSLEM	1898	
BURTON-ON-TRENT	1790	Wilson, Dalrymple & Co.
	1806	Meek, Moulsey & Co.
	1876	

BURTON-ON-TRENT, BOROUGH
    ROAD   1890   Burton, Uttoxeter & Ashbourne Union
                                         Bank.

Branch	Year	Predecessor
BURY	1931	
BURY ST. EDMUNDS	1795	James Oakes & Son.
	1801	Crowe, Sparrow & Brown.
BYFLEET	1949	
CAERNARVON	1792	Roberts & Co.
	1792	Williams & Co.
CALLINGTON	1887	Western Counties Bank.
	1891	Cornish Bank Ltd.
CALNE	1835	North Wilts Banking Co.
	1851	Wilts & Dorset Banking Co.
CAMBERLEY	1924	
CAMBORNE	1885	Devon & Cornwall Banking Co.
	1888	Cornish Bank Ltd.

Cambridge Branches

Branch	Year	Predecessor
CAMBRIDGE	1804	Foster & Co.
	1900	Capital & Counties Bank.
	1905	
CATTLE MARKET	1887	Foster & Co.
CHESTERTON ROAD	1930	
MILL ROAD	1919	
TRINITY STREET	1953	
CAMELFORD	1867	Clymo, Treffry & Co.
	1914	
CANNOCK	1870	
CANTERBURY	1788	Gipps, Simmons & Gipps.
	1896	

Cardiff Branches

Branch	Year	Predecessor
CARDIFF	1819	Towgood & Co.
	1835	*West of England & South Wales District Bank.*
	1879	Bristol & West of England Bank.
	1856	Wilkins & Co.
	1888	County of Gloucester Bank.
CANTON	1897	
CARDIFF DOCKS	1854	*West of England & South Wales District Bank.*
	1879	Bristol & West of England Bank.
	1889	County of Gloucester Bank.
	1890	
	1916	Capital & Counties Bank.
CITY ROAD	1892	Wilts & Dorset Banking Co.
CRWYS ROAD	1922	

Cardiff Branches (contd.)

QUEEN STREET	1898	Capital & Counties Bank.
ROATH	1893	Wilts & Dorset Banking Co.
	1894	County of Gloucester Bank.
ROATH PARK	1910	
ST. MARY STREET	1890	Wilts & Dorset Banking Co.
VICTORIA PARK	1923	
WHITCHURCH	1914	
CARDIGAN	1835	Wilkins & Co.
CARLISLE	1919	
CARMARTHEN	1834	Wilkins & Co.
CARSHALTON	1919	
CATERHAM-ON-THE-HILL	1918	
CATERHAM VALLEY	1886	
CATTERICK CAMP	1925	
CAVERSHAM	1903	Capital & Counties Bank.
CHAGFORD	1890	Devon & Cornwall Banking Co.
	1901	Wilts & Dorset Banking Co.
CHARD	1867	Wilts & Dorset Banking Co.
CHATHAM	1899	Capital & Counties Bank.
	1901	
CHEAM	1923	
CHEAM, NORTH	1930	
CHEDDAR	1885	Wilts & Dorset Banking Co.
CHELMSFORD	1901	Capital & Counties Bank.
CHELTENHAM	1823	Pitt & Co.
	1825	Hartland & Co.
	1836	Cheltenham&GloucestershireBankingCo.
	1875	Worcester City & County Banking Co.
	1889	Bristol & West of England Bank.
	1891	Wilts & Dorset Banking Co.
CHELTENHAM, MONTPELLIER	1883	Worcester City & County Banking Co.
	1908	Capital & Counties Bank.
CHEPSTOW	1914	
CHESHAM	1889	Bucks & Oxon Union Bank.
CHESTER	1793	Williams & Co.
CHESTERFIELD	1921	
CHESTER-LE-STREET	1890	Lambton & Co.
	1896	Hodgkin, Barnett & Co.
CHICHESTER	1864	Hampshire Banking Co.
CHIPPENHAM	1809	Gundry & Co.
	1836	North Wilts Banking Co.
	1852	Everett, Ravenhill & Co.
CHIPPING CAMPDEN	1868	Gloucestershire Banking Co.
CHIPPING SODBURY	1957	

CHOPWELL	1908	
CHRISTCHURCH	1836	Wilts & Dorset Banking Co.
	1837	*Tice & Welch.*
	1896	Capital & Counties Bank.
CHURCH STRETTON	1875	Rocke, Eyton & Co.
CINDERFORD	1869	Gloucestershire Banking Co.
	1884	Bristol & West of England Bank.
CIRENCESTER	1790	Pitt, Croome, Bowley & Brown.
	1796	Cripps & Co.
	1897	Wilts & Dorset Banking Co.
CLACTON-ON-SEA	1920	
CLECKHEATON	1910	Halifax Joint Stock Banking Co.
CLEOBURY MORTIMER	1890	
CLEVEDON	1862	Harwood & Harwood.
	1878	Wilts & Dorset Banking Co. (In premises of *West of England & South Wales District Bank.*)
CLEVEDON, TRIANGLE	1929	[Bank.
COALVILLE	1891	Burton, Uttoxeter & Ashbourne Union
COLCHESTER	1899	Capital & Counties Bank.
COLEFORD	1861	Gloucestershire Banking Co.
	1908	
COLWYN BAY	1915	
COLYTON	1868	R. & H. Williams & Co.
	1872	Wilts & Dorset Banking Co.
COMBE MARTIN	1886	Fox, Fowler & Co.
	1889	Devon & Cornwall Banking Co.
CONNAH'S QUAY	1889	Williams & Co.
CONSETT	1883	Hodgkin, Barnett & Co.
	1900	Lambton & Co.
CORBY	1911	Capital & Counties Bank.
CORSHAM	1857	Wilts & Dorset Banking Co.
	1863	North Wilts Banking Co. (Also 1836–7.)
COULSDON	1921	
Coventry Branches		
COVENTRY	1790	Wyatt, Inge & Lant.
	1810	Eagle, Goodall & Co.
	1835	Coventry & Warwickshire Banking Co.
	1874	
	1885	Worcester City & County Banking Co.
CHEYLESMORE	1949	
EARLSDON	1913	
FOLESHILL	1900	
GOSFORD GREEN	1936	
WALSGRAVE ROAD	1930	

Cowes, Isle of Wight	1862	Hampshire Banking Co. (1837 *Southern District Banking Co.* 1840 Closed after absorption by Hampshire Banking Co.)
Cradley Heath	1913	
Cranbrook	1913	
Cranleigh	1888	Capital & Counties Bank.
Craven Arms	1885	Eyton, Burton & Co.
	1888	Worcester City & County Banking Co.
Crawley	1885	Henty & Co.
Crediton	1878	Devon & Cornwall Banking Co. (Also 1837–1842/5.)
	1881	Fox, Fowler & Co.
Crewkerne	1867	Wilts & Dorset Banking Co.
Crickhowell	1913	
Cricklade	1868	Gloucestershire Banking Co.
Cromer	1889	Lacons, Youell & Co.
Crowborough	1931	
Croydon	1919	
Croydon, South	1925	
Cullompton	1810	Skinner, Brown & Co.
Cwmbran	1919	
Dagenham	1929	
Darlaston	1886	
Darlington	1909	
Dartford	1928	
Dartmouth	1890	Bristol & West of England Bank. (1832 Prout & Stapleton. *c.* 1843 Closed.)
Darwen	1889	Cunliffes, Brooks & Co.
Daventry	1783	Watkins & Co.
Dawlish	1858	Watts & Co.
	1882	Devon & Cornwall Banking Co.
Deal	1896	
	1911	Capital & Counties Bank.
Debden Estate	1953	
Derby	1898	Burton Union Bank.
Derby, The Spot	1953	
Devizes	1775	Sutton, Leach, Bevan & Read.
	1835	North Wilts Banking Co.
	1835	Wilts & Dorset Banking Co.
Dewsbury	1920	
Didcot	1915	
Diss	1919	
Doncaster	1911	
Dorchester	1786	Cox & Co.
	1836	Wilts & Dorset Banking Co.

Dorchester	1897	Devon & Cornwall Banking Co.
	1897	Capital & Counties Bank. (On failure of *Eliot, Pearce & Co.*)
Dorking	1874	Hampshire Banking Co.
Douglas, Isle of Man	1897	Liverpool Union Bank.
Dover	1895	
	1898	Capital & Counties Bank.
Dover, Buckland	1912	Capital & Counties Bank.
Dovercourt	1901	Bacon, Cobbold & Co.
Dowlais	1875	Wilkins & Co.
Downham Market	1919	
Droitwich	1862	Worcester City & County Banking Co.
	1901	Berwick & Co.
Dudley	c. 1791	*Finch & Co.*
Dunmow	1923	
Dunstable	1923	
Durham	1896	Hodgkin, Barnett & Co.
Dursley	1803	Vizard & Co.
	1829	Wood, Pitt & Co.
Eastbourne	1896	Capital & Counties Bank.
	1902	
East Dereham	1881	Lacons, Youell & Co.
East Grinstead	1892	(On failure of *Head's Bank.*)
	1892	Capital & Counties Bank. (On failure of *Head's Bank.*)
Eastleigh	1888	Wilts & Dorset Banking Co.
	1909	
East Molesey and Hampton Court	1925	
Ebbw Vale	1908	
Edenbridge	1892	(On failure of *Head's Bank.*)
	1892	Capital & Counties Bank. (On failure of *Head's Bank.*)
Edgware	1923	
Edgware, Station Road	1954	
Elland	1886	Halifax & Huddersfield Union Banking Co.
	1894	Halifax Joint Stock Banking Co.
Ellesmere	1842	Rocke, Eyton & Co.
	1881	(On failure of *Whitchurch & Ellesmere Banking Co.*)
Ellesmere Port	1952	
Ely	1835	Foster & Co.
Emsworth	1864	Hampshire Banking Co.
Enfield	1886	

EPSOM	1892	Capital & Counties Bank.
ESHER	1931	
ETON	1924	
EVESHAM	1813	Hartland & Co.
	1863	Worcester City & County Banking Co.
EWELL	1931	
EXETER	1818	Sparkes & Co.
	1873	Wilts & Dorset Banking Co.
	1885	Fox, Fowler & Co.
	1903	Capital & Counties Bank.
EXETER, St. Thomas	1893	Devon & Cornwall Banking Co.
EXMOUTH	1863	*West of England & South Wales District Bank.*
	1878	Premises taken over by Wilts & Dorset Banking Co.
	1885	Devon & Cornwall Banking Co.
FAIRFORD	1868	Gloucestershire Banking Co.
	1889	County of Gloucester Bank.
FAKENHAM	1894	Lacons, Youell & Co.
FALMOUTH	1806	Praeds & Co.
	1878	Devon & Cornwall Banking Co.
FAREHAM	1834	Hampshire Banking Co.
	1895	Wilts & Dorset Banking Co.
FARINGDON	1824	Pitt & Co.
FARNBOROUGH	1898	Capital & Counties Bank. (Known as North Camp until 1906.)
FARNHAM	1806	Stevens & Co.
	1916	
FAVERSHAM	1904	Capital & Counties Bank.
FELIXSTOWE	1892	Bacon, Cobbold & Co.
FENTON	1896	
FERNDOWN	1910	Wilts & Dorset Banking Co.
FLEET	1889	Capital & Counties Bank.
FOLKESTONE	1887	Beechings & Co.
	1897	Capital & Counties Bank.
FOLKESTONE, CHERITON & SHORNCLIFFE	1927	
FORDINGBRIDGE	1836	Wilts & Dorset Banking Co.
FOREST HALL AND BENTON	1905	Lambton & Co.
FOWEY	1881	Commercial Bank of Cornwall.
	1897	Devon & Cornwall Banking Co.
FRESHWATER	1883	Capital & Counties Bank.
	1896/7	Wilts & Dorset Banking Co.
	1897	Capital & Counties Bank. (School Green.)
FRINTON-ON-SEA	1935	

FROME	1836	Wilts & Dorset Banking Co.
	1898	Capital & Counties Bank.
GAINSBOROUGH	1919	
Gateshead Branches		
GATESHEAD	1866	Lambton & Co.
	1894	Hodgkin, Barnett & Co.
COASTWORTH ROAD	1907	
FELLING	1909	
LOW FELL	1924	
GIDEA PARK	1928	
GILLINGHAM, Dorset	1836	Wilts & Dorset Banking Co. (Closed 1846–55.)
GILLINGHAM, Kent	1920	
GILLINGHAM, WATLING STREET	1930	(Known as Chatham Hill until 1937.)
GLASTONBURY	1864	Wilts & Dorset Banking Co.
GLOSSOP	1927	
GLOUCESTER	1819	Russell & Skey.
	1831	Gloucestershire Banking Co.
	1834	Gloucester County & City Bank.
	1886	Worcester City & County Banking Co.
	1890	Wilts & Dorset Banking Co.
GODALMING	1808	Mellersh, Moline & Weale.
GOSPORT	1862	Grant, Gillman & Co. (Also 1833–48.)
	1864	Hampshire Banking Co.
GRANTHAM	1919	
GRAVESEND	1904	Capital & Counties Bank.
GRAYS	1900	Capital & Counties Bank.
GRAYSHOTT	1899	Capital & Counties Bank.
GREAT BOOKHAM	1905	Capital & Counties Bank.
GREAT BRIDGE	1876	
GREAT MISSENDEN	1895	Bucks & Oxon Union Bank.
GREENFORD	1928	
GRIMSBY	1914	
GRIMSBY DOCKS	1922	
GUERNSEY	1887	Capital & Counties Bank.
GUILDFORD	1765	Haydon & Smallpiece.
	1913	
GWAUN-CAE-GURWEN	1908	Capital & Counties Bank.
HADLEIGH, Suffolk	1919	
HALESOWEN	1864	Moilliet & Son.
HALESWORTH	1870	Lacons, Youell & Co. (On failure of *Harveys & Hudsons*.)
HALIFAX	1807	Rawson & Co.
	1829	Halifax Joint Stock Banking Co.
HALIFAX, QUEEN'S ROAD	1890	Halifax Joint Stock Banking Co.

HALSTEAD	1920	
HAMPTON	1931	
HANLEY	1877	
HARLOW, OLD TOWN	1947	
HARLOW, TOWN CENTRE	1957	
HARPENDEN	1927	
HARROGATE	1918	
HARROW	1923	
HARROW, NORTH	1927	
HARROW, SOUTH	1931	
HASLEMERE	1891	Capital & Counties Bank.
HASSOCKS	1934	
HASTINGS	1859	Beechings & Co.
	1881	Capital & Counties Bank.
HATFIELD	1956	
HAVANT	1863	Hampshire Banking Co.
HAVERFORDWEST	1832	Wilkins & Co.
HAVERHILL	1810	Sparrow, Brown & Co.
HAWARDEN	1890	Williams & Co.
HAYES, Middlesex	1930	
HAYLE	1908	Capital & Counties Bank.
HAYLING ISLAND	1900	Capital & Counties Bank.
HAYWARDS HEATH	1889	Capital & Counties Bank.
HEATHFIELD	1928	
HEBBURN	1907	
HEBDEN BRIDGE	1874	Halifax Joint Stock Banking Co.
HEDNESFORD	1876	
HELSTON	1879	Cornish Bank Ltd.
	1914	
HEMEL HEMPSTEAD	1856	Bucks & Oxon Union Bank.
HENLEY-IN-ARDEN	1914	
HENLEY-ON-THAMES	1923	
HEREFORD	1862	Gloucestershire Banking Co.
	1881	Worcester City & County Banking Co.
HERNE BAY	1919	
HERTFORD	1905	Capital & Counties Bank.
HESWALL	1895	Liverpool Union Bank.
HEXHAM	1831	Lambton & Co.
	1896	Hodgkin, Barnett & Co.
HIGHBRIDGE	1876	Wilts & Dorset Banking Co.
	1879	Fox, Fowler & Co.
HIGHCLIFFE-ON-SEA	1912	Wilts & Dorset Banking Co.
HIGH WYCOMBE	1812	Wheeler & Co.
HIGH WYCOMBE, DESBOROUGH ROAD	1900	Capital & Counties Bank.

HINCKLEY	1928	
HITCHIN	1856	Wells, Hogge & Lindsell.
HODDESDON	1949	
HOLBEACH	1911	Capital & Counties Bank.
HOLMFIRTH	1907	Halifax Joint Stock Banking Co.
HOLSWORTHY	1875	Gill, Morshead & Co.
	1877	Devon & Cornwall Banking Co.
HOLT	1930	
HOLYHEAD	1919	
HONITON	1891	Devon & Cornwall Banking Co.
	1919	Fox, Fowler & Co.
HORLEY	1891	Capital & Counties Bank.
	1892	(On failure of *Heads' Bank*.)
HORNCASTLE	1819	Garfit, Claypon & Co.
HORSHAM	1839	Henty, Upperton & Olliver.
HOUNSLOW	1926	
Hove Branches		
CHURCH ROAD	1898	(Closed 1943–55.)
PALMEIRA	1909	
PORTLAND ROAD	1930	
TOWN HALL	1891	Capital & Counties Bank.
HUDDERSFIELD	1811	Rawson & Co.
	1881	Halifax Joint Stock Banking Co.
	1918	
HULL	1911	
HULL, PARAGON STREET	1955	
HUNGERFORD	1882	Haydon & Smallpiece.
HUNTINGDON	1919	
HYTHE, Kent	1909	
Ilford Branches		
HIGH ROAD	1922	
ILFORD	1927	
GANTS HILL	1939	
HAINHAULT	1954	
ILFRACOMBE	1872	*West of England & South Wales District Bank.*
	1879	Premises taken over by Fox, Fowler & Co.
	1887	Devon & Cornwall Banking Co.
ILKLEY	1906	Halifax Joint Stock Banking Co.
ILMINSTER	1864	Wilts & Dorset Banking Co.
IPSWICH	1786	Crickett, Truelove & Kerridge.
IPSWICH, DERBY ROAD	1900	Bacon, Cobbold & Co.
IRONBRIDGE	1810	Darby & Co. (Known as Coalbrookdale until 1884.)
IVYBRIDGE	1914	(On failure of *Naval Bank*.)

Jarrow-on-Tyne	1886	Hodgkin, Barnett & Co.
Jersey	1846	*Jersey Joint Stock Bank. (De Carteret & Co.)*
	1862	*English & Jersey Union Bank. (Le Neveu Sorel & Co.)*
	1873	Hampshire Banking Co.
Keighley	1910	Halifax Joint Stock Banking Co.
	1911	
Kendal	1920	
Kenilworth	1884	
Kenton	1925	
Keswick	1920	
Kettering	1876	Northamptonshire Banking Co.
Kidderminster	1857	Worcester City & County Banking Co.
Kingsbridge	1829	Nicholson & Co.
	1832	George Fox & Co.
	1832	Plymouth & Devonport Banking Co.
	1841	Kingsbridge Joint Stock Bank.
	1879	Bristol & West of England Bank.
	1886	Wilts & Dorset Banking Co.
King's Lynn	1889	Lacons, Youell & Co.
Kingston-on-Thames	1921	
Laindon	1950	
Lampeter	1831	Jones, Evans & Co.
Lancaster	1953	
Lancing	1914	
Langport	1913	Fox, Fowler & Co.
Launceston	1832	Gill, Morshead & Co.
	1836	Devon & Cornwall Banking Co.
Leamington Spa	1823	Tomes & Russell.
Leamington Spa, Bath Street	1956	
Leatherhead	1889	Capital & Counties Bank.
Lechlade	1868	Gloucestershire Banking Co.
	1889	County of Gloucester Bank.
Ledbury	1790	Hankins & Co.
Lee-on-the-Solent	1899	Capital & Counties Bank.
Leeds Branches		
Leeds	1813	Nicholson, Brown & Co.
	1903	Halifax & Huddersfield Union Banking Co.
	1903	Halifax Joint Stock Banking Co.
Armley	1914	
Harehills	1927	
Hunslet	1902	
University Branch	1920	(Known as Woodhouse Lane until 1956.)

Vicar Lane	1903	
	1911	Halifax Joint Stock Banking Co.
Leicester Branches		
Leicester	1825	Pagets & Kirby.
Granby Street	1902	Capital & Counties Bank.
Humberstone Park	1934	
London Road	1928	
Melton Road	1928	
Narborough Road	1935	
Leigh-on-Sea	1912	Capital & Counties Bank.
Leigh-on-Sea, Highlands	1930	
Leominster	1862	Worcester City & County Banking Co.
Letchworth	1949	
Lewes	1919	
Lichfield	1857	Stevenson, Salt & Co.
Lincoln	1890	Garfit, Clayon & Co.
	1895	Peacock & Co.
Liphook	1904	Capital & Counties Bank.
Liskeard	1834	Devon & Cornwall Banking Co.
	1864	Clymo, Treffry, Hawke, West & Co.
	1881	Commercial Bank of Cornwall.
Littlehampton	1859	Henty & Co.
Littleport	1889	Foster & Co.
Liverpool Branches		
Liverpool	1835	Liverpool Union Bank.
Allerton Road	1952	
Bold Street	1877	Liverpool Union Bank.
Exchange	1899	Liverpool Union Bank.
London Road	1884	Liverpool Union Bank.
Sefton Park and Mossley Hill	1898	Liverpool Union Bank.
Victoria Street	1921	
Waterloo	1928	
Llandeilo	1842	David Jones & Co.
	1873	Glamorganshire Banking Co.
Llandovery	1799	David Jones & Co.
Llandrindod Wells	1914	
Llandudno	1892	Williams & Co.
Llandyssul	1889	Wilkins & Co.
Llanelly	1837	Wilkins & Co.
	1893	Glamorganshire Banking Co.
Llanfairfechan	1884	Williams & Co.
Llangefni	1889	Williams & Co.
Llanybyther	1903	David Jones & Co.
Longton	1866	

Looe	1866	Clymo, Treffry, Hawke, West & Co.
	1881	Commercial Bank of Cornwall.
	1890	Devon & Cornwall Banking Co.
Lostwithiel	1888	Commercial Bank of Cornwall.
Loughborough	1855	Paget & Co.
Louth	1754	Garfit, Claypon & Co.
Lowestoft	1819	Lacons, Youell & Co.
Ludlow	1825	Rocke, Eyton & Co.
	1840	Ludlow & Tenbury Bank.
	1885	
Luton	1898	Capital & Counties Bank.
Lydney	1840	Gloucestershire Banking Co.
	1908	
Lye	1914	
Lyme Regis	1833	Williams, Cox & Co.
	1907	
Lymington	1788	St. Barbe & Co.
	1800	John West.
	1836	Wilts & Dorset Banking Co.
Lyndhurst	1893	Grant & Maddison's Union Banking Co.
	1898	Wilts & Dorset Banking Co.
	1914	Capital & Counties Bank.
Lynton	1884	Devon & Cornwall Banking Co.
	1890	Fox, Fowler & Co.
Lytham	1949	
Maesteg	1902	
Maidenhead	1842	Stephens, Blandy & Co.
Maidstone	1894	
Malmesbury	1812	Robins, Young & Co.
	1836	North Wilts Banking Co.
Malpas	1919	
Malvern	1847	Berwick & Co.
	1855	Worcester City & County Banking Co.
Malvern Link	1874	Worcester City & County Banking Co.
	1892	Berwick & Co.
Manchester Branches		
Manchester	1819	Cunliffe, Brooks & Co.
Mosley Street and Overseas		
Department	1918	
Oxford Road	1931	
Piccadilly	1911	
Victoria Station	1909	
Mansfield	1915	Capital & Counties Bank.
March	1920	
Margate	1785	Cobb & Co.

MARGATE, CLIFTONVILLE	1899	
MARKET HARBOROUGH	1903	
MARKET WEIGHTON	1954	
MARLBOROUGH	1803	Ward, Brown & Co.
	1836	North Wilts Banking Co.
	1836	Wilts & Dorset Banking Co.
MARLOW	1869	Stephens, Blandy & Co.
	1901	Capital & Counties Bank.
MELKSHAM	1792	Moule & Co. (previously Awdry & Co.).
	1862	Wilts & Dorset Banking Co. (Also 1836–50.)
MELTON MOWBRAY	1835	Paget & Co.
MERE	1836	Wilts & Dorset Banking Co.
MERTHYR TYDFIL	1812	Wilkins & Co. (Opened by Mr. David Evans, later a partner in Wilkins & Co.)
MIDDLESBOROUGH	1910	
MIDDLESBOROUGH, LINTHORPE ROAD	1931	
MIDSOMER NORTON	1903	Wilts & Dorset Banking Co.
MILDENHALL	1827	Brown, Bevan & Co.
MILFORD HAVEN	1901	
MILFORD-ON-SEA	1899	Wilts & Dorset Banking Co.
MILNSBRIDGE	1884	Halifax Joint Stock Banking Co.
	1886	Halifax & Huddersfield Union Banking Co.
MINEHEAD	1884	Fox, Fowler & Co.
	1897	Devon & Cornwall Banking Co.
	1906	Wilts & Dorset Banking Co.
MITCHAM	1927	
MODBURY	1878	Devon & Cornwall Banking Co.
MONMOUTH	1819	Bromage & Co.
	1865	Gloucestershire Banking Co.
MORECAMBE	1956	
MORETONHAMPSTEAD	1891	Devon & Cornwall Banking Co.
	1894	Wilts & Dorset Banking Co.
MORETON-IN-MARSH	1853	Gloucestershire Banking Co.
MORLEY	1902	
MORPETH	1831	Lambton & Co.
	1865	Hodgkin, Barnett & Co.
MOUNTAIN ASH	1890	
MUCH WENLOCK	1889	
NAILSWORTH	1868	Gloucestershire Banking Co.
	1897	Wilts & Dorset Banking Co.
NEATH	1821	Williams & Rowland.
	1910	

NETHERTON	1899	
NEWARK	1809	Peacock, Handley & Co.
NEWBRIDGE, Mon.	1893	
NEWBURN	1910	
NEWBURY	1791	Toomer, Bunney Slocock & King.
NEWCASTLE EMLYN	1890	
NEWCASTLE, Staffs.	1890	
Newcastle-upon-Tyne Branches		
BARRAS BRIDGE	1928	
BYKER AND HEATON	1893	Hodgkin, Barnett & Co.
	1896	Lambton & Co.
CHILLINGHAM	1909	
COLLINGWOOD STREET	1859	Hodgkin, Barnett & Co.
GOSFORTH	1902	Hodgkin, Barnett & Co.
GREY STREET	1788	Davison-Bland & Co.
JESMOND ROAD	1926	
NEWGATE STREET	1923	
OSBORNE ROAD	1901	Hodgkin, Barnett & Co.
QUAYSIDE	1866	Lambton & Co.
WESTGATE ROAD	1893	Hodgkin, Barnett & Co.
NEWENT	1863	Gloucestershire Banking Co.
NEW MALDEN	1926	
NEWMARKET	1844	Foster & Co.
	1893	Lacons, Youell & Co.
NEW MILTON	1900	Wilts & Dorset Banking Co.
NEWNHAM	1834	Gloucestershire Banking Co.
	1884	Bristol & West of England Bank.
NEWPORT, Isle of Wight	1838	
	1914	
NEWPORT, Mon.	1836	*West of England & South Wales District Bank.*
	1879	Bristol & West of England Bank.
	1889	County of Gloucester Bank.
	1890	
NEWPORT, Mon., HIGH STREET	1912	Capital & Counties Bank.
NEWPORT, Mon., MAINDEE	1905	
NEWPORT, Pem.	1891	
NEWPORT, Shropshire	1791	Hordern & Co.
NEW QUAY, Cardiganshire	1903	
NEWQUAY, Cornwall	1883	Cornish Bank Ltd.
	1894	Devon & Cornwall Banking Co.
NEW ROMNEY	1893	
NEWTON ABBOT	1835	Devon & Cornwall Banking Co.
	1842	Watts & Co.
	1887	Wilts & Dorset Banking Co.

New Washington	1899	Hodgkin, Barnett & Co.
Northallerton	1920	
Northampton	1832	Watkins & Co.
	1889	
North Shields	1858	Lambton & Co.
	1859	Hodgkin, Barnett & Co.
North Shields, Bedford Street	1926	
North Walsham	1811	Lacon & Co.
Norwich	1870	Lacons, Youell & Co. (On failure of *Harveys & Hudson*.)
Norwich, Prince of Wales Road	1931	
Nottingham Branches		
Nottingham	1802	Moore, Maltby, Evans & Middlemore.
	1808	Fellows & Co.
Alfreton Road	1881	Hart, Fellows & Co.
Beeston	1947	
Carlton Street	1760	Wright & Co.
West Bridgford	1931	
Nuneaton	1902	
Oakengates	1863	Shropshire Banking Co.
Odiham	1806	Raggett, Seymour & Co.
Okehampton	1888	Devon & Cornwall Banking Co.
	1908	Fox, Fowler & Co.
Oldbury	1864	
Oldbury, Langley	1903	
Oldham	1930	
Old Hill	1905	
Orpington	1930	
Oswestry	1890	
	1910	Capital & Counties Bank.
Ottery St. Mary	1888	Devon & Cornwall Banking Co.
Oxford	1889	
	1900	Capital & Counties Bank.
Oxford, Headington	1930	
Oxford, Summertown	1931	
Oxted	1892	(On failure of *Head's Bank*.) Also 1886–8.
Padstow	1886	Cornish Bank Ltd.
Paignton	1869	Devon & Cornwall Banking Co.
	1890	Bristol & West of England Banking Co.
	1899	Wilts & Dorset Banking Co.
	1915	Capital & Counties Bank.
Paignton, Preston	1915	
Pangbourne	1920	
Peel, Isle of Man	1901	

PEMBROKE	1913	
PEMBROKE DOCK	1913	
PENARTH	1895	
PENGAM	1909	
PENMAENMAWR	1891	Williams & Co.
PENRITH	1920	
PENRYN	1863	Tweedy, Williams & Co.
PENZANCE	1881	Devon & Cornwall Banking Co.
	1882	Cornish Bank Ltd.
	1896	Capital & Counties Bank.
PERIVALE	1936	
PERSHORE	c. 1856	Gloucestershire Banking Co.
	1860	Worcester City & County Banking Co.
PETERBOROUGH	1911	Capital & Counties Bank.
PETERSFIELD	1864	Hampshire Banking Co.
PETTS WOOD	1930	
PEWSEY	1862	Wilts & Dorset Banking Co.
	1863	North Wilts Banking Co.
PINNER	1931	
PITSEA	1928	
Plymouth Branches		
PLYMOUTH	1809	Symons, Soltau & Co.
	1875	Three Towns Banking Co.
	1885	Wilts & Dorset Banking Co.
	1886	Western Counties Bank.
	1888	Cornish Bank Ltd.
	1774	*The Naval Bank.*
DEVONPORT	1832	Plymouth & Devonport Banking Co.
	1891	Capital & Counties Banking Co.
MUTLEY	1893	Devon & Cornwall Banking Co.
ST. BUDEAUX	1948	
STONEHOUSE	1864	Three Towns Banking Co.
	c. 1892	Cornish Bank Ltd.
	1914	(On failure of *Naval Bank.*)
PLYMPTON	1873	Glamorganshire Banking Co.
PONTARDAWE	1913	
PONTARDULAIS	1877	Glamorganshire Banking Co.
PONTELAND	1904	Lambton & Co.
PONTYPOOL	1851	*West of England & South Wales District Bank.*
	1879	Bristol & West of England Bank.
	1890	
PONTYPRIDD	1889	Bristol & West of England Bank.
	1890	Glamorganshire Banking Co.

Poole Branches

POOLE	1821	*Ledgard & Sons.*
	1861	Premises taken over by Wilts & Dorset Banking Co. (Also 1836–8.)
	1900	Devon & Cornwall Banking Co.
LONGFLEET	1914	
PARK GATES	1932	
PARKSTONE	1887	Wilts & Dorset Banking Co.
	1901	Devon & Cornwall Banking Co.
PENN HILL AVENUE	1924	
UPPER PARKSTONE	1896	Wilts & Dorset Banking Co. (Known as Branksome until 1915.)
PORT DINORWIC	1886	Williams & Co.
PORTH	1893	
PORTHCAWL	1919	
PORTLAND	1865	R. & H. Williams & Co.
	1897	Capital & Counties Bank. (On failure of *Eliot, Pearce & Co.*)
PORTSLADE AND WEST HOVE	1899	
	1908	Capital & Counties Bank.

Portsmouth Branches

COMMERCIAL ROAD	1818	Atkins & Sons.
	1888	Grant & Maddison's Union Banking Co.
	1896	Wilts & Dorset Banking Co.
COPNOR BRIDGE	1914	
COSHAM	1896	Capital & Counties Bank.
FRATTON BRIDGE	1921	
HIGH STREET	1787	Grant & Burbey.
	1909	Capital & Counties Bank.
KINGSTON ROAD	1898	Capital & Counties Bank (Known as Landport.)
NORTH END	1897	Grant & Maddison's Union Banking Co. (Known as Kingston.)
PORT TALBOT	1898	
	1904	Capital & Counties Bank.
POTTERS BAR	1956	
PRESTEIGNE	1837	Parsons & Co.
	1875	Worcester City & County Banking Co.
PRESTON, Lancs.	1919	
PRINCES RISBOROUGH	1889	Wheeler & Co.
PURLEY	1899	
PWLLHELI	1916	
RAMSEY, Isle of Man	1900	
RAMSGATE	1866	Hammond & Co.
	1896	

RAYLEIGH	1949	
READING	1790	Micklem, Stephens, Simonds & Harris.
READING, BROAD STREET	1882	Capital & Counties Bank.
REDDITCH	1866	Gloucestershire Banking Co.
	1892	
REDHILL	1890	Capital & Counties Bank.
REDRUTH	1866	Tweedy, Williams & Co. (Also 1834–62.)
	1879	Devon & Cornwall Banking Co.
REIGATE	1891	Capital & Counties Bank.
RHOS-ON-SEA	1919	
RHYL	1920	
RHYMNEY	1906	
RICHMOND, Surrey	1922	
RICKMANSWORTH	1929	
RINGWOOD	1861	Wilts & Dorset Banking Co. (On failure of *Ledgard & Sons*.)
RIPPONDEN	1886	Halifax Joint Stock Banking Co.
ROCHDALE	1932	
ROCHESTER	1901	Capital & Counties Bank.
ROMFORD	1882	Hill & Sons.
ROMFORD, GIDEA PARK	1928	(Closed 1940–51.)
ROMFORD, HAROLD HILL	1954	
ROMSEY	1807	Warner, Newman & Footner.
	1834	Hampshire Banking Co.
ROSS-ON-WYE	1807	Pritchards & Co.
	1836	J. W. R. Hall.
	1878/9	Worcester City & County Banking Co. (On failure of *West of England & South Wales District Bank*.)
ROTHBURY	1869	Hodgkin, Barnett & Co.
	1904	Lambton & Co.
ROYSTON	1834	Foster & Co.
RUGBY	1791	A. Butlin & Son.
RUGELEY	1866	Stevenson, Salt & Co.
RUISLIP	1931	
RUSHDEN	1890	Capital & Counties Bank.
RYDE	1838	*Southern District Banking Co.*
	1906	Wilts & Dorset Banking Co.
RYE	1790	Curteis & Co.
RYTON-ON-TYNE	1904	Lambton & Co.
SACRISTON	1905	
SAFFRON WALDEN	1901	Foster & Co.
ST. ALBANS	1914	Capital & Counties Bank.
ST. ANNES-ON-THE-SEA	1929	
ST. AUSTELL	1833	Devon & Cornwall Banking Co.

St. Austell	1891	Cornish Bank Ltd.
St. Blazey	1882	Commercial Bank of Cornwall.
St. Columb	1882	Cornish Bank Ltd.
St. David's	1891	
St. Ives, Cornwall	1896	Devon & Cornwall Banking Co.
	1897	Cornish Bank Ltd.
St. Ives, Hunts.	1830	Foster & Co.
St. Leonards-on-Sea	1887	Beechings & Co.
	1889	Capital & Counties Bank.
St. Mary's, Isles of Scilly	1891	Cornish Bank Ltd.
	1896	Capital & Counties Bank.
	1903	Devon & Cornwall Banking Co.
St. Neots	c. 1839	Wells, Hogge & Co.
Salcombe	1891	Bristol & West of England Bank.
	1891	Devon & Cornwall Banking Co.
	1891	Wilts & Dorset Banking Co.
Sale	1881	Cunliffe, Brooks & Co.
Salisbury	1811	Everett & Co.
	1835	Wilts & Dorset Banking Co.
	1869	Hampshire Banking Co.
Saltaire	1902	
Saltash	1890	Devon & Cornwall Banking Co.
Sandown	1864	Hampshire Banking Co.
	1909	Wilts & Dorset Banking Co.
Sandwich	1913	Capital & Counties Bank.
Scarborough	1919	
Scunthorpe	1918	
Seaford	1914	
Seaton	1868	R. & H. Williams & Co.
	1872	Wilts & Dorset Banking Co.
	1897	Devon & Cornwall Banking Co.
Seaview	1905	Capital & Counties Bank.
Selby	1915	
Sevenoaks	1898	
	1908/9	Capital & Counties Bank.
Shaftesbury	1816	Storey & Thomas.
Shanklin	1873	Hampshire Banking Co.
Sheffield	1913	
Sheffield, Abbeydale Road	1949	
Shenfield and Hutton	1955	
Shepton Mallet	1864	Wilts & Dorset Banking Co.
Sherborne	1836	Wilts & Dorset Banking Co.
Sheringham	1910	Capital & Counties Bank.
Shifnal	1824	Biddle, Mountford, Pidcock & Cope.
Shipley	1919	

319

SHIPSTON-ON-STOUR	1879	Worcester City & County Banking Co.
SHOREHAM-BY-SEA	1892	Capital & Counties Bank. (Known as New Shoreham until 1913.)
SHOTLEY BRIDGE	1872	Hodgkin, Barnett & Co.
SHREWSBURY	1792	Eyton, Reynolds & Bishop.
	1800	Beck & Co. [land.
	1812	Scott, Burton, Pemberton, Lloyd & Coup-
	1876	
SIDCUP	1926	
SIDMOUTH	1886	Devon & Cornwall Banking Co.
SILVERHILL	1920	
SKEGNESS	1881	Garfit, Claypon & Co.
SKEWEN	1901	Capital & Counties Bank.
SLAITHWAITE	1881	Halifax Joint Stock Banking Co.
SLEAFORD	1792	Peacock, Handley & Kirton.
SLOUGH	1928	
SLOUGH TRADING ESTATE	1927	
SMETHWICK	1876	
SMETHWICK, BEARWOOD	1904	
SOHAM	1904	Capital & Counties Bank.
SOLIHULL	1877	
SOMERTON	1877	Wilts & Dorset Banking Co.
SOUTHALL	1927	
SOUTHAM	1826	Tomes & Russell.
Southampton Branches		
SOUTHAMPTON	1770	Sadleir, Hilgrove, Lowder & Durell.
	1785	Edwards, Harrison, Simpson & Maddison.
	1834	Hampshire Banking Co.
	1837	*Southern District Banking Co.*
	1880	Wilts & Dorset Banking Co.
AVENUE	1896	Wilts & Dorset Banking Co.
	1900	Grant & Maddison's Union Banking Co. (Known as London Road.)
	1911	Capital & Counties Bank.
BITTERNE	1911	Wilts & Dorset Banking Co.
CIVIC CENTRE	1926	
PORTSWOOD	1907	Capital & Counties Bank.
	1907	Wilts & Dorset Banking Co.
SHIRLEY	1896	Capital & Counties Bank.
	1907	Wilts & Dorset Banking Co.
TOTTON	1902	Wilts & Dorset Banking Co.
	1903	
WOOLSTON	1900	Capital & Counties Bank.
	1907	Wilts & Dorset Banking Co.
	1909	

SOUTHBOROUGH	1874	Beechings & Co.
SOUTHEND-ON-SEA	1895	Capital & Counties Bank.
SOUTH MOLTON	1863	*West of England & South Wales District Bank.*
	1879	Premises taken over by Fox, Fowler & Co.
	1889	Devon & Cornwall Banking Co.
SOUTHPORT	1928	
Southsea Branches		
ALBERT ROAD	1897	Grant & Maddison's Union Banking Co.
	1907	Capital & Counties Bank.
CLARENDON ROAD	1941	
ELM GROVE	1890	Capital & Counties Bank.
	1896	Wilts & Dorset Banking Co. (Known as King's Road until 1957.)
MILTON	1912	Capital & Counties Bank.
SOUTH SHIELDS	1859	Hodgkin, Barnett & Co.
SOUTH SHIELDS, HIGH SHIELDS	1898	Hodgkin, Barnett & Co.
SOUTHWOLD	1870	Lacons, Youell & Co. (On failure of *Harveys & Hudsons.*)
SOWERBY BRIDGE	1873	Halifax Joint Stock Banking Co. [Co.
	1886	Halifax & Huddersfield Union Banking
SPALDING	1822	Garfit, Claypon & Co.
	1903	Peacock & Co.
SPENNYMOOR	1907	
SPILSBY	1859	Garfit, Claypon & Co.
STAFFORD	1737	John Stevenson.
STAINES	1927	
STAMFORD	1836	Northamptonshire Banking Co.
STANLEY	1888	Hodgkin, Barnett & Co.
STANMORE	1926	
STEVENAGE	1919	
STEYNING	1827	Henty & Co.
STOCKPORT	1931	
STOCKTON-ON-TEES	1910	
STOKE-ON-TRENT	1922	
STONE	1920	
STONEHOUSE, Glos.	1877	Gloucestershire Banking Co.
STONY STRATFORD	1843	Bartlett & Co.
STORRINGTON	1891	Henty & Co.
STOURBRIDGE	1913	
STOURPORT-ON-SEVERN	1919	
STOWMARKET	c. 1803	Crowe & Co.
	1804	James Oakes & Son.
STOW-ON-THE-WOLD	1821	Cripps & Co.
	1914	

STRATFORD-ON-AVON	1834	Warwick & Leamington Banking Co.
STREET	1884	Wilts & Dorset Banking Co.
STROUD	1798	Grazebrook & Co.
	1830	Watts, Wyatt & Co.
	1834	Gloucestershire Banking Co.
	1885	Bristol & West of England Bank.
	1897	Wilts & Dorset Banking Co.
STURMINSTER NEWTON	1836	Williams, Cox & Co.
SUDBURY	1795	Fenn & Addison.
SUNDERLAND	1831	Lambton & Co.
	1902	Hodgkin, Barnett & Co.
SURBITON	1927	
SUTTON, Surrey	1925	
SUTTON COLDFIELD	1864	
SUTTON COLDFIELD, FOUR OAKS	1921	
SWADLINCOTE	1890	Burton, Uttoxeter & Ashbourne Union Bank.
SWANAGE	1825	Williams & Co. (later R. & R. Williams).
	1896	Wilts & Dorset Banking Co.
	1904	Devon & Cornwall Banking Co.
	1914	Capital & Counties Bank.
Swansea Branches		
SWANSEA	1821	Walters, Voss & Co.
	1828	Eaton, Knight & Stroud. (1809–25 Gibbins & Eaton.)
	1854	*West of England & South Wales District Bank.* (Also 1835–7.)
	1879	Bristol & West of England Bank.
CLYDACH	1889	Glamorganshire Banking Co.
GORSEINON	1900	Capital & Counties Bank.
	1913	
MORRISTON	1873	Glamorganshire Banking Co.
	1913	
MUMBLES	1900	Capital & Counties Bank.
ST. HELENS	1910	Capital & Counties Bank.
UPLANDS	1920	
SWINDON	1807	T. & R. Strange.
	1836	North Wilts Banking Co.
	1876	Wilts & Dorset Banking Co. (Also 1835 for a short time.)
SWINDON, NEW SWINDON	1872	County of Gloucester Bank.
	1875	North Wilts Banking Co.
	1883	Wilts & Dorset Banking Co.
TADWORTH	1910	Capital & Counties Bank.
TAMWORTH	1865	

TAUNTON	1835	*West of England & South Wales District Bank.*
	1879	Premises taken over by Fox, Fowler & Co.
	1864	Wilts & Dorset Banking Co.
	1887	Devon & Cornwall Banking Co.
TAVISTOCK	1791	Gill & Co.
	1836	Devon & Cornwall Banking Co.
TEDDINGTON	1920	
TEIGNMOUTH	1840	Watts & Co.
	1887	Devon & Cornwall Banking Co.
	1902	Wilts & Dorset Banking Co.
TENBURY WELLS	*c.* 1846	Ludlow & Tenbury Bank.
	1887	Berwick & Co.
TENBY	1903	
TENTERDEN	1832	Curteis & Co.
TETBURY	1792	Wood, Pitt & Co.
	1908	Wilts & Dorset Banking Co.
TEWKESBURY	1792	Lechmere & Co.
	1809	Hartland & Co.
	1837	Cheltenham & Gloucestershire Banking Co.
	1906	
THAME	1842	W. Rickford & Son.
THETFORD	1829	Oakes & Co.
THIRSK	1919	
TIDWORTH	1908	Wilts & Dorset Banking Co.
	1915	Capital & Counties Bank.
TIPTON	1921	
TIVERTON	1873	Devon & Cornwall Banking Co.
	1890	Fox, Fowler & Co.
TODMORDEN	1898	Halifax Joint Stock Banking Co.
TOLWORTH	1930	
TONBRIDGE	1815	Beechings & Co.
	1912	Capital & Counties Bank.
TONYPANDY	1889	Bristol & West of England Bank.
TONYREFAIL	1900	
TOPSHAM	1894	Fox, Fowler & Co.
	1911	Wilts & Dorset Banking Co.
Torquay Branches		
TORQUAY	1833	Vivian, Kitson & Co.
	1850	Devon & Cornwall Banking Co.
	1864	*West of England & South Wales District Bank.*
	1879	Bristol & West of England Bank.
	1886	Wilts & Dorset Banking Co.

Torquay Branches (contd.)

St. Marychurch	1877	Devon & Cornwall Banking Co.
	1889	Wilts & Dorset Banking Co.
Torre	1894	Vivian, Kitson & Co.
	1903	Devon & Cornwall Banking Co.
Union Street	1906	Capital & Counties Bank.
Torrington	1865	*West of England & South Wales District Bank.*
	1879	Premises taken over by Fox, Fowler & Co.
	1885	Devon & Cornwall Banking Co.
Totnes	1833	Devon & Cornwall Banking Co.
	1912	Capital & Counties Bank.
	1914	(On failure of *Naval Bank*.) Closed 1916.
Tregaron	1903	David Jones & Co.
Trowbridge	1835	North Wilts Banking Co.
	1836	Wilts & Dorset Banking Co.
	1852	Everett, Ravenhill & Co.
Truro	1771	Sir John Molesworth & Co.
	1807	Turner, Eddy & Co.
Tumble	1906	
Tunbridge Wells	1826	Beechings & Co.
	1902	Capital & Counties Bank.
Tunbridge Wells, Pantiles	1891	
Tutbury	1898	Burton Union Bank.
Twickenham	1929	
Tynemouth	1897	Hodgkin, Barnett & Co.
Uckfield	1923	
Upminster	1930	
Upton-on-Severn	1792	Lechmere & Co.
	1877	Gloucestershire Banking Co.
Uttoxeter	1839	Burton, Uttoxeter & Staffordshire Union Bank.
Uxbridge	1920	
Uxbridge Road	1956	
Ventnor	1862	Hampshire Banking Co.
Wadebridge	1879	Clymo, Treffry, Hawke, West & Co.
	1890	Cornish Bank Ltd.
Wadhurst	1898	
Wainfleet	1889	Garfit, Claypon & Co.
Wakefield	1928	
Wallasey	1953	
Wallingford	1797	Wells, Allnatt, Wells & Wells.
Wallington	1920	
Wallsend	1890	Hodgkin, Barnett & Co.
	1904	Lambton & Co.

WALSALL	1866	
WALTON-ON-THAMES	1922	
WANTAGE	1905	
WARE	1949	
WAREHAM	c. 1833	Williams, Cox & Co.
WARMINSTER	1777	Horlock, Everett, Mortimer, Everett & Co.
	1835	Wilts & Dorset Banking Co.
WARRINGTON	1949	
WARWICK	1791	Dawes, Tomes & Russell.
WATCHET	1877	*West of England & South Wales District Bank.*
	1878/9	Premises taken over by Fox, Fowler & Co.
	1878	Wilts & Dorset Banking Co.
WATERHOUSES	1902	Hodgkin, Barnett & Co.
WATERLOOVILLE	1907	
	1907	Capital & Counties Bank.
WATFORD	1856	Bucks & Oxon Union Bank.
WATFORD, ST. ALBANS ROAD	1898	Bucks & Oxon Union Bank.
WATLINGTON	1885	Bucks & Oxon Union Bank.
WATTON	1904	Capital & Counties Bank.
WEALDSTONE	1895	Bucks & Oxon Union Bank.
WEDNESBURY	1809	S. & W. Addison.
WELLINGBOROUGH	1836	Northamptonshire Banking Co.
WELLINGTON, Shropshire	1805	Reynolds, Charlton & Co.
WELLINGTON, Somerset	1787	Fox & Co.
WELLS	1836	*West of England & South Wales District Bank.*
	1878	Premises taken over by Wilts & Dorset Banking Co.
WELSHPOOL	1816	Beck & Co.
WELWYN GARDEN CITY	1930	
WEMBLEY	1925	
WEST BROMWICH	1882	
WESTBURY	1857	North Wilts Banking Co.
	1866	Wilts & Dorset Banking Co.
WEST BYFLEET	1910	Capital & Counties Bank.
WESTCLIFF-ON-SEA	1901	Capital & Counties Bank.
WESTCLIFF-ON-SEA, LONDON ROAD	1923	
WEST DRAYTON	1930	
WESTGATE-ON-SEA	1877	Cobb & Co.
WEST HARTLEPOOL	1914	
WEST KIRBY AND HOYLAKE	1926	

WESTON-SUPER-MARE	1863	*West of England & South Wales District Bank.*
	1878	Premises taken over by Wilts & Dorset Banking Co.
	1878/9	Fox, Fowler & Co.
	1896	Capital & Counties Bank.
WEST WICKHAM	1928	
WEYBRIDGE	1924	
WEYBRIDGE, QUEEN'S ROAD	1928	
WEYMOUTH	1835	Williams, Cox & Co.
	1861	Wilts & Dorset Banking Co.
	1897	Devon & Cornwall Banking Co.
	1897	Capital & Counties Bank. (On failure of *Eliot, Pearce & Co.*)
WHITCHURCH, Shropshire	1881	(On failure of *Whitchurch & Ellesmere Banking Co.*)
WHITLAND	1890	
WHITLEY BAY	1906	Lambton & Co.
WHITLEY BAY, MONKSEATON	1922	
WHITSTABLE	1863	Hammond & Co.
WILLENHALL	1887	
WILMSLOW	1932	
WIMBORNE	1835	Wilts & Dorset Banking Co.
WINCANTON	1865	Wilts & Dorset Banking Co.
WINCHCOMBE	1842	Gloucestershire Banking Co.
	1888	County of Gloucester Bank.
WINCHESTER	1807	Wickham & Co.
	1915	
WINDSOR	1928	
WINSCOMBE	1911	Wilts & Dorset Banking Co.
	1913	Fox, Fowler & Co.
WINSLOW	1844	Bartlett & Co.
WIRKSWORTH	1780	John Toplis.
WISBECH	1894	Lacons, Youell & Co.
WITHAM	1910	Capital & Counties Bank.
WITNEY	1920	
WIVELISCOMBE	1803	W. Hancock & Son.
WOKING	1887	Capital & Counties Bank.
WOKINGHAM	1949	
WOLVERHAMPTON	1807	R. & W. F. Fryer.
WOLVERHAMPTON, CHAPEL ASH	1930	
WOLVERTON	1892	Bucks & Oxon Union Bank.
WOODBRIDGE	1846	Bacon, Cobbold & Co.
WOOTTON BASSETT	1836	Wilts & Dorset Banking Co.
	1836	North Wilts Banking Co.

WORCESTER	1840	Worcester City & County Banking Co.
WORCESTER (C. & C.)	1772	Berwick & Co.
WORCESTER PARK	1902	Capital & Counties Bank.
Worthing Branches		
WORTHING	1808	Margesson, Henty, Henty & Hopkins.
	1900	
BROADWATER	1936	
GORING ROAD	1935	
WOTTON-UNDER-EDGE	1863	County of Gloucester Bank.
WREXHAM	1889	Williams & Co.
YARMOUTH, GREAT	1791	Lacon & Co.
YEOVIL	1836	Wilts & Dorset Banking Co.
	1882	R. & R. Williams & Co.
	1897	Devon & Cornwall Banking Co.
	1897	Capital & Counties Bank.
YORK	1920	
YSTALYFERA	1908	Capital & Counties Bank.

Appendix 3

BIOGRAPHICAL NOTES

THE following is a list of all the personalities in the history of the bank who have left some mark in the records available. There must unavoidably be many omissions due to lack of information and it is regretted that no note can be made of many men who must have played a significant part in the bank's history.

ABELL, George Edmund. 1839–?
> 1888 General Manager Worcester City and County Banking Co. 1889 Assistant General Manager Lloyds Bank on amalgamation. Deputy Chairman Worcester Royal Porcelain Co.

ADDISON, Samuel. 1766–1849.
> Born at Charnes, Staffs. 1786 Opened a grocer's business in Wednesbury. 1809 Extended his activities to banking.

AGG, Colonel William.
> 1887 Director County of Gloucester Bank. 1893 Deputy Chairman. 1895 Chairman.

ATKINS, Edward. ?–1899.
> 1834 Joined Hampshire Banking Co. 1845 Sub-Manager. 1846 Manager. 1865 Retired. Appointed Director. 1868–79 Chairman.

BACON, Edward. 1772–1860.
> Spent his early working life in India. 1807 Partner in Ipswich Bank on the death of John Kerridge. He lived over the bank for many years.

BACON, George Constantine Edgar. 1813–80.
> Son of Edward Bacon. Trained as a lawyer. *c.* 1850 Partner in Bacon Cobbold & Co., Ipswich. 1862 Mayor of Ipswich.

BAKER, Samuel. 1793–1862.
> See p. 46.

BALDWIN, G. W. 1849–1916.
> Trained in a solicitor's office in Birmingham. 1869 Entered Lloyds High Street office. 1879 Manager of Deritend branch. 1883–9 Sub-Manager at High Street. 1901 Chief Inspector Lloyds Bank. 1913 Retired.

BALDWIN, John Herbert Lacy. 1863–1945.
> Educated at Rugby. 1882 Entered knitting wool firm of J. and J. Baldwin. Director Halifax and Huddersfield Union Banking Company, from 1911 the West Yorkshire Bank. 1897–8 Mayor of Halifax. 1919 Director Lloyds Bank on amalgamation. Chairman West Yorkshire Local Board. 1942 Resigned.

BARCLAY, Hanbury. 1836–1909.
See Lloyds family tree facing p. 362.

BARNETT, Benjamin. 1735–1805.
Son of Curtis Barnett, R.N., who died in 1746 in command of the East Indies squadron. 1761 Partner in Bland Barnett & Co.

BARNETT, Charles Edward. 1848–1937.
1877 Partner in Barnetts Hoares. 1884 Director Lloyds Bank upon amalgamation. Director Alliance Assurance Co. and Cheltenham Original Brewery Co. Chairman Emerald and Phoenix Brewery Co. and New England Breweries Co. Member, Council of Foreign Bondholders and London Board Queensland National Bank.

BARNETT, Charles George. 1816–?
His mother was Elizabeth Canning, sister of Viscount Stratford de Radcliffe. Partner in Barnetts Hoares until amalgamation with Lloyds in 1884.

BARNETT, Francis Carew Charles. 1850–?
Son of Mr. Charles George Barnett. 1877–99 Partner in Stephens Blandy, Reading.

BARNETT, Henry. 1815–96.
1865–74 M.P. for Woodstock. 1884 Partner in Barnetts Hoares at time of amalgamation with Lloyds.

BARNETT, William Edward. 1830–69.
Son of Robert Barnett of Blackheath and nephew of Charles George Barnett. Stockbroker. 1859 Founding partner in Hodgkin, Barnett, Pease, Spence & Co. Newcastle.

BASSETT, Francis, Lord de Dunstanville. 1757–1835.
A leading figure in the Cornish Copper Trade. 1779–1801 Partner in the Cornish Bank, Truro. 1779 Baronet. 1796 Baron.

BATHURST, Charles, Rt. Hon. Lord Bledisloe, K.B.E., G.C.M.G., P.C. 1867– .
Educated at Eton; University College, Oxford; Royal Agricultural College, Cirencester. 1910–18 M.P. for South Wilts. 1911 Director Capital and Counties Bank. 1917 K.B.E. 1918 Director Lloyds Bank on amalgamation. 1924 Retired on joining H.M. Government. Continued on Capital and Counties Section Committee. 1924–8 Parliamentary Secretary Minister of Agriculture. 1926 Privy Council. 1930–5 Governor General New Zealand. Director P. and O. Shipping Co. Ltd., and Australian Mutual Provident Society. 1930 G.C.M.G.

BEATTIE, Joseph. 1829–89.
See p. 36.

BECK, James.
Partner in Beck and Prime of Coventry. 1835 Director and Manager of Coventry and Warwickshire Banking Co. on its formation. Elected Chairman after a few months. 1837 Mayor of Coventry. 1842 Resigned.

BEECHING, Thomas.
> 1767 Came to Tonbridge. Opened a linen draper's shop in Church Lane. *c.* 1789 Believed to have begun transacting some banking business.

BELCHER, Robert Shirley.
> 1839 Shareholder in Burton, Uttoxeter and Staffordshire Union Bank. 1853 Director. 1877–92 Chairman.

BERWICK, Joseph. 1751–98.
> See p. 39.

BEVAN, Robert.
> 1824 Joined J. G. Sparrow and George Brown in partnership in the 'Suffolk and Essex Bank'. 1827 Partnership also in a bank at Diss. 1830 Joined with James Oakes and Co. to form Oakes Bevan and Co.

BLAND, John, ?–1764.
> 1728 Goldsmith at the sign of the Black Horse, Lombard Street.

BLAND, John. 1723–88.
> Son of John Bland and brother to Stamper Bland (d. 1761). A Quaker. At the time of his death he was in partnership with Barnett Hoare and Hill of Lombard Street. See p. 16.

BLANDY, Charles. ?–1875.
> Member of a family of Reading solicitors. Partner in a brewery. 1841 Partner in Stephens Blandy, Reading.

BLANDY, Frederick John.
> 1873 Succeeded his father, William, as partner in Stephens Blandy, Reading.

BLANDY, William. ?–1873.
> Member of a family of Reading solicitors. Partner in a Reading brewery. 1841 Partner in Stephens Blandy, Reading.

BLEDISLOE, Lord. See under BATHURST.

BOORE, William Charles.
> 1859 Appointed General Manager Wilts and Dorset Banking Co. 1863 Retired?

BOSANQUET, Bernard Tindal. 1842–1910.
> 1874 Married Eva Maude, daughter of Sir William James Richard Cotton. 1884 Partner in Bosanquet Salt. Director Lloyds Bank on amalgamation. 1894 Resigned. 1897–8 High Sheriff of Middlesex.

BOSANQUET, James Whatman. 1864–77.
> Educated at Westminster School. 1822 Joined business of Bosanquet Salt. 1873 Retired from Senior Partnership.

BOSANQUET, Samuel. 1768–1843.
> Son of Samuel Bosanquet, Governor of Bank of England 1774. Married daughter of James Whatman. Before 1800 partner in Foster Lubbock. 1801 Joined Beachcroft & Reeves at 73 Lombard Street. Director Palladium Insurance Co.

Bowly, Edward.

1842 Director County of Gloucester Bank. 1867–80 Chairman.

Bowly, James Hinton.

1836 Joint Manager at Cheltenham of County of Gloucester Bank. Hon. Director. 1837 Appointed Inspector. 1861 Resigned.

Bowly, Samuel. ?–1884.

1831 Founding director of Gloucestershire Banking Co. 1862 Deputy Chairman.

Bowman, William (the elder). ?–1799.

Cashier at Smith's Bank. 1770 Founding partner in Hanbury, Taylor, Lloyd & Bowman. Acted as Manager.

Brand, the Rt. Hon. Lord, C.M.G., D.C.L. 1878– .

Educated at Marlborough and New College, Oxford. 1916 Director Lloyds Bank. Director Lazard Brothers. Director The Times Publishing Co. Chairman North British Mercantile Insurance Co. 1919 Financial adviser to Chairman of Supreme Economic Council, Peace Conference, Paris. 1930 Member of Macmillan Committee on Finance and Industry. 1944 Resigned from Board on appointment as Representative H.M. Treasury at Washington. 1947 Re-elected Director.

Brodhurst, Alfred.

1862 Director Moore and Robinson's Nottinghamshire Banking Co. 1865 Chairman. 1892 Resigned.

Brooks, John Brookes Close. ?–1914.

1872 Entered Cunliffe Brooks as clerk. Became Manager and later Managing partner. Also partner in Brooks and Co., 81 Lombard Street. 1900 On amalgamation with Lloyds, District Manager in Manchester. 1901 Director. 1913 Hon. Director on retirement owing to ill health.

Brooks, Samuel. 1792–1864.

Son of William Brooks. Calico printer in Manchester. 1815 Partner in his father's firm. 1819 Opened the Manchester branch of Cunliffe Brooks Bank. 1830 Chairman of first meeting of promoters of Lancashire & Yorkshire Railway.

Brooks, William. ?–1846.

Supplier of cotton to spinners around Whalley and Blackburn. Went into partnership with Roger Cunliffe. 1792 Founded Cunliffe Brooks Bank, Blackburn.

Brooks, Sir William Cunliffe. 1819–1900.

Son of Samuel Brooks. Educated at Rugby under Arnold and St. John's, Cambridge. 1847 Called to the bar. 1864 Sole proprietor of Cunliffe Brooks & Co., Manchester on death of his father. 1864 Opened Brooks & Co., 81 Lombard Street. 1869 Elected Conservative M.P. for East Cheshire. 1886 Knighted.

Brown, Edwin Atkin.

Manager Burton Union Bank. 1872 Given 200 guineas in recognition of his services as Manager. 1899 Retained as District Manager by Lloyds on amalgamation.

BROWN, Ralph.
Before 1860–1907 Partner in Lambtons Bank, Newcastle.

BROWN, William Williams. ?–1856.
1813 Founding partner in Nicholson Brown & Co., Leeds.

BUTLER, Lewis William George.
1891–9 Partner in Stephens Blandy & Co., Reading.

BUTLIN, William. ?–1791.
Draper of Rugby who also transacted banking business. After his death his wife carried on the firm under the title of Anne Butlin & Son.

CHAMBERLAIN, Joseph. 1836–1914.
1861 Married (1) Harriet, daughter of Archibald Kenrick. March 1865 Present at first Provisional Committee Meeting of Lloyds Banking Co. 1865 Director. 1868 Married (2) Florence, daughter of Timothy Kenrick. 1877 Resigned from Board on entering Parliament as M.P. for Birmingham (Liberal). 1876–85 Elected Mayor three times. 1880–5 President Board of Trade. 1886 Local Government Board. 1895–1903 Secretary of State for Colonies.

CHAMBERS, Richard. 1738–1806.
Hardware and leather merchant. 1788 Founding partner in Davison-Bland & Co., later Lambton & Co., Newcastle. 1797 Financial difficulties caused his withdrawal from the partnership.

CHERRY, Arthur Charles.
Brother-in-law of G. E. Martin. Barrister. 1881 Partner in Berwick & Co., Worcester. 1906 Appointed local director by the Capital and Counties Bank upon amalgamation.

CLAY, Henry.
Private banker, Burton-on-Trent. 1839 Director Burton, Uttoxeter and Staffordshire Union Bank when it was formed on the basis of his private bank. 1853–63 Chairman.

CLAYPON, Bartholomew.
1774 Joined William Garfit in partnership in Garfit Claypon & Co. of Boston. His daughter married into the Garfit family.

CLAYTON, John Henry. ?–1924.
1909 Director Lloyds Bank. Also on Liverpool Committee.

COBB, Charles Edward. 1862–1922.
Son of T. E. Cobb. 1881–4 Trained in banking at Lloyds' Head Office, Birmingham. 1884 Director Bucks & Oxon Union Bank. 1902 On amalgamation with Lloyds, General Manager's Assistant under E. Alexander Duff. 1915 Treasurer of the Bank. Close association with Bank Sports Club of which he was Chairman and Hon. Treasurer when he died.

COBB, Timothy Edward. 1830–?

Partner in Cobb Bartlett, Banbury. 1853 Director Bucks & Oxon Union Bank. 1859–92 Chairman.

CHUBB, William.

1863 General Manager Wilts & Dorset Banking Co. 1871 Retired. Elected Director. 1872 Resigned.

COBBOLD, Ernest St. George. 1840–95.

Son of John Chevalier Cobbold. Manager, Woodbridge branch, Bacon Cobbold & Co., of Ipswich for most of his working life.

COBBOLD, Felix Thornley. 1841–1909.

Son of John Chevalier Cobbold. Educated at Cambridge and Lincoln's Inn. 1885–99 Partner in Bacon Cobbold & Co., Ipswich and Cox Cobbold & Co., Harwich. 1885–6 M.P. for North-west Suffolk. 1906–9 M.P. for Ipswich. 1896 Mayor of Ipswich.

COBBOLD, Herbert St. George. 1871–1945.

Nephew of Felix Thornley Cobbold. 1899 Partner in Bacon Cobbold & Co., Ipswich and Harwich. 1905 Local director Capital and Counties Bank on amalgamation.

COBBOLD, John. 1774–1860.

Brewer at Ipswich. 1825 Partner in Crickett Bacon & Co., bankers, Ipswich, to strengthen them at the time of the banking crisis. c. 1839 Partner in Harwich Bank of Cox Cobbold & Co. Director Ipswich & London New Steam Packet Co., Ipswich & Bury St. Edmunds Railway, Eastern Union Railway, Mutual Assurance Benefits Society, Suffolk & General Assurance Co.

COBBOLD, John Chevalier. 1797–1882.

Son of John Cobbold. Brewer, Ipswich. 1825 Together with his father joined Crickett Bacon & Co., bankers, Ipswich. c. 1839 Partner in Harwich Bank of Cox Cobbold & Co. 1841 Mayor of Ipswich. Chairman Eastern Union Railway Co. and Ipswich & Bury St. Edmunds Railway Co. 1847–68 M.P. for Ipswich.

COBBOLD, John Patteson. 1831–75.

Son of John Chevalier Cobbold. Brewer, ship-owner, maltster, corn and wine merchant. c. 1860 Partner in Bacon Cobbold & Co., Harwich. 1867 Mayor of Ipswich. 1874–5 M.P. for Ipswich.

COBBOLD, Nathaniel Fromanteel. 1839–86.

Son of John Chevalier Cobbold. In business in Colchester. 1882 Partner in Cobbold & Co.

COBBOLD, Thomas Clement. 1833–83.

Son of John Chevalier Cobbold. Educated at Charterhouse. 1855–75 Career in the Diplomatic Service. 1875 Partner in Bacon Cobbold & Co., Ipswich. 1876 M.P.

COLLIER, Colonel James Alphonse. ?–1893.

1878 Director County of Gloucester Bank. 1887 Vice-Chairman. 1891 Chairman.

COMMELINE, Thomas.
　　1841 Joined Gloucestershire Banking Co. on probation. *c.* 1860 Manager Stow-on-the-Wold branch. 1861 Manager Cirencester branch. 1872 Manager Gloucester branch. 1886 Joint Manager with Mr. Jewsbury of Gloucester branch, Capital & Counties Bank upon amalgamation.

COPE, William Henry. ?–1885.
　　1835 Director Shropshire Banking Co. at its foundation. 1851–4 Chairman. 1874 Joined Lloyds Board on amalgamation.

COUCHMAN, Charles. ?–1886.
　　March 1865 Member Provisional Committee of Lloyds Banking Company and later Director.

Cox, Anthony. 1767–1839.
　　Government Agent for Packet Boats. Founded bank at Harwich. Deputy Lieutenant of Suffolk. Mayor of Harwich.

Cox, Anthony. 1810–42.
　　Son of Anthony Cox. 1835 Partner in Cox & Son, Harwich. Mayor and High Steward of Harwich.

Cox, Frederick. 1835–1913.
　　Great-great-grandson of Richard Cox. At his death, senior partner in Cox & Co., Charing Cross.

Cox, John Pearson. ?–1897.
　　1880 Member, Committee of Proprietors Moore & Robinson's Nottinghamshire Banking Co. 1888 Director. 1892–7 Chairman.

Cox, Richard. 1718–1803.
　　Secretary to Lord Ligonier, Colonel of 1st Foot Guards (Grenadier Guards). 1758 Agent to disburse the pay of this regiment. From this beginning he built up the Army agent business of Cox & Co. See p. 191.

CROSBIE, Andrew.
　　c. 1865 Clerk in Liverpool Union Bank. Lent to Lloyds to advise on bookkeeping. 1872 Appointed the first inspector, Lloyds Banking Co. 1886 Carried out the first inspection of the London office. 1896 Retired.

CUNLIFFE, James. ?–1854.
　　Son of Roger Cunliffe. Referred to as banker, London. *c.* 1824 Partner in Cunliffe Brooks & Co., Blackburn.

CUNLIFFE, Roger. ?–1822.
　　Member of Congregational Church. Wealthy friend of William Brooks. Calico manufacturer. 1792 Partner with William Brooks in Cunliffe Brooks & Co., Blackburn.

DARBY, Abraham. 1804–1878.
　　1827–49 Manager of the Coalbrookdale iron works. Partner in Darby & Co., bankers of Coalbrookdale. 1839 Director Shropshire Banking Co. 1845 Chair-

man. 1849 Took over iron works at Ebbw Vale and Brymbo. 1852 Resigned from the bank on the grounds of living too far away.

DAUBUZ, John Claude. 1842–1915.
Chairman Cornish Bank Ltd. 1891 Sheriff of Cornwall. 1903 Director Capital and Counties Bank on amalgamation.

DAVIES-EVANS, Col. H.
1903 Took over the direction of David Jones Bank, Carmarthen, when his wife inherited it at the death of her brother Gerwyn Jones. 1909 Sold out to Lloyds Bank Ltd.

DAVISON-BLAND, Thomas.
Landowner. 1788 Founding partner in Davison-Bland & Co., later Lambton & Co., Newcastle. 1790 Retired.

DAWSON, Hon. Richard M. W. 1845–1914.
1894 Director Devon & Cornwall Banking Co. 1907 Director Lloyds Bank on amalgamation.

DE DUSTANVILLE, Lord. See under BASSETT.

DERRY, David. ?–1866.
1832 General Manager Plymouth & Devonport Banking Co., later Devon & Cornwall Banking Co. 1865 Retired.

DEVENISH, Matthew Henry Whitty. 1823–1913.
1856 Joined Wilts & Dorset Banking Co. c. 1868 Assistant Inspector of Branches. 1871 Assistant General Manager. 1894 General Manager. 1911 Retired. Elected Director.

DE WINTON, Wilfred Seymour. 1856–1929.
Educated at Bradfield and Trinity College, Dublin. 1881–90 Junior partner in Wilkins & Co., Brecon. District Manager, Cardiff, on amalgamation with Lloyds. 1909 Director. 1918 Director National Bank of Scotland.

DE WINTON, William. 1823–1907.
Partner in Wilkins & Co., Brecon. 1890 Director Lloyds Bank on amalgamation. Director Brecon & Merthyr Tydfil Junction Railway Co. 1874 High Sheriff Brecon.

DICKINSON, Barnard.
Manager of Darby's iron works at Ketley. 1836 Director and Deputy Chairman Shropshire Banking Co. 1842 Chairman.

DICKINSON, Henry.
Married Deborah Darby of the iron and steel family. 1845 Succeeded his cousin, Barnard Dickinson as Director Shropshire Banking Co. 1854 Chairman.

DILLWYN, Lewis Llewellyn. ?–1892.
By 1860 M.P. for Swansea. 1864–88 Director and Chairman Glamorganshire Banking Co. 1882–92 Remained on Board.

DIXON, George. 1820–98.

Educated at Leeds Grammar School. March 1865 Member Provisional Committee Lloyds Banking Company. Director until 1867. 1866 Mayor of Birmingham. 1867–76 M.P. Birmingham. 1885 M.P. Edgbaston.

DRAPER, W. S.

1880 Entered Brown Janson, Abchurch Lane. 1902 Manager of Lloyds Bank Cheapside Branch, after Brown Janson amalgamation (1900). 1907 Assistant Manager Lombard Street. 1911 Manager Lombard Street. 1918 Joint General Manager. 1929 Retired.

DUFF, E. Alexander. ?–1916.

Educated at Cambridge. 1875 Joined Barnetts Hoares. 1884 Manager of office at 73 Lombard Street. 1885 Manager of St. James's Street branch. 1886 Superintendent of London branches. 1898 Deputy General Manager. 1902 General Manager. 1913 Retired. Elected Director. See p. 59.

EATON, Robert. ?–1840.

1828 Partner in Eaton Knight and Stroud, bankers, Swansea. 1836 Director and Deputy Chairman Glamorganshire Banking Co. at its foundation.

EDWARDS, Frederic.

1870 A junior, contemporary of E. D. Vaisey in Gloucestershire Banking Co. By 1879 Manager Berkeley branch, Gloucestershire Banking Co. 1880 Manager Neath branch, Glamorganshire Banking Co. 1885 Managing Director.

ELIOT, Lord Edward James. 1758–97.

Lord of the Treasury and Kings Remembrancer in the court of Exchequer. Married a daughter of William Pitt, Earl of Chatham. 1771 Founding partner in Sir John Molesworth & Co., Truro.

ELIOT, John, Earl St. Germains. 1761–1823.

Brother of Lord Edward James Eliot. Partner in Biddulph, Cocks, Eliot & Praed of London. 1792 Left this firm. 1803 Founded Praeds & Co., Fleet Street. 1815 Created Earl St. Germains.

EVANS, Alfred S.

1865–9 Director Lloyds Banking Co. Ltd.

FARQUHAR, Walter Randolph. 1842–1901.

Partner in Herries Farquhar & Co. 1893 Director Lloyds Bank Ltd. on amalgamation.

FARQUHAR, Sir Walter Rockliffe. 1810–1900.

Partner in Herries Farquhar & Co. 1846 Senior partner. 1859 High Sheriff of Surrey.

FENWICK, George. 1811–83.

Son of Robert Fenwick. 1833 Partner in Lambton & Co., Newcastle. 1867 Senior partner.

FENWICK, George Anthony. 1840–1912.
> 1857 Entered Lambton & Co. as a clerk. 1861–1907 Partner. Died from a hunting accident.

FENWICK, George John.
> 1843–1907 Partner in Lambton & Co., Newcastle.

FENWICK, Gerard. 1868–?
> 1892–1907 Partner in Lambton & Co., Newcastle.

FENWICK, Hugh. 1843–93.
> 1864 Partner in Lambton & Co., Newcastle. 1893 Left the firm.

FENWICK, Mark.
> 1883–1907 Partner in Lambton & Co., Newcastle.

FENWICK, Thomas. 1772–1852.
> 1788 Entered Davison-Bland & Co., Newcastle. 1795 Partner in Lambton & Co.

FINLINSON, T. H.
> 1884–97 General Manager Halifax & Huddersfield Union Banking Co.

FOSTER, Charles Finch. 1805–66.
> Partner in Foster & Co., Cambridge. 1847–8, 1854–5, 1860–2 Mayor of Cambridge.

FOSTER, Ebenezer. ?–1851.
> A miller in Cambridge. 1804 With his brother, founding partner in Foster & Co., Cambridge. 1836 Mayor of Cambridge. A Baptist.

FOSTER, George Edward. ?–1906.
> Grandson of Ebenezer Foster. Partner in Foster & Co., Cambridge. 1904 Director Capital and Counties Bank on amalgamation.

FOWLER, John.
> 1835 Director North Wilts Banking Co. Usually Chairman. 1843 Managing Director when this appointment was first introduced.

FOX, Charles Alfred. 1848–1929.
> Son of George Fox of Kingsbridge. Educated at Grove House, Tottenham. Went into Lloyd's (London). Became senior partner in Fox Roy & Co., produce brokers, Plymouth. 1893 Director Devon & Cornwall Banking Company.

FOX, George. 1795–1882.
> A Quaker. Considered opening a bank at Kingsbridge in 1826. 1832 Opened his bank after the formation of the Plymouth & Devonport Banking Co. 1833 Absorbed by Plymouth & Devonport Banking Co. for whom he remained manager. 1871 Retired.

FOX, John Howard. 1864–1951.
> Trained in Lloyds Bank. Took an active part in Fox Fowler & Co. 1908 Given partnership. Senior partner. 1921 Director Lloyds Bank on amalgamation until 1949.

Fox, Thomas.
> 1772 Partner in woollen firm of Were & Sons, Wellington. 1782 Married Sarah Smith, daughter of a partner in Smith, Wright & Gray, bankers of Lombard Street. 1787 Issued his own £5 notes and founded Fox & Co., Wellington.

Fryer, William Fleeming.
> Partner in Fryer's Bank, Wolverhampton. 1872 Director Lloyds Bank on amalgamation. 1884 Resigned owing to advanced age.

Furley, John. ?–1854.
> 1788 Clerk in Simmons & Gipps, Canterbury. 1807 Partner. 1846 Retired.

Fussell, William Samuel.
> 1849 Entered Wilts & Dorset Banking Co. as junior clerk. 1855 Assistant Inspector of branches. 1860 Inspector of branches. 1871 General Manager. 1894 Retired. Directors voted 200 guineas for testimonial of plate to him. Elected Director. 1902 Retired owing to ill health.

Fyshe, Alexander.
> 1874 Manager New Street branch, Birmingham Joint Stock Bank. 1883 Deputy manager. 1889 Country General Manager Lloyds Bank on amalgamation. 1912 Retired.

Garfit, Thomas. 1815–1883.
> Corn merchant and shipper at Boston. 1774 Founding partner in Garfit Claytion.

Garfit, William. 1731–1813.
> Corn Merchant and shipper at Boston. 1774 Founding partner in Garfit Claypon & Co., Boston.

Garfit, William. 1840–1920.
> Educated at Harrow and Trinity College, Cambrige. Probably succeeded his father, who died in 1875, as partner in Garfit Claypon & Co., Boston. 1891 Director Capital and Counties Bank on amalgamation. 1892 High Sheriff of Lincolnshire. 1895–1906 M.P. for Boston. 1915 Chairman Capital and Counties Bank. 1918 Director Lloyds Bank on amalgamation.

Garton, Major James William, G.B.E. ?–1941.
> 1905 Director Wilts & Dorset Banking Co. 1914 Director Lloyds Bank on amalgamation.

Garton, Sir Richard Charles, G.B.E. 1857–1934.
> Educated at Owens College, Manchester and Marburg University. 1908 Knighted. 1915 Director Capital and Counties Bank. 1918 Director Lloyds Bank on amalgamation. 1923 Resigned. Director Manbré Garton Ltd. Deputy Chairman Watney, Combe Reid & Co.

Gem, Edward. 1810–1905.
> Member of Edward Gem & Co., merchants, formerly Moilliet & Gem. 1862 Juror of the London Exhibition. 1865 Member Provisional Committee Lloyds Banking Company and later a Director. 1893 Resigned. Chairman Worcester &

Birmingham Canal Co. Director Small Arms & Metal Co., John Bagnall & Sons, and Royal Insurance Co. President Blue Coat School. First Governor Worcester Blind College, and Saltley Training College.

GIBBINS, Joseph. 1787–1870.

Son of Joseph Gibbins, senior. 1809 In partnership with Robert Eaton in Swansea. Founder and Director Birmingham Banking Co. 1831 Trustee Gloucestershire Banking Co.

GIBBINS, William. 1791–1843.

Son of Joseph Gibbins, senior. *c.* 1809–11 Apprenticed to Bassett & Co., bankers, Leighton Buzzard. 1831 Founder and Director Gloucestershire Banking Co. 1836 Listed in share register of Glamorganshire Banking Co. as banker of Falmouth. 1839 Resigned as Director Gloucestershire Banking Co. 1840 Director Glamorganshire Banking Co.

GIBBS, Alexander.

1857 Joined Union Bank of Scotland and rose to be accountant Wick branch. 1865 Joined Bacon Cobbold & Co., Ipswich as assistant manager. 1882 Manager. 1899 Partner—the only non-family partner in that bank's history. 1905 Local director and manager at Ipswich for Capital and Counties Bank on amalgamation. 1909 Mayor of Ipswich.

GILLAN, William Campbell.

1834 Appointed Secretary West of England & South Wales District Bank. Jan. 1835 Services no longer required. Oct. 1835 Organizer of Provisional Committee of Wilts & Dorset Banking Co.

GILLETT, William.

1835 Accountant North Wilts Banking Co. 1843 General Manager. 1847 Resigned.

GOLDNEY, Sir Gabriel, Bt. 1813–1900.

1853 Mayor of Chippenham. *c.* 1865 Joined North Wilts Banking Co. as Director in connexion with its absorption of Everett Ravenhill & Co. 1877 Remained as Director Hampshire & North Wilts Banking Co. later the Capital and Counties Bank. 1865–85 M.P. for Chippenham. 1880 Created baronet. 1893 High Sheriff of Wilts.

GOLDNEY, Sir John Tankerville. 1846–1920.

Son of Sir Gabriel Goldney. In colonial legal service in West Indies. Director Capital and Counties Bank.

GRIFFITHS, Lewis.

1836 Director County of Gloucester Bank. 1839, 1841 Deputy Chairman. 1842–67 Chairman. 1868 Resigned owing to declining health.

GULSON, John. 1813–1904.

Son of Quaker parents. 1832 Entered banking business of Goodall, Wilmot & Goodall, Coventry, in which his father had bought a partnership with a view to providing a career for him. 1834 Partner in Goodall, Gulson, Goodall &

Gulson. 1838 Partnership dissolved. 1839 Business bought by Coventry & Warwickshire Banking Co. from Edward and Richard Goodall. 1838 Went into business as a silk merchant. 1866 Director Coventry & Warwickshire Banking Co. 1867 Chairman. 1867, 1868 Mayor of Coventry. 1879 Director Lloyds Banking Co. on amalgamation. 1886 Resigned.

GWINNETT, William Henry.
1881 Director County of Gloucester Bank. 1887–91 Chairman.

HANBURY, David. ?–1839.
1807 Partner in Sparrow, Brown, Hanbury & Co. with various branches in Suffolk. 1830 Partner in Oakes, Bevan of Bury St. Edmunds but remained at Sudbury to manage their business there.

HANBURY, Osgood. 1731–1804.
See facing p. 362.

HANBURY, Osgood. 1765–1852.
See facing p. 362.

HANBURY, Osgood. 1794–1873.
See facing p. 362.

HANBURY, Osgood. 1826–82.
See facing p. 362.

HANBURY, Phillip. 1802–78.
See facing p. 362.

HANBURY, Sampson. 1827–77.
See facing p. 362.

HANDLEY, Benjamin.
1792 Founding partner in Peacock Handley & Co. of Sleaford. M.P. for South Lincs.

HARRIS, Sir Austin Edward, K.B.E. 1870– .
Educated at Harrow. 1910 Director Lloyds Bank. 1922–47 Deputy Chairman. 1916–18 Chairman Board of Contracts and Assistant Surveyor General of Supply at War Office. 1949 Retired from Board. Remained on Salisbury Committee until 1956.

HARRIS, Robert. ?–1841.
Mealman, Reading. 1791 Founding partner in Micklem, Stephens, Simmonds & Harris, Reading.

HARTLAND, Sir Frederick Dixon. 1832–1909.
Son of Nathaniel Hartland. 1858 Manager Cirencester branch Gloucestershire Banking Co. 1861 Resigned. 1880 M.P. for Evesham. 1891 Baronet. 1895 After various banking connexions joined Lacy Son & Hartland, West Smithfield. 1891 Director London, City & Midland Bank on amalgamation.

HARTLAND, Nathaniel. 1791–1866.
See p. 46.

HARVEY, George Alexander.

1870 Joined staff of Caledonian Banking Co., Grantown-on-Spey. 1873 Joined staff of Hampshire Banking Co. 1888 City Manager Capital and Counties Bank. 1894 Joint General Manager. 1912 Director. 1918 Director Lloyds Bank on amalgamation until 1938/9.

HEARD, John. ?–1865.

1836 Chairman Committee of Proprietors Moore and Robinson's Nottingham-shire Banking Co. 1860 Chairman of the Company. 1865 Retired.

HEATH, Thomas.

A solicitor in Warwick. Director Warwick & Leamington Banking Co. 1866 Director Lloyds Banking Co. on amalgamation. 1872 Retired.

HENDERSON, Robert Cron.

1877 Entered Bank of Scotland, Dumfries. 1880 Joined Birmingham Banking Co. 1881 Joined Capital and Counties Bank. 1894 City Manager.

HENDERSON, William Gavin.

On staff of Bank of Scotland. 1874 General Manager Liverpool Union Bank. 1900 Retired on amalgamation with Lloyds Bank.

HENTY, Arthur.

1871 Partner in Henty & Co., Worthing. 1917 Director Capital and Counties Bank.

HENTY, Edwin. ?–1916.

Partner in Henty & Co., Worthing. 1896 Director Capital and Counties Bank after amalgamation.

HENTY, George. ?–1829.

1808 Founding partner in Henty & Co., Worthing.

HERBERT, Abraham Bucbury.

1835 Director Coventry & Warwickshire Banking Co. 1842–7 Chairman. Continued as Director.

HERRIES, Robert. 1709–91.

Merchant in Amsterdam. 1772 Founding partner in the London Exchange Banking Co. 1780 Resigned in favour of his son, Robert Herries.

HERRIES, Sir Robert. c. 1731–?

Son of John Herries of Halldykes and nephew of Robert Herries. 1754 Established a merchant's business in Barcelona. 1762 Partner in John Coutts & Co., merchants and bankers, Edinburgh, and Herries Cochrane & Co., merchants, London. 1772 Founding partner in the London Exchange Banking Co. c. 1774 Knighted. 1798 Retired from the business. See also p. 193.

HICKLING, John.

1826 Joined Taylor and Lloyd as junior clerk. 1865 Manager High Street office. 1875 Retired.

HICKS-BEACH, Sir Michael E., Earl St. Aldwyn. 1837–1916.
 Educated at Eton and Christ Church, Oxford. 1864–1906 M.P. for E. Glouces-
 tershire and W. Bristol. 1885–6 Chancellor of the Exchequer. 1886 Director
 County of Gloucester Bank. 1893 Chairman County of Gloucester Bank. 1906
 Created Earl St. Aldwyn.

HICKS-BEACH, Hon. Michael Hugh, Viscount Quenington. 1877–1916.
 Son of Earl St. Aldwyn. Educated at Eton and Christ Church, Oxford. 1901–2
 Assistant Private Secretary to Chancellor of Exchequer. 1904–5 Assistant
 Private Secretary to Sir Alexander Head. 1906 M.P. for Tewkesbury. 1911–15
 Director Lloyds Bank. 1916 Killed in action in Egypt.

HILL, Charles. ?–1846.
 1825 Manager of Messrs. Sharpe & Sons Bank, 8 West Smithfield, when it failed.
 Founded his own banking business, to be joined after three or four years by two
 brothers.

HIND, Herbert Wheeler. 1847–1918.
 Senior partner in J. H. Hind and Co., East India Merchants, Liverpool. 1892
 Director Liverpool Union Bank. 1896 Chairman. 1900 Director Lloyds Bank
 on amalgamation. 1900 Chairman Liverpool Local Committee. 1917 Resigned
 from Board but retained chairmanship of Liverpool Local Committee. Director
 Royal Insurance Co., Thames & Mersey Marine Insurance Co., and British and
 Eastern Shipping Co.

HINGSTON, Alfred E. ?–1889.
 By 1851 Manager Plymouth office Devon and Cornwall Banking Co. 1869
 General Manager.

HINGSTON, Joseph. ?–1835.
 Partner in Hingston and Prideaux. 1832 Director and founder, Plymouth &
 Devonport Banking Company.

HOAR, George. 1754–1831.
 Early business connexions with the East India Company. 1788 Founding partner in Davison-Bland & Co., later Lambton & Co., Newcastle. 1790 Retired.

HOAR, William. 1750–1833.
 Barrister. 1788 Founding partner in Davison-Bland & Co., later Lambton &
 Co., of Newcastle. 1806 Recorder of Durham.

HOARE, Edward A.
 On the staff of Barnetts Hoares & Co. March 1884 City Office Manager on
 amalgamation with Lloyds. 1896 Resigned owing to bad health.

HOARE, Edward Brodie. 1841–1911.
 Educated at Tonbridge School and Trinity College, Cambridge. 1864 Entered
 Barnetts Hoares & Co. 1867 Partner. 1884 Director and Chairman London
 Committee after amalgamation of Lloyds Banking Co. and Barnetts Hoares.
 1886–7 Deputy Chairman. 1888 Conservative M.P. for Hampstead. Published

articles on New Zealand. Director The Colonial Bank. 1911 Died as a result of motor-car accident.

HOARE, Sir Henry H. A., Bart. 1865–1947.
Educated at Harrow. 1900 Director Wilts & Dorset Banking Co. 1914–16 Director Lloyds Bank on amalgamation.

HOARE, John Gurney. 1810–75.
See p. 45.

HOARE, Robert Gurney. 1844–99.
Son of John Gurney Hoare. 1859 Partner in Hodgkin, Barnett, Pease, Spence & Co., Newcastle.

HOARE, Samuel. 1751–1825.
See p. 43.

HOARE, Samuel. 1783–1847.
See p. 45.

HOARE, Samuel. 1807–33.
See p. 45.

HOARE, Sir Samuel. 1841–1915.
See p. 45.

HOBSON, Richard. 1836–1909.
Partner in Messrs. R. Hobson & Co., Liverpool. 1893 Director Liverpool Union Bank. 1898 Sheriff of Cheshire. 1900 Director Lloyds Bank on amalgamation. 1908 Resigned from Board but remained on Liverpool Local Committee. Chairman British & Foreign Marine Insurance Co. and James Kershaw & Co. Deputy Chairman Liverpool Overhead Railway Co. Director Liverpool and London and Globe Insurance Co.

HODGKIN, Thomas Edward. 1872–1921.
Son of Thomas Hodgkin. Educated at Cambridge and gained double first in Natural Science. Became partner in Hodgkin Barnett & Co., Newcastle. 1903 Appointed District Manager and then Assistant General Manager Northern District, Lloyds Bank on amalgamation.

HOLDER, Thomas. ?–1896.
1877 Director Liverpool Union Bank. 1889 Deputy Chairman. 1892 Chairman.

HORMAN-FISHER, S. S. H.
1861 Director Glamorganshire Banking Co. 1876–83 Managing Director.

HUNT, George.
1835 Chairman Hampshire Banking Co. at its foundation. 1868 Retired.

HUNT, Zacharias Daniel. 1808–74.
Nephew of William Rickford. Before 1840 partner in Aylesbury Old Bank. 1853 Director Bucks & Oxon Union Bank on amalgamation. 1857 Resigned owing to ill health.

INGOLDBY, John. 1794–1884.

    Clerk in Garfit Claypons & Co., Boston. *c.* 1864 Manager of Boston office. Later a partner.

INVERFORTH, Lord. See under WEIR.

ISAAC, Arthur Whitmore.

    1889 Partner in Berwick & Co., Worcester. 1906 Appointed local director by Capital and Counties Bank upon amalgamation.

ISAAC, Elias. 1755–1803.

    Son of Edward Isaac, senior partner in the banking firm of Isaac, Baldwin and Shapland at Marshfield. 1781 Partner in Berwick & Co., Worcester. Freeman of City of Worcester. 1799 Mayor of Worcester.

ISAAC, Elias. ?–1841.

    Nephew of Elias Isaac. Learned banking with Robarts & Co., London. 1803 Partner in Berwick & Co. on death of his uncle. 1808 Partner also in Lechmere & Co. of Tewkesbury. 1819 Mayor of Worcester. 1821 High Sheriff of Worcester.

ISAAC, John Swinton. 1834–88.

    Son of John Whitmore Isaac. 1859 Partner in Berwick & Co., Worcester. County Treasurer and Treasurer of the City. His wife became a sleeping partner in the bank from his death until 1899.

ISAAC, John Whitmore. 1810–84.

    1844 Partner in Berwick & Co., Worcester. County Treasurer of Worcester.

JAFFRAY, Sir John. 1818–1901.

    Born at Stirling. Educated at High School, Glasgow. Proprietor *Birmingham Daily Post* and *Birmingham Daily Mail*. 1861 Founder and Director Birmingham Joint Stock Bank. 1866–72 Retired from Board owing to ill health. 1878 Chairman. 1888 High Sheriff of Warwickshire. 1889 Director Lloyds Bank on amalgamation until 1894.

JAMES, Thos. S.

    1868 Manager New Street branch, Birmingham Joint Stock Bank. 1888 General Manager.

JANSON, Edward.

    Nephew of Joseph Janson and grandson of John Lloyd through his daughter Lucy. Partner in Brown Janson of Abchurch Lane.

JANSON, Joseph. 1789–1846.

    Lived in Church Street, Stoke Newington. 1813 Founding partner in Nicholson Brown & Co., Leeds, and Nicholson Janson & Co. in Threadneedle Street. His fortune at his death was about £90,000.

JANSON, Thomas Corbyn.

    Nephew of Joseph Janson of Abchurch Lane.

JERVIS, Herbert Jervis White. ?–1934.

Nephew of Felix Thornley Cobbold. *c.* 1880 Manager Cox Cobbold & Co., Harwich. 1886 Partner in Cox Cobbold & Co., Harwich and Bacon Cobbold & Co., Ipswich. 1905 Director Capital and Counties Bank on amalgamation. 1918 Director Lloyds Bank on amalgamation. Chairman Capital and Counties Committee.

JONES, David. 1759–1839.

Married Anne, daughter of Rhys Jones who brought him a fortune of £10,000. 1799 Founded David Jones Bank, Llandovery (The Black Ox Bank). 1825 Sheriff for Carmarthen.

JONES, David. 1810–69.

Grandson of David Jones. Educated at Charterhouse. 1839 Carried on the bank after his grandfather's death. 1851–68 M.P. for Carmarthenshire. 1845 Sheriff of Carmarthen.

JONES, Gerwyn. *c.* 1851–1903.

Son of David Jones. Inherited the Llandovery bank on the death of his two uncles, William and John, who had acted as his trustees.

KAYE, Sir Joseph Henry, Bt. 1856–1923.

Woollens and worsted manufacturer. 1910 Director Halifax Joint Stock Banking Co. (later West Yorkshire Bank). 1923 Created a baronet. Chairman Kaye & Stewart Ltd., Huddersfield, and Gledhill Bros. & Co. Ltd., Huddersfield. Director London Midland & Scottish Railway.

KEEP, Joseph Scrivener. 1820–1907.

1861 Member Provisional Committee and Director Birmingham Joint Stock Bank. 1889 Director Lloyds Bank on amalgamation. 1900 Retired. Chairman Horsley Iron Co. Deputy Chairman Midland Wagon Co. Director Elliott's Metal Co.

KEMP, Sir Kenneth Hagar, Bt. 1853–1936.

Educated at Jesus College, Cambridge. 1880 Called to the Bar. 1893 Partner in Lacons, Youell and Kemp, Yarmouth. Connexions with insurance and hotel companies. 1901 Local director Capital and Counties Bank on amalgamation.

KENRICK, John Arthur. 1829–1923.

Director of Archbald Kenrick & Sons Ltd., West Bromwich. Chairman Union Rolling Stock Company and Nettlefolds. 1877 Director Lloyds Bank.

KENRICK, Timothy. 1807–85.

See p. 36.

KER, Charles, D.L. 1860–1940.

Educated at Glasgow Academy and Glasgow University. Director National Bank of Scotland. 1918 Director Lloyds Bank. Partner in McClelland Ker & Co., Chartered Accountants, Glasgow and London. Director North British & Mercantile Insurance Co. Ltd., and London Midland & Scottish Railway Co.

KING, Henry Samuel. ?–1878.
1857 Became a partner in Smith Elder & Co. of 65 Cornhill. 1868 Took over all the banking and Indian agency side of this business.

KING, Sir Henry Seymour, Bt., K.C.I.E. 1852–1933.
Educated at Charterhouse and Balliol, Oxford. 1873 Entered business as clerk in Henry S. King & Co. 1875 Partner. 1878 On his father's death became senior partner and director of many City companies. 1885–1911 M.P. for Central Hull. 1892 Created K.C.I.E. 1901–2 Mayor of Kensington. 1909 Director Lloyds Bank. 1932 Created baronet in recognition of services as Chairman of Income Tax Commissioners for City of London.

KIRTON, William. 1747–1827.
1792 Founding partner in Peacock Handley & Co., of Sleaford.

KITSON, John. 1836–1911.
Son of William Kitson. Partner in the Torquay bank until amalgamation with Lloyds Bank in 1901.

KITSON, William. 1800–83.
Educated at Blundell's School. Solicitor of Torquay. 1833 Founded a bank in partnership with Captain W. Vivian and Mr. Edward Vivian. Close connexion with local affairs. 1860 Presented with silver plate by the people of Torquay for his services to the town.

KNIGHT, Henry.
1828 Partner in Eaton, Knight and Stroud, bankers of Swansea. 1836 Director Glamorganshire Banking Company at its foundation.

KNIGHT, James. 1803–68.
c. 1830 Purchased the Farnham Bank from James Stevens.

LAMBTON, Ralph Edward.
Before 1860–1907 Partner in Lambton & Co., Newcastle.

LANDELL, David. ?–1793.
Hardware and leather merchant. 1788 Founding partner in Davison-Bland & Co., later Lambton & Co., Newcastle.

LAWRENCE, Walter Lawrence.
1836 Provisional Chairman County of Gloucester Banking Co. Appointed local director for Cheltenham. 1842 Resigned.

LECHMERE, Sir Anthony, Bt. 1767–1849.
1787 Married Mary, daughter of Joseph Berwick. Succeeded his father-in-law as Receiver General. 1792 Partner in Lechmere & Co. of Tewkesbury. 1801 Partner in Berwick & Co., Worcester. 1818 Created a baronet after attracting the attention of the Prince of Wales (later George IV).

LECHMERE, Anthony Hungerford. 1868– .
Third son of Sir Edmund Lechmere. Educated at Charterhouse. 1896 Partner in Berwick & Co., Worcester.

LECHMERE, Sir Edmund Anthony Harley. 1826–94.
Grandson of Sir Anthony Lechmere. Educated at Charterhouse, and Christ Church, Oxford. 1853 Partner in Berwick & Co. 1866 M.P. for Tewkesbury. 1876 M.P. for West Worcestershire. 1886 M.P. for South Worcestershire.

LISSAMAN, Thomas.
1825 Became junior clerk in Beck & Prime, Coventry. 1837 Senior clerk. 1841 Appointed sub-manager Coventry & Warwickshire Banking Co. 1842 Appointed secretary and later manager. 1864 Left the bank.

LISTER, James. 1803–79.
See p. 51.

LLOYD, Charles. 1748–1828.
See p. 26.

LLOYD, Corbyn. 1785–1828.
See facing p. 362.

LLOYD, Cyril Edward. 1876– .
See facing p. 362.

LLOYD, Francis. 1803–75.
See facing p. 362.

LLOYD, Francis Nelson. 1907– .
See facing p. 362.

LLOYD, George Ambrose, Lord Lloyd. 1897–1941.
1912 Director Lloyds Bank. Nov. 1918 Resigned from Board on his appointment as Governor of Bombay. 1924 Joined Board again. 1925 Resigned on his appointment as High Commissioner for Egypt. See facing p. 362.

LLOYD, George Braithwaite. 1794–1857.
See facing p. 362.

LLOYD, George Braithwaite II. 1824–1903.
1841 Entered business as an engineer pupil. Became manufacturer of welded iron tubes. 1 Jan. 1858 Partner in Lloyds & Co. 1865 Director Lloyds Banking Co. Director Midland Railway for 10 years. 1870–1 Mayor of Birmingham. Last surviving partner of the private bank. See facing p. 362.

LLOYD, George Butler. 1854–?
Partner in Eyton Burton & Co., Shrewsbury. 1907 Director Capital and Counties Bank on amalgamation. 1913 M.P. for Shrewsbury.

LLOYD, Henry. 1784–1864.
Son of Sampson Lloyd III. 1807 Interest in the London bank transferred to this son and the two banks separated. See facing p. 362.

LLOYD, Howard. 1837–1920.
See p. 56.

LLOYD, Isaac. 1801–83.
See p. 56.

LLOYD, James. 1776–1853.
See facing p. 362.

LLOYD, James II. 1806–65.
See facing p. 362.

LLOYD, John. 1751–1811.
See facing p. 362.

LLOYD, Nehemiah. 1745–1801.
See facing p. 362.

LLOYD, Richard Borrodaile. 1839–?
1867 Partner in Barnetts, Hoares, Hanbury & Lloyds. 1884 Director Lloyds on amalgamation. Trustee of Bankers Guarantee and Trust Fund. Director Ohlssons Cape Breweries. 1907 Retired from Board owing to ill health.
See facing p. 362.

LLOYD, Richard Harman. 1807–67.
See facing p. 362.

LLOYD, Sampson II. 1699–1779.
See p. 5.

LLOYD, Sampson III. 1728–1807.
See p. 25.

LLOYD, Sampson IV. 1765–1800.
See facing p. 362.

LLOYD, Sampson Samuel. 1820–99.
See p. 32.

LLOYD, Samuel. 1768–1849.
See facing p. 362.

LLOYD, Thomas. 1814–90.
See facing p. 362.

LONG, George. 1823–?
1845 Joined Grant & Burbey, Portsmouth, as apprentice. 1850 Partner. 1888 Director Grant and Maddison's Union Banking Co.

LUCAS, Alexander.
1848–59 Chairman Wilts & Dorset Banking Co.

LUCE, Charles Richard. 1829–?
Educated at Fairfield. 1851 Entered business as brewer at Malmesbury. 1879 Director Wilts & Dorset Banking Co.

LUCY, William Charles. ?–1898.
1884 Director Gloucestershire Banking Co. 1886 Director Capital and Counties Bank on amalgamation.

MCMASTER, John.
1879 Joined Hammond & Co., Canterbury, as a partner. 1902 Retained by Capital and Counties Bank as local director on amalgamation.

MARTIN, Eliot George Bromley. 1866–?
Eldest son of G. E. Martin. 1895 Partner in Berwick & Co., Worcester. 1906 Retained by Capital and Counties Bank as local director on amalgamation. 1915 Director.

MARTIN, George Edward. 1829–1905.
Barrister-at-law. 1860 Partner in Berwick & Co., Worcester. 1882 High Sheriff of Worcester. After his death the bank was amalgamated with Capital and Counties Bank.

MARTIN, Hugo Hamilton. 1858–?
Son of John Martin. Partner in Martins Bank, Lombard Street. 1888 Partner in Berwick & Co., Worcester.

MATHIESON, Kenneth. ?–1925.
Director London and River Plate Bank. 1918 Director Lloyds Bank.

MERRIMAN, Edward Baverstock. 1839–1915.
See p. 54.

MICKLEM, Robert. 1736–93.
Draper, Reading. 1791 Founding partner in Micklem, Stephens, Simmonds & Harris, Reading. Mayor of Reading.

MIDDLETON, Henry N.
Partner in Lambton & Co., Newcastle. 1908 Director Lloyds Bank on amalgamation. 1912 Retired.

MINTY, Alexander Hayward.
c. 1849 Local director for Salisbury, Wilts & Dorset Banking Co. 1859–64 Chairman Wilts & Dorset Banking Co.

MOILLIET, James Keir. 1836–?
Grandson of Jean Louis Moilliet. 1860 Partner in Moilliet & Sons. March 1865 Member of Provisional Committee and then Director Lloyds Banking Company. 1877 Retired.

MOILLIET, Jean Louis. 1770–1845.
Born in Geneva. Came to England at an early age and established himself as a foreign merchant in Birmingham. 1801 Married Amelia, daughter of James Keir, member of the Lunar Society. 1815 Took partnership in Robert Coales bank.

MOLESWORTH, Sir John, Bt. ?–1785.
1774 Founding partner in Cornish Bank, Truro.

MOORE, Thomas. ?–1852.
Partner in Moore & Robinson's Bank, Nottingham. 1836 Director of the joint-stock company formed from this bank. Shared the Chairmanship with Frederick Robinson.

MORCOM, Reginald Keble, Lt.-Col., C.B.E. 1879– .
Educated at Marlborough and Trinity College, Cambridge. 1910–50 Director Lloyds Bank. 1930 Member British Economic Mission to Far East.

1931–56 Member and later Chairman of newly formed Birmingham Committee. Chairman Bellis & Morcom Ltd. Vice-president British Electrical & Allied Manufacturers Association and F.B.I.

MOULE, Frederick. ?–1843.

Practising attorney in Melksham and partner in Moule & Co., bankers. 1835 Manager North Wilts Banking Co., on amalgamation.

MOUNTFORD, Richard.

1837–41 Chairman Shropshire Banking Company.

MUNTZ, George Frederick. 1822–98.

Son of George Frederick Muntz, M.P. for Birmingham from 1840–57. 1862–78 Chairman Birmingham Joint Stock Bank.

NETTLEFOLD, Edward. 1856–1909.

Deputy Chairman Nettlefolds Ltd. 1904–8 Director Lloyds Bank. Director London and North-Western Railway Co., North British Mercantile Assurance Co. Active in Liberal and Unionist Party. Member Imperial Tariff Commission.

NEWSOME, Samuel E. ?–1869.

1848 Director Coventry and Warwickshire Banking Co. 1863 Chairman.

NICHOLSON, Stephen.

1813 Founding partner in Nicholson Brown & Co., Leeds. 1824 Retired.

NICHOLSON, Thomas. ?–1822.

Lived at Roundhay Park, Leeds. 1813 Founding partner in Nicholson Brown & Co., Leeds.

NOBLE, Philip Ernest.

Educated at Eton and Trinity College, Oxford. 1896 Partner in Lambton & Co., Newcastle. 1912 Director Lloyds Bank. 1918 Director National Bank of Scotland. 1922 High Sheriff of Northumberland.

OAKES, James. ?–1829.

Woollen merchant, Bury St. Edmunds. 1795 Founding partner in banking business of James Oakes & Son.

OAKES, Orbell.

1798 Receiver-General for West Suffolk and partner in Bury Bank.

OXLEY, James Walker.

1900 Senior partner in William Williams Brown & Co., Leeds, at amalgamation with Lloyds Bank. Chairman Finance Committee of Midland Railway.

PAGET, Thomas. 1778–1862.

Married Anne, daughter of John Pares, a Leicestershire banker. 1814 Succeeded his father as a partner in Pares bank, Leicester. 1825 Left this partnership and formed Pagets & Kirbys bank. 1831/2 M.P. for Leicestershire.

PAGET, Thomas Tertius. 1807–92.

Son of Thomas Paget. 1862 Succeeded his father as senior partner in Pagets bank, Leicester. 1880 Liberal M.P. for South Leicestershire. 1869 High Sheriff of Leicestershire. Built the Leicestershire Royal Opera House.

PARKER, Alwyn, C.B., C.M.G. 1877–1951.
1919–47 Director Lloyds Bank. Editor *Lloyds Bank Review*.

PARSONS, Cecil. 1786–1876.
Wealthy solicitor in Presteigne. 1837 Founded banking business of Parsons & Co. Sole proprietor until his death when it was absorbed by Worcester City and County Banking Co.

PATTINSON, Arthur Edward. 1868–1939.
Son of John R. Pattinson, Director Liverpool Union Bank. Educated at Harrow. Entered private firm John R. Pattinson & Co., Liverpool. 1917 Director Lloyds Bank. 1924 Chairman Liverpool Committee.

PEARCE, Lt.-Col. William.
1834 Director Gloucester County & City Bank. 1836–43 Director County of Gloucester Bank following its absorption of Gloucester County & City Bank. Appointed local director for Cirencester.

PEASE, Sir Arthur Francis, Bt. 1866–1927.
Educated at Trinity College, Cambridge. 1888 Entered business in Pease & Partners Ltd. and later became Director. Chairman Normanby Iron Works Co. Ltd. 1915 Director Lloyds Bank. 1920 Baronetcy conferred. High Sheriff of Durham.

PEASE, John William. 1834–1901.
Son of John Beaumont Pease. Educated at Grove House, Tottenham. 1859 Entered business and became a founding partner in Hodgkin, Barnett, Pease, Spence & Co. Director North Eastern Railway.

PEASE, John William Beaumont, Lord Wardington. 1869–1950.
Partner in Hodgkin, Barnett, Pease, Spence & Co., Newcastle. 1903 Director Lloyds Bank on amalgamation. 1909 Deputy Chairman. 1918 Director London and River Plate Bank. 1922–45 Chairman Lloyds Bank. 1936 Barony conferred. See facing p. 362.

PHILLIPS, John Spencer. 1847–1909.
See p. 36.

PHIPPS, Pickering. 1861–91.
Brewer. 1847 Sheriff of Northants. Chairman Northamptonshire Banking Co. 1890 Director Capital and Counties Bank on amalgamation.

PLATT, Henry. 1842–1914.
Educated at Cheltenham College, Berlin and Cambridge. Partner in Williams & Co., Chester, until amalgamation with Lloyds. 1877 High Sheriff of Caernarvonshire. 1880 High Sheriff of Anglesey. 1883 Lord Mayor of Bangor.

POCOCK, Thomas Pike. ?–1885.
1860 Became Director North Wilts Banking Co. on amalgamation of Everett

Ravenhill & Co., Warminster, in which he was a partner. 1877 Deputy Chairman North Wilts Banking Co. Director Capital and Counties Bank.

PRAED, Charles Tyringham. 1833–95.
Educated at Eton and Oxford. Partner in Praeds & Co., Fleet Street. 1891 Director Lloyds Bank on amalgamation. 1874–80 M.P. for St. Ives.

PRAED, Sir Herbert Bulkeley. 1841–1921.
Partner in Praeds & Co. until amalgamation with Lloyds in 1891. Director Alliance Investment Trust, Bankers Investment Trust, Campbell Praed & Co., &c. 1906 Baronetcy conferred.

PRAED, Humphrey Mackworth. ?–1802.
1771 Founding partner in Cornish Bank, Truro. 1761–8 M.P. for St. Ives. 1772–4 M.P. for Cornwall.

PRAED, William. 1749–?
Partner in Cocks, Biddulph, Eliot & Praed of London. 1779 Partner in Cornish Bank, Truro. 1792 Left Cocks Biddulph & Co. 1803 Founded Praeds & Co., Fleet Street.

PRANCE, William.
1831–c. 1855 First Chairman Plymouth & Devonport Banking Co., later Devon & Cornwall Banking Co.

PRANCE, William Henry. 1818–?
Educated at Plymouth Corporation Grammar School. 1843 Solicitor in Prance & Prance of Plymouth. 1859 Director Devon & Cornwall Banking Co. 1889–1906 Chairman.

PRICE, William Phillip.
1843 Director Gloucestershire Banking Co. 1862 Chairman. 1886 Director Capital and Counties Bank on amalgamation. 1889 Resigned on being appointed a Railway Commissioner.

PRIDEAUX, Charles. ?–1893.
1839 Appointed Inspector of branches and Secretary to Board of Devon & Cornwall Banking Co. 1866–9 General Manager Devon & Cornwall Banking Co. 1869 Elected Director. 1870–88 Chairman.

PRIDHAM, Arthur E.
1879 Superintendent of branches, Devon & Cornwall Banking Co. 1888–1906 Secretary and Superintendent of branches.

PRIME, Mr. ?–1840.
Partner in Beck & Prime of Coventry. 1835 Continued as sub-manager, Coventry & Warwickshire Banking Co. on amalgamation.

PROVIS, Samuel. 1794–1873.
Timber merchant. 1835 Manager Warminster branch, Wilts & Dorset Banking Co. 1846–59 General Manager Wilts & Dorset Banking Co.

QUENINGTON, Viscount. See under HICKS-BEACH.

RAWSON, Christopher. 1777–1849.

Member of a wealthy Halifax merchant family. 1811 Joined two relatives as partner in John, William & Christopher Rawson & Co., Halifax. 1836–43 Chairman Halifax & Huddersfield Union Banking Company formed out of the private bank.

REDMAN, William.

1856 Director North Wilts Banking Co. 1877 Director Hampshire & North Wilts Banking Co., later the Capital and Counties Bank. 1900 Retired.

REID, William Shiell. 1833–88.

1847 Entered Leith branch, Bank of Scotland, eventually becoming assistant accountant, joint inspector of branches, and assistant manager London branch. 1873 Resigned to become General Manager Hampshire Banking Co.

RICKFORD, William. ?–1803.

1795 Founded Aylesbury Old Bank.

RICKFORD, William. 1769–1854.

Son of William Rickford. 1795 Founded Aylesbury Old Bank with his father. 1808–42 M.P. for Aylesbury.

ROBINSON, Frederick. 1783–1863.

Partner in Moore & Robinson's Bank, Nottingham. 1836 Director of the joint-stock company formed from this bank. Held the offices of Chairman and Managing Director.

RODWELL, William. 1792–1876.

Solicitor. 1825 Partner in Bacon, Cobbold & Co., Ipswich. Prominent in Conservative politics. Represented the Association of Issuing Country Bankers in their dealings with the government. Received testimonials from them in 1844, 1856, and 1865. 1844 Mayor of Ipswich.

ROTHERHAM, Richard Kevitt. ?–1867.

1835 Director Coventry & Warwickshire Banking Co. 1847–63 Chairman.

ROTHWELL, William.

Merchant. 1829–44 Chairman Halifax Joint Stock Banking Co.

ROWLAND, John. ?–1855.

1821 Partner in Williams & Rowland, bankers, Neath. 1836 Manager Neath branch, Glamorganshire Banking Co. 1853 Retired from management and elected Director.

ROWLAND, John Henry.

Son of John Rowland. 1836 Clerk Neath branch, Glamorganshire Banking Co. 1853 Succeeded his father as manager at Neath. 1889–97 Chairman Glamorganshire Banking Co. 1898 Local director Capital and Counties Bank on amalgamation.

RUNDLE, John.

1818 Replaced Elizabeth Rundle in Gill & Rundle, Tavistock. 1835–43 M.P. for Tavistock.

RUSSELL, Thomas.
> 1839 Vice-Chairman Gloucestershire Banking Co. 1842–3 Chairman Gloucestershire Banking Co. 1849 Retired.

ST. ALDWYN, Earl. See under HICKS-BEACH.

ST. BARBE, Charles. ?–c. 1827.
> Grocer and salt manufacturer at Lymington. 1788 Founded St. Barbe's Bank, Lymington.

ST. GERMAINS, Lord. See under ELIOT, John.

SALT, John Charles. 1840–1901.
> Educated at Rottingdean and Rugby. 1859 Entered Stevenson, Salt & Sons at 20 Lombard Street as clerk. Partner in Bosanquet, Salt & Co. (Amalgamated 1867.) 1884 Director Lloyds, Barnetts & Bosanquets Bank on amalgamation. Director National Mutual Life Assurance Society, Bankers' Investment Trust, and Frank Jones Brewing Co.

SALT, John Stevenson. 1775–1845.
> Nephew of William Stevenson. 1800 Married Sarah, daughter of William Stevenson. 1802 Partner in the Stafford bank. 1838 High Sheriff of Staffordshire.

SALT, Thomas. 1802–71.
> Eldest son of John Stevenson Salt. c. 1828 Joined Stevenson, Webb, Salt & Webb at Stafford.

SALT, Sir Thomas, Bt. 1830–1904.
> See p. 34.

SALT, William. 1808–63.
> Third son of John Stevenson Salt. Partner in Stevenson Salt, Lombard Street.

SAMUEL, Samuel, D.L. 1855–1934.
> 1908 Director Capital and Counties Bank. 1913–19 M.P. for Wandsworth and Putney. 1918 Director Lloyds Bank on amalgamation. Director M. Samuel & Co. Ltd., bankers and merchants, Shell Transport & Trading Co., and Anglo-Saxon Petroleum Co. Ltd.

SANDERSON, Oswald. 1863–1926.
> Educated at King's School, Ely. 1906 President Chamber of Shipping of U.K. Managing Director Ellermans Wilson Line, Hull, and Director of other shipping and allied companies. 1916 Director Lloyds Bank.

SELBOURNE, The Rt. Hon. Earl of, K.G., G.C.M.G. 1859–1942.
> Educated at Winchester and University College, Oxford. 1885–95 M.P. for E. Hampshire and W. Edinburgh. 1900–5 First Lord of Admiralty. 1905–10 Governor of Transvaal. 1915–16 President Board of Agriculture. 1919 Director Lloyds Bank.

SHAW, William Dale.
> Partner in firm of Shaw and Shaw, cotton spinners of Huddersfield. c. 1900 Director Halifax & Huddersfield Union Banking Co. Director Northern Counties Investment Trust.

SHEWELL, Edward Warner.
1842 Local director for Head Office at Cheltenham, County of Gloucester Banking Co. 1867 Deputy Chairman.

SHIPTON, James Maurice. ?–1886.
Timber merchant. Formerly Lieutenant R.N. 1831 Founding Director Gloucestershire Banking Co. 1885 Director at time of amalgamation with Capital and Counties Bank.

SIM, Herman Billing. ?–1933.
Director London and River Plate Bank. 1918 Director Lloyds Bank on amalgamation. Director South American Bank. Partner in Goschens and Cunliffe. On Boards of some insurance companies.

SIMONDS, William Blackall.
Brewer, Reading. 1791 Founding partner in Micklem, Stephens, Simmonds and Harris, Reading. 1814 Withdrew from this partnership to found J. & C. Simonds bank (now part of Barclays Bank).

SKILLICORNE, William Nash. ?–1887.
1868 Director County of Gloucester Banking Co. Before 1879 Deputy Chairman. 1880 Chairman.

SLINN, Edward John.
1857 Entered Bucks and Oxon Union Bank as junior clerk. Passed through all grades. 1883 Manager. Director. c. 1895 Deputy Chairman. Chairman West Herts Liberal Club Buildings Co., Watford Gas Co., and Watford Building Society.

SMALL, William.
1871 Director Burton Union Bank. 1892 Chairman. 1900 Director Lloyds Bank on amalgamation. 1911 Resigned owing to advancing age.

SMITH, James. ?–1909.
Partner in Smith Edwards & Co. 1897 Director Liverpool Union Bank. 1900 Member Liverpool Committee, Lloyds Bank after amalgamation. 1908 Director Lloyds Bank.

SMOULT, William.
1788 Founding partner in Davison-Bland & Co., later Lambton & Co., Newcastle. Resided in India during the term of his partnership. 1793 Resigned and had his share of the capital remitted to India.

SPACKMAN, Henry.
1871–1902 Director Wilts & Dorset Banking Co. 1895–6 Chairman.

SPENCE, Robert. 1817–90.
See p. 49.

SQUAREY, Elias Pitts. 1824–1911.
An experienced valuer, founder and president of the Surveyors Institution. 1873 Director Wilts & Dorset Banking Co. 1910 Retired owing to ill health.

STEPHENS, Charles. ?–1867.
  1841 Partner in Stephens, Blandy & Co., Reading.

STEPHENS, Charles.
  Son of Charles Stephens. 1858 Partner in Stephens, Blandy & Co., Reading.
  1891 Retired after a long illness.

STEPHENS, Frederick. 1836–?
  Son of John Stephens. 1858–60 Partner in Stephens, Blandy & Co., Reading.

STEPHENS, Frederick John.
  Son of Frederick Stephens. 1874 Partner in Stephens, Blandy & Co., Reading.

STEPHENS, John. ?–c. 1814.
  Brewer, Reading. 1791 Founding partner in Micklem, Stephens, Simmonds &
  Harris, Reading.

STEPHENS, John. ?–1847.
  1841 Partner in Stephens, Blandy & Co., Reading.

STEPHENS, William. ?–1829.
  1815 Partner in Stephens, Harris & Co., Reading, in succession to John
  Stephens.

STEPHENS, William, junior.
  1814 Partner in Stephens, Harris & Co., Reading. 1841 Retired.

STEVENS, James. 1773–1850.
  Farmer and wool-stapler. Banker at Farnham. 1828 Sold out to John and James
  Knight.

STEVENSON, John. 1706–77.
  Mercer of Stafford. 1737 Banker at Stafford.

STEVENSON, John. 1776–1802.
  Son of William Stevenson. 1801 Partner in the Stafford bank.

STEVENSON, Thomas. ?–1787.
  Son of John Stevenson. Lived at 85 Queen Street, London. 1777 Partner in the
  Stafford bank but more concerned with the 'brief' business in London. 1785
  High Sheriff of Staffordshire.

STEVENSON, William. 1751–1807.
  Youngest son of John Stevenson. Spent his early years farming. 1777 Partner in
  the Stafford bank. 1787 Opened bank in London at 85 Queen Street.

STROUD, William. ?–1854.
  1828 Partner in Eaton Knight & Stroud, bankers, Swansea. 1836 Manager
  Glamorganshire Banking Co. at Swansea on its formation out of the private
  bank. 1854 Died 'by drowning'.

SUMMERFIELD, Henry. 1810–69.
  Son of William Payton Summerfield, brewer, and Anne, daughter of Sampson
  Lloyd III. By 1860 Manager Warwick & Leamington Banking Co. 1866
  Retained by Lloyds after amalgamation. See p. 65.

SUMMERS, Augustus William.
 Director Bristol & West of England Bank. 1894–1909 Director Lloyds Bank.

SUTCLIFFE, Gamaliel. 1842–?
 Descendant of the family which owned the Stoodley Bridge bank which failed
 in 1825. Director Halifax Joint Stock Banking Co. Director Ilkley Brewery and
 Aerated Water Co.

SYKES, Alfred. c. 1845–1915.
 1873 Solicitor. 1899 Director Halifax Joint Stock Banking Co. 1908 Chairman.
 Director Messrs. Joseph Sykes & Co. Ltd., Slaithwaite Spinning Co. Ltd., and
 Globe Worsted Co. Ltd. 1910–11 Chairman Huddersfield Chamber of Commerce. Treasurer to Association of Chambers of Commerce.

TAYLOR, James. 1783–1852.
 See p. 29.

TAYLOR, John, senior. 1711–75.
 See p. 28.

TAYLOR, John, junior, J.P., D.L. 1738–1814.
 See p. 28.

TAYLOR, J. Dixon.
 Manager Stratford-on-Avon branch, Lloyds Bank. 1886 Manager Wolverhampton branch. 1902 Country General Manager. 1907 Resigned owing to ill health.

TAYLOR, William. 1789–1839.
 See p. 28.

TOMKINSON, James. 1840–1910.
 Partner in Williams & Co., Chester. c. 1884 Senior partner. 1887 Sheriff of
 Cheshire. 1899 Director Lloyds Bank. Director Wirral Railways Co. M.P. for
 Crewe (Liberal) in 1900. His death was the result of an accident during the
 House of Commons point to point races.

TOLLEMACHE, Hon. Douglas Alfred. 1862–1945.
 1885 Taken into partnership in the Ipswich bank of Bacon, Cobbold & Co. by
 Mr. N. F. Cobbold who was at the time sole surviving partner. 1899 Left Bacon,
 Cobbold & Co. in order to join Oakes, Bevan & Co. of Bury St. Edmunds.
 Partner and Director of Tollemache's Ipswich Brewery.

TUNSTALL, William Crewdson. 1818–75.
 Nephew of William and Joseph Gibbins. 1854 Manager Gloucester branch,
 Gloucestershire Banking Co. 1859 General Manager. 1866 Relinquished duties
 owing to ill health but invited to take a seat on Board. 1866 Managing Director
 of reorganized Birmingham Banking Company.

TURNER, James Aspinall. 1797–1867.
 Educated at Grammar School, Bolton-le-Moors. Cotton manufacturer and
 merchant in Manchester, North Shore Mills. 1845 Director Liverpool Union
 Bank. 1857–65 M.P. for Manchester. 1858 Chairman Liverpool Union Bank.

TWEEDY, Robert. 1806–98.

> Son of William Tweedy. 1834–59 Manager, Redruth branch, Cornish Bank. 1849 Partner in the Cornish Bank. 1859 Manager Head Office. 1879 Managing Director. 1865–90 Chairman Cornwall Railway Co.

TWEEDY, William. 1766–1854.

> 1804 Manager Praeds & Co., Truro. 1830–54 Partner in the same bank, now Tweedy, Williams & Co.

TWINING, George. 1778–1850.

> One of the three sons of Richard Twining I. 1805 Joined the tea firm of Twining & Co. 1824 Gave special attention to the banking business opened in conjunction with this firm. 1826 Member Goldsmiths Company. 1838 Prime Warden Goldsmiths Company.

TWINING, Herbert Haynes, J.P. 1849–1935.

> Son of Samuel Harvey Twining. 1869 Joined Twining & Co. 1876 Became a partner, devoting most of his attention to the bank. Joint manager with Samuel Twining at 215 Strand. 1892 Remained joint manager Strand branch, Lloyds Bank, after the amalgamation. 1917 Retired.

TWINING, Richard. 1807–1906.

> See p. 42.

VAISEY, Ernest Dent. 1853–1928.

> 1870 Joined Gloucestershire Banking Co. 1875 Moved to North Wilts Banking Co. 1881–9 Manager Ludgate Hill branch, Capital and Counties Bank. 1887 Comptroller of branches. 1894 Joint General Manager. 1918 Director Lloyds Bank on amalgamation. 1921 Retired from General Managership but remained director. 1926 Resigned owing to ill health but remained on Capital and Counties Section Committee.

VASSAR-SMITH, Sir Richard Vassar. 1843–1922.

> See p. 38.

VIVIAN, Edward. 1809–93.

> 1833 Partner in the Torquay bank. 1879 Received a testimonial from the people of Torquay.

VOSS, John Matthew. ?–1845.

> Partner in Walters, Voss & Walters, bankers, Swansea. 1841 Manager Glamorganshire Banking Co. on amalgamation.

WALL, Samuel. 1734–1812.

> Came of a Herefordshire family. Married Millicent, daughter and heiress of William Ellis of Worcester. c. 1760 Partner with Samuel Crane as linen draper and haberdasher. 1781 Founding partner in Berwick & Co., Worcester. Did not take a very active part in the bank in later years.

WALL, William. 1766–1844.

> Son of Samuel Wall. Employed in Berwick & Co., Worcester. 1801 Partner. 1808 Partner also in Lechmere & Co., Tewkesbury.

WARD, John Whiteley. 1826–*c*. 1914.

1882–1908 Chairman Halifax Joint Stock Banking Co. Director until 1914 (by this time West Yorkshire Bank).

WARDINGTON, Lord. See under PEASE, John William Beaumont.

WATERS, John. ?–1894.

1860 Local director Wilts & Dorset Banking Co., Salisbury. 1865 Chairman Wilts & Dorset Banking Co. until death.

WEBB, Edward John. 1819–1896.

Partner in Webb & Co., Ledbury. Deputy Lieutenant of Hereford. 1883 Local director Gloucestershire Banking Co. on amalgamation.

WEBB, Thomas. 1776–1837.

1815 Took over the banking business of Hankins & Co., Ledbury. Deputy Lieutenant of Hereford.

WEIR, Andrew, Lord Inverforth. 1865–1955.

1916–39 Director Lloyds Bank. 1919 Baronetcy. 1919–21 Minister of Munitions. President Andrew Weir Shipping & Trading Co. Hon. President Cable & Wireless (Holding) Ltd. Chairman United Baltic Corporation Ltd.

WHATMAN, George Dunbar. 1846–1923.

Educated at Eton and Exeter College, Oxford. Partner in Bosanquet Salt & Co. 1884 Joined Board of Lloyds. Director Bank of British North America, Provincial Bank of Ireland, Anglo-Foreign Banking Co., United States Brewing Co. 1921 Resigned from Board of Lloyds owing to ill health.

WHEELER, Owen. 1870–1948.

Son of Francis Wheeler (d. 1887). Educated at Winchester. 1892 Joined staff of Wheeler & Co., High Wycombe. 1894 Junior partner. 1896 Remained on staff of Capital and Counties after amalgamation. Later manager of their branches at Godalming and Canterbury.

WHEELER, Robert. 1777–?

Born at Witney (Oxon.). 1812 Came to High Wycombe and opened a bank (Wheeler & Co).

WHEELER, Thomas. 1783–1870.

1835 Director North Wilts Banking Co. until his death.

WHITWORTH, Robert. 1854–1923.

1872 Entered business. Chairman Whitworth & Co. Ltd. Before 1894 Director Halifax & Huddersfield Union Banking Co. 1910 Director Halifax Joint Stock Bank on amalgamation (later West Yorkshire Bank). 1919 Joined Lloyds Board on amalgamation.

WILLEY, Col. Francis Vernon, C.M.G., C.B.E., M.P.

1919 Director Lloyds Bank. 1928/9 Retired.

WILLIAMS, Henry. ?–1877.

Iron and coalmaster in partnership with his brothers, Philip and Walter. 1865 Only surviving partner in P. & H. Williams, Wednesbury. Director Lloyds Banking Co. on amalgamation.

WILLIAMS, Rees. ?–1849.

1821 Partner in Williams & Rowland, bankers, Neath. 1836 Director and Chairman Glamorganshire Banking Co. at its formation until his death.

WILLIAMS, William. ?–1904.

Vice-Chairman Glamorganshire Banking Co. 1899 Director Capital and Counties Bank.

WILSON, James. 1817–1891.

A self-made man who came to Liverpool and built up a successful corn merchants business. 1864 Director Liverpool Union Bank. 1867 Deputy Chairman. 1868 Chairman until his death.

WINTERBOTHAM, Lindsay. 1800–71.

Son of a nonconformist minister. Trained and practised as a solicitor at Tewkesbury. 1834 Invited to become Mr. Nathaniel Hartland's assistant in superintending branches of Gloucestershire Banking Co. 1860 Joint Managing Director, and manager Stroud branch. 1865 Relieved of management of Stroud in order to give all his time to supervision. Succeeded by his son, E. W. Winterbotham.

WOODWARD, Robert. 1840–1921.

Educated at Exeter College, Oxford. Barrister. Director Worcester City and County Banking Co. 1890 Director Lloyds Bank.

WORTHINGTON, William.

1839 Director Burton, Uttoxeter & Staffordshire Union Bank. 1868 Chairman.

WRIGHT, Ichabod Charles. 1767–1862.

1791 Joined his father's bank in Nottingham as a clerk. 1794 Succeeded his father as partner. 1807 Accepted command of a troop of yeomanry.

WRIGHT, Ichabod Charles. 1795–1871.

Son of Ichabod Charles Wright. Educated at Eton and Christ Church, Oxford. 1825 Joint manager Wright's Bank, Nottingham. 1862 Senior partner. Various publications on currency matters and Greek classics.

WRIGHT, John Skirrow. 1822–80.

A Baptist. Partner in Smith & Wright, Birmingham, button manufacturers and tin-plate workers. He gave annual bonuses to his work-people in order to give them an interest in the business. 1872 He retired in order to devote himself to mercantile affairs. 1877 Director Lloyds Banking Co. Chairman Birmingham Chamber of Commerce. 1880 M.P. for Nottingham.

WRIGHT, William. 1838–1900.

1892 Director Moore & Robinson's Nottinghamshire Banking Co. 1897–1900 Chairman. Chairman Farm & Colonization Co. Director Trafford Park Estate, Starey's Carriage Works, and Horse Repository Co.

YOUNG, Archibald.

Manager Brighton branch, Hampshire Banking Co. 1877 City manager Hampshire & North Wilts Banking Co., later Capital and Counties Bank. 1888–94 General Manager Capital and Counties Bank.

YOUNG, George.

Manager National Provincial Bank, Gloucester. 1854 Appointed manager Glamorganshire Banking Co. at Swansea. 1876 Retired.

YOUNGER, George, Viscount Younger of Leckie. 1851–1929.

Educated at Edinburgh Academy and University. Chairman George Younger & Son, Brewers, Alloa. 1906–22 M.P. (U) Ayr Burghs. 1911 Baronetcy conferred. 1918 Director Lloyds Bank. 1923 Raised to peerage. Lord Lieutenant County of Stirling. Vice-Lieutenant County of Clackmannan.

INDEX

Note. This index does not include Appendix 2: Branches of Lloyds Bank.

* indicates a reference on the Table facing p. 362

PRINTED IN
GREAT BRITAIN
AT THE
UNIVERSITY PRESS
OXFORD
BY
CHARLES BATEY
PRINTER
TO THE
UNIVERSITY